Economics
and
Society

Louis A. Dow
Professor Emeritus
University of Alabama at Birmingham
Birmingham, AL

Fred N. Hendon
Professor of Business
Samford University, Birmingham, AL

Prentice Hall, Englewood Cliffs, New Jersey 07632

Library of Congress Cataloging-in-Publication Data

Dow, Louis A.
    Economics and society / Louis A. Dow, Fred N. Hendon.
    ISBN 0-13-224551-5
    1. Economics.   I. Hendon, Fred N.   II. Title.
    HB171.5.D626   1991
    330—dc20   89–25481
                                                               CIP

Editorial/production supervision and
    interior design: Keith Faivre
Cover design: Ben Santora
Manufacturing buyer: Pete Havens

© 1991 by Prentice-Hall, Inc.
A Division of Simon & Schuster
Englewood Cliffs, New Jersey 07632

Printed in the United States of America

10   9   8   7   6   5   4   3   2   1

ISBN 0-13-224551-5

Prentice-Hall International (UK) Limited, *London*
Prentice-Hall Australia Pty. Limited, *Sydney*
Prentice-Hall Canada, Inc., *Toronto*
Prentice-Hall Hispanoamericana, S.A., *Mexico*
Prentice-Hall of India Private Limited, *New Delhi*
Prentice-Hall of Japan, Inc., *Tokyo*
Simon & Schuster Asia Pte. Ltd., *Singapore*
Editora Prentice-Hall do Brasil Ltda., *Rio de Janeiro*

Contents

PART II
The Circular Flow of Economic Activity

PART IV
Microeconomics: Theory and Policy

Preface

A NOTE TO THE STUDENT

We believe that economics is an exciting and important subject. Exciting because economics relates to many of the most significant and controversial issues of the day—the environment, jobs, poverty, inflation, economic growth, and competitiveness. Important because a solid understanding of basic economic principles is a necessary prerequisite for devising and implementing policy to help solve these problems.

Too often students consider economics a difficult and boring subject. They often feel more confused than enlightened upon finishing the course. To some extent, this may be the result of the way it is presented, of what appears to be a mass of disjointed theoretical detail, more suitable in preparing the student for advanced study than for basic understanding of how the world works. We hope this book will give the students who will go no further in the subject that basic understanding, and yet at the same time be complete enough not to preclude further study.

NATURE OF APPROACH

Our whole approach is organized around the circular flow model of economic activity. At its most basic level, the circular flow stresses the interrelatedness of two basic sectors of the economy—households and business firms. This approach allows us to emphasize that all markets are interrelated. For example, households, given their current incomes, purchase goods and services; they may also postpone consumption by saving. Business firms, motivated by profits, attempt to give the households the composition and amounts of products they desire. They also borrow the savings of households in order to expand their operations or to start entirely new businesses. In doing so, business firms demand and pay for the services of the productive resources owned by households. Thus the act of production by business firms to satisfy consumer wants, both now and in the future, determines the amounts of income flow to households, the original means for consumer demand. Indeed, we emphasize that the markets for goods and services and the markets for resources are interrelated. We then integrate the role of government and the international sector into this discussion for a complete picture. Another device we use through the book is repetition of concepts and ideas. Our experience in the classroom has convinced us that students understand and remember more when important ideas and concepts are repeated at appropriate places in the text. The book also contains a glossary of important terms and concepts.

PROCEDURE FOR STUDY

The best advice that one can give students is to study the material *before* class lectures or discussions. Prior preparation is essential for getting the most out of the classroom presentation. The student who has already studied the chapter is not only better able to understand the lecture and discussion but can ask appropriate questions about things he or she doesn't understand.

We suggest that the following steps be taken prior to class coverage of each chapter. First, the student should skim the chapter, reading the chapter preview, major definitions, conclusions, and summary. The idea here is to get a broad grasp of the chapter's subject matter. Second, the student should read the entire chapter carefully and make a list of the most important ideas. By using this procedure, classroom notetaking can allow time for the student to think about what the instructor is saying and to ask questions rather than write notes.

A FINAL COMMENT

It is no exaggeration to say that we have enjoyed writing this book. It is truly a joint product—it is almost impossible for either of us to say that this section, or that page, or that chapter is entirely his own contribution. Every page reflects a continuing collaboration and agreement.

We could not, of course, have completed the work as it now stands had it not been for the constructive comments of a number of reviewers. The usual caveat that we alone are responsible for any errors must be made. So, with no further ado, we acknowledge the help of the following: Karla Eiland, Kay Sutton and Sara Brittian for their patient and diligent retyping of several drafts; and to our wives, Marley and Gery, for their patience and understanding.

Louis A. Dow

Fred N. Hendon

1

Utopias and Economic Reality

chapter preview

• Utopias in which everyone consumes all that he or she wants and has no work to do are but idle dreams.

• They are doomed, if for no other reason, because of the scarcity of economic resources—land, labor, and capital.

• *Land* is the term used to designate natural resources.

• *Labor* is comprised of many types of effort and degrees of skill.

• *Capital* are items that have been manufactured for the purpose of producing further goods and services.

• Every society faces a scarcity of resources and thus must answer the four important questions of *what, how much, how,* and *for whom* goods and services should be produced.

• There are three ways in which these questions can be resolved—by custom, by command, and by markets. Most economies are mixes of all three methods.

• The United States has a mixed economy which is dominated by free, voluntary markets.

• In a market-type economy, the economy's scarce resources are allocated and reallocated through markets in response to voluntary decisions.

• These decisions are expressed in terms of supply and demand in markets.

• Changes in consumer demand cause changes in prices, and these act as a signal to producers to change supply.

• Changes in demand thus cause resources to flow from some uses into other uses.

There is a far land, I'm told, where cigarette trees and lemonade springs abound; the hens lay soft-boiled eggs; the trees are full of fruit, and hay over-flows the barns. In this fair and bright country there's a lake of stew and of whiskey too. "You can paddle around 'em in a big canoe." There ain't no short-handled shovels, no axes or picks. Its a place to stay, where you sleep all day, "where they hung the jerk that invented work." Its called the Big Rock Candy Mountain, but its ancient name is the land of Cockaigne.[1]

This quotation summarizes a folksong that was popular in the United States during the Great Depression of the 1930s when economic problems were so severe for so many workers and their families. It expresses a longing for some sort of Utopia in which there are no such problems and in which there are bountiful benefits to all with a minimum of labor effort.

The idea, however, was not new to the 1930s. To the contrary, the dream of Utopia has a rich history and is found in many guises in many societies at many times. Consider, for example, this medieval folksong:

In Cockaigne we drink and eat
Freely without care and sweat,
The food is choice and clear the wine,
At fourses and at supper time.

I say again, and I dare swear,
No land is like it anywhere,
Under heaven no land like this
Of such joy and endless bliss.

There is many a sweet right,
All is day, there is no night,
There is no quarreling nor strife,
There is no death, but endless life;
There is no lack of food or cloth,
There is no man or woman wroth . . .
All is sporting, joy and glee,
Lucky the man that there may be.[2]

What a golden age! What enchantment! In Cockaigne and the Big Rock Candy Mountain all things are so abundant that they are free—they are simply there for

[1]Sebastian de Grazia, *Of Time, Work, and Leisure* (New York: Twentieth Century Fund, 1962; Doubleday Anchor edition, 1964). The quotation is from the Doubleday Anchor paperback, p. 363.

[2]Found in I. Tod and M. Wheeler, *Utopia* (London: Orbis Publishing, 1978), pp. 10–11.

2

the taking. There is no need to worry about hunger and labor, no need to pay prices for things, no need to put something aside for the future, no need to worry about taxes, government deficits, foreign trade, paying interest, and the like. For that matter, there would be no need for a book of this sort, for there would be no need to study economics. In this fair and far-off land, there are no serious economic problems.

A. SCARCITY: THE RUIN OF UTOPIAS

Has there ever been a Cockaigne? Not really. The continent of Atlantis was supposed to have been one, but it presumably sank into the seas and remains lost to this day (if, indeed, it ever existed). Utopia, or Cockaigne, seems to have existed only in people's imagination. And many famous writers—Plato, Sir Thomas More, the Marquis de Condorcet, Campanella, and William Godwin, to mention only a few—have dreamed of Utopia and have put their visions in writing, usually in great detail and all too often with a strong totalitarian bent. But it remains true that *utopian* is merely what the word implies, for *Utopia* is derived from two Greek words that mean "nowhere."[3] There is a simple but overwhelming reason why no such state of bliss exists in the world today, and that is *the scarcity of economic resources.* Every society, no matter what form or structure it may have, no matter whether it is ancient or modern, and no matter what political system it may have, faces the same crucial problem of scarcity of economic resources. This is as true of the United States today as it was of ancient Greece. And it is as true of the Soviet Union, Peru, Japan, Cuba, Ireland, the People's Republic of China, Chad, and Ethiopia.

> Scarcity of economic resources is a basic problem common to all human societies. Put otherwise, in every society resources are scarce *relative* to the demands imposed upon them—that is, wants are *unlimited* with respect to the *limited* means of producing the goods and services people demand.

But just what are these economic resources that are so scarce? Some brief definitions will suffice for now. Economic resources are typically classified into three categories—land, labor, and capital:

Land. This is really a misleading term, for it refers to much more than fertile fields and building sites. It includes all the natural resources of the society—mineral deposits, oil and gas supplies, water, air, and so on. "Land," therefore, is truly a catchall word.

Labor. This refers to all the human resources, both intellectual and

---

[3]A few utopian experiments, however, have been attempted—for example, the short-lived (1825–26) New Harmony Community of Equals in Indiana. Some other experiments were Joseph Warren's Utopia community in Ohio and later his Modern Times community on Long Island; Saint-Simon's society in France; and the Oneida community in New York, which survived from 1848 to 1879.

physical, in the country. There are, of course, many types of labor, and the more industrially advanced the society is, the greater the diversity of tasks and skills to be performed. "Labor," therefore, is also a catchall word, including, as it does, the skilled physician, the janitor, the college chancellor, the garbage collector, the professional basketball player, the plumber, and so on. Our society's "labor" is made up of a large heterogeneous group of workers. The skills, education, and native ability embodied in individuals are referred to as *human capital*. A unique and important type of labor takes the form of risk-assuming entrepreneurs.

Capital.   This refers to the plants, buildings, machines, and inventories that *have been manufactured for the purpose of producing further goods and services*. The automobile assembly plant in Michigan with all its robots, tools, and parts is capital; so is the one-man barber shop. The computers of a large insurance company are capital; so is the automobile driven by a salesman. Note, however, that all these examples are taken from the private sector of the economy. They represent *private capital*. There is also what is called *public capital*—e.g., highways, fire stations and their equipment, educational facilities, and the like. Thus, like "land" and "labor," the term "capital" is a catchall word.

As long as these productive resources are scarce, the goods and services they are used to produce are also scarce. In short, there are no *free goods*, things that are found only in the mythical land of Cockaigne where resources are so abundant that no one lacks anything desired. Economic goods are, by definition, *scarce goods*. The next chapter elaborates on the role and importance of scarcity. For now let's only say this: Utopias and their creators aside, it remains a hard and unpleasant fact that for each society there simply are not enough resources to produce everything that everyone wants (or, for that matter, needs).

Conclusion: *Scarcity* is the hard core from which all economic activity springs, and it is therefore the source of the study of economics. All societies must face up to and somehow or other resolve the problems created by the scarcity of economic resources.

B. FOUR QUESTIONS: *WHAT, HOW, HOW MUCH,* AND *FOR WHOM?*

The shortage of resources gives rise to four essential questions or problems. First, some decisions must be made (how they are made we leave unanswered for the moment) about *what* goods and services and *how much* of each are to be produced. Next, decisions must be made at the same time about *how* the economy's scarce resources are to be used in producing the selected goods and services—i.e., in what proportions are resources to be combined. And, finally, some decisions must be reached about who is going to get those goods and services—that is, *for whom* they are produced. This set of questions is unavoidable and must be settled by all societies, no matter how different they may be in other respects. They must, for example, be answered by such socialist states as the Soviet Union, such capitalist states as the United States, such economically lagging third-world countries as Kenya, and even such primitive people as the bushmen of the Kalahari desert. Let's look at each of these questions in more detail.

1. A Patchwork of Choices: The *What* and *How Much* Questions

What goods and services should society's resources be used to produce? Remember, resources are scarce, and therefore when more of one thing is produced, then less of some other thing or things must be produced. Scarcity of resources gives substance to the old saying "You can't have your cake and eat it too." So, should our scarce resources be used to produce more automobiles or more medical services or more television entertainment? Or should some of them be allocated toward eliminating poverty, providing adequate housing for all, and cleaning up the environment? Perhaps more resources should be directed toward building up our defense program. Or perhaps more should be used for new capital, both private and public, so that more goods and services can be produced at some future date. These *what* and *how much* questions are important, and the way they are answered will affect our economic well-being both now and in the future.

2. More Capital or More Labor? The *How* Question

Suppose there has been some determination of what goods and services are to be produced. The question now arises as to *how* they are to be produced—that is, how should our scarce resources be used in the production process? For instance, should the goods and services be produced by methods that emphasize the use of labor and reduce the use of capital? This technique is commonly used in countries in which there are a multitude of people and hence "labor is cheap"—countries such as India and China. Such methods of production are called *labor-intensive*.

On the other hand, the techniques used may rely much more heavily on capital equipment or small amounts of highly trained labor (i.e., human capital) and may therefore tend to minimize the employment of unskilled labor. Such methods are termed *capital-intensive* and are typically found in the industrially advanced economies, such as the United States, Britain, Sweden, Japan, Canada, and West Germany.

No matter which method is in fact used, the one selected should always be as efficient as possible (that is, it should produce the desired output with a minimum amount of resources). After all, since our resources are so scarce, we do not want them to be used wastefully. To the contrary, they must be used as productively as possible. We must "economize" them.

3. Who Gets What? The *For Whom* Question

Finally, there is the all-important question of how the total output pie is to be sliced up and divided among the members of society. Put otherwise, how should the goods and services being produced be distributed among all concerned? Are there any hard and fast rules about *income distribution?* Not really. In fact, a number of alternatives present themselves. At one extreme, there is the notion of perfect equality— i.e., everyone receives an equal share of the pie, no matter how much he or she contributed to the size of the pie. At the other extreme could be a society in which the tyrant (or the ruling class) claims the lion's share of total output. This latter pattern of income distribution is much more prevalent in the world today than is the former. Indeed, there is no society in which the distribution of income is perfectly equal, but in many third-world countries there are great and grinding inequalities in income distribution.

Still another method of income distribution is that each member of society is to take back an amount of the total output pie equivalent to the amount he or she contributed. This, of course, means that the aged and infirmed would have no income, since they contribute nothing. In this event, government is likely to step in and through its taxing programs transfer some income from those who have to those who have not.

All sorts of thorny problems and heated debates emerge when we discuss how income *should* be distributed, but we can hardly deal with the matter here. Yet it is actually dealt with in many ways by many societies. Despite the difficulties of this question, each society must (and, in fact, does) decide how income is to be divided among its members.

C. CUSTOMS, COMMANDS, AND MARKETS

Even though the scarcity of resources is universal, this doesn't mean that all societies face up to the problem in the same way. Some societies rely heavily on central government planning to determine what is to be produced, as well as the methods of production to be used in the process of production. Indeed, the central plan also determines who will get what—that is, the distribution of income. Other societies, however, rely heavily on the voluntary interaction of demand and supply in the marketplace to answer the basic economic questions. Still others find themselves dominated by customs and traditions in answering the same questions.

Actually, no economic society is completely a command economy or a market economy or a tradition economy. Instead, any particular society contains all three elements—command, market, tradition. Economies are truly mixtures of all three.

1. Command-Type Economic Societies

In some economies, the command elements are so dominant that they can be classified as "command-type," even though they may possess some important market features and customs. Good examples of command-type economies would be Albania, the Soviet Union, the People's Republic of China (P.R.C.), and Yugoslavia. Consumers in these countries typically have little to say about how resources are used—e.g., whether steel is to be used for refrigerators or for construction and guns. Nor do they have any say about how much cement is to be used for highways and how much for apartment buildings. All of these and a myriad of other decisions are made by the economic planners in a command-type economy, and if the consumers do not like the results, there is virtually nothing they can do about it. Some of the consequences and reactions are discussed in Exhibit 1–1.

In recent years, however, and particularly in the P.R.C., the authorities seem to be relying more and more on markets as a means of allocating some of the country's resources. This tendency has generally been applauded, but evidently the command-type economies continue to be dominated by central economic planning.

2. Tradition-Type Societies

In some countries, tradition and custom almost completely control how resources are used, what is produced, and who gets what. In most of these societies, if you happen to be the son of a fisherman, you become a fisherman; if you happen to be the daughter of a hunter, you may have to marry a hunter at some point in time.

Not only will occupations be determined by convention, but the fruits of production will be divided according to custom. Consider this example of an actual kill:

> The Gemsbok had vanished. . . . Gai owned two hind legs and a front leg, Tsetchwe had meat from the back, Ukwane had the other front leg, his wife had one of the feet and the stomach, the young boys had lengths of intestine. Twikwe had received the head and Dasina the udder.
>
> It seems very unequal when you watch Bushmen divide the kill, yet it is their system, and in the end no person eats more than any other. That day Ukwane gave Gai still another piece because Gai was his relation, Gai gave meat to Dasina because she was his wife's mother. . . . No one, of course, contested Gai's larger share, because he had been the hunter and by their law that much belonged to him. No one doubted that he would share his larger amount with others, and they were not wrong, of course; he did.[4]

Again, and more generally:

> A man does not normally earn his right to a particular share of output by contributing a particular piece of work. His claim to a share is based on his membership and on his status in the social group, household, camp, club, et cetera for which the work is being done. He works in order to fulfill his social obligations, to maintain his prestige and the status to which his sex, age, rank, et cetera may entitle him.[5]

[4]Found in R. Heilbroner, *The Economic Problem* (Englewood Cliffs, NJ: Prentice Hall, 1970), pp. 16–17.

[5]D. Forde and M. Douglas, "Primitive Economics," in G. Dalton, ed., *Tribal and Peasant Economies: Readings in Economic Anthopology* (Garden City, NY: Doubleday, 1967), p.20.

EXHIBIT 1–1
Command Decisions and Queues

What is a queue? A *queue* is a line of people waiting for something, as when people queue up to buy tickets for a ballgame or a concert. Or it can also be a line of cars, as when cars queue up on the freeways during peak-load traffic. There are many kinds of queues.

Although the word is not widely used in the United States, it is rather common in Europe and Asia. There, people with their carts of groceries don't *line* up at the checkout counters of the supermarket. They *queue* up.

Most visitors from the United States and western Europe are impressed by the queues they see in Russia. These queues of consumers often materialize quickly on the streets and may be as long as one hundred to two hundred people, no matter what the weather may be. Each person patiently waits his or her turn in the line, hoping to buy whatever the queue is for.

Why are these queues so common? Let's suppose that the decision makers have decided that the tin and steel resources of the economy are far more important for the military program and the construction of new factories than they are for, say, canned fruit. They therefore allocate only a very limited amount of these resources for canned fruit. Once consumers get wind of the fact that there is a consignment of canned fruit available, they queue up for it. Who gets the limited amount of the canned fruit? Simply those who arrive at the head of the queue first. It is merely a matter of first come, first served. Those who get there too late will be more careful in the future to get there earlier (if they know of the availability and location of the good in question).

This is a very costly way of shopping. Often the consumer will stand in line for hours only to be told that there is no more of the item when he or she gets to the head of the queue. Look at the cost involved—that is, consider all the other things the individual could have been doing but didn't because of being in the queue. This is inconvenient and costly.

How common is this type of situation in Russia? Very! There are queues for such things as fresh fish, canned fruit, ice cream, eggs, and toilet paper. There are even queues for taxis in Moscow, and often a person may have to wait as long as twenty minutes on a cold winter's day to get a taxi. (The same is true in large U.S. cities.)

This is one way of allocating the scarce amount of an item. Simply let the buyers queue up and then sell on a first come, first served basis. It is so rare in the United States that one wonders why the Russian consumers accept such a costly, clumsy method of allocation. However, they do, and with a modest amount of grumbling.

Thus, even though there may be traces of market activity in and between such societies, it is clear that custom and tradition dominate economy activity.

3. Market-Type Economic Behavior

The *what, how, how much,* and *for whom* questions are resolved in the United States, Britain, West Germany, Canada, and a number of other economies largely by means of the market system. Here the pattern of resource use is usually determined by the decisions of private individuals and organizations, and with much less emphasis on command elements. To be sure, government does influence economic activity in the United States, but the lion's share of decisions is made by private parties. Government does not tell us what is to be produced, nor does it determine the techniques of production. These are, to repeat, largely matters of individual choice and behavior. Government, however, does have a major role to play in income distribution, a matter to be taken up later. Still, it is safe to say that the *for whom* question is also mainly determined by individuals and businesses interacting freely in markets. Let's look at the market system in more detail.

D. FOOTBALL, RADIOS, AND TVs

Every autumn a strange and exciting phenomenon takes place in the United States—the onset of the football season. Millions of fans sit in the warm fall sun to cheer their team on to victory; they even brave snowy and rainy days to cheer for their teams. The football season, whether professional, collegiate, or high school, is an exciting time of the year.

"But," you may ask, "what does this have to do with economics?" Just this. Let's suppose that your school has a football stadium that is not large enough to seat everyone who wants to go to the games. The demand for the seats is there, and so is the supply of seats, but in this case the amount demanded outstrips the amount supplied. It may well be that plans are being made for the construction of a larger stadium, but that is not the point for now. The important thing is that there is a scarcity of seats relative to demand. So, for the moment, the serious issue is that somehow or other the limited number of seats must be divided among those who want to watch the game.

How is this to be done? The question is crucial. It is merely a microscopic version of the question that applies to the entire economic system: How are scarce economic resources to be divided among all the competing uses of them?

1. Command Decisions

One way of resolving the football problem is to have the school's administration simply decide on its own who gets a seat, where the seat is, and what game the viewer may attend. In short, centralized command decisions divide the scarce resources according to the rules of the decision makers. This is quite arbitrary; indeed, some would say it is dictatorial.

Fortunately, such detailed command elements are rare in this country, although there are undoubtedly some traces of them. For instance, the school's administration may decide which sections students may sit in. There is also an arbitrary decision about whether there will be admission prices, how these prices will be charged, and what the student and nonstudent prices will be.

However, such centralized command decisions about how scarce resources are to be divided are relatively rare in the United States. But as our football example shows, they are not completely absent. And it is also true that some very significant decisions flow from government—consider, for example, tax laws, regulation of public utilities, and minimum wage legislation. But in the overall picture of resource allocation, command elements count very little. Certainly they are far removed from the magnitude one finds in such economies as the Soviet Union, the People's Republic of China, and Cuba. Ours is truly a market system, but let's not forget that there are command elements in it.

2. Traditional Patterns

As we have seen, custom and tradition may be used to decide how resources are to be divided among different uses. We cannot imagine this happening for our football problem, but a hypothetical situation might be like this: As the community has grown, it has become a tradition for students to sit in certain sections and for nonstudent spectators to sit in others. Also, custom may dictate that the older spectators get the better seats and that the fans of the visiting team have the seats facing the sun or in the end zones. And so on.

Far flung? Sure it is. But at the national level, a number of customs and traditions can influence economic activity. Religious holidays, the closing of many businesses on Sunday, the idea of summer vacations for students—all of these affect economic behavior. Still, they are, like the command elements, merely traces in the market system of the United States.

3. The Market Answer

How might the football problem be dealt with under the market system? The answer to this question goes as follows.

There is a limited supply of seats and hence tickets. In fact, there is such a shortage of tickets that demand is greater than supply. Now, if the tickets are put on the market for sale, the excess of demand over supply will surely drive ticket prices up. Thus, only those who are *willing to pay* and are *able to pay* the higher price are the ones who will go to the game. The rest of the students and nonstudents have been cut out of the market.

Does this sound harsh? Isn't it undesirable that many who would really like to go to the game are not able to because they cannot pay the price? It may be. But let's not lose sight of the fact that the decision not to pay the higher price is a voluntary one. No one commanded some students to buy tickets and others not to buy. Not in the market system. Decisions are voluntary.

> **Example:**   Suppose the price of a ticket per game is $10.00. Suppose also that Kathy happens to have $10.00 to spend on anything she wants, including a ticket. Suppose finally that Kathy also happens to be a fairly good thinker and is careful about how she spends her money. Now, what she will do is to look around at the other things she can spend the $10.00 on, and in the process may decide that she would much rather use it to buy a new scarf. Thus she has voluntarily decided not to buy the ticket at $10.00, but rather to obtain something else that she figures will give her more satisfaction.
>
> Martha, on the other hand, also has $10.00, and because of her love of football and school spirit, she immediately decides to buy a ticket. Again, her decision is voluntary.
>
> Let's return to Kathy for a moment. Remember that at the price of $10.00 per ticket, she opted not to go to the game. But what if the market price had been bid to only $7.50? In this case, Kathy might well reconsider her options and decide to go to the game and use the remaining $2.50 for something else. In other words, in our example, she would go to the game at the lower price; but at the higher price she would voluntarily drop out of the market.

When we turn to the economy as a whole, the same sort of thing applies. Consumers are free to spend their money as they see fit, and how they spend it depends largely on the relative prices of the things they buy. Just as Kathy does, they respond differently to higher and lower prices. If the price of butter goes too high for some, they reduce their purchases of butter and buy more margarine. If the price of beef rises, some consumers will cut back on it and buy more pork or chicken if these goods are cheaper. And so on. People tend to buy more of something when its price is lower and less when its price is higher. They are continually shifting their purchases as they respond to relative price changes. It is important to remember that all these choices are voluntary. Note that *price is the device that rations the available amounts among potential buyers.*

Furthermore, producers are free to produce what they want to, and once they have decided on the goods or services to produce, they are also free to determine the methods of production to be used. In all of this, they are strongly influenced by the profit motive. If, for example, a farmer finds it more profitable to grow corn instead of soybeans, he will shift his land and other resources from soybeans to corn. Also, if he finds it more efficient to use more fertilizer and less seed (given his amount of land), he will use the lower-cost method of production. And all of this is done voluntarily and clearly influences how the economy's resources are used. Note again that the relative prices of goods determines what is profitable to produce. Using the example above, if the price of corn were to rise as a result of greater relative scarcity, then corn would be more profitable relative to soybeans. This would prompt the farmers to transfer land from soybean to corn production.

4. Televisions and Radios

All of this economic behavior is described in more detail in the next few chapters. Still, a final example may prove helpful in understanding how the system works. Suppose consumers in general decide voluntarily that they want more television sets and fewer radios. The market system responds to this change in demand as follows:

> **Example:**   As the demand for TVs increases, the price of TVs will also rise. This means that there are more profits in the TV industry. At the same time, the decreases in the demand for radios means lower prices and profits in the radio industry.
>
> Now, the TV industry will respond to the higher prices and profits by increasing output (supply); and the radio manufacturers, facing lower prices and profits, will cut back on their production, thereby reducing the supply of radios.
>
> Since more resources—land, labor, and capital—are needed in the TV industry, they will then tend to flow into it, particularly as the TV firms are apt to pay a higher price in order to get them. Where do these resources come from? Well, at least some will be coming from the radio industry, since fewer resources are now needed there.
>
> But note what has happened. Resources have been reallocated between the two industries in response to the change in demand. Consumers wanted more TVs and they got them; they wanted fewer radios and consequently the output of radios has fallen. All of this is done voluntarily in response to profit potential and with no government laws or orders being necessary.

In sum, in the market system, resources are allocated and reallocated among different uses in response to voluntary decisions based on personal desires. In this allocative and reallocative process, prices and profits play leading roles. This is why the market system is often called the price system and the profit system. The task of the rest of this book is to examine the operations of the market system. As we shall see, the system doesn't always function perfectly. In fact, at times it can get way off track. But all of this comes later.

E. SUMMARY

The scarcity of economic resources means that any society must answer four questions: *What* is to be produced? *How much* is to be produced? *How* is the production to occur? and *For whom* are the goods to be produced? Generally speaking, there are three types of economic societies that answer these questions differently—the command-type economy, the tradition-oriented economy, and the market-oriented economy. In reality, all economic societies are mixtures of these three. Still, some nations may be classified as predominantly command (e.g., the Soviet Union), others as predominantly tradition (e.g., some of the third-world countries), and still others as predominantly market (e.g., the United States).

The market system, which is the focus of this book, answers the *what, how much, how,* and *for whom* questions mainly by relying on the voluntary decisions and actions of private individuals and businesses taking place in markets. Changes in demand cause changes in prices, and these in turn signal producers to revise their actions in their pursuit of profits. In our example, more television sets were produced and the supply of radios fell. This change in outputs was accompanied by a new pattern of resource use as land, labor, and capital flowed from the radio industry into the television industry.

Terms and Concepts to Remember

Land	*What, how, how much, for whom*
Labor	Market economy
Capital	Command economy
Scarcity	Tradition economy

Questions for Review

1. Why would the *what, how, how much,* and *for whom* questions be irrelevant in a Utopia (even though we know that Utopias don't exist)?

2. When Robinson Crusoe found himself stranded and alone on his island, which of the basic economic questions was he able to ignore? Why couldn't he ignore the others?

3. Why are different methods of road construction used in the United States and India?

4. What are some elements of tradition that affect economic decisions in the United States? Do these elements have much impact on how the economy's scarce resources are used?

5. What are some command elements in our economy? Do they have much influence on how the basic economic questions are answered? Explain.

2

Scarcity, Opportunity Costs, and Diminishing Returns

chapter preview

• Scarcity of economic resources means that trade-offs and opportunity costs are inevitable.

• Trade-offs occur at all levels of economic activity, from the individual up to the total economy.

• Opportunity costs are sacrifices— that is, they represent what is given up by doing one thing rather than another.

• Since the economy's resources are scarce, every time they are used to produce something, there is an opportunity cost because something else cannot be produced.

• Economics can be defined in terms of opportunity costs.

• Because of the complexity of the economy, we need to make use of economic road maps (models) as guides.

• No model can ever be completely descriptive of reality. This is as true of economic models as it is for other types of models. Hence, economic models are by definition unrealistic, but they are very useful in allowing us to understand how the economy functions.

• This usefulness is illustrated by the production-possibilities model—our first economic road map. The production-possibilities curve shows alternative uses (and costs) of the economy's resources.

• Changes in technology, net investment, and the total amount of resources will cause the production-possibilities curve to shift.

• The law of diminishing returns, a basic and unavoidable phenomenon, explains the shape of the production-possibilities curve.

• The law of diminishing returns also explains why opportunity costs rise as more and more resources are used for the production of one good at the expense of other goods.

Scarcity of economic resources, the theme of the last chapter, leads to the important idea discussed in this chapter, namely, TANSTAAFL. Translated, this means: "There Ain't No Such Thing As A Free Lunch," and that is what scarcity and economics are all about.[1] If there are no "free lunches," then all lunches must cost something. As this chapter shows, everything has a cost attached to it, including the very air you breathe. Let's examine this idea first as it applies to the individual and then as it applies to society and the economy as a whole.

A. TRADE-OFFS AND OPPORTUNITY COSTS AT THE INDIVIDUAL LEVEL

We begin with the notion of a *trade-off,* which is well illustrated by the old saying "You can't have your cake and eat it too." This clearly tells us what a trade-off is. If, for example, you go to a movie, then you can't attend a football game or study for an exam at the same time. You can do either one or the other; you can't be in more than one place simultaneously. Thus, if you decide to go to the movie, you give up (i.e., trade off) going to the game, studying for the exam, or going to a party. Time constrains us all. Since we can't be in two or more places simultaneously, we must always give up something. In our example, the decision to go to the movie means that you must sacrifice the benefits that you could have received from the other activities.

This also illustrates what is meant by the concept of *opportunity cost,* for here the cost of going to the movie is not being able to enjoy the benefits of something else. Note: At no place in our example have we considered the money price of the movie admission. At the moment we are not at all concerned with the fact that the ticket may have cost you, say, four dollars. Indeed, we will even assume that someone is buying the ticket for you, so that you don't have to part with any money. Someone might argue that the movie, in this case, is truly a "free lunch" for you. But recall that since you can't spend the same time doing something else, there is a real cost, and the real cost is the lost benefits you could have experienced if you had spent the time in the next-best alternative. This is the opportunity cost of your "free" movie.

How do we apply the opportunity cost concept in the event that you use your own money to buy the theater ticket? There would still be the cost mentioned above

[1]To our best knowledge, this term was coined by Robert Heinlein; see his *The Moon Is a Harsh Mistress* (New York: Berkley Publishing Corp., 1968). First published by Putnam's, 1966.

due to the constraint of time, but there would now be an additional opportunity cost. This new opportunity cost would be in the form of the benefits you could have acquired by spending the four dollars on something else, such as a pizza or a paperback novel. The benefits from what you would otherwise have spent the four dollars on would be the opportunity cost of your buying the theater ticket.

These examples may seem mundane; in fact, they are, and that is the point. They pertain to commonplace activities and decisions. But they also symbolize the countless similar decisions you make every day of your life. The important thing to remember is that every time you make a decision, there are opportunity costs that you should rationally consider. This is true whether you are contemplating going to a movie, buying a book or a cassette, or taking a nap. It is also true when you consider large purchases, such as an automobile or a fine sound system; and it is equally true when you must make major decisions about going to college, selecting a job, buying a house, and so on.

> **Definition:**   To take advantage of any one opportunity, you have to sacrifice the benefits that could be obtained from the opportunities you must pass up. *Opportunity costs, therefore, are the forgone benefits involved in doing one thing rather than something else.* Normally we think of cost as the monetary outlay needed to acquire a product. But the real costs are the benefits of the other things we could have obtained with the same dollar outlay. The opportunity cost that is relevant is the benefits given up by sacrificing the *next-best alternative* use of your time and money.

Trade-offs and opportunity costs are therefore unavoidable. They are everywhere, and they continually confront every individual whose time and income are limited. What is true of the individual is also true of the family. Nearly all families have limited incomes— that is, they simply don't have enough money to buy everything they want (or perhaps need).

This is illustrated by Figure 2-1, which looks something like a pie. This diagram shows us how the average American family spends its income. The largest slice of the pie, as you might suspect, is for housing, although the food slice is also very large. When you hear people grumbling about the cost of food and the mortgage (or rent) payment, now you know why. These two things alone absorb almost half of the family's income. All the other slices of the pie, except for transportation, are much smaller. This, however, does not mean that they are unimportant to the family. To the contrary, each plays its own significant role in the family's well-being.

Does your family spend pretty much like this one? Probably not, for the pie diagram in Figure 2-1 tells us how the "average" American family spends, and it is highly unlikely that your family is exactly "average." That is, your family has its own budget—its own pie chart, with its own slices.[2] Now let's suppose that your family is thinking about buying an *extra* car. In other words, you want to make the

---

[2]It would be a useful and instructive exercise for you to construct a similar chart for your family and compare it with Figure 2-1 (see Exhibit 2-1).

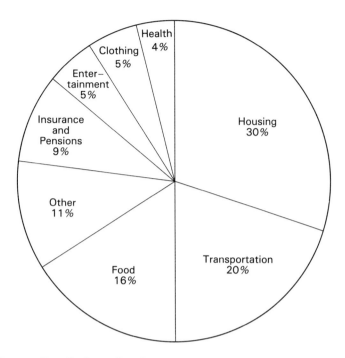

FIGURE 2-1   Family Spending Pattern   The largest chunks of the family budget go for food, housing, and transportation. The high prices of gasoline since OPEC's emergence have caused the transportation slice of the budget to rise to second place in the past decade and a half.
Source: U.S. Department of Agriculture, *Family Economic Review,* 1987, #4, p. 35.

transportation slice of the pie a little bigger. To do this, however, you will have to get the money to make monthly payments on the car from somewhere, and since your family's income is given, this means that you must cut down on the size of some other slice or slices of the pie. And that is your family's opportunity cost, that is, obtaining the car means having to give up the benefits derived from consuming some other things. Let's suppose that in order to get the monthly wherewithal to make payments for the car, your family decides to eat only inexpensive foods, make do with the same old clothes for another year, and go out less often. Thus the cost of getting the car is no new clothes for a while, less steak, and fewer movies and meals out; the clothing, food, and entertainment slices are trimmed back.

Is it worthwhile, given all these costs, to buy the additional car? This of course is a personal judgment and will vary from family to family (see Exhibit 2-1). However, a generalization can be made, and it applies to all the preceding examples as well as to all the cases that involve opportunity costs.

Conclusion: As long as the anticipated benefits to be derived from the action are greater than the opportunity costs—i.e., the forgone benefits of the next-best alternative—then carry through on the action. (In our case, buy the car.) On the other hand, if the anticipated benefits are less

EXHIBIT 2-1
Budgets and Opportunity Costs

The idea of opportunity costs is crucial to any reasonably sound method of making decisions, and once you start using it (more consciously than you have been), you will see its importance. This will become clearer once you consider the role of a family budget.

A *budget* is a plan or schedule of expenditures for a certain period based on the income of that period. Since nearly every household has a given (or limited) income, a budget is a good device for estimating how that income is to be allocated among different uses.

There are different methods by which a family may set up its budget. Unfortunately, a common procedure is for the head of the household to spend the family's income as he or she sees fit, and without any consultation with the other members of the family. The usual justification for this type of behavior is, "Well, it's my money, I make it, and I can spend it as I please." Or it may be that the head of the household genuinely feels that he or she knows what is really best for the family. Even if the head of the household is benevolent and loving and has the well-being of the other members at heart, this method of carrying out a budget procedure may create many resentments and much anxiety and bitterness.

At the other extreme is the "democratic" procedure, by which the entire family participates directly in the budget-making process. At any rate, everyone has a chance to put in his or her "two cents worth" on how the family's income is to be spent. In this respect, a pie chart such as Figure 2-1 (or similar method of presentation) will prove helpful. Everyone will then have a better picture of how enlarging any one slice can occur only by cutting or reducing another slice. There is no assurance that this approach will eliminate conflicts and resentments, but it will probably tend to reduce them. An awareness of opportunity costs always makes for better decision making.

than the opportunity costs, then forgo the action. (In our case, do not buy the car.)

This generalization always serves as a rational guide to decision making and action. There may be some problems involved in attaching even reasonably accurate weights to the benefits and costs, but the problems will be greater if the attempt isn't made.

B. REAL COSTS AT THE SOCIAL LEVEL

Do the problems of opportunity costs, trade-offs, and TANSTAAFL apply to the economy as a whole? There is a simple, but accurate, answer to this question. Yes! As we saw in Chapter 1, if resources were superabundant, our society would be more like the Big Rock Candy Mountain than it is. Unfortunately, however, since resources are scarce, every time society decides to use its scarce resources one way rather than another, there are opportunity costs and trade-offs.

It is true that new resources are constantly being discovered. It is also true that technological advances eventually make our existing resources less scarce by making them more efficient. It is even true that some resources—e.g., the labor force—become larger due to natural forces. Under these circumstances, then, why are our resources so scarce? The simple reason is that our demands for goods and services are so great that they put enormous pressure on our resources. Put otherwise, there are not enough resources in the economy to produce everything that everyone wants. Thus, just as a family must "economize" on how it spends its limited income, so must society "economize" on how it uses its scarce resources. Note also that even the steadily increasing quantity and efficiency of our resources can't seem to keep up with our demands. Demands seem to be unlimited, and therefore there is no relief from the pressures on resources. It seems that the more we get, the more we want; and in the race between resources and demands, the latter are the clear winners. If this is the case, it follows that resources continue to be scarce relative to demands.

Accordingly, trade-offs and opportunity costs continue to dominate the economic scene. If, for example, more steel is used in the production of more automobiles, then this steel is not available for other uses, such as for bridges, dishwashers, office buildings, and nails. The opportunity cost of having more automobiles, then, is the forgone benefits of having fewer of these other things. Consider another example. The resources used in the military program of the United States are not available for uses in the civilian sector, and thus there are opportunity costs in the form of benefits forgone due to a smaller output of civilian goods and services. These are only two examples; countless others abound. TANSTAAFL is a basic economic phenomenon that is inescapable; "there ain't no such thing as a free lunch" because every resource use carries in its wake an opportunity cost for someone. Indeed, there can't even be a "free lunch" program in our public school system for the simple reason that the resources used for the lunch program carry with them an opportunity cost. The taxpayers must ultimately pay for the resources used in the free lunch program, and therefore someone "goes without lunch so that others may eat."

C. WHAT IS ECONOMICS?

Perhaps enough has been said to allow us to give a preliminary definition of economics.

> **Definition:** *Economics* is the study of the benefits and opportunity costs flowing from choices made in allocating scarce resources among alternative, competing uses. These choices occur at all levels, ranging from the individual to the society as a whole.

This definition is based on the points that have been stressed so far—namely, that resources are scarce, that choices about their different uses entail trade-offs and opportunity costs, and that rational decisions entail a comparison of the anticipated benefits with the anticipated costs. It is the job of economics to study these costs and benefits so that we can make more rational choices about how our resources are to be used.

D. ECONOMIC MODELS

By this time it has undoubtedly occurred to you that the economic world is an incredibly complex reality with its millions of producers and consumers interacting in hundreds of thousands of markets. If we wish to understand how the economy functions so that we can understand and predict future behavior, we must somehow simplify this complexity. This process of simplification lets us cut through all the detail and concentrate only on those factors that are considered to be important for answering the questions or problems at hand.

The simplified picture of reality that we construct is called a *model,* and since we are concerned with many problems, there are many models. Nonetheless, any model is a scaled-down version of reality. In this sense, the model is unrealistic with respect to the real world about us. Consider some basic illustrations. From childhood on, you have been aware of such things as model airplanes and dollhouses— that is, reality is scaled down so that the child can play pilot or housewife. Many toys, indeed, are scaled-down versions of reality. At a different level, stores often make use of models in displaying their clothing and other wares. And at still a different level, model airplanes and automobiles are used in wind tunnel tests to examine design specifications that may later be incorporated into the real thing. Models of all sorts are obviously used for a variety of reasons.

Suppose a group of us are walking down a street and the driver of an out-of-state auto asks us for directions to the airport (which, we assume, is a considerable distance away). We have a problem. If we are to be completely "realistic" (and had enough paper and time), we may attempt to draw a map on a one-to-one scale, showing all the streets, buildings, houses, parks, and trees between here and the airport. Now this, of course, would be impossible to do, and even if we could draw such a map, it would be of no use. Imagine the confusion that would set in as the map became longer and more detailed. In fact, it would be impossible to describe true reality.

At the other extreme, if we are impatient (or inconsiderate) and want to be on our way, we may point vaguely in the general direction of the airport. Clearly, this approach, while better than nothing at all, is of little practical use. The best procedure would be for us to draw a map, not necessarily to scale, indicating the major streets, landmarks, and approximate distances along the best route to the airport, leaving out everything else. The driver could then reach his destination with a minimum of difficulty. In fact, this would be a least-cost method of doing so.

This example illustrates the process of simplifying reality in order to solve (or at least cope with) a problem. Note that the map we drew contained just enough information to get the job done, but not so much as to be unnecessarily complex. In this sense, the map we drew was "unrealistic"; it ignored much of reality. Yet it was realistic enough to get the job done.

So it is with good economic models (or theories). They are simplified descriptions of the real economic world; they contain only the information needed for the job at hand. This doesn't mean, however, that a model, once constructed, never changes. It does change. Once the basic model is understood, we can then add more complexities to it, making it less unrealistic. Even so, a model, by its very nature, can never be realistic. As one leading economist put it, ". . . never do we come to real life, however closely we may approach it, for reality is always more complex than the economist's picture of it."[3]

So, let's turn to our first map of the economic society.

E. THE PRODUCTION-POSSIBILITIES MODEL

The importance of scarce resources and the presence of opportunity costs can be explained very neatly with the production-possibilities model.

Definition: The *production-possibilities curve* shows the various combinations of two goods (or two classes of goods) that the economy's scarce resources can be used to produce at full employment and with a given technology.

Consider Table 2–1 in which we list the various combinations of the two things that we assume that our economy can produce—tractors and tanks. In this example, tractors are used as a symbol of the output for the civilian sector of the economy and tanks are used to symbolize output for the military sector.[4]

TABLE 2-1   The Economy's Production-Possibilities Schedule

Possibility Points	Tractors (in thousands)	Tanks (in thousands)
(1)	(2)	(3)
A	25	0
B	24	10
C	20	19
D	15	27
E	8	31
F	0	33

[3]Or, for that matter, anyone else's view of reality. The quotation is from K.E. Boulding, *Economic Analysis* Vol. I, *Microeconomics* (New York: Harper & Row, 1966), p. 13.

[4]Other appropriate classifications would be capital goods and consumer goods, luxuries and necessities, manufactured goods and services, and so on.

1. Opportunity Costs Illustrated

Table 2-1 clearly illustrates what is meant by opportunity costs. The first column is headed "Possibility Points," and each point (*A, B, C,* etc.) shows a particular combination of tanks and tractors that the economy can produce. Note that the points are *mutually exclusive;* the economy can't, for example, be at point *B,* producing 24,000 tractors and 10,000 tanks, and also be at point *D,* producing 15,000 tractors and 27,000 tanks. It can be at either one or the other, or at any other listed point, but not all at once. The economy can settle *only at some one or another* of these points. Where it will in fact settle is a matter for later discussion.

The data given in Table 2-1 have been transferred to Figure 2-2, in which we have plotted the quantity of tractors along the vertical axis and the quantity of tanks along the horizontal axis. The curve connecting all the "possibility points" is what we call the *production-possibilities curve.* It shows graphically the various possibilities of producing tractors and tanks from which the economy may choose.

Consider first point *A.* This is truly an extreme use of the economy's resources, for here all resources will have been allocated to the production of tractors and, therefore, none to the production of tanks. The economy would have 25,000 tractors but zero tanks. In our modern world, this is a rather unlikely point at which the economy would settle.

Consider now the other extreme at point *F.* In this case, all resources would have been directed toward the production of tanks and none to tractors. The economy would have 33,000 tanks but zero output of tractors. Again, this would be an

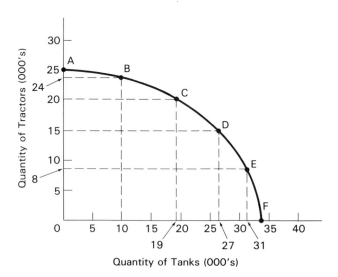

FIGURE 2-2   The Production-Possibilities Curve for the Economy   This curve shows graphically the several "possibility points" in Table 2-1. Where society ends up on the curve is the outcome of private and public decisions. The economy, nonetheless, can be at only one (and not more than one) point at any particular time.

unlikely situation, for even in an "all-out" military effort, people need to be fed and clothed.

More likely, of course, the economy will end up at some point on the production-possibilities curve between these two extremes. Let's assume that at present resources are being allocated so that we are at point *B* (24,000 tractors, 10,000 tanks), but that political pressures push the economy down the curve to point *C*. If this were to occur, the economy would now have 19,000 tanks, and a greater military preparedness would exist. But since "there ain't no such thing as a free lunch," there must be an opportunity cost involved, and there is. That cost is the benefits from the 4,000 tractors that must be sacrificed as more resources are used to produce the 9,000 extra tanks. At point *C,* the total production of tractors has fallen from 24,000 to 20,000 as resources have been bid away from the civilian sector over to the military sector in order to increase the output of tanks from 10,000 to 19,000. The opportunity cost is the benefits forgone from the lost output of tractors.

We can always read the opportunity costs from the production-possibilities curve. Figure 2–3 repeats the production-possibilities curve of Figure 2–2. Note that as the economy moves from point *B* to point *C*, the output of tanks rises by *GC* amount (i.e., 9,000) while the output of tractors falls by *BG* amount (i.e., 4,000). We say, then, that the opportunity cost of *GC* more tanks is the *BG* amount of tractors forgone. Furthermore, a movement from point *C* on the curve to point *D* means that the opportunity cost of *HD* more tanks is the *CH* lesser amount of

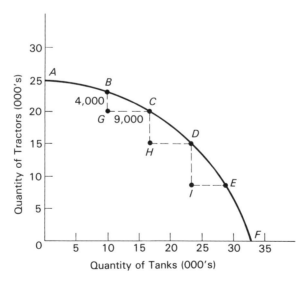

FIGURE 2-3   Production-Possibilities Curve Showing Opportunity Costs
We can read the opportunity costs of getting more of either good as the amount that must be given up of the other good. Actually, this is not quite right; the opportunity cost is the lost benefits that could have been received from the sacrificed good. Also, rather than use numbers, from now on we will probably use letters or other symbols in reading our graphs. Thus the opportunity cost of *IE* more tanks is *DI* fewer tractors.

tractors. Thus it is easy to infer the opportunity cost of more of either good—it is merely the amount of the other good that has to be given up or, more correctly, the benefits expected from those goods.

2. Points Beneath the Curve

Recall the assumptions stated in our definition. We assumed that the economy's resources are fully employed. Yet that is rarely the case. More often than not, there is some unemployment of the labor force, and the capital stock of the economy is not always being used at its full capacity. Indeed, in 1986 the unemployment rate was over 7 percent of the labor force. This was high, but not nearly as high as the 25 percent unemployment rate of the early 1930s. In recent years, unemployment has fallen and hovered around 7 percent of the labor force. At the same time, the unemployment of the capital stock has ranged close to 20 percent—i.e., our plants and factories have been working at about 80 percent of full physical capacity.

How do we alter our economic road map (model) to take this bit of reality into account? We do so in Figure 2-4, where we have plotted a point *U beneath* the production-possibilities curve. This point shows that the economy is operating at *less than full employment,* and this is truly a waste. The opportunity cost is the lost output of tanks and tractors shown by the shaded area *UCD.* This output, when

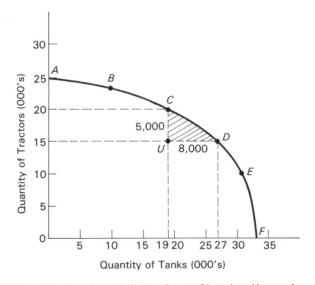

FIGURE 2-4   Production-Possibilities Curve Showing Unemployment   If the economy settles at any point beneath the production-possibilities curve, it is not using its scarce resources wisely. Any point under the curve—such as point *U*—simply means that not all potential output is being produced. In this case, if the economy is at *U,* only 19,000 tanks are being produced, along with only 15,000 tractors. Thus *UC* more tractors can be produced with no loss of tank output; or *UD* more tanks can be produced with no loss of tractor output. The shaded area *UCD* shows different lost combinations of output, and this lost output is the opportunity cost of unemployed resources.

lost, can never be regained. It obviously is wasteful to allow our scarce resources to go unemployed. In this case, the output of tractors can be increased by *UC* amount (= 5,000 tractors) at no cost to the output of tanks. Similarly, the output of tanks can be increased by *UD* quantity (= 8,000 tanks) without the output of tractors being reduced. Between these two extremes, the output of *both* tractors and tanks can be increased as the economy moves from point *U* up to the production-possibilities curve anywhere between *C* and *D*.

Much of the material in Parts II and III of this book focuses on how the economy gets beneath its production-possibilities curve and, in turn, what sort of government policies can be used to get the economy back to the curve—i.e., at or near full employment.

3. Economic Growth

Let's add to the economic model of the production-possibilities curve in still another way. Ultimately at any point in time, society has only a given amount of resources. Over longer periods of time, however, the quantity of resources in the economy can grow or decline. For instance, resources grow when the labor force expands from year to year as persons who were born earlier come of age and enter the workplace. Resources decline, for instance, when worn-out capital is not replaced. Also, it seems that new resources are always being unearthed, and people are constantly extending the amount of natural resources by such means as irrigation and draining swamps.

The results of such a growth of resources are shown in Figure 2–5. Earlier, say a few years ago, the production-possibilities curve was P_1P_1, which indicates the amount of resources available at that time. The growth of resources since then, however, will have shifted the curve to P_2P_2. Larger outputs of both goods can now

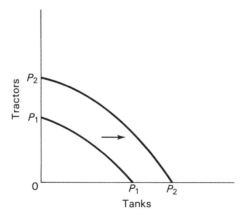

FIGURE 2-5   Production-Possibilities Curves Showing Growth   A growing amount of resources will, over time, shift the economy's production-possibilities curve to the right (from P_1P_1 to P_2P_2). This is simply because a greater amount of resources can produce more tanks and tractors than before.

be obtained, and for the simple reason that the economy has more resources. This, in a very general sense, is what is meant by economic growth.

Growth, however, may come about for another reason. Let's now drop the assumption of a static technology and accept the fact that technological advances do occur. A *technological advance* is a change in technique that increases the efficiency (productivity) of the economy's *given* resources. Consider, for example, how much more efficient a farmer is when he is working with technologically advanced equipment than he would be if he were limited to shovels, hoes, and rakes. Many of our resources today are much more efficient because of technological advances in the past. Because of this we have experienced economic growth.

The impact of technology is shown in Figure 2–6. Note that in Figure 2–6(A), the technological advance has been directed only toward the production of, say, pizzas (which we plot on the horizontal axis). It is not at all relevant for the manufacture of magazines (which we plot on the vertical axis). Thus, if all the economy's resources were to be allocated toward the production of magazines, we would still be at that point P_1 on the vertical axis. The reason for this is that the efficiency of resources in magazine production has not been affected. Resources now, however, are much more efficient in pizza production, so that if all resources were allocated to the production of pizzas, we would be at point P_2 on the horizontal axis. The new production-possiblities curve, therefore, is P_1P_2.

Figure 2–6(B) shows how the production-possibilities curve will shift as a result of a technological advance relevant for magazines only. The new curve ($P_3 P_1$) originates at P_1 on the horizontal axis, as before, because in this case pizza production is not affected by the new technology. With the new method, however, the economy's resources can produce considerably more magazines than before.

Finally, Figure 2–6(C) shows how the curve shifts when the new technology affects both pizzas and magazines. The entire curve shifts to the right. However, there is no reason to believe that the production of both goods will be equally affected by the new technology. Thus the new production-possibilities curve ($P_4 P_4$) need not be—in fact, typically will not be—parallel to the original one.

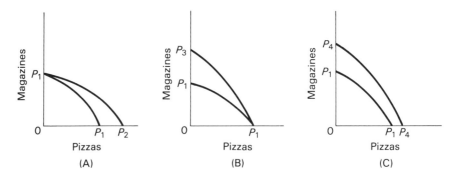

FIGURE 2-6   Production-Possibilities Curves Showing Changes in Technology   Technological advances shift the *P–P* curve to the right because they make the economy's scarce resources more efficient. It is unlikely, however, that technological advances will equally affect the production of all goods and services, and therefore the new *P–P* curve will probably not be parallel to the original one.

4. Net Investment and Economic Growth

There is still another reason for this production-possibilities curve to shift to the right, and that is by the economy allocating resources away from the production of consumer goods over to the production of more capital goods. This increase in the output of capital goods is called *net investment,* and historically it has served as a major source of economic growth in industrially advanced economic societies. The analysis here also illustrates another important point—namely, that while increased net investment may impose opportunity costs in the short run, the gain in long-run benefits swamps these costs.

First, consider Figure 2-7(A). Here we have country's original *P–P* curve (P_1P_1). Note that we have plotted capital goods (K) along the horizontal axis and consumer goods (C) along the vertical axis. Let's suppose that the economy is at point *B* and then events take place that encourage a greater production of capital goods—i.e., the economy moves to point *E*. The net investment, in this case, is *DE* amount of new capital goods. But note that the opportunity cost is *BD* less consumer goods. Thus the cost of the new capital investment is borne by the consumers who have less to consume in the *present*. However, once the new plant, machines, and inventories are available for production, the entire *P–P* curve will shift to the right. The reason for this is that we simply have more plant and buildings and machines to produce more goods and services. To be sure, there is an immediate cost imposed on consumers; but note that the future benefits are greater. More of both capital and consumer goods are then available because of the economic growth stimulated by the net investment.

In the preceding case, nothing was said about technology; we implicitly assumed it to be constant. What, however, would happen to the *P–P* curve if new

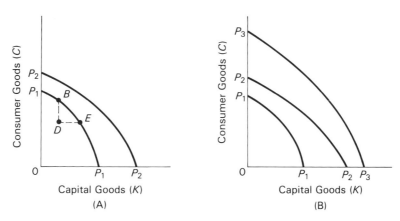

FIGURE 2-7   Production-Possibilities Curves Showing Effects of New Capital Formation   New capital formation, as in panel (A), will shift the *P-P* curve to the right (from P_1P_1 to P_2P_2), but when the new capital goods have new technology incorporated into them, the *P-P* curve will shift even farther to the right, as shown in panel (B). It is unlikely that the new capital formation and the new technology will equally affect the production of *C* and *K*, and thus the new *P-P* curves will not be parallel to the old ones.

technological advances were incorporated into the new capital goods? In this instance, not only would the curve shift to the right because of more capital goods, as in Figure 2–7(A), but it would shift still farther out because of the new technology. This is shown in Figure 2–7(B), in which $P_3 P_3$ lies farther to the right than $P_2 P_2$ in panel (A) of the same figure.

All told, net, new investment is very important as a source of economic growth, not only because of its own contribution but because it harbors new technologies.

F. THE LAW OF DIMINISHING RETURNS

Thus far nothing has been said about why the production-possibilities curve is drawn as *concave* to the point of origin—that is, bows outward. Figure 2–8 once again shows this concavity. Why does the curve bow outward? The answer to this question involves one of the most important principles in economics—the *law of diminishing returns*. This famous law underlies nearly all of modern economic thought, and a thorough grasp of it is essential for understanding what follows.

1. An Illustration of the Law

We can use our original example of the production-possibilities curve to illustrate the law of diminishing returns—see Table 2–2 and Figure 2–8. Let's start with point *A,* at which no tanks are being produced and 25,000 tractors are being turned out in the private sector of the economy. Let's also assume that 500 units of resources can be used in varying combinations to produce either tractors or tanks. Thus, at point *A* all 500 units of resources are devoted to the production of tractors and none to tanks.

Now suppose that increased military tensions induce the government to produce 10,000 tanks, and suppose further that this means that 100 units of resources

TABLE 2–2   The Economy's Production-Possibilities Schedule—Production Effects of Resource Transfers

Possibility Points	Tractors (000's)	Tanks (000's)	Net Transfer of Resources	Net Gain in Tank Output (000's)	Net Loss in Tractor Output (000's)
(1)	(2)	(3)	(4)	(5)	(6)
A	25	0			
B	24	10	100	10	1
C	20	19	100	9	4
D	15	27	100	8	5
E	8	31	100	4	7
F	0	33	100	2	8

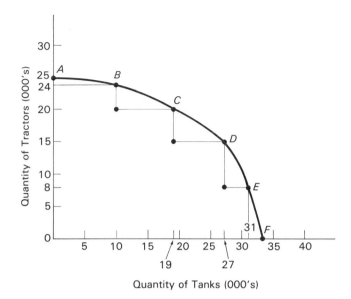

FIGURE 2-8   Production-Possibilities Curve Illustrating Diminishing Returns   This curve shows graphically the several "possibility points" in Table 2-2. Note that the curve is bowed out from the origin (i.e., is concave); this is due to diminishing returns. As more and more of either good is produced, greater amounts of the other good must be given up. The "law of increasing costs" flows directly from the law of diminishing returns.

must be allocated from the civilian sector of the economy over to the military sector—that is, the economy moves from point *A* to point *B* on the production-possibilities curve. Note that in order to increase its military preparedness, the economy has to give up 1,000 tractors. This sacrifice of tractors is the opportunity cost of the 10,000 new tanks.

Now, if international tensions continue to build up, government may decide to allocate an additional 100 units of resources to the military sector, so that we slide farther down the curve to point *C*. In this case, the net gain in tank output is 9,000 and the net loss (opportunity cost) of tractors is 4,000. Furthermore, an additional transfer of 100 units of resources would slide the economy down to point *D,* which means a net gain of 8,000 tanks and a net loss of 5,000 tractors. And so on down to point *F.*

The really important observation to make about this illustration is that in each case, as the economy moves down the production-possibilities curve, the *net* gain in tanks is *less than the preceding net gain.* This is shown in column 5 of Table 2-2. Put otherwise, *the output of tanks per unit of resources becomes smaller and smaller as more resources are allocated from the production of tractors over to the production of tanks.* This is what is meant by diminishing returns and can be expressed very neatly:

Net gain in output of tanks/Net transfer of resources

In this example, the net transfer of resources is always 100 units, and therefore the denominator remains constant at 100. But the net gain in tank production declines, and accordingly the gain in output per unit of extra resources diminishes. Table 2–3 shows this in detail. Note how, in column 3, the extra output per unit of extra input diminishes.

This explains why the production-possibilities curve is concave to the point of origin (0). Each additional 100 units of resources produces fewer extra tanks than the preceding 100 units of resources. The reason, to repeat, is the law of diminishing returns.

2. The Law Itself

But what is this law? Why does it prevail? It can be stated as follows:

> **Definition:**   As additional units of a variable input (e.g., labor) are added to a fixed amount of other inputs (e.g., capital, land), the extra output per extra unit of the variable input will eventually decline—it becomes smaller and smaller.

In our example, resources are transferred from the production of tractors to the production of tanks. Some of the resources, however, which are quite essential for the production of tanks, are fixed in supply (at least in the short run). Engineers, scientists, and technical machinery are good examples. These resources are scarcer than others (for example, land, unskilled labor, and concrete), and thus, by our definition, they constitute the fixed inputs. The other resources are the variable inputs.

Accordingly, as more and more of the variable resources are allocated to the production of tanks, the fixed resources become overworked and hence less efficient. They can't keep up with the pressures and demands imposed on them, as they have to cooperate with an increasing amount of variable inputs.

More important, however, is the fact that *the variable inputs also become less efficient.* For example, the first lab assistant working along with a scientist in a given laboratory setting may be very efficient, and so may a second, and perhaps

**TABLE 2-3   Diminishing Returns and the Economy's
Production-Possibilities Curve**

Net Transfer of Resources	Net Gain in Tank Output	Net Gain in Tank Output per Unit of Extra Input
(1)	(2)	(3) = (2)/(1)
100	10,000	100
100	9,000	90
100	8,000	80
100	4,000	40
100	2,000	20

even a third. But after a point—say, the fifteenth assistant—the additional worker won't be of much help. Certainly the one hundredth assistant won't be of any help. Put otherwise, the first lab assistant will have a rather high productivity, as probably will the second one. But as the fixed inputs (in this case, the scientist and his laboratory) become more crowded, the scientist will become overworked with supervising all of his assistants, and the laboratory will become too crowded for anyone to be able to work efficiently.

In fact, the productivity of the variable input declines because the fixed input becomes more and more crowded and overworked. Going back to our original example, the extra output of tanks produced by additional units of resources becomes smaller and smaller because some of these resources are fixed in supply.

The example is reversible, at least as long as some of the resources needed in the production of tractors are fixed in supply. If, for example, a special type of land is essential for the production of tractors, and it is fixed in quantity, then as resources are allocated from tanks to tractors, (a) this land will become overcrowded and less efficiently used, and (b) the productivity of the cooperating variable inputs will also decline.

3. The Law of Increasing Costs

The law of diminishing returns can easily be restated as the law of increasing costs. Recall that every time the economy slides up or down along the production-possibilities curve, more of one good is acquired but at the cost of giving up some other goods. This loss is, of course, the opportunity cost of acquiring the extra output.

The law of diminishing returns, as we noted above, implies the law of increasing opportunity costs. This is shown in Table 2–2. As the economy moves toward more and more tanks, fewer and fewer tractors can be produced. This means that the opportunity cost of getting more tanks rises as tank production rises (see column 6 of Table 2–2). In other words, the diminishing returns in tank output (column 5) are accompanied by increasing opportunity costs in tractor output (column 6). Why are there increasing costs whenever the output of the other good is increased? Purely and simply because of the law of diminishing returns. The decreasing efficiency of the inputs as tank output rises is reflected in rising opportunity costs.

G. SUMMARY

Trade-offs and opportunity costs exist at all levels of society as long as there are relatively scarce resources. This is why the TANSTAAFL principle—i.e., ''there ain't no such thing as a free lunch''—is everywhere relevant. In fact, this chapter defines economics in terms of benefits and opportunity costs: Economics is the study of the benefits and opportunity costs flowing from choices made in allocating scarce resources among alternative, competing uses.

Models—we have called them economic road maps—are used to penetrate the complexity of the economic system and give us a better picture of economic activity, benefits, and costs. A model, by its very nature, is a simplified picture of reality, and in this sense it is always "unrealistic." Yet models are necessary for us to understand the economy and how it functions.

Our first model is the production-possibilities curve of alternative combinations of goods that can be produced by the economy's scarce resources. It illustrates the concepts of opportunity costs (i.e., trade-offs) and benefits very well. Any movement along an economy's production-possibilities curve means that more of something is being obtained at the expense of giving up increasing amounts of something else.

The production-possibilities model is also used to explain not only the opportunity costs that flow from unemployed resources but also the meaning of economic growth. This growth can occur as a result of any one or more of three things: the growth in the supply of resources; technological advances; and net, new investment.

Finally, the production-possibilities curve is drawn as bowed out from the point of origin. This shape is due to the law of diminishing returns, which states that as long as any one or more of the resources used in production are fixed in quantity, the additional units of output due to an extra unit of the nonfixed (variable) input will eventually begin to decline. This law of diminishing returns is also the source of the increasing opportunity costs that result from a movement along the production-possibilities curve.

Terms and Concepts to Remember

Opportunity costs	Net investment
Real costs	Law of diminishing returns
Economics	Fixed inputs
Model	Variable inputs
Production-possibilities model	Law of increasing costs

Questions for Review

1. Can you think of any trade-offs relating your study time to other alternatives such as watching TV or going to a party? What are some specific opportunity costs that occur when you decide to engage in activities other than studying for classes? Can these be translated into monetary and psychological costs? Discuss.

2. What are the opportunity costs of attending college? What economic benefits do you hope will offset these costs? What are the opportunity costs of not attending college?

3. Using the concept of opportunity costs, discuss each of the following:
   a. Time is money.
   b. You can't be in two places at the same time.
   c. A bird in the hand is worth two in the bush.

4. Draw a hypothetical production-possibilities curve for an entire economy, with capital goods on one axis and consumer goods on the other. Where would the economy operate at full employment? What would cause a movement along the *P–P* curve? Where would the economy operate at less than full employment? How could the curve be shifted outward?

5. Farmer Cardwell has a 500-acre farm, the size of which can't be changed. When he purchased his first tractor, the farm's output increased by 100 percent. If he purchased two tractors, would his output increase by 200 percent? If he purchased ten tractors, would his output increase by 1,000 percent? Explain in detail.

3

Specialization, Exchange, and Money: Markets Revisited

chapter preview

- A market exists wherever supply and demand come together to set price. Every economic good and service has a market in which it is supplied and demanded.

- Markets exist because of the extensive presence of division of labor, an economic phenomenon that increases the productivity of the economy's scarce resources tremendously.

- The important idea of specialization (or division of labor) was introduced into economics by Adam Smith.

- Specialization is applicable to all economic resources—land, labor, and capital—and it pervades the entire economy.

- Advances in specialization shift the economy's production-possibilities curve to the right.

- Specialization means that the specialists produce an output far in excess of their own needs; thus they exchange the surpluses among themselves.

- The exchange among specialists— that is, their respective demands and supplies—make up the various markets in the economic society.

- Exchange, however, will take place only if the parties involved will benefit from it; in other words, exchange occurs when there is a range of mutual benefit between the trading parties.

- Economic conflict may occur within the range of mutual benefit, and if it is severe, may eliminate the rage of mutual benefit.

- Barter, as a method of exchange, is very clumsy and inefficient. Money, on the other hand, greatly aids the market exchange system.

- *Money* is defined as anything that is generally accepted as a medium of exchange.

- Both commodities (e.g., gold and silver) and paper money have been used to facilitate the exchange process, but in modern societies the most important form of money is "checkbook" or "bank" money.

The economic system of the United States is called a *market system* because it is made up of hundreds of thousands of markets. There is indeed a market for every good and service that is traded or exchanged. There are also markets for the resources to produce these goods and services. For example, there is a market for blue jeans; there is a market for haircuts; a market for bicycles; one for corn; another for motorcycles; still another for labor; and even a market for money. There is a foreign exchange market, many capital goods markets, a stock and bond market, and so on and on and on. To repeat, there is a market for every economic resource, good, and service, no matter how important it may be (e.g., housing) or how insignificant it may seem (e.g., yo-yos). A moment's reflection will also tell you that there are many illegal markets (e.g., for cocaine, stolen goods, and pornography). Markets truly abound in our economic system.

But just what is a market and how does it function? The next chapter answers this and other questions in more detail; for now we will say only this:

> **Definition:** A *market* is a place or a process in which buyers express their demands for a good or service and sellers provide their supplies of that good or service. It is a place or an arrangement in which demand and supply come together, interact, and set prices and the quantities exchanged.

Some markets, like the wheat market, are as broad as the whole world. Other markets are as narrow as a teenager's neighborhood for mowing lawns during the summer. But no matter how broad or how narrow it may be, supply and demand are always at work in the market; they continually interact with one another. It is this interaction that sets the prices of goods and services, determines how much of each will be produced, and how much of each will be consumed. Moreover, changes in supply and demand cause prices to change, and this in turn influences production, consumption, and resource allocation.

Markets, therefore, are crucial in determining the quality and direction of economic activity, and we will examine them in later chapters. But for now there are some questions that must be considered: Why are there markets in the first place? What accounts for the presence of markets? Also, what do markets in general imply about such things as exchange and money?

A. PINS, NAILS, AND PRODUCTIVITY

More than two centuries ago, a Scottish philosopher by the name of Adam Smith published the first important book on modern economics, *An Inquiry into the Nature and Causes of the Wealth of Nations* (usually referred to as *The Wealth of Nations*). One of the major things that Smith did in this seminal work was to expound on the idea of division of labor and make it the basic foundation of market activity. Here are a few of Smith's examples of division of labor and its impact:

> To take an example, therefore, from a very trifling manufacture; but one in which the trade or division of labor has been very often taken notice of, the trade of the pin-maker; a workman not educated to this business . . . , nor acquainted with the use of the machines employed in it . . . , could scarce, perhaps, with his utmost industry, make one pin in a day, and certainly could not make twenty. But in the way in which this business is now carried on, not only the whole work is a peculiar trade, but it is divided into a number of branches, of which the greater part are likewise peculiar trades. One man draws out the wire, another straightens it, a third cuts it, a fourth points it, a fifth grinds it at the top for receiving the head; to make the head requires two or three distinct operations; to put it on is a peculiar business, to whiten the pins is another; it is even a trade by itself to put them into the paper; and the important business of making a pin is, in this manner, divided into about eighteen distinct operations. . . . I have seen a small manufactory of this kind where ten men were only employed, and where some of them consequently performed two or three distinct operations. But though they were very poor, and therefore but indifferently accommodated with the necessary machinery, they could, when they exerted themselves, make among them about twelve pounds of pins in a day. There are in a pound upwards of four thousand pins of a middling size. These ten persons, therefore, could make among them upwards of forty-eight thousand pins a day. Each person, therefore, . . . might be considered as making four thousand eight hundred pins in a day. But if they had all wrought separately and independently, and without any of them having been educated to this particular business, they could not each of them have made twenty, perhaps not one pin in a day.[1]

What a fantastic increase in productivity—from 20 to 4,800 pins per person per day. This is the great beauty of division of labor: It increases the productivity of the worker tremendously. Surely the greater the division of labor, the greater the output per worker, *and therefore the higher the country's level of living.*

In another example, Smith observed that a blacksmith working alone ". . . can seldom with his utmost diligence make more than eight hundred or a thousand nails in a day." However, he continued:

> I have seen several boys under twenty years of age who had never exercised any other trade but that of making nails, and who, when they exerted themselves, could make, *each of them,* upwards of two thousand three hundred nails in a day.[2]

[1]Adam Smith, *An Inquiry into the Nature and Causes of the Wealth of Nations* (New York: Random House, 1937), Modern Library ed., pp. 4–5.

[2]Ibid. p. 8.

This again is a great increase in productivity from, say, 1,000 nails per worker to around 2,300 nails, more than a doubling of output per worker due solely to division of labor.

Thus far our discussion of division of labor implies that the concept is restricted to labor alone. This is not the case, however, for it applies equally well to the other productive resources—capital and land. Perhaps we should use the term *specialization* instead of *division of labor*. Either term is acceptable, however, and we will use them interchangeably to designate the same fundamental concept. (See Exhibit 3–1.)

EXHIBIT 3–1
Adam Smith: The Founding Father of Modern Economics

Adam Smith wrote about many more things than pin and nail factories. In fact, his role in the development of our economic and democratic political thought has been tremendously important. It is perhaps no coincidence that his famous *Wealth of Nations* was published in 1776, the year that means so much in the history of our country. In 1776, Smith showed the world how to achieve individual economic freedom; in the same year, the United States showed the world how to achieve individual political freedom. We have combined the two types of freedom into a democratic, free-enterprise market system; and in doing this we have gone a long way in showing that Smith was right. He argued that free choice and free action in the marketplace are the best way to provide for the economic welfare of the citizens of a country. Government, in his view, has but few economic functions: (1) to make sure that the market system remains competitive; (2) to provide for defense; (3) to provide for education, the court system, and other basic necessities of government; and (4) to provide necessary public works. Other than those, government is to keep its "hands off" economic affairs. The "hands-off" policy is also known as *laissez faire* (a French phrase that means "allow them to do")— that is, allow consumers and producers to do their own thing, as long as they operate within the broad, general framework of the law. (*Laissez faire* doesn't mean allowing murder for profit, for example.) The basic idea is that we ourselves know better than government what is best for us. Chapter 4 explains how this happens. So does Part IV of this book.

But there is so much more in *The Wealth of Nations*. It describes the process of economic growth, it sets forth rules of taxation that are still relevant today, and it shows the benefits of free international trade. These are only a few—a *very* few—of Smith's contributions to modern economic thought. *The Wealth of Nations* is a book that is still well worth reading; it remains, even after two centuries, amazingly modern.

There is much specialization in the use of land. Land in the South, for example, is best suited for producing cotton and peanuts; land in the Midwest, on the other hand, is best suited for corn, wheat, and soybeans. Kentucky and West Virginia specialize in the production of coal; Texas and Oklahoma in oil and cattle; and Washington and Oregon in timber and fruits and vegetables. Some land is better suited for farming, other land for urban development, and still other land for recreational purposes. Therefore, as in the case of labor, there is a great deal of specialization in the uses of land.

The same is true of capital. Capital can take many forms as it is used to produce the economy's output. Some is specialized in the production of steel, some in the production of electronic equipment, and so on. There is also specialization within a plant, as on the assembly line of an automobile factory. Specialization of capital has been carried so far that robots now perform many of the tasks that humans used to do on the assembly line.

There is also specialization in marketing, sports, medicine, education, and government. Indeed, there is specialization in nearly every walk of life. Division of labor is very widespread. Moreover, it is essential if we want to have economic growth and rising standards of living. Specialization in the use of land, labor, and capital makes the economy's scarce resources more productive and hence allows greater output per unit of resource input.

We can use the production-possibilities model to illustrate the significant impact of specialization on our scarce resources. Figure 3–1 shows the production-possibilities curve of pins and nails before division of labor. Note how far to the left the P_1P_1 curve lies. Now let's introduce division of labor into the production of both commodities. This is the same thing as an improvement in technology. Consequently the curve shifts to the right to P_2P_2, showing that with greater division of labor, the same resources can produce much larger amounts of both pins and nails.

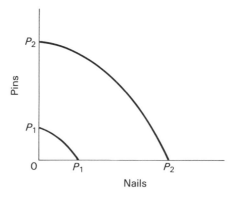

FIGURE 3-1   Production-Possibilities Curves, or Smith's Pins and Nails   The P_1P_1 curve shows the various combinations of pins and nails that can be produced with little division of labor and capital. However, as Adam Smith's analysis shows, the productivity of these resources increases tremendously with the introduction of division of labor. Hence the production-possibilities curve shifts far to the right. This is the same thing as an advance in technology.

Division of labor, which can be considered a form of technology, is thus a prime source of economic growth.

B. THE EXCHANGE PROCESS

Certain major consequences flow from the widespread application of division of labor. We have just discussed one of these—the growth in productivity of resources. Another consequence is that we all become very dependent on others for our economic well-being and, indeed, for our very survival. In a society in which there is much division of labor, no one person is able to provide for all of his or her needs. None of us is a jack-of-all-trades; we are instead all specialists of one sort or another. As the eighteenth-century poet Charles Churchill put it:

> By different methods different men excel;
> But where is he who can do all things well?

As specialists we each depend on others to provide us with the various things we need and want. A farmer who specializes in wheat must depend on other specialists to provide him with food, clothing, shelter, health care, and so on, just as these other specialists depend on him for wheat. This interlocking dependency clearly shows itself when activities in any one specialized area of production wane or cease.

A good analogy of this is a television set, which consists of numerous specialized parts. As long as all the parts are functioning harmoniously, the set will produce both good audio and good video. Yet let only one small piece malfunction, and the quality of both video and audio will deteriorate; indeed, either or both may disappear. Thus, in a highly specialized environment, all the parts must interact smoothly if the entire system is to operate efficiently.

Still another consequence is important in understanding the market-exchange system, for the very nature of specialization leads to an exchange process. The reason for this is that every specialist produces a surplus. For example, doctors produce many more medical services than they will ever need; farmers grow more corn than they can ever consume; and workers in a furniture factory create far more furniture than they will ever use. Certainly Smith's pin worker will never need all the 4,800 pins per day that division of labor allows him on average to produce.

At the same time, the doctors and furniture workers don't (indeed, can't) grow all the food they need—they rely on the farmers for this commodity—and the farmers, in turn, rely on the doctors for medical services and on the furniture workers for tables and chairs. This, however, goes further than the interdependency noted above, for now everyone must, in some way or another, exchange his or her surpluses for some of the surpluses produced by other specialists. And here we come to a basic principle.

> **Conclusion:** Specialization creates surpluses that must be exchanged among the specialists if they are to receive the full benefits of specialization.

Here, of course, we have the reason why there are markets. All exchanges of surpluses take place in markets. *All* specialists *supply* their own surpluses and *demand* the surpluses of others. In other words, supply and demand come together in the market as these surpluses are being swapped back and forth among the specialists. Thus our major conclusion for now is: Specialization leads to exchanges and these exchanges make up what we call markets. Let's look at the exchange process in more detail.

1. The Benefits of Exchange

In a free-enterprise market economy, all exchanges are voluntary (except for some illegal activities). No government officials tell us or order us to buy what we buy or to work where we work. This is not a command economy. Instead exchanges are made freely and voluntarily. Moreover, they are made because *they yield benefits for the parties involved.*

Let's take an example. Suppose you purchase a chair from a furniture dealer for, say, $195. Let's suppose also that you have gone through the decision-making process discussed in the preceding chapter—that is, you have already drawn up a budget and have considered all the relevant opportunity costs involved in purchasing the chair. What this means is that you have decided that you will get more benefits from the chair than you will by spending the $195 on anything else.

At the same time, the furniture dealer is willing to part with the chair for $195 (he must be, for that is what he has priced it at) because he feels that the money (or what he can buy with the money) will give him more benefit than the chair does. In other words, he also will benefit from the exchange between the two of you.

> **Conclusion:** Voluntary exchange is a process that mutually benefits both parties. If it didn't, exchange wouldn't take place. Exchange creates value.

This simple, but important, point is worth repeating: If the exchange doesn't benefit both parties, it won't take place. It doesn't matter that either one or the other would benefit; what does matter is that *both* must gain from the exchange.

2. The Range of Mutual Benefit

The benefits created by voluntary exchange are essential to the ongoing market economy. Let's pursue this matter with another example. Suppose a certain Mr. Sellers has a car that he is willing to part with but has decided that he won't sell it at any price below $4,000. Suppose also that a neighbor down the block, Mr. Byers, is in the market for a used car but has decided not to pay, say, any price above $3,000. In this case, there won't be an exchange—the demand and supply of these two persons don't come together in the market. Therefore each will look elsewhere in the used-car market. There won't be an exchange because there is no possibility of *mutual benefit.*

Let's stick with Mr. Sellers and suppose that, after his disappointing session with Mr. Byers, he uses the Want Ads section of the newspaper to advertise his car. His ad is read by a number of people, including a Mr. Bigger who is in the market to buy a used car. Suppose too that Mr. Bigger has decided that he is willing to pay a price up to $6,000, but no more. We now have the opportunity for exchange, and the reason is that Mr. Sellers's *minimum offer price* ($4,000) is less than Mr. Bigger's *maximum offer price* ($6,000). In this case, there is a *range of mutual benefit.*

Figure 3–2 illustrates this range of mutual benefit. On the vertical scale, we have plotted different possible prices of the automobile. The dashed arrow, which originates at the price of $4,000, shows the prices at which Mr. Sellers is willing to sell. Note that these prices are at and above $4,000, his minimum offer price. The solid arrow, originating at Mr. Bigger's maximum offer price of $6,000, shows the prices at which Mr. Bigger is willing to buy. Observe that there is a range (shown as *MB)* in which these two arrows overlap. This is what we call the *range of mutual benefit,* and it must exist if there is to be voluntary exchange. If Sellers and Bigger get together and reach an agreement, then exchange between them will take place somewhere *within this range.*

Where within the range will the exchange take place? Will the exchange take place smoothly and harmoniously? Strange as it may seem, there is room for some economic conflict within the range of mutual benefit. This is because, even though both parties will benefit, each wants to benefit as much as possible. Thus Sellers wants to sell at as high a price as possible, and as long as he is dealing only with

FIGURE 3–2   Range of Mutual Benefit   As long as the buyer's maximum offer price is greater than the seller's minimum offer price, there will be a range of mutual benefit from exchange between the two. Here the range is shown as *MB.*

Bigger, he would prefer the price of $6,000. Bigger, on the other hand, would prefer a lower price, in fact, as low as point *B* in Figure 3-2—that is, as low as Sellers's minimum offer price. The stage is set, therefore, for bargaining and negotiation, and this is a form of economic conflict. The final outcome will depend largely on the bargaining strength and skills of the two men.

> **Conclusion:** Even though both parties experience gains within the range of mutual benefit, either one can obtain greater gains only at the expense of lesser gains for the other. Mutual benefit and conflict are not contradictory.

In some cases, however, the conflict swamps the possibility of mutual benefits, and in these cases the conflict may be severe and costly (not only to the parties involved but to outsiders as well). Consider the case of collective bargaining between a labor union and management shown in Figure 3-3. Here the two arrows don't overlap; there is no range of mutual benefit as perceived by the two parties. The union's minimum wage offer lies above the employer's maximum offer, and unless either or both parties modify their demands, conflict in the form of a strike is apt to occur and continue until some range of mutual benefit has been established.

Nevertheless, our major conclusion is that as long as a range of mutual benefit exists, voluntary exchange will take place between the involved parties. There may be some conflict as negotiations are being carried on, but conflict and benefit are quite compatible in the market system. In some cases, however, conflict may temporarily disrupt the voluntary exchange process.

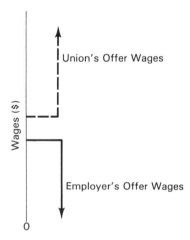

FIGURE 3-3 Economic Conflict with No Range of Mutual Benefit In this case, there is no range of mutual benefit because the seller's minimum offer price lies above the buyer's maximum offer price. Accordingly, no mutually beneficial exchange can occur, at least until the conflicting offers are reset so that a range of mutual benefit emerges.

C. MONEY IN THE EXCHANGE PROCESS

So far in this chapter we have seen how exchange and division of labor benefit the members of society. Division of labor increases the productivity of relatively scarce resources by allowing people and other resources to specialize more efficiently in particular tasks. Exchange, then, becomes necessary because each specialist produces more than he or she can consume of one thing and, at the same time, produces nothing at all of other things he or she needs. Thus the surpluses must be exchanged, and we know they will be as long as there are ranges of mutual benefit.

1. Barter

Exchange, however, has to be carried out some way or other, and historically two methods have emerged. One of these is the barter method—the mutual swapping back and forth of physical goods and services. This method of exchange is very common in many of the traditional-type economic societies that we mentioned in Chapter 1. It was also widely used in the early history of the United States, particularly on the frontier. In fact, it is used wherever and whenever there is little or no money in the economy, and hence people are paid an "income in kind." This means that the workers are paid in the form of their contribution to the output of the goods they help to produce. Let's go back to Adam Smith's pin factory. Recall that in this example, a worker could, *on the average,* produce 4,800 pins per day. Suppose the employer keeps out 800 pins for his profits and to cover the other costs of production. Then he pays the worker a daily wage of 4,000 pins. Thus the 4,000 pins are the worker's income in kind.

You can undoubtedly see how clumsy and inefficient the barter method of exchange is. The worker can't survive on his income in kind, on pins alone. He needs many more items than pins to exist. In fact, he probably needs very, very few of the 4,000 pins—maybe none at all. But he does need food and clothing, shelter and drink. So now he must look about for other people who have surpluses of these things but who also need pins. For example, if our pin worker needs a loaf of bread, he must find some baker who has a surplus of loaves of bread *and who also needs pins*. This is called the "double coincidence of wants." Only in this case will there be a range of mutual benefit so that exchange will take place. It doesn't matter that the baker has a surplus of bread; as long as he demands no pins, exchange won't occur. There is no range of mutual benefit.

However, it may be that the baker needs some cloth. Now, if our pin worker is fortunate enough to find someone who has a surplus of cloth and a shortage of pins, then the pin worker is in business. He can exchange his pins (or some of them) for cloth, which he can then take to the baker and swap for the bread. At last he can eat; but, unfortunately, he now has to go through the same process to get milk, shoes, a chair, and so on and on and on.

All very clumsy and inefficient, isn't it? Too much so! Indeed, had we not allowed the pin worker to find the cloth right away, he might still be searching. Then think of all the time and effort he must devote to exchanging his pins for everything else that he needs. Ranges of mutual benefit may exist, but discovering them is another matter. In fact, in a barter system, more time will be spent in the search for ranges of mutual benefit than will be expended on production. In this case, the benefits of division of labor will be lost. Indeed, in a barter-type economic society, there will be very little division of labor.

2. The Role of Money in Exchange

It is at this point that money enters the economic scene, and money, as we shall see, is necessary for a smoothly functioning market system of exchange. Money facilitates the exchange process and allows it to work more smoothly and efficiently.

But just what is money? And what is the historical background of the types of money we use in our society today? First, a provisional definition.

> **Definition:** *Money* is anything that is generally accepted as a means of payment. Put otherwise, money is anything that performs one basic, essential function—it must be generally accepted as a medium of exchange.

As we shall see, a variety of things may perform—indeed, have performed—this basic function of money.

3. Commodity Money

The first form of money to be used as societies developed was some good or commodity that was itself exchanged in markets. Actually, over the centuries and across different cultures, many strange and wondrous things have served as money. Barley, cattle, fur skins, shells, silver, gold, and beads—to mention a few—have been used as money in times past. Even in recent modern history some rather strange things have served as money in times of crisis. Nylon stockings and cigarettes, for example, were widely accepted in exchange in Europe during the chaos following World War II.

The interesting thing about commodity money is that it has two values—a *value in use* (as a commodity) and a *value in exchange* (as money). In other words, commodity money is a useful good that also circulates as money. All the commodities mentioned above have had these two values; but the two goods that have played a major role in the evolution of money have been gold and silver. These two commodities have particular attributes that make them very well suited as forms of money. First, they are universally desired because of their great beauty and other attributes. Second, and equally important, they are both relatively scarce in supply. The result of this relatively high demand and relatively low supply is a high unit value. That is, a small amount or weight of gold and silver can be exchanged for a lot of other goods. Third, both gold and silver are easily divisible. Both are soft metals that can easily be melted down and worked into different shapes. Consequently, they are ideal for money in the form of coins, which are convenient for making change in market transactions. Finally, the metals are very durable and thus don't deteriorate or wear out (like cattle, barley, and cigarettes).

4. Paper Money

Paper money evolved directly out of the use of commodity money. In fact, paper money originally was merely a warehouse receipt for gold or silver. During the Middle Ages, merchants in Europe had need for a safe, secure place to keep their gold and silver. Goldsmiths and silversmiths, artisans who worked the precious metals into plate and jewelry, had vaults for the safekeeping of their raw materials. As time passed, it became customary for the merchants to keep their gold in the goldsmith's vaults for security purposes. The goldsmith would then issue a paper receipt to the merchant in return for the gold. When the merchant wished to use his commodity money, he would present his receipt to the goldsmith and thus obtain his gold.

Gradually, however, a mutual trust began to build up between the goldsmiths and the merchants. Under these circumstances, it was not necessary for the merchant to bring his gold to the market. Instead the warehouse (vault) receipt could be, and was, used as payment for his purchases. The real money—the physical gold—remained in the vaults. The end result was that paper receipts circulated as a medium of exchange while the gold that "backed" them tended to stay in one place.

Over the centuries, the gold backing of these pieces of paper has disappeared while the paper continued to circulate. In this way, therefore, commodity money evolved into paper money. Note, however, an important point: Although commodity money has both use value and exchange value, paper money has no intrinsic, or use, value, but only value in exchange. To put it more simply, *paper money is wanted only for the things it can buy in the market. It has no value in and of itself.*

5. Bank Money

The most recent step in the evolutionary process of money is the appearance of checking deposits, or what we refer to here as "bank money." Checking accounts of various kinds have largely replaced paper money as a medium of exchange in the industrially advanced economies. Most of us receive our wages and salaries in the form of a check on payday instead of getting a pile of paper money. Some of us have our wages and salaries paid directly to our banks; we never even see a check, let alone paper money.

Then, as we make purchases, we write checks against our accounts, ordering the banks to transfer balances from our accounts to the accounts of others. The checks that we write are not money; they are merely orders to the banks to move funds. The actual movement of money (funds) takes the form of electronic orders moving balances from one bank to another (see Chapter 11).

The important point for now is that in the modern world, money continues to evolve rapidly. Credit cards, traveler's checks, and the so-called debit cards are some of the more modern variations on the theme of checkbook money.

6. Money in the United States

Checkbook money dominates the scene in advanced economies. For example, roughly 90 percent of the value of total transactions in the United States is accounted for by checkbook money. This is actually the most important type of money in our society.

Still, we continue to make use of both paper money and coins. Our paper money is issued by the Federal Reserve System (our central bank), and it ranges all the way from one-dollar bills and five-dollar bills to much higher denominations. Unlike the old warehouse receipts, which were backed by gold, our modern paper money is backed only by the credit-worthiness of the issuing institutions. Paper money is what is called *fiat money*—that is, it is decreed as money by the issuing government. It has little or no value as a commodity, but as long as the public has faith that the issuer is trustworthy, it will continue to serve as a medium of exchange.

Metal coins—pennies, nickels, dimes, quarters, and a few half-dollars and dollars—are minted by the U.S. Treasury. They are sometimes referred to as *token coins* because the market value of the metal in them is less than the face value of the coins. For example, there isn't a nickel's worth of metal in a nickel. But since nickels are accepted at face value in exchange, it doesn't matter that they are token. We use these coins because they are accepted as money, not because of the value of the metals in them. They are not commodity money.

All forms of money today—checkbook, coins, paper—are fully interchangeable at face value. They have no value in and of themselves (no use value); the only value they possess is that they are generally accepted as a medium of exchange.

The subject of money has become very complex in the modern world. In this chapter we have merely introduced the subject.

7. Back to the Pin Maker

Let's return now to the harried and distressed pin worker and relieve him of the burdens of barter exchange. Instead of having him paid with income in kind (4,000 pins), let's have him paid in the form of money wages. The amount of these money wages (in our example) is the money market value of 4,000 pins. Suppose our pin worker is paid by check, which he then deposits in his checking account. Before or at the time of deposit, he may keep out some of the wages as coins and paper money for his small, routine transactions. The rest of his transactions are made by check. Remember, all of these types of money are generally accepted in the exchange process. Thus he can now easily buy the loaf of bread he wants from the baker. And the baker is happy with the pin worker's money because he, in turn, can exchange it for the cloth and the other items that he needs.

So, in the modern world, as in the past, *money allows the exchange process to function efficiently (at least cost) so that we can attain the full benefits of the division of labor.* It is, as Adam Smith put it, "the great wheel of circulation, the great instrument of commerce" that furthers the operation of the market exchange economy.

D. SUMMARY

Our market economy has grown out of the processes of specialization and exchange. Specialists produce far more than they themselves can consume, and then they exchange these surpluses among themselves. The advantage of specialization is that it increases the productivity of the means of production. But it also requires some sort of exchange process so that the surpluses may be swapped back and forth. In our society, this exchange takes place through markets. Hence, reading each arrow as "leads to," we have:

$$\text{Markets} \rightarrow \text{Specialization} \rightarrow \text{Exchange}$$

Exchange in markets can be carried out by barter, but barter is very inefficient. Instead we use money, which is anything generally accepted as a medium of exchange. Money has historically evolved from commodity money and coins to paper money to checkbook money. Money, however, is crucial as a means of facilitating the exchange process. The exchange of goods for money is far more efficient than the exchange of goods for goods. Money is therefore an integral part of the smoothly functioning, efficient market exchange process.

Terms and Concepts to Remember

Division of labor (special-
    ization)
Exchange
Range of mutual benefit
Barter
Income in kind

Money
Commodity money
Bank money
Fiat money
Token coins

Questions for Review

1. Write a short answer that explains why Adam Smith's pin worker's productivity increases because of the division of labor. Now think of some modern-day examples that have the same general economic impact.

2. What is meant by the range of mutual benefit? How does it relate to the idea of markets?

3. An early twentieth-century British economist, F. Y. Edgeworth, presented an analysis

that concluded that conflict and exchange are not mutually exclusive. Using our concept of the range of mutual benefit, explain why Edgeworth's conclusion is valid.

4. What is money? What forms does it take in our society?

5. Why does commodity money have two values? What has happened historically to commodity money? Why?

6. Define and illustrate each of the following: (a) token coins, (b) fiat money, and (c) income in kind.

4

The "Mystique" of the Market

chapter preview

• Prices are set by the interaction of supply and demand in markets. Supply and demand represent the private decisions of the sellers and buyers, respectively.

• The "law of demand" establishes an inverse relation between the price and the quantity demanded of a product.

• In addition to price, demand is affected by tastes, incomes of buyers, prices of other goods, expectations, and the number of buyers.

• The demand curve is drawn under the assumption that only the price of the product can be varied. All other factors that affect demand are assumed not to change.

• A change in any of these other factors will shift the demand curve. An increase in demand is shown by a rightward shift of the curve; a fall in demand is shown by a leftward shift.

• The "law of supply" establishes a direct relation between the price and the quantity producers are willing to sell.

• In addition to price, supply is affected by prices of resources, technology, expectations, and the number of producers.

• A supply curve is drawn under the assumption that the other factors that affect supply don't change. A change in any of these will shift the supply curve to the right (an increase) or to the left (a decrease).

• The interaction of market demand and supply sets the equilibrium price at the level where the quantity demanded equals the quantity supplied. Any other price is a disequilibrium price and will move toward the equilibrium level.

• Changes or shifts of either supply or demand curves cause changes in equilibrium price and quantity.

How is it that when we go to the grocery store to buy bread, milk, canned goods, breakfast cereal, coffee, and canned soup there are sufficient quantities of these things on the shelves? Why do clothing and department stores have available supplies of dresses, suits, blouses, and pants? And why do bakeries have rolls and doughnuts when we want them, and shoe stores have the shoes that we want, bookstores the books, and furniture stores the furniture? When you consider the millions of different goods that we consumers demand and the quantities of them that we acquire every day of the year, year in and year out, it is amazing that these things are available at all, let alone in sufficient amounts and at the proper places and times.

This result is even more amazing once we recall that in our society we don't rely on central commands to tell us what is to be produced, in what quantities, by what techniques, for whom and when. No central planner says, "Today we will produce three million doughnuts for New York City, three thousand for St. Louis, and none for Albuquerque." That wouldn't work in our society. If not, then what is it that determines how much of anything is to be produced? The answer is simply this: *The exchange process as it unfolds in the various markets in the economy.*

> **Conclusion:** Our society relies very heavily on private decisions as they are voluntarily expressed in free markets to answer the *what, how, how much,* and *for whom* questions. And out of the literally billions of individual decisions made by all the participants in the economic society, order, not chaos, emerges and prevails. There is actually a sort of mystique or magical quality in how the market system serves as a coordinating mechanism, bringing as it does far more harmony than discord out of all these decisions.

The task of this chapter is to unravel this mystique, and we begin by stressing the role that prices play in coordinating the market system. Prices serve as a guide to action, as we saw earlier in Chapter 1 with regard to the TV and radio markets. Buyers and sellers respond to prices and price changes and hence influence how the economy's scarce resources are used. In a sense, prices are the heartbeat of the market system.

How are prices set? What causes them to change? And how do they help in coordinating economic activity? The simple answer to these questions is *supply and demand.* These two basic economic forces (supply, demand) are continually interacting in the marketplace to determine prices and to cause prices to change. Supply and demand! The analysis of supply and demand constitutes the essence of economic thinking in a market economy. We now turn to this analysis.

A. THE DEMAND SIDE OF MARKET PRICE

There is something rather puzzling about the role of the consumer in the market system. Any one single consumer is apt to find that the market is a very large and impersonal force. Indeed, the single consumer is so small in the market that he or she has no influence on the prices of goods and services. For example, you may ask, "What do I have to say about the price of shirts? Nothing! I go to a store—I even shop around among several stores—and every time I look at a shirt, there is a price tag on it. I can't even bargain with the clerk about the price. In effect, he tells me, 'Take it or leave it. If you don't want it at this price, then leave it. Someone else will buy it.' I don't have anything to say about the matter."

You are right! You alone, acting only by and for yourself, really have little to say about how high or low the price of shirts will be. You, as a single, solitary consumer in the market, are forced to act as a *price taker*—that is, you take prices as given and beyond your direct control. And, given these prices, you do the best you can to make your limited income go as far as possible when you buy goods and services.

However, and this is the important point, you are not alone. Most products have thousands of consumers; many have millions. And all of you acting collectively (even though you do not know one another) have a very definite impact on prices, more than any one of you might think. There are millions of consumers of shirts, and if all of you decide, for some reason or another, to reduce your demand for shirts, you can bet your bottom dollar on one thing—the market price of shirts will fall! It may not fall immediately, but fall it must. Thus, while you alone may be insignificant in acting as a price taker, all consumers acting together participate powerfully in setting prices.

1. The Law of Demand

Let's begin our analysis by supposing that you have a limited income and that you are in the market for shirts. More specifically, let's suppose that you are thinking about spending a part of your limited income to add some new shirts to your wardrobe. Let's also suppose that these new shirts are of the same style and quality as those you already have.

Look at what we have done in this example. We have stated that two of the major factors affecting your demand for shirts are *given*—that is, set and unchanging—namely, your income and your tastes. There is no need to explain that your income is given except to say that we assume it as given for only the time period in question. Over time, of course, it will change; but for a shorter time period—say, a month or even a year—we may reasonably assume your income is unchanging.

What do we mean, however, when we say that your tastes are also given?

Surely desires and preferences are always changing; so why do we take them as set? The answer is that your tastes are assumed to be given only for sake of the analysis. Later on, after we have developed the model of consumer behavior far enough, we may drop the assumption of given tastes and see what this implies. But for now we simply assume that the new shirts you are contemplating buying are to be of the same type and quality as those you already have.

Since we have already taken two of the factors influencing your demand as given, let's go one step further and assume that two other factors influencing your demand for shirts are also given: the prices of all other goods and services; and your expectations about what will happen to the price of shirts in the near future.

Thus far, then, we have taken as given—i.e., we ignore for the moment—four important things that influence demand: (a) income, (b) tastes, (c) prices of all other goods and services, and (d) expectations. We may add a fifth, and that is the number of consumers of the product. What is left? Well, what is left is the *actual market price* of shirts. If you act rationally, then you will shop around and look for lower-priced shirts. Remember that quality and style are the same; and given your income you will undoubtedly be very conscious of the prices charged for the shirts. In fact, it seems reasonable to argue that if the price of the shirts is very high, you won't buy as many as you would if the price of the shirts were lower.

This allows us to state another basic economic principle—the *law of demand.*

Conclusion: The higher the price of a good or service, the lower the amount you will demand, *ceteris paribus*, that is, all other things being equal. The reverse is also true: The lower the price, the greater the amount you will demand (again, *all other things being equal*).

The law of demand thus states that there is an *inverse relationship* between the price of the item and the *quantity demanded*. This sounds reasonable. All other things given, the consumer will buy fewer shirts at a higher price and more shirts at a lower price. Indeed, the law of demand holds generally among products and consumers. That is why it is called a "law."

So far we have stated the law of demand in words only. There is another way of stating it, and that is to use a table or, as we call it, a schedule. Let's suppose that, given your tastes, income, and so on, the schedule in Table 4–1 represents your

TABLE 4-1   Your Demand Schedule for Shirts

(1) Price	(2) Quantity	(3) Point on Demand Curve in Figure 4–1
$50	0	A
30	1	B
20	2	C
16	3	D
8	4	E

demand for shirts pretty closely. This means that at some very high price ($50), your quantity demanded is zero—that is, at that price you will simply make do with the shirts you already have. However, the demand schedule in Table 4-1 also shows that at lower prices your quantity demanded will increase until, at the low price of $8, you will demand a quantity of four shirts.

The information in Table 4-1 can be stated in still another way. In Figure 4-1, we have plotted physical quantities of shirts along the horizontal axis, and we have plotted prices along the vertical axis. Now consider the price of $20 per shirt, at which the quantity demanded is two shirts. This particular price-quantity demanded combination is shown as point *C* in Figure 4-1. This point tells us that at the price of $20 per shirt, the quantity demanded is two shirts.

If we do the same thing for point *D*, we see that the price of $16 per shirt, the quantity demanded is three shirts. Similarly, point *B* tells us that when the price is higher ($30), the quantity demanded is lower (one shirt), and at the lower price of $8 per shirt, the quantity demanded is four shirts (point *E).*

The next step is simply to connect all of these various price-quantity demanded combinations (*A, B, C, D,* and *E).* This gives us your *demand curve* for shirts. Note that the demand curve begins at point *A,* which lies *on* the vertical axis. This means that at the price of $50 per shirt, your quantity demanded is zero. What it really means is that at $50 you have been priced out of the market.

Note also that the demand curve in Figure 4-1 runs downhill from left to right—that is, it has a *negative slope.* This is what we would expect of the law of demand. Any curve that has a negative slope tells us that there is an *inverse relationship* between the things plotted on the two axes—in this case, price and quantity demanded. That is, the higher the price, the lower the quantity demanded; and the

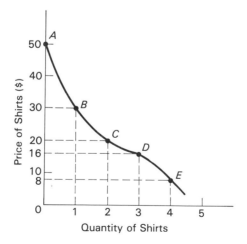

FIGURE 4-1   An Individual's Demand Curve for Shirts   The downward-sloping curve running through points *A, B, C, D,* and *E* is your hypothetical demand curve for shirts. This negative-sloped curve shows that there is an inverse relationship between price and quantity demanded.

lower the price, the higher the quantity demanded. The negative-sloped demand curve in Figure 4–1 is merely a picture of the law of demand as it applies to you and shirts.

2. The Market Demand Curve

You, of course, aren't the only one demanding shirts. Millions of consumers have their own individual demand curves for shirts. As might be expected, the producers (the suppliers) of shirts are far more interested in the *total demand* of all these consumers than they are about your individual demand. Economists, likewise, are much more concerned about the *market* (or total) *demand curve* than they are about any one consumer's demand curve.

What is this market demand curve? It is nothing more than all the individual demand curves added together horizontally. That is, it is simply Jones's demand curve *plus* Smith's demand curve *plus* Carpenter's demand curve and so on. To repeat, the market demand curve is the demand curves of all the consumers of shirts *added together* from left to right.

This is illustrated in Figure 4–2, which shows how we add together the demand curves of our three consumers. Although there are millions of consumers of shirts, these three illustrate the point. The three individual demand curves in Figure 4–2

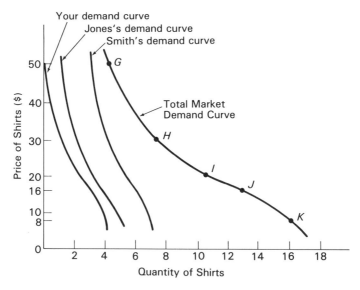

FIGURE 4–2   From Individual Demand to Market Demand   To get from the demand curves of all the individual consumers of the product to the total market demand curve, we merely add together all the individual demand curves horizontally—i.e., from left to right (not from top to bottom). Since all the individual demand curves adhere to the law of demand, so does the market demand curve.

TABLE 4-2   Summing Up Individual Demand Curves

	(1) +	(2) +	(3) =	(4)	(5)
Price	Your Demand + Schedule	Jones's Demand + Schedule	Smith's Demand = Schedule	Total Demand Schedule	Point on Market Demand Curve in Figure 4-2
$50	0	1	3	4	G
30	1	2	4	7	H
20	2	3	5	10	I
16	3	4	6	13	J
8	4	5	7	16	K

have been taken from Table 4-2. Observe that these demand schedules (hence the demand curves) are different from each other. Why? For any of a number of reasons. For instance, each consumer will have a set of tastes that differs from that of others, incomes will be different, as will expectations of future price changes. Thus, while you decide to be "priced out of the market" at the price of $50, Jones is willing to demand a quantity of one shirt. Smith, who may have a higher income or may like shirts very much, is willing to purchase a quantity of three shirts at that price. As long as we have different tastes, and as long as we have different incomes and future expectations, our demand curves are apt to be different, even for the same goods.

Therefore, at the price of $50, the total quantity demanded is four shirts (zero for you, one for Jones, and three for Smith). This total quantity demanded is shown in column 5 of Table 4-2 and as point G in Figure 4-2. If we do the same thing with the quantities demanded at the price of $20, we get the total quantity demanded of ten shirts (two by you, three by Jones, and five by Smith); this is shown by point I on the demand curve. Thus, by summing up the quantities demanded at each price, we get the market demand curve. Note that it too has a negative slope, running downhill from left to right. The reason is simply that each individual demand curve in it has a negative slope.

B. CHANGES IN DEMAND

So far we have stressed that, all other things given, the quantity demanded of a good varies inversely with price. These other things are the incomes of consumers, prices of other products, tastes, consumer expectations of future prices, and the number of consumers themselves. In reality, of course, "all other things" are *not* given, and when any one or more of them changes, there is a *change in demand*. This is shown by a shift of the entire demand curve either to the right (an increase in demand) or to the left (a fall in demand). Let's look at the effects of changes in each of these other things.

1. Changes in Preferences

A change in tastes that increases consumers' preferences for a shirt will cause the entire demand curve to shift to the right. This is shown in Figure 4–3. Consider first the price of $20 per shirt. Before the change in preferences, consumers were demanding a quantity of 22 million shirts at that price. This particular price-quantity demanded combination is shown as point *A* on the original demand curve D_1D_1. But once tastes change in favor of shirts, consumers are willing to buy the larger quantity of 30 million shirts at the same price ($20). This is shown as point *B* on the new higher demand curve D_2D_2.

Note that demand is also higher at other prices. In our example, at the price of $10 per shirt, demand has increased from 35 million to 45 million; and at the price of $30 per shirt, demand has increased to 15 million shirts (from about 12 million).

> **Conclusion:**   When demand increases, the entire demand curve shifts to the right, showing that consumers are willing to buy more of the good or service at each price.

Note also that the new demand curve D_2D_2 is not parallel to the original D_1D_1 curve. The reason for this is that the change in tastes is not uniform at all prices of shirts. This example assumes a greater change in preferences for shirts at lower prices. But this is an example only: We could just as well have assumed that the stronger preferences were for shirts at the higher prices, in which case the new de-

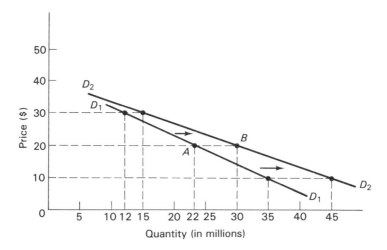

FIGURE 4–3   An Increase in Demand   Here the demand curve has shifted in its entirety to the right from D_1D_1 to D_2D_2. Such a shift shows an increase in demand at each price—i.e., consumers are, for whatever reason, willing to buy more even though price remains the same.

mand curve would have been steeper than the original line. In any event, it is unlikely that a change in tastes will affect demand equally at all prices.

What would happen to the demand curve if tastes were to change in the opposite direction? In this event, demand would fall, and the demand curve would shift
to the left, as shown in Figure 4–4.

> **Conclusion:**   When demand falls, the entire demand curve shifts to the
> left, showing that consumers are willing to buy smaller amounts of the
> good or service at each price.

Again we have drawn the new demand curve D_3D_3 to be not parallel to the original
D_1D_1 curve. What does this tell us about the change in tastes that we have assumed?

2. Changes in Income

Changes in income are also important. When their incomes rise, consumers tend
to increase their purchases of many goods and services. When their incomes fall,
consumers reduce their demand for many goods and services. But again the shift of
the curve need not be parallel. The main reason for this is that the income change
won't be uniform for all consumers of shirts; and even if it were, not all consumers
have the same tastes.

3. Changes in the Prices of Other Goods

The third cause of a change in demand is a bit more complicated. Here we must
distinguish between two categories of goods: substitutes and complements. Let's
look first at substitute goods.

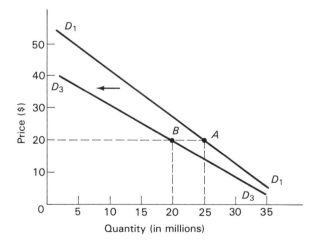

FIGURE 4–4   A Fall in Demand   A leftward shift of the entire demand curve reflects a fall in demand. Here, for example, consumers are now willing to purchase only
20 million shirts at the price of $20 per shirt, a fall in demand from 25 million shirts.

Definition: *Substitute goods* are those that compete with each other in the consumer's budget.

Beef, pork, and chicken are examples. Coca-cola and Pepsi-Cola, cabbages and peas, and movies and television are other examples.

Now, what will happen to the demand for one good when the price of the substitute changes? The answer may be obvious. For example, when the price of beef rises, people will buy less of it and more chicken, even though the price of chicken remains unchanged. That is, consumers increase their demand for chicken in response to the higher relative price of the substitute.

The argument is reversible. If the price of beef were to fall, people would increase their *quantity demanded* of it and thus reduce their *demand* for chicken.

Conclusion: Whenever the price of a good changes, then, all other things equal, the demand for the substitute will change in the *same* direction

Complementary goods present a different situation.

Definition: Two goods are *complementary* when they must be consumed together in order for the consumer to gain satisfaction from either.

An automobile doesn't provide much pleasure to its owner if there is no gasoline to operate it. Other examples: golf clubs and golf balls, horses and saddles, beer and chips, cereal and milk, and hog jowl and black-eyed peas.

What will be the effect of a change in the price of golf clubs on the demand for golf balls? Again perhaps the answer is obvious.

Conclusion: When the price of the one good changes, the demand for the complementary good will change in the *opposite* direction.

Thus when the price of golf clubs falls, the demand for golf balls will rise. Similarly, a rise in the price of automobiles will reduce the demand for tires and batteries.

4. Changes in Expectations of Future Prices

A change in consumer expectations about future prices will cause the demand curve for a product to shift. If consumers anticipate that the price of the product is going to fall in the future, they are apt to postpone their purchases until the price does in fact fall. On the other hand, the expectation that price is going to rise is likely to cause the demand curve to shift to the right as consumers increase purchases to beat the anticipated price increase.

5. The Number of Consumers

One final factor affecting demand should be mentioned. All other things equal, a change in the number of consumers will shift the demand curve for a product. Clearly, a decrease in the number of consumers in the market will result in a leftward shift of the demand curve, while an increase in the number of consumers (again, all other things equal) will cause it to shift to the right. Changes of this sort, however, generally occur over longer periods of time than do changes in income, tastes, other prices, and expectations. These can change very abruptly.

6. An Interim Summary

- The law of demand states that there is an *inverse relationship* between price and quantity demanded. Put otherwise, the demand curve has a *negative slope.*
- Whenever the price of the product changes, therefore, there is a change in *quantity demanded*—i.e., when price rises, *quantity demanded* falls; and when price falls, *quantity demanded* rises. These changes are shown as movements along a stable nonshifting demand curve.
- The original demand curve (such as D_1D_1 in Figures 4–3 and 4–4) is drawn on the assumption of "all other things given." That is, the other factors that influence consumer behavior are assumed to be constant and unchanging, *and as long as they remain given, the demand curve will maintain its original position. It will not shift.*
- These other factors are tastes, income, expectations, the prices of other goods and services, and the number of consumers.
- A change in any of these other factors, however, will cause the demand curve to shift. Depending on the nature of the change, the demand curve may rise (as D_2D_2 in Figure 4–3) or fall (as D_3D_3 in Figure 4–4). We illustrate these shifts of the demand curve by considering the effects of a change in tastes, a change in consumers' income, a change in the prices of other goods, and a change in the number of consumers.

Now that we have laid down these basic principles of demand, let's turn to the supply side and develop some further principles.

C. THE SUPPLY SIDE OF THE MARKET

If we are going to consume things, those things must of course be available—they have to be produced and supplied. This is the major function of all the *privately owned* business firms in the market economy. They produce (supply) nearly all the goods and services that we consume; and they typically do so with one major purpose—to make a profit. So once again we see the importance of market price, for price is one of the three things that determine what profits are. The other two are the costs of production and technology (see Chapter 17). Thus, whenever price changes, producers respond by altering production. Put more accurately, *whenever demand changes, causing price to change, the amount supplied will also change.* In a consumer-oriented market economy, the consumer plays a powerful role indeed (see Exhibit 4–1).

1. The Law of Supply

We have already seen that there is a law of demand. There is also a *law of supply!* This law, as might be expected, differs from the law of demand; in fact, it is just the reverse of the law of demand (which states that there is an inverse relationship between price and quantity demanded).

EXHIBIT 4–1
The Consumer as King (?)

Here is Adam Smith again. In *The Wealth of Nations,* he placed the consumer on a pedestal. He put it this way:

> Consumption is the sole end and purpose of all production; and the interest of the producer ought to be attended to, only so far as it may be necessary for promoting that of the consumer.[1]

This seems very clear; and our chapter has shown how producers respond to consumer demand. This is as it should be. Who else are the producers to produce for and sell to? Themselves only? No, Smith was right—the sole end and purpose of production is for the consumer. It is for this reason that in our type of economic system, the consumer is often referred to as "king."

The American economic system generally works rather well in responding to consumer demand. If we want more jeans and T- shirts, we get them— maybe with a lag and at higher prices, but we get them. If we want more fishing boats, we get them. And if we want fewer neckties, fewer of them will be produced.

This doesn't mean, however, that consumers get everything they want at the prices they are willing to pay. Such a result is impossible. But it does mean that consumers have far more clout than, say, in the Soviet Union or in any other command-type economy. If there is any doubt in your mind about this, please go back to Chapter 1 and reread Exhibit 1-1. The contrast is remarkable.

Consumers, however, have much to complain about. Sometimes the advertising that influences them is misleading and perhaps downright dishonest.

[1]Adam Smith, *The Wealth of Nations* (New York: Random House, 1937), Modern Library ed., p. 625.

At other times the products they get are of inferior, and even shoddy, quality. And it is true that monopolistic elements in the economy can create higher prices than might otherwise exist. Thus the consumer may be king in the market economy, but often enough the king is taken advantage of.

There is an old saying—*caveat emptor*—which means "let the buyer beware." That is, one buys at his or her own risk. For many years in this country, this was a practical rule. Rarely did consumers have any direct means of protecting themselves, and if they purchased a faulty product, they often had no recourse. The whole idea was that sellers would not produce faulty products, that they would not commit such an act.

Yet experience reveals that this wasn't the case. One result was the creation of the Consumer Product Safety Commission in 1972, which followed from efforts and disclosures by Ralph Nader and other consumer advocates. Also, other legislation that indirectly protects the consumer has been around for some time—for example, the Federal Trade Commission (1914), which forbids misleading advertising. We will say more about these regulations in Chapter 21, but for now we merely want to point out that such legislation is designed to increase the consumer's sovereignty.

Our major conclusion, however, is this: In the market economy of the United States the consumer, while maybe not really a king, is a powerful actor in the economic drama. Producers and sellers must still cater to the consumer; and, as we shall see, the more competitive the economy, the more powerful the consumer.

Definition: The *law of supply* states that (all other things given) the higher the price, the greater the quantity supplied; and the lower the price, the lower the quantity supplied. Thus both price and quantity supplied *change in the same direction*—i.e., they show a *positive relationship* with one another.

Table 4–3 gives us the supply schedule of a small, hypothetical shirt producer. These figures are transferred to Figure 4–5 as the firm's supply curve. Note that the firm's supply curve has a *positive slope*—it runs uphill from left to right. Note also that at point *A* on this supply curve, quantity supplied is zero. This means that at the low price of $8 per shirt, our hypothetical firm will cease production. Producing even one shirt will create a loss for the firm, and thus the firm will not produce at all.

At points *B, C, D,* and *E,* on the other hand, the firm will indeed produce because at these higher prices it will be making a profit. Also, the higher the price (say, $20), the greater the quantity supplied (2,000 shirts, as at point *C*). At still some higher prices, the quantity supplied will also be higher (e.g., 4,000 shirts at the price of $50 per shirt, giving us point *E* on the firm's supply curve). Thus the

TABLE 4-3 A Firm's Supply Schedule of Shirts

Price	Quantity	Point on Supply Curve in Figure 4-5
$50	4,000	E
30	3,000	D
20	2,000	C
16	1,000	B
8	——	A

firm's supply curve has a positive slope. This sounds reasonable enough. Ask any competitive business manager what he or she would do with the firm's output as price rises, and the answer would be, "Increase it."

Our small, hypothetical firm, however, provides only a very small share of the total market output of shirts, and we are concerned with its supply curve only inasmuch as it is a part of the *market supply curve.* To get the market supply curve, we must add together the supply curves of all the firms in the industry. This is done for three firms in Figure 4-6; but remember, these are only three firms out of hundreds of firms producing shirts. The real market supply curve, then, is made up of the supply curve of all the firms in the industry. Figure 4-6 is for purposes of illustration only.

Since each individual firm's supply curve obeys the law of supply—i.e., has a positive slope—then the market supply curve must also have a positive slope, since

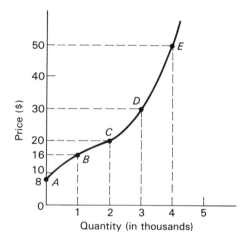

FIGURE 4-5 A Single Firm's Supply Curve The curve connecting points *A* through *E* is the single firm's supply curve. Observe that it slopes up from left to right (i.e., it has a positive slope). This shows how price determines the amount that the firm will supply. The higher the price, the greater the quantity supplied; and the lower the price, the lower the quantity supplied. This is the law of supply.

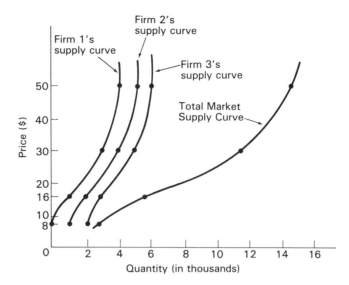

FIGURE 4-6   From Individual Supply to Market Supply   Getting to the market supply curve means that we must add horizontally the supply curve of all the individual firms producing the product. Since all of these individual supply curves reflect the law of supply, so does the market supply curve.

it too reflects the law of supply. Remember, according to that law, the lower the price, the lower the quantity supplied; and the higher the price, the higher the quantity supplied.

2. Changes in Supply

Just as the demand curve may shift back and forth in response to, say, changes in incomes and tastes, so too will the supply curve shift, although for different reasons.

> **Conclusion:**   An increase in supply is shown by the entire supply curve shifting to the right. This means that firms are willing to produce a larger amount at each price. Furthermore, if producers decide to reduce supply, this is shown by the curve shifting to the left.

What could cause supply to increase, that is, shift from S_1S_1 to S_2S_2, as shown in Figure 4–7? A number of things, as we shall see. One of these is an increase in the number of firms in the industry. Suppose profit opportunities in the industry have risen; this will then lure new firms into the industry and induce existing firms to expand, hence shifting the supply curve to the right. Also, as we shall see later, an improvement in technology will cause the supply curve to move to the right. So will a reduction in the costs production and marketing.

On the other side of the coin, a fall in supply is shown by a leftward shift of the supply curve, as from S_1S_1 to S_3S_3 in Figure 4–7. This could be caused by a

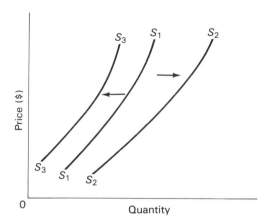

FIGURE 4-7 Changes in Supply Changes in supply (as opposed to changes in quantity supplied) are shown by shifts of the entire supply curve. A shift to the right shows that supply has increased, whereas a shift to the left reflects a decrease in supply.

lessening of the number of firms in the industry or by a rise in the costs of production.

3. A Recap

Supply and demand curves will be discussed at length in Chapters 15–17. For now we merely want to assert the following:

* The law of supply shows that there is a *positive relationship* between price and quantity supplied.
* Whenever the price of the product changes, therefore, there is a change in *quantity supplied.* When price rises, *quantity supplied* rises; and when price falls, *quantity supplied* falls. These changes are shown as movements along a stable, nonshifting supply curve.
* The original supply curve (such as S_1S_1 in Figure 4–7) is drawn on the assumption of "all other things equal." That is, the other factors that influence producer behavior are assumed to be constant and unchanging. *As long as they remain given, the supply curve will maintain its original position. It will not shift.*
* These other factors are the number of firms in the industry, costs of production, and technology.
* A change in any of these other factors will cause the supply curve to shift. Depending on the nature of the change, the supply curve may rise (as from S_1S_1 to S_2S_2 in Figure 4–7) or fall (as from S_1S_1 to S_3S_3).

D. THE INTERACTION OF SUPPLY AND DEMAND IN THE MARKET

We are now ready to see how supply and demand interact in setting market price. Consider Figure 4-8, in which we have both the market demand curve and the market supply curve.

The important point we want to establish is this: As long as the two curves are stable, the market price will end up at the level shown by the intersection of the curves. In Figure 4-8, this occurs at the price of $20 per shirt. Note that at this price, the quantity demanded of 25 million shirts is the same as the quantity supplied of 25 million shirts.

To see why the market price will settle at the level at which quantity demanded is equal to quantity supplied, let's see what would happen if quantity supplied actually exceeds quantity demanded.

1. Quantity Supplied Greater Than Quantity Demanded

Let's begin by assuming that the market price is, for whatever reason, as high as $50 per shirt. The producers, as we might expect, definitely like this price because they think it means higher profits for them. As Figure 4-8 reveals, they are willing to supply a quantity of 35 million shirts at that price. Thus the *quantity supplied* is 35 million; this is a *market surplus*.

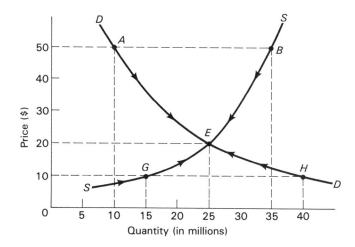

FIGURE 4-8   Market Equilibrium and Disequilibrium   The intersection of the market demand and supply curves indicates where the equilibrium price will be. At that price, consumers are demanding exactly the quantity that producers are supplying. Any other price is a disequilibrium price. A price that is too high (i.e., above the equilibrium level) will induce a *market surplus;* a price that is too low (i.e., below the equilibrium level) will lead to a *market shortage.* In both cases, however, the disequilibrium conditions of the market will be eliminated by the automatic functioning of the market.

What the firms so happily start out doing, however, turns into a bad mistake. Why? Because, while the firms are supplying a quantity of 35 million shirts at the price of $50, consumers are willing to demand a quantity of only 10 million shirts at that price. The price of $50 is just too high for many consumers. Although some are willing to purchase shirts at that price, most will make do with the shirts they already have. They are, as it were, priced out of the market, and hence the quantity demanded is a mere 10 million shirts.

Here, then, is the problem for the producers. What serves as a stimulus for them to *increase* their quantity supplied—the high price of $50 per shirt—serves also as an inducement for consumers to *reduce* their quantity demanded. In this case, the quantity supplied is 35 million. Since the producers can sell only 10 million of their output of 35 million shirts, then unplanned, unwanted inventories of 25 million shirts pile up in the warehouses. These excess inventories of 25 million are shown by the distance between point *A* (quantity demanded) and point *B* (quantity supplied) in Figure 4–8. Here we have another important conclusion.

> **Conclusion:**   As long as quantity supplied is greater than quantity demanded, excess inventories will build up. There is a *surplus* of the product in the market.

How will the producers respond to this situation? First, they will cut price to move the excess inventories out of their warehouses. The price reduction is transmitted to the wholesalers, and from the wholesalers to the retailers. The retailers, in turn, will lower the price at which they sell the shirts to us. This means that some consumers now get back into the market at the lower price. In terms of the law of demand, now that price has been cut, there will be an increase in quantity demanded. Thus the inventories will be reduced and will continue to be reduced as consumers respond to price cuts by increasing quantity demanded. This is shown by the arrows pointing down the demand curve from point *A* in Figure 4–8.

But price cutting is not the only thing that the firms will do. It is extremely unlikely that they will continue producing the same quantity of shirts that got them into trouble. Instead, they will start cutting back on production. Put in terms of the law of supply, as price falls, quantity supplied also falls. This is shown by the arrows pointing down the supply curve from point *B* (Figure 4–8). We are now ready to draw another important conclusion.

> **Conclusion:**   Whenever quantity supplied exceeds quantity demanded, both price and quantity supplied will fall. Quantity demanded, however, will rise. These responses will continue as long as there is an excess of quantity supplied over quantity demanded.

In the case of market surplus, therefore, price falls.

2. Quantity Demanded Greater Than Quantity Supplied

Let's now suppose that for some reason or other, the producers are supplying an output of 15 million shirts (point *G* on the supply curve in Figure 4–8). Let's suppose also that they set price as low as $10 per shirt. If they do behave in this way, they will once again discover that they have made a serious error. What is their mistake now? Simply this: At the current output, quantity demanded is 40 million shirts, whereas quantity supplied is but 15 million. At such a low price, consumers demand far more than the amount being supplied, and now there exists a *market shortage.* This shortage is shown by the distance between point *G* (quantity supplied) and point *H* (quantity demanded) and, in this case, amounts to 25 million shirts.

This situation will not continue, however, since some consumers are willing to pay a price higher than $10, and since they want shirts, they start bidding the price up. This is shown by the arrows pointing up the demand curve from point *H.* In other words, the law of demand continues to prevail, and as the price rises, the quantity demanded falls, thus reducing the shortage.

Also, as the price rises, the law of supply holds, and firms will increase their quantity supplied. Thus the market shortage tends to be reduced.

> **Conclusion:** Whenever quantity demanded exceeds quantity supplied, both price and quantity supplied will rise. Quantity demanded, however, will fall. These responses will continue as long as there is an excess of quantity demanded over quantity supplied.

In the case of a market shortage, therefore, price rises.

3. Quantity Demanded Equals Quantity Supplied: The Equilibrium Price

Recall that when price was so high that quantity supplied exceeded quantity demanded, price began to fall. This was our case of market surplus. But the fall in price did two things: first, it increased quantity demanded; second, it reduced quantity supplied. These two responses reduced the surplus and they will continue as long as there is a surplus, no matter how small.

On the other hand, when price was so low that quantity demanded exceeded quantity supplied, price began to rise. This was our case of market shortage. And the rise in price did two things: first, it increased quantity supplied; second, it reduced quantity demanded. These two responses reduced the shortage, and they will continue as long as there is a shortage, no matter how small.

Thus, all other things equal, price always tends toward the level at which there is no market surplus or shortage. This occurs at the intersection of the demand and supply curves (at point *E* in Figure 4–8). At this point, the quantity demanded equals the quantity supplied at 25 million shirts. In fact, that is how we define market equilibrium.

> **Definition:** A *market equilibrium* exists when quantity demanded equals quantity supplied, all other things given. But if one of these "other things" changes, the equilibrium is disturbed; the market, however, will tend toward a *new* equilibrium price at which once again quantity supplied equals quantity demanded.

The fascinating thing is that all of this occurs spontaneously and with no government intervention. In the free market system, both consumers and suppliers respond freely and voluntarily to disequilibrium price changes, and the market creates a new equilibrium.

4. The Equilibrium Price as Compromise

Will everyone be happy with the equilibrium price? Not really! Most people, consumers and producers alike, will probably be unhappy with it. The sellers would like the selling price to be higher, for this would mean more profits for them. However, *given* the market demand curve and *given* the market supply curve, the sellers are limited to the equilibrium quantity of 25 million shirts.

Consumers would of course like to get their shirts at some lower price. Indeed, they would purchase more at any price below $20. But, for the moment, that doesn't matter; *given* their own demand curve for shirts, and *given* the producers' supply curve, they too are stuck with the price of $20 and the quantity of 25 million shirts.

Thus we have a situation in which, at the equilibrium price, producers want a higher price (but can't get it), and consumers want a lower price (but also can't get it). In this respect, the equilibrium price is something like a *compromise price*. Like most prices, it leaves most parties at least a bit unhappy. Nonetheless, there it is! That is how the market works.

E. THE EVER-CHANGING MARKET

There is no reason to believe that an equilibrium price, once reached, will continue through time for very long. Instead demand and supply conditions always seem to be changing, and therefore market prices are also in a state of flux. To see why, let's start out with the market price of T-shirts being in equilibrium at price P_1 in Figure 4–9 and see what happens when we upset the equilibrium. From now on, we will use the letter P to stand for price and the letter Q to stand for quantity. We will not specify what these P's and Q's are, whether $20 and 25 million. From now on we are interested only in the direction of movements of the P's and Q's, not precise numerical figures.

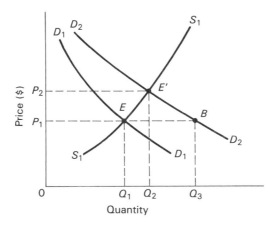

FIGURE 4-9   Adjustments to an Increase in Demand   Here we have demand rising relative to supply, and as a consequence both the equilibrium price and the equilibrium quantity rise. The rise in demand disturbs the initial equilibrium at E by creating a market shortage of EB amount at the price P_1. Consequently, market price will rise to P_2 where quantity demanded (Q_2) equals quantity supplied (Q_2).

1. A Change in Demand

Now suppose a T-shirt fad sweeps the country, so that the demand curve in Figure 4-9 rises from D_1D_1 to D_2D_2. What will be the consequence of this, all other things given? As long as the supply curve remains constant at S_1S_1 (as we have assumed), then we find that the old equilibrium price P_1 is now a *dis*equilibrium price, for at P_1 quantity demanded (Q_3) is greater than quantity supplied (Q_1). This is a case of a market shortage—i.e., consumers are demanding a larger quantity at P_1 than suppliers are willing to provide (in fact, by EB amount). Our analysis, however, argues that in the case of a market shortage, price will be bid up so that the shortage will be eliminated. The new equilibrium is at E'. At the new equilibrium price, P_2, quantity demanded equals quantity supplied at Q_2. Note, however, that the new equilibrium quantity (Q_2) is greater than the original equilibrium quantity (Q_1); note also that the new equilibrium price (P_2) is higher than the original equilibrium price (P_1).

> **Conclusion:**   When demand rises, all other things given, the new equilibrium price and quantity will be greater than the original price and quantity.

The reverse of this is true. If demand were to fall, all other things constant, both the new equilibrium price and the new equilibrium quantity would be lower than the original equilibrium levels.

2. A Change in Supply

Suppose now that the supply curve rises for some reason or other—say, more new firms begin manufacturing T-shirts. Note that this is the only thing we allow to

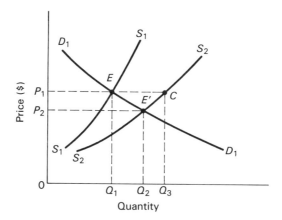

FIGURE 4-10   Adjustments to an Increase in Supply   When supply increases relative to demand, a market surplus is created. In this case, the market surplus is *EC* amount at the old equilibrium price of P_1. A market surplus, however, means that price will fall, eliminating the surplus. Thus price falls to P_2, the new equilibrium level at which quantity supplied (Q_2) is equal to quantity demanded (Q_2).

change—i.e., we hold the demand curve constant. What will be the consequence of this? In this event, the original equilibrium price of P_1 (in Figure 4-10) is now a *dis*equilibrium price, for now at P_1 the quantity supplied (Q_3) is greater than the quantity demanded (Q_1) by *EC* amount. Thus we have a case of market surplus; and as shown above, whenever a market surplus exists, price will fall. And fall it will toward the new equilibrium level of P_2. The new equilibrium quantity is Q_2, which is greater than the original quantity of Q_1.

> **Conclusion:**   When supply rises, all other things equal, the new equilibrium price will be lower than the original price and the new equilibrium quantity will be greater than the original quantity. In this case, price and output move in opposite directions.

The reverse of this is also true. If supply were to fall, all other things given, price would rise to a new equilibrium level and output would fall to a new equilibrium level.

All the possibilities are summarized in Table 4-4.

3. A Puzzling Case

In Figure 4-11, we have the original equilibrium price (P_1) and quantity (Q_1). Suppose now that *both* demand and supply curves shift to the right. In this case, what will happen to equilibrium price and quantity? Will price rise or fall? Will quantity rise or fall? Is there any neat, definite answer? In one sense, yes! Quantity will definitely rise. But in another sense, no! Whatever will happen to *P* depends on how

TABLE 4-4   Price and Quantity Responses to Changes in Demand and Supply

If this change occurs,	then price will	and quantity will
Demand rises	↑	↑
Demand falls	↓	↓
Supply rises	↓	↑
Supply falls	↑	↓

far *each* of the curves shifts to the right. As a good exercise in supply and demand analysis, you should figure out the alternatives. Be sure to do the same thing for leftward shifts of the curves.

F. LAGS AND IMPERFECTIONS IN MARKET ADJUSTMENT

A final point is in order. The market for most goods and services doesn't work as smoothly and as quickly as our discussion in this chapter may imply. For one thing, it takes time for prices to adjust to changing market conditions.

To illustrate this, let's go back to a new T-shirt fad sweeping the country. This, as we saw in Figure 4-9, causes the demand curve to rise from D_1D_1 to D_2D_2.

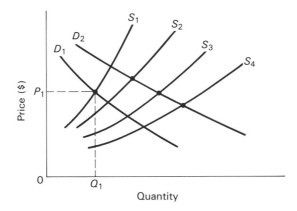

FIGURE 4-11   Alternative Responses to a Change in Demand   When both curves shift to the right, we can definitely say that quantity bought and sold in the market will rise. But what will happen to price? It all depends on how far to the right the supply curve shifts relative to the demand curve shift. In one case (S_2), the new equilibrium price will be higher than the old P_1. In another case (S_3), the new equilibrium price will settle at the old level P_1; and in the last case (S_4), the new equilibrium price will dip beneath P_1.

Consumers go dashing into retail stores to buy more T-shirts at price P_1, and retailers are certainly more than happy to sell out their stocks at the price of P_1. Just moving their inventories is good enough for them; they don't raise price, at least not yet.

This may seem odd at first, for our analysis has led us to believe that when demand rises, *ceteris paribus,* price will also rise. Yet, in this example, there has been no price rise. But do not fear; there will be a price rise somewhere down the line.

The retailers, once their inventories have been worked down, will place new orders with the wholesalers who handle T-shirts. But price will probably not yet rise, for these wholesale firms will sell at the same price. But once their shelves are bare, they too place new orders with the manufacturers. So far, there has been no price rise as a result of the increase in demand.

Now, at the manufacturer's level, we find forces coming into play to raise prices. One of the basic ingredients used in T-shirts is cotton. As a result of the increased demand for T-shirts, the demand for cotton rises. This has to be the case if the manufacturers of T-shirts are going to increase production to satisfy the higher demands of wholesalers. But cotton is limited in supply. Only so much was grown last season, and it is used for many more things than simply T-shirts. So the only way the producers of our product can get the necessary cotton is to pay a higher price for it. Thus the costs of production of T-shirts have gone up.

The manufacturers of T-shirts now sell their new output to wholesalers at a higher price to cover the increased costs of production. The wholesalers, in turn, pass the price increase on to the retailers. So eventually you will go to the store to buy a new T-shirt and find out that its price is P_2, not P_1. You complain, and the owner replies, "I'm sorry, but I have to charge the higher price because my costs have gone up."

So now the market price has moved toward the new equilibrium level of P_2 (Figure 4-9). It took a while for it to start rising, but rise it did. When consumers increase their demand for any good in the market, they can expect to end up paying a higher price, even though there may be a time lag.

Will P_2 remain the equilibrium price? Probably not. This higher price may well cause new producers of T-shirts to set up business and start turning out their product. In other words, the supply curve will shift to the right from S_1S_1 to S_2S_2, as shown in Figure 4-10. This will cause price to start dropping toward the new equilibrium. But even that equilibrium won't be maintained, not if demand changes again.

The actual market price is like a frustrated hunter. It is always seeking its target (the equilibrium level), but conditions are constantly changing, hence moving the target from one point to another. That's the way the market works.

Our description of how the market works has ignored a lot of things. For instance, it has left government regulation out of the picture. It has also pushed off to one side the problems created by the monopolies, the labor unions, and the impact of foreign trade. But we have accomplished what we set out to do, and that was to present the basic explanation of how the market system works. It is continually allocating and reallocating resources as supply and demand change. In a market economy, resources are allocated and reallocated by voluntary decisions. We say a lot more about all of this in Part IV.

G. SUMMARY

In a market economy, prices are set by the interplay of supply and demand; and prices change as supply and demand change. These prices serve as signals of how resources are to be allocated among alternative uses.

The law of demand states that there is an inverse relationship between price and quantity demanded. The law is reflected in the downward-sloping market demand curve, which is the horizontal summation of all individual consumer demand curves for the product.

The demand curve, however, is constructed on the assumption that all the other factors that affect consumer behavior are constant. These are income, prices of other goods, tastes, expectations, and number of consumers. A change in any of these will cause the demand curve to shift either to the right (an increase) or to the left (a decrease). Demand will increase when any of the following occurs: consumers' incomes rise, preferences for the product increase, the prices of substitutes rise, the prices of complements fall, expectations are that future price will rise, and the number of consumers rises. The reverse of all of these will cause demand to fall.

The law of supply postulates that the market supply curve is positively sloped, showing a direct relationship between price and quantity supplied. The market supply curve is the horizontal sum of all the individual firm supply curves of the product. This supply curve assumes that prices of productive resources, technology, expectations, and the number of firms in the industry are constant. Thus a change in any of these will cause the supply curve to shift either to the right (a rise in supply) or to the left (a fall in supply). The following will cause supply to rise: a fall in the prices of productive services, an advance in technology, expectations of rising input prices, and the number of firms supplying the product. The supply curve will fall if the reverse of these happens.

The intersection of the demand and supply curves indicates the equilibrium price at which quantity demanded equals quantity supplied. Any other price is a disequilibrium price, and market forces will push it toward the equilibrium level. A market surplus exists when quantity supplied is greater than quantity demanded. This happens when price is too high, but price will fall and eliminate the excess of quantity supplied over quantity demanded. A market shortage prevails when price is too low and thus quantity demanded exceeds quantity supplied. However, price will rise, eliminating the shortage.

Market equilibrium thus occurs when there is no tendency for price to change—that is, when quantity demanded equals quantity supplied. Actual market prices, however, are seldom equilibrium prices. The main reason is that in a dynamic economy, supply and demand are always changing. Very rarely are all other things constant.

Terms and Concepts to Remember

Law of demand	Market supply
Inverse relationship	Change in quantity sup-
Market demand	plied
Change in quantity de-	Change in supply
manded	Market price
Change in demand	Equilibrium quantity
Law of supply	Equilibrium price
Positive (direct) relation-	Disequilibrium price
ship	

Questions for Review

1. List the factors that affect demand. Describe a product and state how the demand for this product is affected by changes in these determinants of demand.

2. Advertising attempts to alter people's tastes and preferences and to increase the number of buyers in the marketplace. Can you think of a product that really isn't very important to our continued existence, but for which there has been demand created through advertising?

3. What is the real meaning of a downward-sloping (negative slope) demand curve? Can you describe real-life examples of this type of economic behavior? (*Hint:* Seasonal white sales or quantity discounts.)

4. What happens to the supply of oranges when the wages of migrant labor increase? What happens to the supply of oranges when there is freezing weather in central Florida? What happens to the price of California oranges when there is a freeze in central Florida? Why and how do these changes occur?

5. Can you describe an economic *shortage* of some product with which you are familiar? How and why were quantities demanded greater than quantities supplied? (*Hint:* Think in terms of the ticket situation for a Michael Jackson concert.)

6. Can you describe an economic *surplus* of some product with which you are familiar? Why did quantities supplied exceed quantities demanded?

7. Define and describe a *disequilibrium price*. Why are disequilibrium prices a temporary phenomenon? Answer in terms of both a market shortage and a market surplus.

5

The Circular Flow of Economic Activity

chapter preview

• The circular flow model shows how the markets for goods and services are interrelated with the markets for productive resources.

• Households play a dual role in the circular flow of economic activity— they demand the output of business firms and at the same time supply productive services to business firms to produce that output.

• Business firms also play a dual role in the circular flow—they supply the goods and services demanded by households and at the same time demand the use of the resources needed to produce that output.

• The production of output by business firms generates a flow of income to households sufficient to purchase that output.

• Households allocate a portion of their income to saving. By itself, this saving drains purchasing power from the economic system.

• Savings, however, flow into financial institutions because of the lure of an interest return to the savers.

• Business firms demand these savings for capital investment purposes.

• Financial institutions channel the savings of households toward business firms that desire to invest in new capital. Financial institutions are thus intermediaries between households and business firms.

• By itself, saving is a leakage from the circular flow of spending; investment, however, is an injection into the spending flow.

• If the savings leakage is matched by the investment injection, the circular flow will be in equilibrium and the level of economic activity will not change.

• Investment plans of business firms are likely to be different from the saving plans of households. When this happens, the circular flow of spending will change.

• When saving exceeds investment, the circular flow contracts; when investment exceeds saving, the circular flow expands.

We all consume. Every time we buy something, whether it be a pair of socks, a house, a ticket to a hockey game, a car, or a videocassette recorder, we perform an important act on the demand side of the market. Clearly, households (consumers) play a vitally important role in economic activity.

But there is more to economic activity than simply consumption and demand. There is also the production (supply) side. Here is where business firms enter the picture, for they produce and supply the various goods and services demanded by consumers, and as we have seen, they attempt to do so for a profit. Business firms, therefore, play out their role in the supply side of the economy.

Government, too, gets into the act. Although government in the United States directly produces few goods and services, it is nonetheless the largest single demander of the things produced in the private sector. The federal government is also tremendously important in financial markets; it has now amassed a debt of about $3 trillion. Consequently, its role in economic activity is crucial.

Finally, it is impossible for us to overlook the part played by foreigners, for we are truly a part of the world economy. Goods and services are constantly flowing in to and out of the country as we here at home exchange some of our surpluses for some of the surpluses produced abroad. The idea of mutual benefit discussed in Chapter 3 is just as relevant for international exchanges as it is for domestic interchanges. Accordingly, the foreign sector plays a major role in the flow of economic activity. In fact, the impact of foreign trade on our economy has increased tremendously in recent years.

The interaction of all of these economic units—consumers, business firms, government, and foreigners—determines the magnitude and direction of economic change. And the overall picture of the economy reveals a ceaseless ebb and flow of our scarce resources among alternative uses as these various actors make their decisions and exchanges of goods and services.

What we need now is another economic road map, another economic model, that will help explain all of this activity. The next section introduces this new model—the *circular flow* model. As always, we begin with the simplest version of the model and then add realistic complications to it. Thus we start by considering the basic roles played by only two actors in the economic drama—households and business firms. The other major players, government and foreigners, will be introduced in the next two chapters. For now, however, we don't want the stage to be overcrowded.

A. THE CIRCULAR INTERACTION: BUSINESS FIRMS AND HOUSEHOLDS

We begin with Figure 5–1. All of the 55 million or so households in our society are lumped together in a box on the right-hand side. And all of the nearly 17 million business firms are lumped together in the box on the left-hand side.

Let's look at this diagram more closely; it deserves a lot of attention. Note how the boxes are tied together by two sets of arrows. First, there is a solid arrow that flows round and round in a counterclockwise direction. It emerges from the business firms box and flows to the households, only to pass through the households box and flow again back to the business firms. Second, there is the dashed arrow that flows around in a clockwise direction. Starting again with the business firms, it flows through the households and back to the firms. Both of these arrows indicate a continually flowing process, round and round. This is the basic picture of the economy as a circular flow process.

1. The Real Flows

But what do these arrows represent? Let's look first at the households box. This box represents all the families (including single persons) in the economy; they are the consumers of goods and services in the marketplace. They are the ones behind the demand curves discussed in the last chapter. There is no question about it; households as consumers play a central role in the economic system.

They also play another equally important role—namely, as providers of productive services. All the households must obtain incomes in order to buy the goods

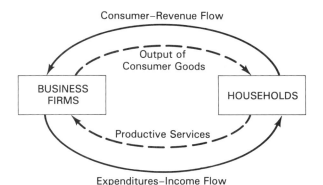

Consumer–Revenue Flow

Output of
Consumer Goods

BUSINESS
FIRMS

HOUSEHOLDS

Productive Services

Expenditures–Income Flow

FIGURE 5-1   The Basic Circular Flow   The circular flow model shows how economic agents—households and business—are interrelated in the economic system. The act of production by businesses generates a flow of income to the households. Households use this same income to purchase that which has been produced by business. Here, solid arrows indicate money flows while dashed arrows measure physical goods and resource flows.

and services they are demanding. A demand without an income backing it up is an unfulfilled want. But how do households get their incomes? Simply by selling the productive services they own to business firms (which need them, of course, in order to produce the goods and services being demanded). Some households own land that they may rent to others and receive a *rental income.* Some may have savings that they have invested in business for *profit income.* Alternatively, they may have lent their savings for use by others, in which case they receive an *interest income.* (Saving is the way households provide for future consumption.) The great majority of households, however, receive a *wage* or *salary income* by selling their labor services to business firms. This labor may be highly skilled (e.g., a nuclear engineer), managerial (e.g., the president of a corporation or the head of a small business), semiskilled (e.g., a lathe operator), or unskilled. For our purposes now, it doesn't matter what jobs or positions are involved; the main point is that the vast majority of households receive a wage or salary income. Wages and salaries hovered around two-thirds of national income for most of the post–World War II period, although in recent years employee compensation has approached the three-fourths mark (see Table 5-1).

Now let's return to the dashed arrows in Figure 5-1. All the households sell some sort of productive service or other to business firms. In all cases, what is being sold consists of *real physical productive services,* and that is what the dashed arrow in the bottom part of the diagram—the one flowing from right to left from the households box to the business firms box—stands for. This arrow, or better, this flow, is a hodgepodge of the different kinds of productive activities provided by the owners of land, labor, and capital.

The business firms in the economy acquire these services for one reason and one reason only—to employ them in the production of goods and services. The things that consumers want to buy cannot be made out of thin air. Business firms must combine the physical services of natural resources, labor, and capital in order to produce outputs. In fact, this is the major economic function of business firms— to obtain and combine the productive services provided by households in order to

TABLE 5-1   Factor Incomes as Percentage of National Income (The Functional Distribution of Income)

Year	1950	1965	1970	1980	1985	1986	1987	1988
National Income:	100.0	100.0	100.0	100.0	100.0	100.0	100.0	100.0
Compensation of employees	64.0	70.0	75.4	76.0	73.0	74.0	73.0	73.3
Proprietors' income	16.0	10.0	8.0	5.0	8.0	8.3	8.2	8.3
Rental income	4.0	3.0	3.0	2.0	*	*	*	*
Corporate profits	16.0	13.0	9.0	9.0	8.9	9.0	9.6	8.4
Net interest	.6	3.0	5.0	9.0	9.7	8.7	8.2	9.9

*Negligible percentage.

Note: Small error in percentage totals due to rounding.

produce the goods and services demanded by them. What they produce, of course, are *real physical goods and services,* such as bicycles, stereos, haircuts, books, food, houses, and movies. This total output of material goods and services is represented by the dashed arrow in the upper part of Figure 5-1, the arrow flowing from left to right, indicating the tremendous variety of the goods and services made available to households.

In sum, the dashed arrows in Figure 5-1, those flowing in a clockwise direction, represent the flow of *real* goods and services. In the lower part of the diagram, we have the flow of physical productive services from households to businesses. These factor services are then transformed by business firms into tangible things for household consumption, as shown by the dashed arrow in the upper part of the figure.

Remember, each of these flows represents a fantastic variety of real things.

2. The Money Flows

As Chapter 3 pointed out, barter is a clumsy, inefficient way to exchange goods and services, and thus we use money to facilitate the exchange process. Indeed, money is essential in a market exchange economy, and this means that we need to introduce money into the circular flow diagram. What really needs to be done is to translate the real dashed flows of Figure 5-1 into their monetary equivalents, and that is what the solid arrows do.

In the bottom part of the diagram, there is a solid arrow flowing left to right from the business firms box to the households box. This arrow (or flow) represents *(measures)* the money payments made by businesses for the productive services provided by households; it consists of wage and salary payments, interest payments, rental payments, and profits. In this respect, as it flows out of the business firms box, the arrow represents the expenditures made by the firms—that is, their costs of production. These firms must of course pay wages, salaries, rents, and interest and must provide profits to their owners if they are to continue operating. But note that what are expenses for the firms are the same thing as money income for households, and it is this money income that households use to purchase goods and services. Hence we will label the solid arrow flowing from businesses to households the *Expenditures-Income flow;* it is the money value of all the real productive services contained in the dashed arrow flowing from households to firms.

There is another solid arrow, the one in the upper part of Figure 5-1, flowing from the households back around to business firms. It, too, is a monetary arrow—that is, it measures the total money values of all the material goods and services purchased by households. We will label this the *Consumer-Revenue flow.*

Thus the solid arrows in Figure 5-1 depict the money-spending flows of the economy. The Consumer-Revenue flow measures the amount of money spent by households as they buy consumer goods and services. The revenue that business firms receive from these sales is used to cover their expenses. These expenditures, in turn, become income for the households, as shown by the Expenditures-Income flow, and once again households use their money income to purchase the goods and services produced by businesses. And so it goes; each flow is transformed into the other as we follow the ceaseless flow of economic activity around the circular flow.

> **Conclusion:** The dollar amount of the Expenditures-Income flow is always equal to the dollar amount of the Consumer-Revenue flow.

B. MARKETS IN THE CIRCULAR FLOW

How do the markets we discussed in Chapter 4 fit into the circular flow model? Figure 5–2 tells us. (The circular flow in Figure 5–2 is the same as the one in Figure 5–1. We are just adding some new elements to it.) Remember, there are countless demands of households making up the Consumer-Revenue flow—one for cars, one for books, one for lawn mowers, one for pencils, and so on and on. They are so numerous, in fact, that we couldn't possibly draw very many of them in Figure 5–2 without a great deal of clutter. One, however, is all that we need to make our point, and we have singled out the demand curve for blue jeans. This demand curve has been drawn above the households box in Figure 5–2, and it will serve as a point of departure for the following discussion.

1. Resource Markets

Now, in order to buy blue jeans, households must have an income, and as we saw earlier, they obtain this income by selling their productive services in resource markets. These are the markets in which supply and demand interact in setting the prices of productive services—wages, salaries, rents, etc. There are therefore labor markets, capital markets, and so on; but all of these, we concentrate on the labor market because most households receive the bulk of their income by supplying their services in that market.

The supply curve of labor is shown in the diagram directly beneath the households box, and like all the supply curves we met in Chapter 4, it too has a positive slope—that is, the *law of supply* holds for labor services just as it holds for any other good or service. Thus the lower the price of labor services (i.e., the wage rate), the lower the quantity supplied for labor; and the higher the wage rate, the greater the quantity of labor services supplied in the market. The only difference between this supply curve and the ones in Chapter 4 is that we plot the wage rate on the vertical axis, but that is permissible because the wage rate is the price of labor services.

Switch over now to the business firms box. Below that box we have drawn the demand curve of business firms for labor services. Note that like any other demand curve, it obeys the *law of demand*. Accordingly, the lower the wage rate, the greater the quantity of labor demanded; and the higher the wage rate, the smaller the quantity demanded.

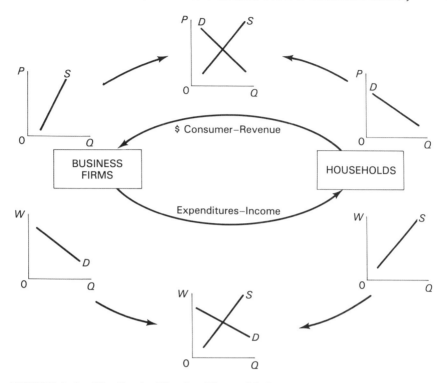

FIGURE 5-2 **The Basic Circular Flow with Product and Resource Markets**
This version of the circular flow shows that business firms and households are tied together through product and resource markets. Households are simultaneous suppliers of productive factors and demanders of products. Business firms simultaneously demand factor services and supply output. Thus the economy has two broad types of markets—resource and product—which are interrelated.

The bottom part of Figure 5-2 is nearly completed. All we need do is bring the demand curve for labor together with the supply curve, as we have done in the diagram at the very bottom of Figure 5-2. This diagram shows how supply and demand come together and interact in the labor market to set the wage rate. Any change, of course, in either demand or supply (or both) will cause the wage rate to change and hence alter the amount of labor employed.

There are also supply and demand curves for each type of productive service. All of these markets constitute the *resource* markets of the economy, and it is in these markets that wages, salaries, rent, interest, and profits are determined.

2. Product Markets

The upper part of Figure 5-2 contains what are called the *product markets*. We have already looked at the demand curve in one of these markets (blue jeans). The supply side is now an easy matter. Business firms, once they have acquired productive services in the resource markets, use them to produce (supply) consumer goods and services. Of all the millions of firms in the economy, there are some that produce blue jeans, as shown by the supply curve that lies just above the business firms box. This supply curve, then, is brought together with the demand curve at the very top of Figure 5-2; and here we have one product market, the one for blue jeans. But of course this is merely one of numerous *product markets.*

Note that we saw above how households play a dual role in the economy—simultaneously they are suppliers in resource markets and demanders in product markets. Business firms likewise play a dual role—simultaneously they are demanders in resource markets and suppliers in product markets.

It is clear that all markets are closely related in the circular flow of economic activity, and a change in any one market will have repercussions in other markets. These interactions are examined in Part IV of this book. However, one important interrelationship embedded in the circular flow calls for further discussion now.

C. SAVING AND INVESTMENT IN THE CIRCULAR FLOW

The circular flow model undoubtedly gives us some insights into the complexities of our economic society. Despite these advantages, you may well be ready to ask some critical questions about the model, at lease as far as it has been presented. As noted earlier, our simplistic model purposely omits government and international trade; these are added, however, in the next two chapters.

But two further omissions need to be filled in here. First, we have assumed that households *do not save* any of their current income. In fact, we have assumed that they spend all of their income on currently produced goods and services. But this isn't true; households do save a portion of their income—about 4 percent in 1988—and we must take this into account.

Second, the simple model assumes that no capital goods are being produced. Indeed, it has all production for the satisfaction of consumer demand. But we know that capital goods must be produced, and we must also take this into account.

Look at Figure 5-3 on page 84. We now have *two* arrows flowing out of the households box. One of these is labeled *C* and is the Consumer-Revenue flow (as before). The other arrow is labeled *S,* and it shows that households save a part of their incomes. Although the diagram can't show it, the *C* arrow is much, much larger than the *S* arrow, nearly $3.4 *trillion* in 1988 as compared with about $145.0 billion of saving (see Exhibit 5-1).

Two problems immediately arise. First, saving is a *leakage from the total spending stream;* that is, saving is the portion of a household's income that is *not spent.* This being the case, saving (which, to repeat, is *not spending)* would cause the circular flow of economic activity to contract, resulting in reduced output and unemployment. This is a serious problem, but before we can deal with it, we must

EXHIBIT 5–1
The Rate of Household Saving

Actually, the income that we are concerned with is what is called disposable income. *Disposable income* is the income that households have after they have paid all their taxes; it is what is left to dispose of as they see fit—that is, to spend or save, or both. Chapter 8 expands on this concept. The point we want to stress, however, is that households *in general* don't spend all of their disposable income, although they do spend the greater part of it. That portion which isn't spent is called *saving*.

Not all households, of course, save. Some indeed don't save anything, and others have negative saving (that is, they spend more than their income). But in the overall picture, more households save than dissave, so that in 1988 personal saving was $145 billion.

The accompanying chart tells us what has been happening to personal saving as a percentage of disposable income. During the past few years, the savings rate has drifted downward, so that in the aggregate households were saving only about 3 to 5 percent of their disposable income. In Japan and West Germany, on the other hand, the saving rates were at least twice as high as those in the United States.

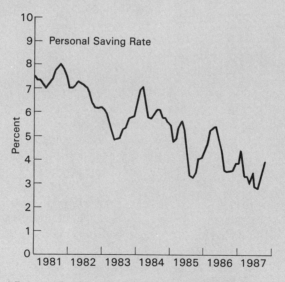

Source: Federal Reserve Bank of Cleveland, January 1988.

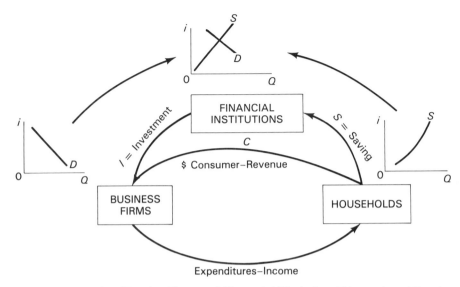

FIGURE 5-3   The Circular Flow and Financial Markets   This version of the circular flow is expanded to highlight the role of financial markets. Financial institutions specialize in intermediating or transferring funds from those economic agents who currently save part of current income to other agents who wish to spend beyond current income for investment.

consider the second problem. What form does saving take, and where do we put our savings?

1. Where Do Savings Go?

Probably the most extreme way of saving is *hoarding*. This amounts to squirreling away money in mattresses, or in the cellar, or in the backyard. Few people, however, save in this manner. Occasionally you will read or hear about an older person who has died and left hoards of cash hidden away somewhere. But such events are so rare that when they do occur, they are considered newsworthy.

Most of us save in a quite different way. We place our savings in some sort of financial institution, usually a commercial bank. There are, however, many types of financial institutions that are more than willing to hold our savings for us. Savings and loan associations are widely used, mutual banks to a lesser extent, and credit unions to an even lesser extent. Mutual funds and pension funds are important outlets for saving. But no matter what type of financial institution we may prefer, nearly all personal savings find their way into such organizations. Note that the main reason households save today is to provide for future consumption in excess of future income. Retirement, education of children, and travel are among the major motives for current saving. All well and good, but why put our money in the hands of others?

Probably the main reason why we put our savings in these institutions is that we receive an interest income on them. If we didn't, we might as well hold our savings as hoards (except that there is the ever-present danger of their being stolen). These "thrift" institutions, as they are also called, encourage us to save a part of our income by offering to pay an interest rate on our savings.

In fact, we can show this by another supply curve, but this one is a supply curve of savings flowing from households. This curve is drawn in just above the households box, and like any other supply curve, it has a positive slope. Note that we have put the *rate of interest* (*i*) on the vertical axis. Why? Because the *interest rate* is the price of saving—that is, it is the price that you must be paid to induce you to save a part of your income. The *law of supply* is as applicable here as anywhere else: The higher the rate of interest offered us, the greater the amount of saving; the lower the rate of interest, the smaller the amount of saving.

You may well question this conclusion. You may be in an income situation in which you can't save anything, or, at best, very little. Does this mean that the law of supply isn't present? Hardly! It is necessary that we keep in mind that we have included all 55 million families in the households box, and as noted above, nearly two-thirds have savings in some amount or another. Thus, *in the aggregate*—that is, taking *all* households together—there were personal savings of over $120 billion in 1987.

2. Financial Institutions as Middlemen

Why would financial institutions want to collect the savings of households and actually pay us interest? The reason is that some businesses come to the financial markets to borrow these savings, and they demand our savings for a number of reasons. For one thing, many existing businesses may want to expand the size of their operations—that is, they want to acquire new plants, machines, and inventories in order to increase the total output of the products they are producing. Other businesses may also want to introduce new products, and they too, therefore, must build new plants. Finally, all sorts of new businesses are springing up, and like the others, they require new plants, equipment, and machinery for their planned operations.

These ventures, of course, must be financed, and the business firms obtain the funds they need by borrowing from the financial institutions. This is why we have drawn a demand curve for savings directly above the business firms box. Business firms demand the use of the savings that households have supplied.

Financial institutions, therefore, play a major role in the circular flow of economic activity. They constitute the *financial markets,* and they are specialist middlemen in that market. There are millions of households that may be willing to lend their savings to business firms, just as there are millions of firms that are willing to borrow those savings and pay an interest. The only problem is that those on the supply side of the market don't know who the demanders are; nor do the demanders know which households are saving.

It is here that the financial institutions perform their role in the economic scene. They stand between those who save and those who want to borrow those savings. They bring supply and demand together in the financial markets, as shown in the upper part of Figure 5-3.

Conclusion: Financial institutions channel the savings leakage from the circular flow through the financial market to those who want to borrow the savings. In this way, then, the leakage may not remain a leakage. Business firms borrow the savings for spending on plant, equipment, and inventories, and so they reenter the spending-income flow.

In all of this, of course, the financial institutions hope to make a profit; and they do so by simply charging a higher rate to borrowers than they pay to the saving households.

3. An Important Definition

We have already pointed out that business firms demand funds to finance their expansion plans. At this juncture, it will be useful for us to pause and consider two things: first, to recollect an earlier definition; and second, to provide a new one.

Much earlier we defined an important economic resource, capital, as follows:

Capital is comprised of man-made things used as a means for the further production of goods and services.

Capital is thus a means to an end; it is a means of producing more consumer goods and services than could otherwise have been produced. The most obvious forms of capital are buildings of all sorts (factories, office buildings, retail stores, etc.), machinery and equipment (typewriters, lathes, rolling mills, etc.), and inventories of both resources and finished output. All of these, along with labor, are essential in the production process. And now for our new definition (which, as it turns out, is not all that new):

Definition: *Investment* is spending by business firms on *real, physical capital* in the form of plant, equipment, and inventories. Another term economists use for this type of activity is *capital formation*.

To sum up: By not consuming, that is, by saving, households free up resources in the business sector to be reallocated to the production of new capital (investment). Savings provide the purchasing power for the business sector to acquire this new capital. The interest rate paid by businesspeople for loans is then the cost of obtaining the funds used to purchase the new capital. The interest rate is then the price of new capital.

Please don't confuse the term *investment,* as it is used in economics, with spending on stocks, bonds, insurance policies, certificates of deposit (C.D.'s), and the like. From now on, whenever we use the word *investment* without qualification, we will mean spending by business firms on plant, equipment, inventories, and residential construction, all of which are necessary to produce other goods. If and when we discuss the purchase of stocks and bonds, we will use the term *financial* investment. It's important that we always keep this distinction between *economic* investment and *financial* investment in mind.

4. Savings as a Leakage: Economic Contraction

Now back to the circular flow model. We have introduced savings into the model by means of the S arrow flowing from the households box up to financial institutions at the top of Figure 5-3. The important thing to keep in mind about this saving is that it is a leakage from the spending flow; unless it reenters the spending stream, the circular flow of activity will contract. Let's see why and how.

Suppose the business firms in Figure 5-3 are turning out $1,000 of goods and services. The expenditures they made (including profits) are therefore $1,000; households consequently receive an income of the same amount. Remember, spending is income—that is, the Expenditures-Income flow is $1,000 as it leaves the business firms box, and it is also $1,000 as it enters the households box.

To begin, let's assume that households aren't doing any saving, that they spend their entire incomes on goods and services. The Consumer-Revenue flow, therefore, is $1,000 as it leaves the households box, and it enters the business firms box as $1,000 of revenue (income). In this case, the total demand by households ($1,000) is equal to the total supply provided by firms ($1,000)—that is, the economy is in a state of equilibrium, and the circular flow will continue to go round and round unless something happens to upset it and create a disequilibrium.

Let's do just that. Let's create a disequilibrium to see what will happen, and we will do so by supposing households decide to save $100 out of their income and hide it in the cellar. This means that they must reduce their consumption by $100, while the S arrow now becomes $100. In other words, total demand for goods and services has fallen.

Business firms, however, are as yet unaware of this. Households don't announce that they have changed their plans. Why should they? But firms soon find out, for now demand is but $900 and production is $1,000. Thus they discover that they are producing $100 more output than is being demanded. Put otherwise, business begins to experience an unplanned and certainly unwanted pileup of inventories. And here is the clue for them to alter their plans, and they do so by reducing output to $900 in order to bring supply into line with the new, lower demand.

A new equilibrium, however, isn't established by this action, for as firms lay off workers and cut back production to $900, the income of households is also reduced to $900. Households cannot now spend and save as much as they could before, so they must cut back more on their demand for goods and services. Firms, as you might expect, react to this still lower demand as they did earlier—by further reducing output and employment. And so it goes. An economic contraction is under way in our circular flow model. Every time each household and business tries to draw back and cut down on its spending, it forces the other to contract even more. In this way, then, the economy can go into a cumulative tailspin or contraction.

Recall that all of this happens simply because of a leakage from the circular flow of spending and income. In this case, the saving leakage took the unlikely form of hoarding. If the saving is hoarded, it can't reenter the flow. Thus we have an important conclusion.

> **Conclusion:**   If there is a saving leakage from the circular flow of spending income that doesn't reenter the spending-income stream, the circular flow model will contract. There will be a general economic contraction with falling levels of output and employment.

However, as we pointed out earlier, hoarding is an improbable method of saving. Let's look at what happens to the circular flow if saving takes more conventional forms.

5. Economic Stability: Saving = Investment

The top part of Figure 5-3 tells us that business firms enter the financial market to borrow households' savings; and they will borrow them in order to finance their investment plans. Thus we have a route by which the saving leakage can reenter the flow of spending.

Let's suppose that by some happy coincidence the demand for savings to be used by businesses for economic investment is just equal to the supply of savings flowing from households. In this instance, the saving leakage (the S arrow in Figure 5-3) passes through the financial market and is transformed into investment spending (the I arrow in Figure 5-3). This being the case, we have two types of spending— consumption spending (C) by households and investment spending (I) by business firms. Moreover, as long as the saving leakage (S) is absorbed by investment spending (I)—that is, $S = I$—there is no need for the circular flow to contract.

> **Conclusion:**   As long as investment spending equals saving, there is no tendency for the general level of economic activity to change. $S = I$ implies economic stability or, in our terms, *equilibrium*.

6. Economic Contraction: Saving Greater Than Investment

Earlier we discussed the possibility of an economic contraction because of $S > I$, but in that case we did not allow for the hoards to reenter the spending-income stream. That case was unrealistic because saving is rarely in the form of hoarding. Yet there remains the possibility of saving in conventional forms being greater than investment, at least in the short run. How can this be? The answer to this question is that investment plans are made by one set of economic actors and that saving plans are made by another set; consequently, there is no reason to conclude that these plans will always be in harmony at one point in time. Quite the contrary, they are not apt to mesh at all. Thus it is conceivable that the saving arrow flowing into financial institutions can be greater than the investment arrow. Consider, for example, an economic scene in which businesses become very leery of future events and accordingly decide that it is in their best interests to revise their investment plans down. In a free economic system, there is no one telling them that they can't do this. And what will be the result? The same as before, for as long as $S > I$, for whatever reason, the circular flow of spending income will contract. As we shall see in Part III, fluctuations in investment plans and spending are a major cause of economic instability.

7. Economic Expansion: Investment Greater Than Saving

The question now is, What will happen if business firms wish to invest more than households are saving? At first this seems impossible, for it seems that the flow of savings is the only thing that can be directed back into the spending stream. Put otherwise, it seems that the flow of savings would put a lid on the level of investment activity. This, however, is not the case. As Chapter 11 will show, financial institutions can actually allow business firms to invest more in plant and equipment than is being saved by households. And they do this by creating money and credit, a power that some of our financial institutions clearly possess.

In terms of our previous example, if businesses are producing $1,000 of output, then household income will be $1,000. If households spend only $900 on goods and services, then saving will be $100. What, however, would happen if business firms had investment plans of $200 of new capital formation? If they can obtain *new* money and credit from financial institutions to carry out these plans, then we have the possibility of investment being greater than saving ($I > S = \$200 > \$100$). In our circular flow model, the spending injection ($200) is greater than the saving leakage ($100). Since the total amount of the two types of demand ($C + I$) is greater than the amount being produced (i.e., $1,100 > $1,000), businesses must hire more workers in order to meet the higher demand. This rise in employment leads to greater household income, which in turn results in further consumption demand and spending, and so on. Thus the circular flow of spending will expand.

> **Conclusion:** As long as economic investment is greater than personal savings, the general level of economic activity will tend to rise.

Is there any market force that over longer periods of time might act to equalize savings (S) and investment (I)? Yes! The interest rate performs this function. If, for example, saving exceeds investment, financial institutions have excess funds that they are willing to lend, and therefore interest rates tend to fall. This fall encourages more investment and discourages saving. When the demand for new capital investment is strong ($I > S$), interest rates tend to rise and stimulate saving. Thus interest rates, the price of capital, tend over time to change to bring saving and investment into equality.

D. SUMMARY

This chapter has two major objectives: (1) to show how, in a simple way, the different parts of the overall economy are interrelated, and (2) to show what happens when saving and investment get out of line with each other. The circular flow model was developed in order to explain these two objectives.

The lower part of the model represents resource markets. It is there that the supply of and demand for the different productive resources interact. This interaction determines household income. The solid arrow flowing from business firms to households represents the money income payments made by firms to consumers.

The upper part of the model represents product markets. It is there that the money income is exchanged for consumer goods and services. The total consumer demand is shown by the solid Consumer-Revenue flowing from households to businesses.

Not all income, however, is spent. Some of it is saved, and this is a leakage from the circular flow spending stream. If that saving doesn't reenter the spending stream, the circular flow will contract: The economy will experience a contraction (depression). But if it does reenter by the same amount, the circular flow will remain constant. One of the major ways for it to get back into the spending stream is as investment. Business firms may borrow the saving of households to finance the building of new plant and equipment.

Financial intermediaries are important as specialized middlemen in bringing the supply of and the demand for saving together. However, saving and investment aren't always equal. Sometimes saving is greater than investment, and the economy contracts. Sometimes investment is greater than saving, and the economy expands.

Terms and Concepts to Remember

Money flows
Real flows
Expenditure-Income flow
Consumer-Revenue flow
Product markets
Reserve markets
Resource markets

Saving
Investment
Financial institutions
Circular flow equilibrium
Circular flow disequilib-
rium

Questions for Review

1. Explain how the act of production generates household income and demand for goods and services.

2. Explain how the household demand for goods and services generates household income.

3. Explain how saving by itself can cause economic contractions.

4. Explain the term *investment* as defined in this chapter.

5. What is the role of financial institutions in the circular flow?

6. An equilibrium exists in the circular flow when injections equal leakages. Explain.

7. Disequilibrium exists in the circular flow when injections do not equal leakages. Explain.

Appendix:
Types of Business Organizations

In the United States, business firms can operate under any of a variety of legal forms. Only three of these, however, are important: the individual proprietorship, the partnership, and the corporation. How do the three basic legal forms of business organizations differ from one another? What are the legal and economic advantages and disadvantages of each? Finally, how do the legal and economic characteristics interact in determining the advantages and disadvantages?

A. INDIVIDUAL PROPRIETORSHIP

There are more proprietorships in the United States than partnerships and corporations combined. In fact, 76 percent of the total number of businesses are individual proprietorships. This implies that there are certain legal and economic advantages underlying this form of organization, and there are. But, as we shall see, there are also substantial disadvantages.

1. Legal Ease of Getting Started

There are few legal problems involved in a person's starting a proprietorship. All she has to do is to say (after obtaining a business license), "I am now a business" and begin operations. This statement, moreover, is literally true, for in many respects under the law there is no distinction between the person and the business. The profits of the business are hers to do with as she pleases (after personal taxes), and the losses are also hers. She can hire whom she pleases, can contract for supplies, and can open or close shop at her own convenience. In fact, she and her business are so indistinguishable that it dies when she dies.

2. Being One's Own Boss

Very often the cliché about being one's own boss is cited as an advantage of the proprietorship form of organization. Yet this can be a questionable advantage. To be sure, as noted above, the owner may open and close shop as she sees fit; but her hours had better roughly coincide with her creditors' ideas about a normally managed business. Bankers, for example, can get very upset when the business they have lent money to in good faith is closed, say, half the time. And they are apt to put some pressure on the businessperson to keep better hours. "Being one's own boss" doesn't mean complete freedom to do as one sees fit with the business. The proprietor, in fact, often has to work long and arduous hours just to survive. This is especially true during the "gestation" period (the period between conception and birth). Conception is the starting date; birth occurs when the firm becomes a viable economic unit and operates more often with profits than losses. But during gestation the proprietor faces difficult times, for this is when costs generally exceed revenues. It is this period in which the proprietor must struggle to build total sales and reduce total costs. It is also the period in which the owner may wonder about the advantages of being her own boss.

3. Low Financial Requirements

The amount of funds required for a firm to get started varies considerably from one line of business to another. In the fields in which proprietorships are dominant—agriculture, services, and retail trade—these requirements are seldom prohibitive. Although the rate of failure of small firms is high, more new firms are started every year than go out of business. A major reason for this is the modest financial requirements.

4. Inadequate Division of Labor and Working Capital

There are two significant disadvantages that accompany the individual proprietorship of business organization. Both of these are due to the smallness of size, not the legal aspects. The first is inadequate division of labor. Given the smallness of her operations, the proprietor must diversify her talents and skills over a broad range of activities. Not only is she president of the firm, she is also the vice-president of finance, the personnel manager, the accountant, and often the custodian. In other words, there is little division of labor in the small proprietorship, which tends to reduce managerial efficiency. According to the experts in these matters, managerial inefficiency is one of the two major causes of the failure of small firms.

The second disadvantage frequently encountered is inadequate working capital. The individual proprietor often finds it difficult to obtain sufficient funds for survival. The amount of money required to start the business may not be great; but starting is one thing, staying in business is another—it is the acid test. Remember, every firm has to pass through a gestation period. Thus the firm needs an adequate source of money capital to see it through this difficult period. In fact, according to the experts again, inadequate working money capital is the second major cause of the high rate of failure of small firms. Unfortunately, if the proprietorship runs into a shortage of working capital, the proprietor finds it difficult to borrow the necessary funds, since she is already in financial trouble.

5. The Legal Disadvantage of Unlimited Liability

At this point, a crucial legal disadvantage rears its ugly head: Namely, the proprietor is subject to *unlimited liability*. This means that the creditors may claim the proprietor's personal assets, if need be, in order to satisfy their legal demands. Remember, the proprietor and her business are indistinguishable, and therefore she is personally liable for all her business debts in the event of failure. The creditors will force liquidation of the so-called business assets first, but if they still find themselves short they can force liquidation of the proprietor's personal assets. There is no limit, other than satisfaction of their legitimate claims, as to how many assets they may liquidate. Many a car and home have been lost in this way, although most states have legislation that allows the bankrupt proprietor to maintain ownership of a minimum amount of assets.

B. THE PARTNERSHIP

Are there any significant advantages of the partnership form of business organization? Well, yes and no! *Yes* in the sense that when two or more persons operate the business, there can be more division of labor and larger sources of financial funds as the partners pool their dollars. *No* in the sense that partnerships are typically small-scale firms and therefore still have problems in raising financial funds and obtaining the degree of division of labor that permits maximum managerial efficiency. Partnerships constitute only about 8 percent of the total business population. The intriguing thing about the partnership form of business organization is its legal framework.

1. Legal Ease of Getting Started

Partnerships, like proprietorships, don't encounter any significant legal problems in getting established. The partners must, of course, enter into some sort of partnership arrangement that specifies the contribution of each partner, his or her obligations, his or her share of the net profits, and so on. The agreement may be verbal or spelled out in a formal statement. To avoid conflicts, the latter procedure is preferred.

2. The Agency Rule

In the usual partnership agreement, each partner acts in the name of the firm—that is, acts as an agent of the firm. He or she can enter into contracts with suppliers and customers, commit the firm to debt, grant wage increases to employees, and so on. The firm is bound by such acts, even though the other partners didn't consent and perhaps were even unaware of what was going on. Obviously such actions can cause conflicts and enmities.

3. The Problem of Dissolution

The life of a partnership is rather tenuous. If any partner dies, becomes "insane," or voluntarily withdraws from the firm, the partnership ceases its legal existence. A new partnership may replace it. Even if all but one of the original partners continue to run it, the firm is legally a new entity.

4. Unlimited Liability

Unlimited liability is also present in the case of the partnership, although with some modifications. If the firm goes bankrupt, the creditors can still attach the personal assets of the partners if the business assets do not suffice. But now creditors have a choice. Since there are perhaps several partners, they will tend to select the partner (or partners) with the greatest amount of personal assets.

C. THE CORPORATION

A corporation is a legal entity, something separate from the owners themselves. Remember that if a proprietor or a partner dies or leaves the business, the firm ceases to exist. Not so with the corporation. If an owner dies or transfers his or her ownership to someone else, the business continues its existence. Under the law, a corporation is a legal "person" separate from its owners and thus can survive its owners. It can sue and be sued; it can contract in its own name.

However, to operate as a corporation and to be recognized as a legal person, the firm must have a charter. When a corporation comes into existence, the owners must obtain the charter from some state, although it need not necessarily be the state in which it does most of its business. Some states in fact have very lenient laws affecting the birth and powers of corporations—for example, Delaware and New Jersey—and many corporations are formed in these states.

Among other things, the charter stipulates what field of activity the corporation will operate in and the length of life (say, ninety-nine years) of the firm. While these provisions may at first seem to be somewhat restrictive, they are not. The statement pertaining to the field of activity is usually so vague that there is actually no restriction on the type of activity the corporation may pursue. The charter can easily be renewed, so that for all practical purposes the corporation legally has a perpetual life.

1. Ease of Raising Funds and Limited Liability

Usually it is argued that the corporate form of business organization has a decided advantage in raising money capital. This, however, depends on the size of the firm. A small struggling corporation will have as much difficulty obtaining funds as a small struggling proprietorship. Nevertheless, the corporate form of organization does have a definite advantage in this respect, for it can offer the benefit of *limited liability* to its owners—that is, to its stockholders.

Let's look first at the two basic ways by which a firm may raise funds, and then consider what is meant by limited liability. If the corporation wants to raise long-term funds, it can do so by selling stocks or bonds, or both. *Stocks* are shares of ownership. The stockholders own the corporation, although individually they often have little say-so in the operation of the firm. This task is left to the board of directors and to the officers appointed by the board.

Stockholders have a voting privilege (one vote per share). They have the right to vote for the members of the board of directors, significant organizational changes, important board issues, and so on. Stockholders also share in the net profits of the corporation, but only after other obligations have been met. The bondholders must receive their interest payments before any dividend can be declared for the stockholder. Stockholders, in other words, receive only a residual share of the net profits, and not even that if the board of directors does not declare a dividend. In the most usual case, a portion of the net profits is paid as dividends; the rest is retained as undistributed corporate profits.

Bondholders are creditors of long-term funds. Upon lending money to a corporation, they receive a bond certificate that stipulates the rate of interest that must be paid by the corporation, the time to maturity of the bond, and the principal amount of the bond. The corporation must pay interest on bonds and pay off the principal at maturity. In fact, the interest must be paid before dividends are paid to stockholders.

Owners or stockholders have *limited liability*. What does this mean? Simply that when you buy a share of stock in a corporation that later becomes bankrupt, you are only liable for the value of stock. The rest of your personal assets are safe from the creditors of the corporation. This feature obviously serves as a strong inducement for the purchase of ownership shares.

2. Managerial Efficiency

Large corporate firms also have the advantage of a greater division of labor, usually at all levels of operation. This is particularly important at the managerial level, for a high degree of division of labor means greater managerial efficiency. It should be stressed, however, that this advantage is the result of size, and not legal form, unless the legal form itself is conducive to large size.

D. A COMPARISON

Our discussion of the three major types of business organizations has said little about their comparative size. We observed that proprietorships are found mainly in agriculture, services, and retail trade. These are typically small enterprises, and the data in Figure 5A-1 support this inference. In fact, a large number of firms (76 percent of the total number of businesses) account for only 8 percent of total sales of all businesses. Small, indeed.

Partnerships are also relatively small, although they are larger than proprietorships. They account for about 8 percent of total business firm populations, but they only account for about 4 percent of total sales.

The large firms are the corporations, although there are many small corporations. They account for only 16 percent of all firms combined but account for 88 percent of total sales. On average, then, corporations are very large relative to partnerships and proprietorships.

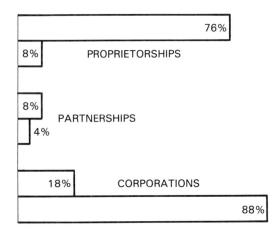

FIGURE 5A-1   Forms of Business Organizations   The top bars show the relative percentage of each type of business organization. The bottom bars indicate the percentage of total sales for each type of organization. Proprietorships clearly dominate with respect to numbers of firms, whereas corporations account for the lion's share of all sales.

6

Government in the Circular Flow

chapter preview

• Government plays a central role in the economy, although there are no uniform views on what this role should be.

• Government provides a number of private and social benefits—e.g, collective goods, regulation of monopoly power, regulation of externalities, changing the distribution of income, and stabilization of the economy.

• A collective (public) good is one that, when provided to any one citizen, is automatically provided to all and at no extra cost.

• An externality is an unintended consequence of some private activity pursued in the market. Some externalities are negative; some are positive.

• Most federal government spending is on transfer payments, notably income security, followed by national defense.

• The bulk of federal revenues is raised through the personal income tax.

• The bulk of state and local spending is on roads, highways, and education. This spending has, in recent years, increased more rapidly than federal spending. State and local governments receive the bulk of their revenue from sales and property taxes.

• The federal government influences the level of economic activity by altering the flows of its revenues and expenditures.

• There are now two leakages from the circular flow (i.e., saving and taxes) and two injections (i.e., investment and government spending on goods and services).

• When these two leakages *combined* are equal to the two injections *combined,* the circular flow will be in equilibrium.

The circular flow model of the last chapter tells us a lot about how the economy functions. However, it is incomplete in two major respects. First, it leaves government out of the picture, and this is a serious omission that needs to be set right. Government obviously plays a significant role in the economy. Second, the model ignores the fact that the United States trades with a host of countries. This, too, is a serious omission, for our position in the international economy directly affects the level of economic activity here at home.

It is now time to fill these gaps. This chapter deals with the place and impact of government in the circular flow. The next chapter does the same with international trade. Then Chapter 8 brings all four economic sectors—households, business firms, government, and the international sector—together in a consistent manner.

A. SOME BASIC IDEAS ON GOVERNMENT

The role played by government in the economy has become increasingly influential and powerful. Figure 6-1 shows how government spending has mushroomed, and Figure 6-6 (see p. 113) reveals that spending by the federal government has often exceeded tax revenues, forcing the government into more and more debt.

This pattern of behavior has generated much public debate over the proper role of government in our society, and the quarrel is far from being settled, if it will ever be. Some people argue that there is nothing wrong with a strong government if it acts only to correct the inefficiencies and inequities spawned by the market system. From their perspective, therefore, government has a positive role to play. It needs to prevent profit-seeking businesses from inflicting harm on consumers, workers, and the environment. These people also affirm government's functions in the areas of education and welfare.

But other people vigorously contend that government has become too large and abusive. They argue that government is very inefficient and is much too demanding in our personal economic lives. These opponents of large government point out that it restricts private actions and personal freedom in at least two ways. First, regulation of business enterprise dulls initiative and inventiveness; second, increased intervention takes up more and more economic space and hence crowds private actors off the stage.

In any event, our economic society is far removed from the classical ideal of *laissez faire,* which is essentially the philosophy that the best government is the least government. Laissez faire may still appeal to some, but the fact is that government

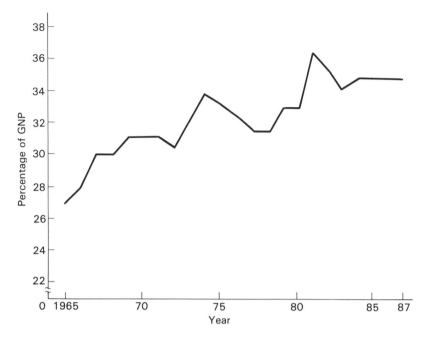

FIGURE 6-1   Total Government Spending (Federal, State, and Local) As a Percentage Of GNP 1965-87   The rising level of government spending as a percentage of GNP illustrates the increasing importance of the public sector in the U.S. economy.

Source: Economic Report of the President, February 1988, p. 341.

has become so large and economically influential that laissez faire remains just that—an appealing ideal apparently beyond reach.

1. Inconsistent Views

Much of the controversy surrounding the proper economic role of government abounds with misleading ideas and notions. Also, many of the opinions are based on inadequate information. Let's look at some of the confusing (and confused) arguments. After that, we will look at some pertinent data.

In the first place, we are often inconsistent in our views on the proper role of government. Our own self-interest may lead us into contradictions and discrepancies. This may be difficult for us to admit, however.

Consider, for example, the businessman who bitterly complains about welfare payments to families; he feels that such payments reduce the incentive to work. Yet he strongly favors a tariff that protects him from foreign competition. The tariff, of course, is really nothing more than a subsidy for him. So the question arises, If welfare subsidies actually reduce incentives, then won't the tariff reduce his incentives to become more efficient? Or is he somehow different from the others? If so, why and how?

Look at another example. Homeowners often grumble over paying property taxes, but at the same time they demand more and better schools and police and fire protection. There is a conflict here. Section D of this chapter shows that the property tax is a major source of tax revenue for local governments. Thus, if homeowners really want more of these benefits, they are probably going to have to pay higher property taxes.

Finally, consider the student who gripes about government aid to families with dependent children. This is what is called a transfer payment. Government has a number of such transfer payment programs, and they all entail transferring income from some members of society to others. But, as we point out below, public education is also partially financed by a transfer payment. Might it not be, then, that the student considers some transfer payments to be quite all right while others are utterly wrong?

These three examples show how contradictions can abound when government enters the discussion. All that we ask for now is that you try to be as neutral as possible on this matter as you read further. Holding on to inconsistent views, if you have any, will do you no good, anyhow.

2. Obvious Costs—Hidden Benefits

One reason why we hold so many inconsistent views on government is that it is often difficult to make a basic comparison—it is difficult for us to relate the tax burden we feel when we pay taxes to the benefits that flow back to us when the tax revenue is spent. We can of course make this comparison if we try, but there are some good reasons why it may be puzzling.

For one thing, it is usually difficult for us to measure the benefits we receive from government. This is quite the opposite of our experiences in the private economy. As we work to earn a living, we feel a number of burdens: getting up to go to work, fighting the traffic to be at work on time, putting in the required hours behind the desk or counter or on the assembly line or in the field—all of these are burdens for most of us. But when we get our paycheck, we are rewarded for our efforts. It is easy, in this case, to associate the reward with the burden. The connection is direct and clear.

The matter is quite different when we try to connect the burden of taxation with the benefits of government. When income tax is withheld from our paychecks, when we pay sales taxes on our purchases, when we pay excise taxes (which are included in the prices of the commodities taxed, such as gasoline and liquor)—in all these intrusions, we feel the burden of taxation directly. Part of our income has been taken from us, depriving us of the pleasure of spending it on things we want for our own consumption.

On the other hand, we may not (and often do not) directly see the benefits resulting from the tax revenues as they are being spent. This is because the benefits usually go to society as a whole, and hence they come back to us in an indirect way. None of this is to deny that there aren't benefits that never got back to us because they get lodged with special-interest groups. These cases, to be sure, do exist and need to be examined. But our first task is to look at why the general benefits seem to be so difficult to measure (as they in fact are). To fulfill this task, let's look at a number of areas of government intervention that seem to be generally accepted. In each case, we want to look for the indirect benefits as well as the direct burdens.

3. Collective (or Public) Goods

Government, among other things, provides us with what are called *public* or *collective* goods. The reason why it has taken on this obligation is simply that the private market system has not provided them, and it would probably not provide them under any circumstances. Yet these goods are deemed desirable and necessary.

> **Definition:** A *collective good* is one that, when provided to any one citizen (consumer), is automatically provided to all. One person's consumption does not reduce the ability of others to consume the same good.

A good example is national defense, for in order to be effective, the defense program must be collective; it must, by its very nature, be a program that benefits all, not just a few. Can you conceive of a system of defense that would effectively protect a citizen in Chicago without, at the same time, protecting all citizens? Besides, even if we could, why do it? As our definition points out, a public good is one that benefits all when it benefits any part. And it does this at no extra cost when another person is benefited. It costs no more to protect all than to protect Chicago alone. Nor does it cost any more when another citizen is born. (See Exhibit 6-1 for a discussion of lighthouses and street signs as public goods.)

There is another important feature about a collective good—it has no market price and therefore can't be allocated as other goods are. National defense can't be sold in the domestic market like peanuts or shoes. To demonstrate this, let's suppose that there is a private domestic market for defense, even though there isn't. We do this only to show that national defense is truly a collective good. Now, in this hypothetical market, what would (could) you, as an individual, buy outright? A tank, a part of a jet fighter? Remember, these are tremendously expensive items. How about a portion of a battleship and a fraction of a missile? Moreover, even if you could buy weapons in a domestic market, you would also have to buy the technical proficiency needed to operate them effectively. Who among us is capable of flying a jet fighter over enemy territory or driving a tank across hostile terrain? Sounds rather ridiculous, doesn't it? Well, it sounds that way because it is ridiculous.

But there is an even deeper problem. Even if you could buy a share of the national defense program, you might actually decide not to. You might think about it and conclude that the reasonable thing for you to do was not buy into the defense system at all. Why? Because, at heart, you might be a free loader (free rider). You might simply sit back and reason as follows: "If my neighbors and the people in the next block are buying enough defense to protect themselves, then they are buying enough to protect me too. No problem; I'll let them buy enough to protect me, and I won't have to spend a penny.''

Definition: *A free loader* (free rider) is one who doesn't pay for a good or service and yet benefits by consuming it.

EXHIBIT 6-1
Lighthouses and Street Signs; But What of Parks?

Most people would probably agree that street signs are necessary in a society like ours in which privately owned automobiles are the major means of transportation. Just consider what it would be like without them. People wouldn't be able to locate new places, businesses couldn't deliver the goods, and collision insurance rates would become prohibitive. Clearly, street signs are essential. Yet they aren't provided through the market system. Nor will the private market system provide traffic control signs. When a street sign or a stop sign is placed at an intersection, it isn't because some business found it profitable to put it there as a means of traffic control. And, since all drivers (and others) benefit from the sign (and at no extra expense), street signs are a collective good.

Lighthouses at the ocean's edge are also collective goods—well, they serve as public goods, even though today most of them are privately owned. When the lighthouse sends out its beam, all the ships in the area benefit from it (and at no extra cost). Of course, those ships that don't help pay for the lighthouse are free loaders. Free riders exist because the benefits from the lighthouse, once provided, can't be rationed by price.

Now, what about state and national parks? Are they collective goods? And what about public education? Isn't it too a collective good? Be careful. Don't hasten to say, "Yes, these are all examples of collective goods." They aren't.

There is, however, a hidden problem for free loaders: There may be too many of them. If there are a lot who think just as you do, then there is a fly in the ointment. If enough people think and act as you do, then not enough protection will be bought for all. Too many free riders spoil the ride.

This being the case, and since there can be no private domestic market for defense, the only way adequate protection can be provided for all is for government to provide it. And since it must be paid for, government finances it by taxing us all. We do end up paying for it, therefore, but via purchases (taxes) through the government sector, not through a market.

National defense isn't the only public good; there are many others: police and fire protection, public health, research at public institutions, spraying for mosquitoes, and street signs—all of these are collective goods, although not all are pure public goods like defense.

Do these collective goods benefit the taxpayer? It would seem so, but the benefits are difficult to quantify in any significant way. You may, on the one hand, be able to say, "I paid $7,532.89 in taxes last year to the federal government," but it is outlandish to ask the government to give you a dollar-and-cents statement of your share of the defense program, since defense can't be rationed by price. The same holds true for all the other collective goods; nonetheless, the benefits are present. Look at them in a negative way: What would happen to your state and sense of well-being if they weren't present?

4. Regulation of Monopoly Power

The private market system doesn't always work as smoothly as Chapter 4 implies, and an additional reason why it doesn't is because of monopolies. A monopoly firm faces no direct competition. Therefore it is able to enrich itself by restricting output, and as a result consumers pay higher prices. In short, competitive markets benefit consumers; monopoly markets exploit them. President Andrew Jackson (as long ago as 1832) put it this way: "Every monopoly and all exclusive privileges are granted at the expense of the public. . . ."[1] And much earlier (1763), Adam Smith said that the "single advantage which the monopoly procures to a single order of men is in many ways hurtful to the general interest of the country."[2]

Government has taken it upon itself to do something about regulating monopolies in order to protect the consumer from the abuses of monopoly power. Indeed, from as early as 1890 (the Sherman Antitrust Act) to as late as 1950 (the Celler-Kefauver Act), government has taken an active role in regulating and restricting monopolies.

Government responses to monopoly can best be discussed at a later stage (see Chapters 20 and 21). Suffice it to say that this form of intervention, if carried out properly, can be beneficial to the taxpayers as consumers. The gains are in the form of lower prices than they would otherwise pay.

5. Regulation of Externalities

In recent years, a new style of regulation has entered the economic scene. This new approach isn't concerned with monopoly; instead it concentrates on such broad social economic problems as pollution of the environment, safety standards, and employment opportunities. In these instances, the problems occur because supply and demand in the private markets don't accurately reflect the costs and benefits to society as a whole. There is, in other words, a gap between private costs and costs to society and private benefits and benefits to society.

[1]Cited in George Seldes, ed., *The Great Thoughts* (New York: Ballantine Books, 1985), p. 202.

[2]Adam Smith, *The Wealth of Nations* (New York: Random House, 1937), Modern Library ed., p. 579.

Consider, for example, a steel mill whose smokestacks spew pollution over the surrounding community. In this case, the firm is an active, job-generating participant in the private market. Its management will argue that it is using the most efficient methods of making steel and that any interference by government to reduce the amount of pollution will result in undesirable consequences—namely, it will raise the cost of production and hence the price of steel, which will in turn force the plant to lay off workers.

Critics, on the other hand, will argue that the steel mill is imposing many costs on members of society, costs in the form of respiratory illness, higher cleaning bills, destroyed forests, lakes, and streams, and a generally ugly environment. As long as the mill continues to pollute, it is imposing these (social) costs on other parts of society. The firm, of course, doesn't cover these social costs and understandably won't; it is concerned only with its internal private costs.

This is an example of what is called a negative externality.

Definition: An *externality* is an unintended consequence of some private activity pursued in the market. This activity may impose costs on others, in which case we call it a *negative externality;* or it may actually create benefits for others, in which case we call it a *positive externality.* In all cases, however, the costs and benefits are byproducts of private activity undertaken for profit or private consumption. And in all cases, the externalities are external to the firm or consumer—that is, they aren't considered an integral part of the firm's operations or the individual's consumption.

Another example of a negative externality flowing from private production is water pollution. Suppose, as is unfortunately too often the case, firms dump waste byproducts from their manufacturing processes into streams and rivers. The major perpetrators in this respect are certain high-tech industries, which must dispose of the chemicals they use in the production process, such as salts, solvents, acids, heavy metals, and other strong toxins. These chemicals contaminate drinking water and are suspected of being a major cause of cancer. Nuclear power plants also have disposal problems that create negative externalities. Nor should the negative externalities resulting from noise pollution be overlooked.

Some examples of negative externalities caused by private consumption are the costs imposed on nonsmokers by smokers; the growing amounts of litter found along the highways and streets; and the tremendous pollution of the atmosphere due to the emission of waste from the millions of privately owned and operated automobiles.

These externalities (and others) are so important in our lives, not only now but also for the future, that government at all levels has responded to them. The major form of regulation is to force the guilty firms to pay for the external costs; and the foremost piece of legislation in this respect is the National Environmental Policy Act of 1969. The overseer of this law is the Environmental Protection Agency (EPA). Although the EPA has both critics and supporters, it now seems to be a permanent part of the economic landscape. In any event, negative externalities affect large parts of our society, and this logically places the matter directly in the realm of politics. It must be kept in mind, however, that these externalities can never be completely eliminated, because to drive them to zero would be prohibitively expensive. These costs must be considered when planning reductions in externalities.

There are, however, some positive externalities that cast their benefits widely. Let's take an obvious example, education. Clearly, the educated person benefits economically from being educated. Many studies show that earning power is directly related to a person's quantity and quality of education. It also is true that education increases a person's sense of self-worth. But this isn't the point right now. What is important is that we *all* benefit economically from other people being better educated.

What should government do when externalities, both positive and negative, are present? Here is a good generalization about government and externalities.

> **Conclusion:** If it is considered desirable to reduce negative externalities, then a tax should be imposed on them. On the other side, if it is considered desirable to expand positive externalities, then government should subsidize them.

A tax imposed on the discharge of wastes into streams, for example, would raise the cost of producing pollution. If the tax were set at the correct level, it would create incentives for the firm to install waste facilities and thus reduce pollution.

The positive benefits of public education have long been recognized. Our nation has a rich history of subsidizing primary and secondary education. Public colleges and universities are also subsidized to the extent that students pay only a fraction of the total costs of their education.

An alternative method of regulation, and the type that is most often used, is direct intervention. For example, EPA sets both engineering and performance standards to which firms must adhere. Performance standards, as with EPA auto emissions, limit pollution by firms. Engineering standards are even more direct. They tell firms exactly what they can and can't do. For example, newly constructed coal-fired power plants must install devices designed to reduce acid rain. Most studies of pollution abatement indicate that its costs have been very high. Again, there are benefits from this sort of governmental intervention, but they are difficult to measure.

6. Government and Income Distribution

Another area in which government has voluntarily interfered in the private sector is in resource markets, particularly the labor market. Remember, nearly all households receive most, if not all, of their income via the sale of their labor services. The way labor markets operate, therefore, is important to most people.

As it turns out, labor markets have functioned in such a way as to leave many persons unemployed, unemployable, or low on the earnings scale. Thus our government has assumed the responsibility for redistributing income among various groups and classes of people. In other words, we have, through the political process, decided that worthwhile benefits are involved in transferring some of the nation's income from the more fortunate to the less fortunate among us—for example, social security (as a pension fund); unemployment compensation; aid to families with dependent children; food stamps; and health insurance.

A number of these programs were introduced during the Depression years of the 1930s, but it was during the 1960s that a revival of interest in income inequalities propagated many new programs and extended others.

Income that passes through these and similar programs is called *transfer payments.* Such payments represent an income for the recipients for which no work or productive activity is performed.

> **Definition:**   *Transfer payments* are a redistribution of income between members of society for which the recipient performs no direct productive activity and which are paid out of tax revenues.

Government also provides transfer payments to certain sectors and areas of the economy that are thought to be in the public interest. Public education, the merchant marine, large parts of agriculture, and public housing are good examples (see Exhibit 6–2).

As might be expected, conflicting views abound over the purpose and importance of transfer payments. Yet government has believed that the aggregate benefits outweigh the costs. We will have much more to say about transfer payments in Chapters 8 and 10.

7. Government's Role As "Stabilizer" of the Economy

Finally, we come to the self-imposed obligation of economic "stabilization." This responsibility was first formally adopted in the Employment Act of 1946 and was reaffirmed in the Full Employment and Balanced Growth Act of 1978 (usually referred to as the Humphrey-Hawkins Act).

A glance ahead to Figures 9–1 and 9–5 (see pp. 168 and 172) will reveal why government assumed this responsibility. The economy has been on a roller coaster of boom periods followed by busts. At times, there has been widespread unemployment. At other times, inflation has imposed its hardships on households and businesses.

The market economy seems to have failed us in this respect, just as it has failed us in all the things discussed so far in this section. If the economy were truly competitive, and if it always behaved so that the savings leakage in the circular flow was matched by the investment injection, then there would be no need for this function of government. Under these ideal conditions, the economy would continually generate full employment levels of operation everywhere.

But, as Chapter 5 showed us, this is seldom the case. Instead we typically find that either saving is greater than investment or investment is greater than saving, and so the roller coaster runs on. It is because of this that government has taken on

EXHIBIT 6-2
More on Transfer Payments: Agriculture and Public Education

Transfer payments are really income security (welfare) payments, or at least the bulk of them are. This is certainly true of most cash payments (e.g., unemployment compensation and social security benefits) and of most in-kind payments (e.g., food stamps). And we usually think of transfer payments going to the lower-income strata of society. But a closer examination reveals some interesting things.

First, what about the payments made by the federal government to the farmer to induce him *not* to produce? This is a crucial part of the agriculture policy at present in the United States; the government pays farmers to keep their land out of production. It may also restrict the number of acres that can be devoted to a crop (e.g., peanuts) so that, by restricting output, price may be driven up and farmers' incomes increase. Now, if the farmer is paid cash not to produce or a higher income to restrict production (as in the case of peanuts), this is as much a transfer payment as, say, a cash payment to an unemployed worker. In both cases, there is a payment made for *not* producing.

Second, what of public education? It isn't, as you might at first think, a public good, for education can be provided to some without having to be provided to all. It can be rationed and allocated by price. Since public education doesn't fit the definition of a public good, it is best to treat it as a transfer payment. It is generally available, even to those who pay minimal or no taxes; on the other hand, it is financed by all taxpayers, even those who don't directly use the schools.

the threefold task of (a) maintaining a reasonably stable level of full employment, (b) sustaining a reasonably stable level of prices, and (c) providing for continued economic growth.

8. An Interim Summary

Government has responded to a number of ways that the private market system fails to provide benefits to the citizenry. It has therefore interfered in the market to provide these benefits. Whether it has succeeded in this respect isn't the point at issue here, but keep in mind that the benefits are rarely seen as a direct result of government activities when in fact they are present. Briefly these interventions are as follows:

- The provision of collective goods that the private market system can't produce
- The regulation of monopolies to prevent them from exploiting consumers and others
- The regulation and taxation of negative externalities that are imposed on unde-

serving citizens by the operation of privately owned business firms; and to subsidize positive externalities that have widespread benefit

- The provision of income support for economically disadvantaged persons and groups who seem to be unable to participate fully in the market system
- The effort to counteract the instability in the levels of production, employment, and prices that the private economy generates

B. FEDERAL TAXING AND SPENDING

As government has performed all these functions, it has had to exercise its powers of taxation and spending. Refer again to Figure 6-1 to see how much government spending has risen over the years, especially since the late 1960s. That picture, however, is a bit too general, for it includes spending by all levels of government—federal, state, and local. Now it's time to look at each of these, and we begin with the biggest of the three.

1. Spending Patterns of the Federal Government

The top line in Figure 6-2 tells us that spending by the federal government has grown more rapidly than spending by state and local governments. But what has the federal government spent its revenue on? The pie chart in Figure 6-3 shows the breakdown of federal outlays in 1987. Note that national defense accounts for slightly over a quarter of the total federal budget. Even though defense spending has grown in recent years, it has declined as a percentage of outlays from as high as 40 percent to a level of 28 percent.

Transfer payments, on the other hand, have grown rapidly in recent years until they are now nearly 40 percent of the budget. Actually, the figure would be higher if we included interest on the national debt and public education in this category (see Exhibit 6-2). Interest on the national debt is a transfer payment because it isn't a payment for current productive services.

A final point on spending. It is important to remember that almost all the funds spent by the federal government are actually received by individuals and businesses. With few exceptions (e.g., the postal service and TVA), the federal government doesn't engage in the direct production of goods and services. Instead it purchases what it needs from private businesses and persons. For example, when the air force buys a fighter plane, it acquires it from a private company. When the government builds roads, it purchases the construction services from private businesses. And cash payments are made by check to individuals and businesses, which in turn respend their receipts in the private sector of the economy. What perhaps needs to be stressed here is that rising federal government spending has nothing to say about or to do with socialism. It does mean that government has a significant role to play in our economy as it performs its various functions, but this isn't socialism in any meaningful sense of the term. Socialism exists when government owns some significant proportion of the means of production, but our government owns

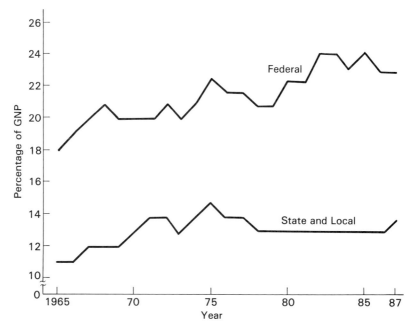

**FIGURE 6-2   Federal and State and Local Spending as a Percentage of GNP
1965–87**   From 1965 to 1975, federal spending and state and local spending both increased as a percentage of GNP. Since that time, the increasing relative size of the
public sector is the result of federal spending.

Source: Economic Report of the President, February 1988, p. 341.

as unusually small amount of productive resources as compared with other economies.

2. Revenue Patterns of the Federal Government

The wherewithal for federal spending comes from two sources—tax revenues and
borrowing. We look at tax revenues as a source of funds here; Section C of this
chapter reviews borrowing by the government.

Figure 6-4 shows the breakdown of federal tax revenues in percentage
amounts. The largest source of revenue is the individual (or personal) income tax,
which accounts for 42 percent of total tax revenues. The second largest source is
social security contributions, which amount to 39 percent of total tax collections.
All the other levies combined, including the corporate income tax and excise taxes,
amount to only a 19 percent slice of the pie. Let's take a closer look at some of
these taxes (also see the appendix to this chapter).

Personal income taxes are just that—taxes on the personal incomes of households. Not all personal income, however, is taxed; there are certain "exclusions."
Social security benefits, welfare payments, and some interest on state and local bond
issues are exclusions—that is, they are nontaxable. In addition, certain deductions

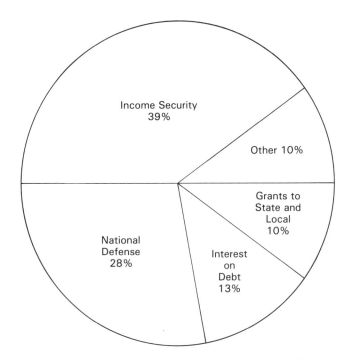

FIGURE 6-3   Type of Federal Expenditures as Percentage of Total 1987   The three largest types of federal expenditures as a percentage of the total are income security, 39 percent; national defense, 28 percent; and interest on the national debt, 13 percent.

Source: Economic Report of the President, February 1988, p. 343.

are allowed before the final tax payment is computed. For example, interest payments on home mortgages, a certain amount of medical and dental expenses, charitable contributions, and state and local income tax payments are allowed as deductions. Finally, exemptions for the taxpayer and household members further reduce the income on which taxes are levied.

Until 1986, when the Tax Reform law was enacted, the personal income tax rate was nominally very progressive. What does this mean? Simply that as a family's taxable income rose, the fraction or percentage to be paid out as taxes also rose. Indeed, the percentage tax burden increased as income increased. For all practical purposes, the effective marginal tax rates varied from a minimum of 14 percent to a maximum of 64 percent (see the appendix for more on the idea of progressivity).

The Tax Reform Act, however, significantly reduced the progressivity of the personal income tax by reducing the number of tax brackets to two—15 percent and 28 percent (by 1988). The law also increased exemptions, reduced (in some cases eliminated) deductions, and decreased the tax rates and burdens on corporations. These changes will undoubtedly affect the contribution of the personal income tax to federal revenues; indeed, the share may very well rise.

The second major source of federal tax revenues is social security taxes. The

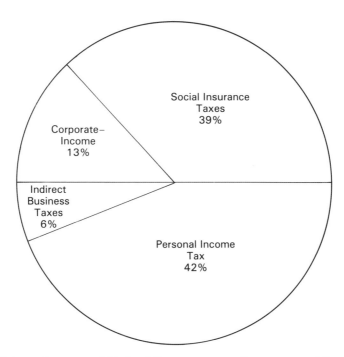

FIGURE 6-4   Sources of Federal Revenues as a Percentage of Total Tax Re-ceipts, 1987   The personal income tax continues to be the main tax revenue source of the federal government, although social security is a close second. The percentage of the corporate income tax has declined in recent years.

Source: Economic Report of the President, February 1988, p. 343.

purpose of the social security system is to provide old age insurance (actually a retirement program) and also to provide unemployment insurance, financed through a separate unemployment tax on firms, for those who are involuntarily out of work. Under this program, welfare grants are provided to the states, which in turn match the grants and distribute the funds to the poor under state administration. Social security taxes are paid by employers and employees in equal amounts.

These contributions to total federal tax revenues have increased dramatically in recent years. One main reason is that the social security law has been amended, bringing more persons under its coverage. Another is that rates have been increased significantly. Currently, the programs under the Social Security Act are (a) old age assistance, (b) aid to the permanently and totally disabled, (c) aid to the blind, (d) aid to families with dependent children, (e) Medicare, and (f) Medicaid.

Finally, the corporate income tax deserves a brief look. Back in the 1950s and 1960s, this tax provided as much as 20 percent of the federal government's tax revenue. Over the years, however, legislation has whittled away at this source until in 1987 it provided 13 percent of the total. What will happen to this share as a result of the Tax Reform Act is unknown. Prior to the act, corporations were subject to tax rates ranging from 15 percent to 46 percent, this last being the rate on taxable income in excess of $100,000. Under the new law, the rate structure has been considerably simplified (see the appendix for the new rates). This is surely an advantageous change for corporations. But, on the other side of the coin, the deductions (investment tax credits and depreciation allowances) have been eliminated or pared down considerably. Thus, what will happen to the tax burden carried by corporations remains to be seen.

C. THE FEDERAL BUDGET: BALANCE VERSUS IMBALANCE

Figure 6-5 shows the behavior of federal tax receipts and expenditures over time. The relationship between these expenditures and revenues constitutes the federal budget. Figure 6-6 shows the same data from a different perspective; it calculates federal government surpluses and deficits as a percentage of GNP.

In some respects, this budget is almost like your own budget. Both your budget and the federal budget have a revenue side—income in your case, tax revenues in the federal case. And both budgets have an expenditures or outlays side. Moreover,

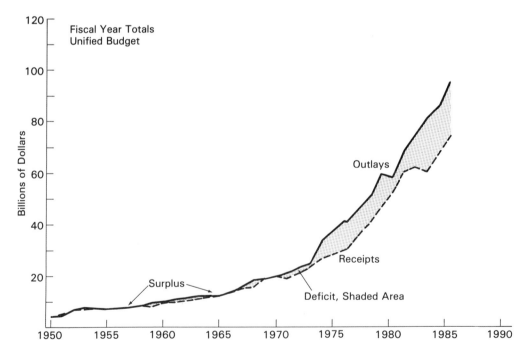

FIGURE 6-5   Federal Budget   Since the early 1970s, federal budget deficits have been annual events and have increased substantially.

Source: Board of Governors, *Historical Chart Book 1986,* Federal Reserve, p. 51.

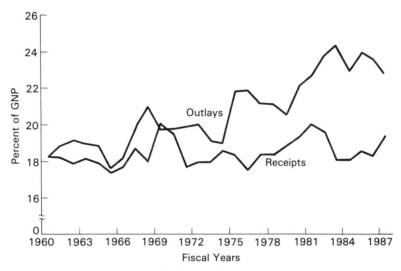

FIGURE 6-6   Federal Receipts and Outlays as Percentage of GNP   Since the early 1970s, federal budget deficits as a percentage of GNP have been enormous by recent historical standards.

Source: Economic Report of the President, February 1988, p. 31.

your budget may be in balance (when your spending equals your income), or it may be imbalanced (when you spend more or less than your income).

Suppose your family has an income of $30,000 but spends only $29,000 on goods and services. If this occurs, your family budget is in imbalance—that is, it is running a *surplus* of $1,000. We usually refer to this surplus as savings when we talk about a family budget. No matter what the name, when income (revenues) exceeds expenditures, there is a surplus.

However, the family may find its budget in another type of imbalance— namely, a deficit. If, for example, your family spends $32,000 over the course of the year, it is running a *deficit* (or, we could say, it is *dissaving)* in the amount of $2,000. How can you finance this deficit? For one thing, you can dig into the family's savings that have been built up over the past; or, you can borrow. Usually, a family's deficit is financed by purchasing things on credit (installment credit, charge accounts, and the like). In fact, deficit financing of this sort (consumer credit) by households has risen consistently over the years. Add on to this the residential mortgage debt of over $2 trillion, and we have to conclude that households are heavily engaged in deficit financing.

Much of this is true of government. It too, more often than not, has engaged in budgeting imbalance. Figures 6-5 and 6-6 reveal that, since 1950, the federal budget has sometimes run a surplus—that is, government collected more in taxes than it spent—in 1950, 1955-57, 1959-60, and 1968-69. The deficit periods, however, have been more frequent, and the deficits have on average been larger than the surpluses. This means that total government tax revenues have generally been less than total government spending. As a result, the federal government has had to borrow to fill the deficit gaps; and as the yearly deficit has been piled on top of each deficit of the preceding years, the national debt has been built up to nearly $3 *trillion* (i.e., $3,000,000,000,000) in 1987. This is a staggering public debt.

How is it that the federal government can continue to assemble such a gigantic debt by borrowing year after year to cover its deficits, and what attitude should we take toward this debt? Here the comparison between your family's budget and the federal budget breaks down. If your family (or you, for that matter) were to go on doing what the federal government does—that is, continue building up debt—you would eventually either have to declare bankruptcy voluntarily or be forced into court by your creditors. This doesn't happen to the federal government, and for two reasons. First, its life is theoretically unlimited, and therefore, unlike a person with a restricted life, it can remain in debt indefinitely. Second, the government has the ability to tax or print money; this means that (theoretically at least) the government has the power to raise the necessary funds to pay off its debt.

Of course, government shouldn't go into debt for any frivolous reason. As a rule of thumb, the government shouldn't borrow simply to meet current expenses, such as payroll. Borrowing for the purpose of acquiring long-term public capital is a different matter. As with productive private capital, public capital yields its benefits to society into future years. Under these conditions, it is rational to borrow today and repay over the future as the public capital yields its benefits. Since the federal budget isn't split into current and capital items, it is difficult to separate total federal spending neatly into these two categories. However, several economists have tried. Estimates differ widely, but all show capital items to be a significant percentage of federal spending.

D. STATE AND LOCAL GOVERNMENTS

Like federal spending, the spending by state and local governments has also increased dramatically over the past few years; indeed, Figure 6-2 shows that in some years it has increased more rapidly. For a number of years, the main reason for this growth was increased spending on education and on highways. The higher education needs resulted from the surge in the post–World War II birthrate, as well as the greater emphasis on education in the age of space exploration and high-tech revolution. As for highway spending, it increased in our society (already a society on wheels) when the move to suburbia required more new roads and a higher level of road maintenance. However, now that the birthrate has been lowered and the rush to suburbia has slowed down, these two areas of spending may taper off. On the other hand, there has in recent years been an increased amount of spending at state and local levels because of the upsurge in transfer payments we commented on above. Many of the programs are partially financed by the federal government but administered at the state and local level.

A glance at the pie charts in Figure 6-7 tells us a lot about sources of revenue

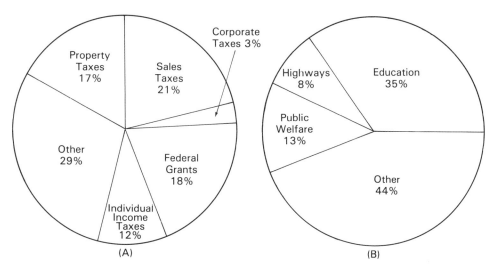

FIGURE 6-7   Sources of State and Local Revenue and Types of Spending as Percentage of Total (1985–86)   The largest single source of state and local revenue is sales taxes followed by grants from the federal government and property tax receipts. The largest single type of state and local spending is for education.

Source: Economic Report of the President, February 1988, p. 345.

and patterns of spending. Panel (A) shows that there are three roughly equal sources of revenue for state and local governments: first, sales taxes; second, property taxes; and third, revenue from the federal government. This last is used to fund a number of programs—Medicaid, highway construction, and income security programs. Note that, even combined, the personal and corporate income taxes do not generate much income for state and local governments.

On the spending side, we find that, as panel (B) tells us, education imposes the greatest demands on state and local budgets. Other major types of expenditures are highways, welfare, health programs, and police and fire protection.

E. GOVERNMENT IN THE CIRCULAR FLOW

We are finally ready to fit government into the circular flow model developed in the preceding chapter. A brief reminder of what that chapter said will be helpful. Recall that this model emphasizes the interdependency of households and business firms. Recall also that personal saving by households is, *in and of itself,* a leakage from the spending stream. However, we had these savings flowing into financial institutions, which made them available as investment funds to be used by businesses for net, new capital formation (investment). Recall, finally, the possible relationships between saving (*S*) and investment (*I*). Investment must be treated as an injection into the spending stream. Thus, as long as the saving is channeled into investment— i.e., the leakage (*S*) equals the injection (*I*)—the circular flow remains in equilibrium. The level of general economic activity will remain constant. (Chapter 5 also pointed out that if *S* and *I* are unequal, the level of economic activity will change; but we aren't concerned with these possibilities right now—in a moment we will be.)

When government is added to the model, additional leakages and injections must be taken into account. The government drains dollars out of the flow of private spending by imposing various kinds of taxes on society—the most important of these are the personal income and social security taxes. These leakages are shown in Figure 6-8 by the arrows flowing into the government box, and in so doing they reduce the size of the Expenditures-Income flow. In a very important sense, these tax leakages are just like the personal savings leakage. *If the taxes are not injected back into the spending stream, the general level of economic activity will fall.*

Government, of course, balances the tax leakages by spending the revenues it collects. It does this in two ways. First, government purchases many goods and services directly from business firms; this is shown by the arrow labeled *G* as it flows from the government box to the business firms box. Thus a portion of the tax leakages reenters the spending stream as the government buys goods and services directly from business firms. The second way the tax leakages are injected back into the spending stream is by means of transfer payments. This route of reentry is shown by the arrow flowing from the government box back into the Expenditures-Income flow as it nears the households box. Thus transfer payments are treated as income by households that can now spend them. This clearly shows how these payments are truly transfers: Income is transferred from the taxpayers (via the tax arrows) to the receiving households.

Since taxes are a leakage from the circular flow of income-spending, and since

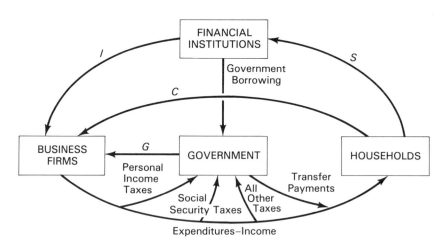

FIGURE 6-8   Government in the Circular Flow   Government affects the circular flow by collecting taxes from households and business (leakages) and then redirecting the funds back into the system, namely through direct expenditures on goods and services and transfer payments to households.

government expenditures are an injection, the government can potentially change the level of economic activity. Can you see how? It can do this by (1) altering its level of spending, or by (2) changing its taxes, or by (3) changing both simultaneously.

This sort of activity is called *fiscal policy* and is discussed in Chapter 13 in more detail. But we can reach some important conclusions even at this early stage. What do you think would happen, for example, if the following economic scenario were to occur? Suppose that the private sector of the economy is in equilibrium (i.e., *S = I)* and that government leaves its spending programs unchanged, and, at the same time, cuts tax rates. In the short run, this would probably force the government into running a deficit, but it would probably also cause the circular flow to expand. Why? Because households now have more income after taxes (taxes have, remember, been cut, and so take-home pay is greater). This in turn means that households will increase their demands for consumer goods, the revenues of business firms will grow, firms will probably increase output and employment, causing households to receive more income (even after taxes), and so it goes. In this event, an expansion of the circular flow results.

Similarly, if the private sector is in equilibrium with *S = I,* and if government now leaves tax rates unchanged but increases its spending on goods and services, the circular flow will expand. This time business firms receive more revenue as government increases its demands, and they must increase employment and output to satisfy these higher demands. But once more, households have a larger income and increase their consumption spending, and an expansionary process gets under way. (What would happen if taxes were cut and spending on goods and services rose at the same time?)

In both the preceding cases, the government runs a *deficit* and hence must borrow. We show this by the arrow dropping down from the financial institutions box to the government box. This arrow reveals that government sometimes competes with private business firms in borrowing the savings of the economy.

Conclusion: Budget deficits due to a rise in government spending on goods and services, all other things equal, or due to a cut in taxes, all other things equal, or both, tend to expand the level of general economic activity.

The reverse of this is also true. If government cuts its spending or raises taxes, or both, the circular flow of economic activity will tend to contract. If, for example, government were to raise taxes while it kept its spending on goods and services constant, households would have less spending power, business firms would . . . you trace it through and see how a contraction might well set in. Furthermore, a cut in government spending on goods and services, all other things given, would also generate a contraction. In both these instances, the government is engaging in *surplus financing* (or reduction in deficit).

Conclusion: Budget surpluses (or deficit reductions) due to a fall in government spending on goods and services, all other things equal, or due to a rise in taxes, all other things equal, or both, tend to contract the level of general economic activity.

One final point: Now that government has been introduced, we must consider *two leakages* from the spending-income stream—savings and taxes. We must also consider *two injections*—private investment in plant and equipment and government spending. However, the same general relationship between leakage and injection holds true.

> **Conclusion:** If the two leakages *combined* are exactly matched by the two injections *combined,* the circular flow will neither expand nor contract, but rather be in a state of *equilibrium.* Total output and employment tend to remain stable.

Note: It isn't essential that saving equal investment and government spending equal tax revenues. That's asking far too much. What is necessary for an equilibrium is that investment plus government spending are equal to taxes plus saving.

> **Conclusion:** When the two injections (expenditures) are greater than the two leakages (savings and taxes), the level of economic activity will rise (assuming idle capacity exists). When the two leakages are greater than the combined injections, the level of economic activity will tend to fall.

F. SUMMARY

Government performs many functions, but in the economic sphere the five most important are (1) providing collective goods, (2) stabilizing the level of economic activity, (3) redistributing income, (4) regulating business, and (5) regulating externalities. All of these provide private and social benefits, but we seldom associate the benefits we receive with the tax burdens we feel as we hand over part of our income to government.

The major source of tax revenues for the federal government is the personal income tax. Second is social security, and third is the corporate income tax. Property and sales taxes are the major source of revenue for state and local governments.

On the spending side, the federal government spends the largest share of its revenues on income maintenance programs, and defense spending comes in second. State and local governments spend mainly on education and their highways.

As this chapter has stressed, revenues and expenditures are rarely in balance. For the federal government, expenditures typically exceed revenues. That is, there is usually a budget deficit. Such deficit financing tends to be expansionary. On the other hand, surplus financing (when revenues exceed spending) tends to contract the circular flow of economic activity.

Finally, when government is introduced into the picture, two leakages from the spending stream must be taken into account—personal savings and taxes. There are also two injections—investment in plant and equipment and government spending. If the two leakages are equal to the two injections, the level of economic activity will remain constant. It will fall, however, if the two leakages exceed the two injections, just as it will rise if the injections are greater than the leakages.

Terms and Concepts to Remember

Laissez faire	Public (collective) good
Transfer payment	Progressive tax
Free rider	Regressive tax
Deficit financing	Proportional tax
Surplus financing	
Externality, positive and	
negative	

Questions for Review

1. One reason why people are so critical of government in our society is that they are unable to measure many of the benefits that government provides them. Do you agree? What are some of these "hidden" benefits?

2. According to this chapter, what major benefits does government provide? Discuss each briefly.

3. What is a *collective good?* Defense is usually referred to as a *pure* public good. Education, police and fire protection, and national parks aren't pure collective goods. Why aren't they?

4. Suppose Pureville's waterworks is located down river from a chemical plant that spews its toxic wastes into the river. How does this affect the economic well-being of Pureville's citizens? What can they do about it? Answer in terms of externalities.

5. What are the major sources of revenue and types of expenditures by (a) the federal government, and (b) the state and local governments.

6. Suppose the federal government increases tax revenues and, at the same time, decreases expenditures. Other things being equal, what will happen to the level of economic activity?

7. Suppose the economy is in a recession. What fiscal policies could you recommend to raise the level of output and employment?

Appendix: Adam Smith Again: The Four Maxims of Taxation

The great economist Adam Smith argued that every nation's government has definite obligations that it owes to its citizens, and these must of course be financed out of tax revenues. The duties that Smith saw as inescapable are (1) the expense of defense; (2) the support for a system of justice; (3) the provision of public works, such as roads, canals, and harbors; and (4) the expense of institutions of public education. We have met most of these in the text of this chapter. What distinguishes those that are public goods? Which of them are transfer payments?

These various expenditures must be financed, and Smith considered a variety of different types of taxes. (He also considered deficit financing.) But, no matter what type of taxation government may use, Smith cautioned that all taxes should follow his four maxims. These are, and we quote:

I.   The subjects of every state ought to contribute towards the support of the government, as nearly as possible, in proportion to their respective abilities; that is, in proportion to the revenue which they respectively enjoy under the protection of the state. [This is the ability-to-pay principle.]

II. The tax which each individual is bound to pay ought to be certain, and not arbitrary.

III. Every tax ought to be levied at the time, or in the manner, in which it is most likely to be convenient for the contributor to pay it.

IV. Every tax ought to be so contrived as both to take out and to keep out of the pockets of the people as little as possible, over and above what it brings into the public treasury of the state.[3]

These maxims can be summarized as (I) the greater the benefits granted by the state, the higher the tax; (II) taxes should be clearly and openly stated, not hidden from the taxpayer's view; (III) payment of taxes should be convenient; and (IV) taxes should raise only the revenue needed and no more.

Let's look at the various taxes in the United States to see how well they fit Smith's maxims. We aren't going to tell you whether they do; instead you should consider the possibilities.

Consider, first, what is called a *proportional tax*. This tax is stated as a given

---

[3]The duties are covered in Chapter I of Book V of *The Wealth of Nations;* the four maxims of taxation are in Chapter II of Book V.

percentage of income, no matter what the income level is. If, for example, the tax rate is 15 percent, then a household with an income of $20,000 per year would pay $3,000 in taxes; and a household receiving, say, $200,000 would pay $30,000. This example assumes that there are no deductions and no exemptions allowed. This is truly a "flat tax." The Tax Reform Act of 1986, as we shall see, was a tentative step in this direction.

A *progressive tax* is one whose tax rate rises as taxable income rises. Prior to the Tax Reform Act, there were fifteen tax brackets (ranging from 11 percent to 50 percent) in the personal income tax. We show here the earlier progressive corporate income tax structure because it is shorter. Under the old law, taxes had to be paid according to these rates:[4]

Taxable Income	Tax Rate (percent)
$25,000 or less	15
25,001–50,000	18
50,001–75,000	30
75,001–100,000	40
Over $100,000	46

Under the new law, things appear simpler:

Taxable Income	Tax Rate (percent)
$50,000 or less	15
50,001–75,000	25
Over $75,000	34

Despite the simplification, the corporate income tax remains progressive. So does the personal income tax, but now with only two tiers. For example, married persons filing joint returns pay a tax rate of 15 percent on taxable income equal to, or less than, $29,750, and a rate of 28 percent on taxable income above this amount. The new law, therefore, significantly reduces the degree of progressivity.

Finally, many of the taxes we pay are *regressive*—that is, they impose a heavier percentage burden on lower-income households and a lighter burden on higher-income households. One of the most important is the social security tax. Excise taxes, such as gasoline taxes, are also regressive. Suppose each of five families drives the same number of miles per year and, in fact, pays the same amount in gasoline taxes ($300). The main difference between these families is their incomes and thus the *percentage of their incomes* going for gasoline taxes.

---

[4]Taken from *The Price Waterhouse Guide to the New Tax Law* (New York: Bantam, 1986), pp. 4, 141–42.

Household Income Per Year (1)	Gasoline Taxes Paid (2)	Percentage of Income to Pay Gasoline Taxes (3) = (2) ÷ (1)
$10,000	$300	.0300
20,000	300	.0150
40,000	300	.0075
60,000	300	.0050
80,000	300	.0038

The figures in column 3 may not seem extravagant, but consider the burdens imposed by sales taxes, social security taxes, and other excise taxes. All of these are important, and all are regressive.

Now, what of Adam Smith's maxims? Do excise taxes follow III? (How much of the price that you pay per gallon of gasoline is tax?) Do sales taxes adhere to II? What about the progressive personal income tax? Does it follow II? What about federal, state, and local governments withholding taxes from our paychecks? What we want you to do is to look at the various taxes we pay, as well as the way we pay them, and ask which of Smith's four maxims is (are) relevant to them.

7

International Trade in the Circular Flow

chapter preview

- Nations trade with each other because of mutual advantage. Trade takes place whenever there is a range of mutual benefit.

- Nations trade because of absolute or comparative advantages.

- These advantages exist because countries possess different quantities and qualities of resources.

- Free trade results in specialization and hence benefits for the citizens of the trading countries.

- Despite this, nations tend to reject free trade. They erect barriers to trade in the form of tariffs, quotas, and other nontariff restrictions.

- Trade restrictions benefit special interest groups at the expense of consumers in general. Domestic consumers pay higher prices, and domestic producers make higher profits.

- The flow of trade and funds between a country and the rest of the world is recorded in the country's balance of payments.

- Imports and exports are recorded in the Current Account of the balance of payments.

- Money flows are recorded in the Capital Account of the balance of payments.

- If exports exceed imports, there is a surplus in the current account. If imports exceed exports, there is a deficit.

- If money capital inflow is greater than money capital outflow, there is a surplus in the Capital Account. If more money capital flows out of the country than flows in, there is a deficit in the Capital Account.

- The Current and Capital Accounts reflect the supply and demand for a country's currency in world markets.

- The value of each country's currency is determined by the supply and demand for that currency.

- This value is referred to as an exchange rate—that is, the rate at which one currency exchanges for another.

- Imports, like saving and taxes, are leakages from the circular flow. Exports are an injection into the circular flow.

- The circular flow is in equilibrium when all of the leakages are offset by all of the injections. If injections exceed leakages, economic activity expands; if they are less than leakages, contraction results.

Thus far we have strongly emphasized exchange, trade, and the functioning of markets. In Chapter 3, we saw how individuals and businesses specialize and trade back and forth among themselves. The circular flow model in Chapter 5 also stressed the exchange, or trading, that takes place between households on the one hand and business firms on the other. Then Chapter 6 pointed out that there is trade between the public sector (government) and the private sector (households and businesses). Ours is truly an exchange economy.

But trade is not restricted to exchange within the American economy. There is also a large and growing volume of trade between nations. In fact, many countries rely on international trade to provide the variety of products that constitute a decent standard of living. This is especially true of such small countries as Belgium, The Netherlands, Taiwan, Korea, and Denmark. These countries obtain a large percentage of goods consumed internally from abroad through imports. They pay for these imports by means of their own exports.

International trade, however, is not limited to small countries alone. Large countries, such as the United States and Canada, also engage in international trade, and for exactly the same reasons that small countries do. True, the United States has a very large resource base as compared, let's say, with Denmark. We are, indeed, blessed with an abundance of resources. However, not all of our resources are abundant; some, in fact, are relatively scarce. And when things are produced that require relatively scarce resources, the prices of these goods and services will be higher. Other countries, however, have more of these resources than we do and, therefore, can produce the same things at lower costs and prices. It is for this reason that we, also like the small economies, import from abroad. We can get these things much more cheaply than if we produced them at home.

At the same time, we can, with our relative abundance of other resources, produce many different goods and services much more cheaply than other nations can. Since so very many of these items are in demand throughout the world, we also export. And, just as the small nations pay for their imports with their exports, so do we. At times, we may import more than we export, and at other times, we may export more than we import, but in the long run, exports pay for imports. The important conclusion for now is that the United States is a major part of, and plays a major role in, the international economy.

Trade among nations has grown rapidly over the years. It is no accident that this growth has coincided with the rising standards of living throughout a large part of the world during this period. In fact, the growth of international trade has contributed to these rising standards of living.

This chapter's subject, then, is international trade. It begins by explaining why nations benefit from trading with each other; and it ends by describing how international trade figures in the circular flow model and, therefore, affects the level of economic activity. In between, it stresses the importance of free trade and shows the disadvantages of such barriers to trade as tariffs and import quotas as well as non-tariff barriers. It also explains how trade is financed with monetary payments.

A. WHY DO NATIONS TRADE?

Nations trade because it is to their advantage to do so. They trade among themselves for the same reason that individuals and regions within a country trade among themselves. This may be obvious, but let's look at it in more detail.

1. Trade within an Economy

Recall Adam Smith's pin factory that we discussed in Chapter 3. That example showed that when labor concentrates on more and more specialized tasks, pin production is dramatically increased. The average efficiency of each worker in the factory increases remarkably because of division of labor. Recall also that this increased productivity gives each worker many more pins than he himself can consume, and little or nothing of the other things he consumes. Thus he exchanges his surplus output of pins for part of the surplus outputs of other specialists in other activities. Hence exchange (trade) flows from specialization, and in the process everyone benefits.

But the benefits of specialization and exchange are not limited to individuals alone. They also exist among the states or regions of a country. California, for example, is a large state with a diversity of abundant resources. Conceivably, therefore, at least in a hypothetical sense, California could cut itself off from all contact with the other states and still be able to produce many of the goods necessary for an adequate standard of living. True, that standard of living would be much lower than it is now, but it could be done.

However, would it be worthwhile? The obvious answer is no! California's climate and soil are ideally suited for producing citrus fruits. In fact, the state is very efficient in producing this type product. Certainly, it costs less to grow oranges in California than it does in, say, Maine or Wisconsin. The climate and soil of these two states would make the costs and prices of producing oranges there very high indeed.

It is for this reason that California concentrates a lot of land, labor, and capital equipment in the production of citrus fruits. But, in doing so, the state produces many more oranges than Californians could possibly consume. Therefore concentration of resources in this line of activity yields a surplus of oranges far above the local demand.

What, then, does California do with this surplus? Californians trade it to people in other states that have specialized and produced surpluses of their own—

surpluses of things produced much more efficiently than California could ever manage. Therefore some of the surplus oranges are traded for surplus automobiles from Detroit and for surplus cheese from Wisconsin.

Now, this is beneficial to Californians, but only on one condition—namely, that they end up with more oranges, cheese, and automobiles than they would have had if they had tried to produce all these products themselves. In other words, specialization and trade are beneficial only if all states are better off after trade than they were before. And, in our case, they will be. Californians can get automobiles a lot cheaper than they can produce them themselves, and Michiganites can get oranges a lot cheaper than if they had tried to grow them in such a cold climate.

All of this probably seems pretty obvious. After all, we have grown up in the United States where there is free trade among the states. In fact, virtual free trade is maintained within this country because we know, experience, and appreciate its benefits.

But then again, maybe it isn't all that obvious. Although we recognize the benefits of free trade here at home, we often close our eyes to the similar benefits that flow from free trade between the United States and other countries. That is a bit strange, for we engage in trade internationally for exactly the same reasons that we engage in free trade among the states. So let's take a look at the benefits we derive from international trade.

2. The Benefits of International Trade

A hypothetical example is the best way for us to see the gains and benefits of foreign trade. Let's suppose that there are only two countries in the world—Texas and Labrador. They produce only two products—cotton and fish—and these are all that are needed for survival. Now, as it turns out, both of these countries have abundant land and offshore fishing grounds. However, the moderate climate and soil conditions in Texas make cotton farms much more productive than the cotton farms in Labrador. Labrador's waters, on the other hand, teem with fish because of the Gulf Stream, so that fishing is much more productive there than it is in Texas. Next, in our example, let there initially be no trade between these two countries. This means that, without trade, each country must produce both products for its citizens.

There are two final things about the example. First, suppose we measure production costs in terms of labor-hours only. Our main point can more easily be made if we use labor productivity as our measure of cost. Second, suppose *output per unit* of labor time remains constant as output changes. Thus, if it takes one hour of labor to produce one pound of fish in Texas, then it takes only one hour per pound of fish whether ten pounds or one million pounds are caught. In other words, costs of production (measured as hours of labor per unit of output) remain constant for both products in both countries. There are no diminishing returns in either commodity.

Table 7–1 shows how much of the two products one hour of labor can produce in both countries. In Texas, one hour of labor can produce either one pound of fish or four pounds of cotton. Clearly, labor is much more productive in producing

**TABLE 7-1   Pounds of Output of
One Hour of Labor**

	Texas	Labrador
Fish	1	6
Cotton	4	1

cotton than it is in catching fish. In Labrador, on the other hand, one hour of labor can produce either six pounds of fish or one pound of cotton. Therefore labor is more efficient there when used to catch fish.

Since one hour of labor yields six pounds of fish in Labrador but only one pound in Texas, we say that Labrador has an *absolute advantage* in the production of fish. That advantage is 6-to-1. Texas, on the contrary, can produce four pounds of cotton with an hour of labor, whereas Labrador can produce only one pound. Therefore Texas has an *absolute advantage* of 4-to-1 over Labrador in cotton production.

> **Definition:**   An *absolute advantage* exists when a country is able to produce a good at an absolutely lower cost than other countries can.

This cost is measured in terms of labor required to produce the good. In Texas, the cost of one pound of fish is one hour of labor. In Labrador, the cost of one pound of fish is one-sixth of an hour (i.e., ten minutes) of labor, since one hour of labor catches six pounds. Thus the *absolute advantage* that Labrador has in fish means that the labor costs of production per pound of fish are lower than in Texas.

3. Pretrade Production and Consumption

Earlier we assumed that there was no trade between Texas and Labrador. This means that each country will have to use its labor force to produce both fish and cotton. Thus if each country has 1,000 hours of labor available, it will have to split these hours between the production of both products.

How will these hours be divided between fish and cotton? It all depends on consumer demand in each country. Let's suppose that *each* country—Texas and Labrador—divides its 1,000 hours of labor equally between the two goods, that is, 500 for catching fish and 500 for growing cotton. Table 7–2 shows the production and consumption in both countries.

What Table 7–2 tells us is that 500 hours of labor in Texas can catch 500 pounds of fish (500 hours × one pound per hour = 500 pounds), and the same number of hours will produce 2,000 pounds of cotton (500 hours × four pounds per hour = 2,000 pounds). In Labrador, 500 hours of labor will produce 3,000 pounds of fish (500 hours × six pounds per hour = 3,000 pounds) and 500 pounds of cotton (500 hours × one pound per hour = 500 pounds).

**TABLE 7-2   Pretrade Output and Consumption in Pounds
(1,000 hours of labor time in each country)**

	Texas	Labrador	Total Output
Fish	500	3,000	3,500
Cotton	2,000	500	2,500

Total output for *both* countries would therefore be 3,500 pounds of fish and 2,500 pounds of cotton. This is all without trade, but now we have to determine whether opening up trade between the two countries would improve or benefit both.

4. Gains from Trade

Let's take our example a bit further and imagine that a Texan takes a vacation trip to Labrador. While there he is impressed by the abundance of fish. He is also impressed by the lower price of fish in terms of cotton. This of course means that cotton will be expensive in terms of fish. He then recalls that back home in Texas cotton is plentiful relative to fish, and hence its price is low and the price of fish is high.

What does all of this mean? Well, if our Texan is smart, it means that he will see some profit for him if he engages in some international trade with Labrador. He will sell the low-priced Texas cotton to Labrador at a much higher price than at home. Furthermore, the low-priced fish in Labrador will be sold at a higher price in Texas. Under these conditions, trade between the two countries will open up.

However, the opening up of trade between the two countries begins to affect the pattern of production in both. Texans, finding that they can get fish cheaper in Labrador by trading cotton, begin to concentrate more labor on the production of cotton. Labradorians, on the other hand, allocate more labor toward catching fish because they can trade the fish for the cheaper cotton in Texas.

Let's take our example to the limit and suppose that trade finally leads to complete specialization—Texas produces only cotton, and Labrador produces only fish. The top part of Table 7–3 shows the output in both countries after complete specialization.

Remember that in Texas, it takes one hour of labor to produce four pounds of cotton. Since there are 1,000 labor-hours, Texas ends up producing 4,000 pounds of cotton. This is much more than it was producing before trade opened up (2,000 pounds in Table 7–2), because before trade it had to use some of its labor to produce fish.

Up in Labrador, we find a somewhat similar result. Before trade, it was producing only 3,000 pounds of fish because some labor had to be used for producing cotton (see Table 7–2). Now, with complete specialization, Labrador's output of fish is 6,000—that is, all 1,000 labor-hours are devoted to catching fish. Since each hour of labor yields six pounds of fish, total production is 1,000 × six pounds = 6,000.

**TABLE 7-3 Posttrade Production and Consumption
in Pounds**

	Texas	Labrador Production in Pounds	Total Production
Fish	0	6,000	6,000
Cotton	4,000	0	4,000
		Consumption	
Fish	3,000	3,000	6,000
Cotton	2,000	2,000	4,000

What is important is a comparison between Table 7-2 and the top part of Table 7-3. The opening up of trade and the specialization by each country increases world production of both goods dramatically. Before trade, total fish output was 3,500 pounds. After trade begins, it is 6,000 pounds, a fantastic increase of 2,500 pounds. As for cotton, its total output has increased by 1,500 pounds—from 2,500 pounds before trade to 4,000 pounds now.

Conclusion: One of the gains from trade is that specialization increases the world output of goods.

But that isn't all. There are still further gains, as the bottom part of Table 7-3 tells us. Not only does total output rise, but also total consumption. Let's assume that each country maintains the pattern of consumption it had before trade opened up. Again, we have to compare Table 7-2 with Table 7-3, but this time the bottom part of Table 7-3. Prior to trade, Texas had only 500 pounds of fish and Labrador had only 500 pounds of cotton. But in Texas, the residents want to consume only 2,000 pounds of cotton. Since total production of cotton is 4,000 pounds, they swap the surplus 2,000 pounds of cotton for fish. This means that their consumption of fish rises from 500 pounds to 3,000.

Where did the 3,000 pounds of fish come from? From Labrador, of course, for the residents up there have a surplus of 3,000 pounds of fish. Remember, we are assuming that they want to maintain their pretrade consumption of 3,000 pounds. But with complete specialization, they produce 6,000 pounds and trade the surplus for cotton. That's where the 3,000 pounds of fish in Texas come from.

Note, too, that cotton consumption in Labrador has risen to 2,000 pounds (as compared with the pretrade 500 pounds). And where did this 2,000 pounds come from? You answer the question.

Conclusion: Another benefit of trade is that consumption in both countries rises beyond what was possible before trade.

In the example just cited, the fact that each country had an *absolute advantage* in terms of labor in producing a single commodity led to trade and gains in living standards in both countries. Trade and benefits can also occur even if one country has an absolute advantage in the production of *both* commodities. This may sound strange at first, but the nineteenth-century economist David Ricardo demonstrated how trade could still be mutually beneficial (see Exhibit 7–1). Suppose an hour of labor could produce 12 pounds of fish and 8 pounds of cotton in Texas while conditions in Labrador remain as before. Texas would now have an 8-to-1 advantage in cotton production and a 2-to-1 advantage in fish. Under such conditions, could trade be beneficial? The answer is yes! Consider that Texas has an advantage of 8-to-1 in cotton, but only 2-to-1 in fish. In other words, even though Texas has an absolute advantage in both, its greater advantage is in cotton. Therefore we would say that Texas has a *relative advantage* in cotton and a *relative disadvantage* in fish.

EXHIBIT 7–1
David Ricardo: Discoverer of the Principle of Comparative Advantage

David Ricardo (1772–1823) was the leading and most influential economist during the first half of the nineteenth century.

He was not an academic economist like Adam Smith. Instead, he retired from a highly successful business career at the age of forty-two and devoted most of his time thereafter to the study of economics. He also was a member of Parliament for a brief time and gave many speechs on theoretical economics to his fellow parliamentarians. (Whether they understood him is another matter.)

Ricardo published extensively in the newspapers, but his lasting contributions to economics can be found in his *Principles of Political Economy and Taxation* (first published in 1817). It is here that he describes his labor theory of value; his argument that since savings always flow into investment, there is never any lasting or important contraction of the circular flow; his views on taxation, population, and deficit financing; and his theory of comparative advantage.

Economists had known for a long time that there were benefits from free trade when the trading countries each possessed some sort of *absolute advantage*. Ricardo, however, took the argument an important step further and argued that all nations should trade by specializing in whatever goods they could produce at opportunity costs lower (relatively) than their trading neighbors' costs. (This is spelled out in the appendix to this chapter.)

If, however, nations are to benefit from comparative advantage, trade between them must be unrestricted. There must be free trade, and nearly all the economists of the nineteenth century were champions of free trade. The history of most countries, however, shows that the arguments in favor of protection (no matter how weak they may be) have won out over the economic arguments for free trade based on the law of comparative advantage.

Labrador, on the other hand, has an absolute disadvantage in both, but a relative advantage in fish, because its absolute disadvantage is less. Ricardo clearly showed that countries could still benefit by trading under such conditions. The result has come to be known as the *law of comparative advantage.* An example of how the law of comparative advantage works to the advantage of both trading countries is given in the appendix to this chapter.

5. The Gains from Trade in General

Do these benefits, both higher levels of production and greater consumption, occur when we move away from our simple illustration and out into the world? The real world is, of course, comprised of hundreds of countries and millions of products. Yet the results are the same. Whenever countries specialize in producing goods in which they have an advantage and then trade the surpluses, both output and consumption rise. This being the case, we can only conclude that free international trade raises the standard of living in each country and for the world as a whole.

> **Conclusion:**   International trade, in other words, extends the benefits of specialization and exchange beyond national boundaries.

B. TRADE BARRIERS

With all the benefits that flow from free international trade, it is surprising that so many nations have set up barriers to the free flow of commerce. A case in point is the United States. Americans have accepted free *interstate* trade as being in the best interests of all. At the same time, however, they tend to look upon free *international* trade with some fear and skepticism. The same inconsistency is found in other countries.

We want to consider two important questions here. First, what are the main types of barriers to trade that nations use? Second, what are the major reasons given in defense of these barriers?

1. Tariffs, Quotas, and Non-Tariff Barriers

There are two basic types of trade barriers—quotas and tariffs. Many nations, including the United States, set up quotas of various types.

> **Definition:**   A *quota* is a restriction on the physical volume of goods moving into the country.

A quota can be stated in terms of an absolute amount (e.g., so many pounds or tons may be imported); or it can be stated as a percentage of the domestic market (e.g., only 10 percent of the demand for the good may come from abroad). The United States has established quotas on a number of imported goods, such as sugar and textiles. There are also informal quotas on Japanese automobiles.

The purpose of the quota, of course, is to protect the domestic producers from foreign competition. Once the small amount from abroad is bought up, then consumers must buy from domestic producers. Thus the purpose of the quota is achieved—the producers at home are protected from foreign competition. But isn't there also another effect? Surely! Recall that trade between countries results from some countries being more efficient in producing what they export. Since they are indeed more efficient, they sell at a lower price. But the quota prevents us here at home from buying the less-expensive foreign-made goods and forces us to buy the more-expensive domestically produced goods. What is beneficial for the producers is hardly beneficial for the consumer; one small group gains at the expense of the many.

Far more common than quotas is the use of tariffs. Nearly every country uses tariffs of one kind or another.

Definition: A *tariff* is a tax imposed on the price of an imported good.
Like the quota, it protects domestic producers from foreign competition.

Since the tariff is tacked on to the price of the good, it makes it more expensive for the consumer to buy the commodity. This gives the domestic producer an advantage, especially if the tariff is high enough to raise the price of the imported good above the price of the good produced at home.

There are basically two types of tariffs: ad valorem duty and specific duty. An *ad valorem duty* is a certain percentage of the value of the good—for example, 5 percent of value. A *specific duty* is a fixed dollar amount per unit of the good, no matter what the price may be—for example, one dollar per pound. The United States uses both ad valorem and specific duties to protect its domestic markets, whereas European countries mainly use ad valorem duties.

Since tariffs have the effect of raising the prices of imported goods, they give domestic producers a price advantage over foreign competitors. As a result, domestic producers can increase their sales at the expense of foreigners. But again, the domestic producers gain at the expense of domestic consumers, for as consumers we are forced by buy higher-priced domestically produced goods and not the less-expensive foreign goods. Once again, we are being deprived of the benefits of free international trade.

In the post–World War II period, there has been a significant lowering of tariffs worldwide under the General Agreement of Tariffs and Trade (GATT). During the same period, however, many countries have engaged in a variety of restrictive practices known as non-tariff barriers. Such practices include discriminating government procurement policies, restrictive customs procedures, exchange rate controls, and complex technical regulations on imports. The latter include domestic content requirements and product safety standards beyond what is reasonable. Also, the 1980s witnessed a strong surge of demands for tariff protection.

2. Arguments in Favor of Protection

Since tariffs and quotas are so harmful to consumers, why do we have them? Why don't our lawmakers get rid of them and thereby raise our standard of living? Four arguments have been advanced to justify tariffs and quotas. Some of these are better than others.

First, there is the keep-the-money-at-home argument. This boils down to the argument that if we restrict imports, our money stays here instead of flowing out of the country and into the pockets of foreigners. Presumably, keeping the money at home yields us some sort of benefit.

Now, let's consider the logic of this argument. When an American importer buys a Volkswagen from Germany, he may well pay for it with dollars. The German exporter, however, has no need for dollars—he lives in Germany and, therefore, needs marks to pay his workers and cover his other costs of production. What he does, then, is go to his bank and change the dollars into marks. Thus the German bank now holds the American dollars.

What will the German bank do with the dollars? It will hold on to them because it expects to sell them later. What is this? Selling dollars? True enough, for there are other Germans who will need them later because they are importing goods from the United States. The German importers buy the dollars with marks and then use the dollars to pay off the American exporters. Thus the dollars paid out for imports return to us as we export.

What we have said about the dollars and West Germany holds for all the other countries that engage in international trade with us. Therefore the dollars that we spend on imports *must ultimately* be used to buy exports from the United States. Indeed, if we aren't willing to buy goods from foreigners and pay for them with dollars, we can't expect them to buy from us. They need those dollars to pay us off.

Let's use an example from here at home to illustrate this point. If other states don't provide California with dollars for its oranges, Californians won't have enough dollars to buy, say, peanuts from Georgia and wheat from Kansas. Therefore the dollars spent by Georgians and Kansans will flow back from California. Furthermore, the dollars spent by Americans will flow back as foreigners acquire them to pay for goods they have purchased from the United States.

Moreover, look what would happen at home if we had high enough quotas and tariffs to keep our money here. Not only would we, as consumers, suffer by having to pay higher prices, there would be other disadvantages as well. We have a number of export industries—agriculture and aircraft to mention only two—that are extremely dependent on the world market. And if we don't provide the rest of the world with dollars to pay these industries for their exports, there will be some serious domestic unemployment and waste of resources.

What is the moral of all this? It is that in order to be able to sell our exports to other countries, we must buy from them. Ultimately the dollars spent on imports can only be used to buy our exports. In an important sense, then, the dollars never really leave the country.

The second argument used to defend tariffs and quotas is based on differences in wage *rates* between countries. The argument runs as follows. Many foreign producers can sell their goods as cheaply as they do in the United States because they use cheap labor. Since they pay such low wages, they sell more cheaply than American producers can sell. This is bad because the low-priced imports reduce the sales of American products, and this causes the unemployment of many higher-paid

American workers. Tariffs, therefore, raise the prices of the imports, cause demand to swing back over the American-made goods, and thus protect jobs in this country.

This argument has a certain appeal, but the way it is presented doesn't make it a very strong argument. What is important isn't wage levels alone, but average wage costs per unit of output. In other words, the ability to compete depends on average costs of production, and these in turn depend on both the wage and the efficiency (productivity) of the worker. A superior worker may be paid a high wage, but the wage costs per unit of output would be much lower than the same costs if an inefficient low-paid worker were employed.

In fact, a very strong argument can be made that wages are usually low because the workers are inefficient. The reverse is also true. As Chapter 18 points out, wages in the United States are as high as they are because American labor has traditionally been very productive. The large amounts of capital it works with, as well as the technology we have, make our labor force much more efficient than most. But despite the high wages the American worker gets, the high productivity keeps the cost per unit of output low. Considering the great variety of our exports to so many countries, we must conclude that this is rather widespread in the United States.

Of course, in some cases high wages here and low wages abroad actually do prevent us from competing with foreign producers. But this only tells us that we don't have an advantage in these cases. Therefore we should import the goods in question and take advantage of the superior foreign efficiency.

The third argument in favor of tariffs is the so-called infant industry argument. It goes like this: "We are now importing commodity X from abroad, but we can produce X here at home. If we did, however, it would at first be at a much higher cost and hence higher price. The reason is simply that the foreign producers have had a head start on us and can therefore undersell us. But give us enough time and we can become much more efficient than they are. In other words, foreign producers can undersell us only when our X industry is in its infancy stage. Protect us during this stage and then, when we reach maturity, we can drop the tariff."

The United States has historically used this argument to protect small struggling industries, many of which have now matured. And here is the major drawback of the argument: Who decides when an industry has become mature? Many industries that started out with tariff protection continue to argue for continued protection long after they have passed the infancy stage. More than that, they actually continue receiving the protection. In large part, this is undoubtedly because once a tariff has been established, it becomes politically difficult to remove it. But there may be another reason why the tariff is continued—it could be that the older industries are still less efficient than their foreign competitors. If this is the case, then we, as consumers, continue to be deprived of the benefits of trade.

The last argument pertains to defense, and it justifies certain tariff protection. If we were to open up free trade in all items, we might end up with a questionable result. We might, that is, end up being completely dependent on foreign sources for important military equipment. Recall that under free trade, there is a tendency for each of the trading nations to become increasingly specialized in the goods in which it has an advantage. This means, of course, that it becomes increasingly dependent on its specialized trading partners.

Now, what would—or could—happen, if war broke out? For one thing, it would be quite easy for the enemy to sever the trade channels between us and the countries providing us with essential equipment. That would make us quite vulnerable. Even worse, what if the enemy itself were the supplier of equipment essential to our winning the war? Sounds bleak, doesn't it?

There is merit to this argument. The difficulty, however, is to decide which industries are crucial to the defense of this country. Obviously, some—such as the aerospace industry—are essential. But what about the steel or textile industry? Perhaps an argument can be made that these two industries are essential in the event of a war. However, if this line of reasoning is carried far enough, it will lead to the conclusion that nearly all industries become crucial to the effort. This doesn't mean, does it, that we should grant tariff protection to most of the industries in the United States?

C. THE BALANCE OF PAYMENTS

A major difference between international trade and interstate trade is that here at home we use the same type of money in all the states, but internationally all different types of money are used. If a retailer in Alabama buys Wisconsin cheese, he naturally pays the seller with dollars. He writes a check on his account in an Alabama bank and sends it to the Wisconsin dairyman. The dairyman then deposits the check in his bank. The end result is very simple—the cheese moves to Alabama and the dollars flow northward to Wisconsin. There is no problem here: The dollars are equally acceptable anywhere in the United States.

However, the situation would be quite different if the same Alabama retailer bought cheese from Switzerland. He would have to make his final payment, not in dollars, but in Swiss francs. The Swiss exporter doesn't want dollars; he wants the money that is generally accepted in his country. And if he were to get dollars, he would sell them immediately for Swiss francs.

How would the Alabama retailer pay off the Swiss exporter? He would use his dollars to buy the necessary Swiss francs from a bank and would then use the Swiss francs to pay the exporter in Switzerland. In the same way, a British importer of American goods would have to use his pounds to buy dollars to pay the American exporter. And so it goes. Currencies (different kinds of money) are continually being traded for one another. Exhibit 7-2 lists all the major, and some of the not so major, currencies used in the world today.

There has to be a financial system that links or connects all the currencies so that trade between countries can be carried on. There is indeed such a financial system, and it is called the *foreign exchange market*. It is a loosely knit, worldwide network of banks, both private and public, that stay in constant touch with each other by means of telephone and cable. As long as the foreign exchange market

EXHIBIT 7–2
Money, Money, Money

There are over 135 countries in the world, and each has its own currency. As we have seen, there is a foreign exchange market for all these currencies, so that each can easily be converted into another. Listed below are some of the leading currencies in the world today.

Country	Name of Currency
Australia	Australian Dollar
Belgium	Franc
Brazil	Cruzado
Canada	Dollar
China, People's Republic of	Yuan
Denmark	Krone
East Germany	Ostmark
Finland	Markka
France	Franc
Greece	Drachma
Hong Kong	Hong Kong Dollar
India	Rupee
Iran	Rial
Iraq	Dinar
Israel	Shekel
Italy	Lira
Japan	Yen
Jordan	Dinar
Luxembourg	Franc
Mexico	Peso
Netherlands	Guilder
Norway	Krone
Spain	Peseta
Sweden	Krona
Switzerland	Franc
U.S.S.R.	Ruble
United Kingdom	Pound
United States	Dollar
West Germany	Deutsche Mark

functions smoothly and efficiently, it facilitates the flow of trade of physical goods; it does this by facilitating the flow of money among the trading nations.

For the most part, the major participants in foreign exchange markets are the large, privately owned banks in the main financial centers of the world, such as New York, London, Tokyo, Hong Kong, and Paris. These banks keep deposits of all sorts of foreign currencies in many other banks scattered around the world. For example, a New York bank will have deposits of pounds in a London bank, guilders in an Amsterdam bank, marks in a Frankfurt bank, and so on. At the same time, the major foreign banks hold deposits of dollars in the United States. It is this way that our Alabama retailer, who bought cheese from Switzerland, was able to exchange his dollars for francs. The foreign exchange market means that businesspeople and travelers are always able to get the foreign exchange they need.

Nearly every country engages in trade with numerous other countries, and this involves thousands upon thousands of different goods and services. It also, as we have seen, involves millions of different foreign exchange transactions among the trading nations. Each country, of course, must have an accounting system to keep its position with respect to the "rest of the world" up to date. This accounting system is called the balance of payments. For example, the transactions between the United States and the rest of the world are recorded in our balance of payments statement.

> **Definition:**   The *balance of payments* is an annual statement of all the international transactions between a country and the rest of the world.

The term *balance of payments* is, in a sense, misleading. As we shall see, the balance of payments of a country is *always* in balance. Yet, you might have heard recently on television or read in a newspaper that the United States has a "deficit" in its balance of payments. But a deficit means that more is going out than is coming in. So how can it be that the country's balance of payments is always in balance and still can be running a deficit? Confusing? Maybe for right now, but once we run through how the balance of payments is actually set up, you will find that it really isn't confusing at all.

1. The Basic Transactions

There are two basic types of transactions in a country's balance of payments account: receipts and payments. This makes sense, for we are dealing with money flows. Let's look at each of these more closely.

On the receipts side, as we have seen, when Americans export to other countries, they expect payment in dollars, not marks, francs, or drachmas. This means that the foreign importers must exchange their currencies for dollars; they do this in the foreign exchange market.

The important thing to keep in mind is that importers from the United States must and do demand dollars to pay the American exporters. They satisfy this demand by exchanging their currencies for dollars in the foreign exchange market.

Another important point is that when they use these dollars to pay the Americans, the dollars are receipts for the United States. Thus *receipts for this country can be viewed as the foreign demand for dollars.*

So far we have considered only the demand for dollars by importers of American exports. But foreigners want dollars for other reasons as well. What are these? Many foreigners like to travel in the United States, and, again, they need dollars for this. And some foreigners may want to invest in capital equipment—i.e., start a business, buy an already existing business, or purchase stocks and bonds—in the United States. Or they may want to buy real estate. There are all sorts of reasons why foreigners demand dollars; and, remember, these dollars flow into the United States and are counted as receipts in the balance of payments.

What about the payments side? The payment items are the opposite of the receipt items. *Payments are those transactions that involve a demand for foreign currencies by people in this country.* From the point of view of our balance of payments, we can obtain these currencies only by supplying dollars in the exchange market. Thus, payments = the supply of dollars by Americans, just as receipts = the demand for dollars by foreigners. And here we are again, back to supply and demand.

Americans supply dollars to get foreign currencies for the same reason that foreigners demand dollars. We travel overseas, we import from abroad, and we invest in the land, capital, and stocks and bonds of other countries.

We can now define what is meant by a deficit in the balance of payments as well as what is meant by a surplus.

> **Definition:**   A *deficit* occurs when the payment items, that is, our supply of dollars to foreigners, exceed the receipt items, that is, the foreign demand for dollars. In other words, supply is greater than demand for dollars, and consequently more dollars are flowing out of the country than are flowing in. A *surplus* exists when the receipt items exceed the payment items, that is, demand exceeds supply, and more dollars are flowing in to the country than flowing out. Finally, if the payment items and receipt items are equal, there is an equality of the amount supplied and the amount demanded. Thus the amount of dollars flowing in is the same as the amount flowing out.

2. The Actual Accounts

Let's now take a look at the balance of payments of the United States for a recent year. We want to determine how the different kinds of international transactions affect the supply of and demand for dollars.

Table 7–4 shows the payments and receipts of the United States for 1986. Included are transactions in commodities, services, and flows of money capital. The two major accounts that contain these items are the Current and Capital Accounts.

The actual international purchases and sales of goods and services are recorded in the Current Account (items 1–7). Most of this Current Account consists

TABLE 7-4   Balance of Payments for the United States, 1986 (Billions of $)

	Payments (−) (Supply of dollars)	Receipts (+) (Demand for dollars)	Balances (Net Supply of dollars − or Net Demand of dollars +)
1. Exports		+224	
2. Imports	−369		
3. *Merchandise Trade Balance* (1 − 2)			−145
4. Service Transactions (Net)		+18	
5. *Balance on Goods and Services*			−127
6. Transfers (Net)	−16		
7. *Balance on Current Account*			−143
8. Capital Outflow	−96		
9. Capital Inflow		+213	
10. *Balance on Capital Account* (9 − 8)			+117
11. *Basic Balance* (7 − 10)			−26
12. Change in Official Reserves	−2		
13. Statistical Discrepancy		+24	
14. Net Balance			0

Source: Economic Report of the President, February 1988. Adapted from Table B99, pp. 364–65.

of merchandise imports and exports (items 1–3). For example, our exports at that time were $224 billion and imports were $369 billion. Therefore the Merchandise Trade Balance had a *deficit* of $145 billion. As a result, the supply of dollars exchanged to buy imports exceeded the demand for dollars to buy exports by $145 billion.

Item number 4, Net Service Transactions, narrowed the trade deficit by $18 billion to $127 billion. Service transactions measure imports and exports of services and net income on overseas investments. Examples of service exports would be foreign tourist travel in the United States, as well as financial, insurance, and transportation services for foreign entities. Service imports, would of course include not only foreign travel by U.S. citizens but financial, insurance, and transportation service provided by foreign firms to U.S. entities. The main reason for net receipts of $18 billion in service transactions, however, is the enormous excess of investment income earned by American businesses overseas over investment income earned by foreign businesses in the United States. The result, item 5, the Balance on Goods and Services, is a $127 billion deficit.

One other thing must be considered before we get the Balance on Current Account (item 7), and that is Net Transfers (item 6). Transactions here include foreign aid, as well as funds sent by people and businesses here at home to people abroad. Gifts to relatives in other countries and pension checks sent to retired Americans living abroad would fall into this category. This entry was a negative (or payment) figure of $16 billion, and thus the deficit on Current Account was $143 billion, very large by historical standards.

The next two items in Table 7–4 (items 8 and 9) record the movement of funds of a capital nature. Capital Outflow records the supply of dollars in foreign exchange markets during the year as Americans bought foreign stocks, bonds, and bank balances and invested in plants and equipment overseas.

The $96 billion capital outflow was more than offset by a capital inflow of $213 billion. That is, foreigners bought U.S. stocks, bonds, real assets, and bank balances in enormous amounts during the year, almost offsetting the Current Account deficit. The main point here is that a country can cover deficits in the Current Account by capital funds from abroad. When foreign institutions lend to us, that is, of course, a capital inflow. From the point of view of foreign countries, they are covering their Current Account surplus with us by lending us money. The Basic Balance, which is the net of Current Account and capital movements, thus shows a deficit of $26 billion.

This Basic Balance deficit was then covered by a reduction in Official Reserves assets of $2 billion and a mysterious Statistical Discrepancy of $24 billion. Statistical Discrepancy includes a wide variety of unrecorded transactions. A large amount of this undoubtedly consists of foreign funds moving to the United States for safekeeping through domestic agents, and it is therefore not recorded as capital inflow. At any rate, line 14, the Net Balance, is zero in conformance with good accounting practice.

The above discussion explains how the value of the dollar in foreign exchange markets could rise so dramatically in the early 1980s, even in the face of an increasing current account deficit. A current account deficit implies that the supply of dollars exceeds the demand, and this by itself should cause the value of the dollar to drop in exchange markets. Why, then, did the dollar rise? Part of the answer is that high interest rates in the United States relative to rates in other countries attracted a large money capital inflow—i.e., an excess demand for dollars in the capital account. As a matter of fact, the surplus on capital account exceeded the deficit on current account, creating a basic balance surplus in the early 1980s. Overall, then, the demand for dollars exceeded the supply, putting upward pressure on the dollar exchange rate. Many economists point out that the high dollar itself has been the main reason for the huge trade deficit. In other words, the high dollar makes foreign goods less expensive to us and makes our exports more expensive to foreign buyers. In the mid 1980s, the exchange value of the dollar began to fall against most European currencies and the Japanese yen. The decline of the dollar is a result of a reduced international demand for dollars as a result of a number of factors, among them a fall in U.S. interest rates relative to foreign rates. The fall in the dollar value has, after a long and painful time lag, begun to shrink the trade deficit.

D. FOREIGN TRADE AND THE CIRCULAR FLOW

We will wind up this chapter by seeing how foreign trade fits into the circular flow model. Figure 7–1 shows the model with the international sector added.

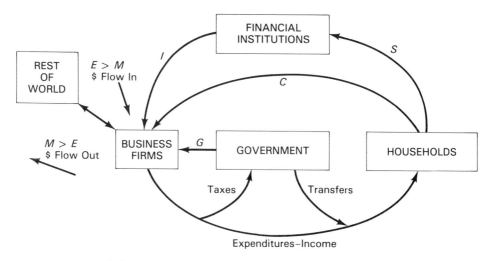

FIGURE 7-1   Foreign Trade in the Circular Flow

Some part of the expenditures of both households and business firms goes for the purchase of foreign goods and services. These of course are imports, and they constitute a leakage from the spending stream. Unless this leakage is offset elsewhere, the levels of output and employment here at home will contract.

But as we have seen, foreigners also spend a part of their income on our goods and services—that is, we export things—and the payment of these exports constitutes an injection of dollars into our economy. By themselves, therefore, exports tend to expand the circular flow model and to raise the levels of domestic output and employment.

However, as we have also seen, we must take the outflow of dollars and the inflow together to determine the net effect. But which of the balances we mentioned in the preceding section is the relevant one for the circular flow? It is the Current Account, for here we consider the expenditures made on the imports and exports of goods and services. These expenditures have a direct and immediate impact on output and employment and therefore influence the size of the circular flow.

Changes in foreign trade flows between the United States and the rest of the world will affect the size of the circular flow. An increase in exports adds to the total demand for domestically produced goods and services and then increases household incomes. On the other hand, an increase in imports reduces domestic demand for output and decreases the income flow. Whether activity in the circular flow will expand or contract depends on the difference between exports and imports. If exports exceed imports ($E > M$), the circular flow expands. If imports exceed exports ($E < M$), the circular flow contracts.

Conclusion: If there is a surplus in the Current Account, then the foreign sector exerts a net expansionary effect on the economy. On the other hand, if there is a deficit in the Current Account, leakages exceed injections, and the level of economic activity tends to fall.

TABLE 7-5

Relationship	Circular Flow
$S + T < I + G$	Expands
$S + T = I + G$	Remains constant
$S + T > I + G$	Contracts
$S + T + M < I + G + E$	Expands
$S + T + M = I + G + E$	Remains constant
$S + T + M > I + G + E$	Contracts

Once the foreign sector—that is, imports (M) and exports (E)—has been included, we must add to the conclusions of the preceding chapter. There, we saw that the leakages of saving (S) and taxes (T) must be offset by the injections of investment (I) and government spending (G) if the circular flow is to remain unchanged. But, if the leakages exceed the injections—that is, $S + T > I + G$—the level of economic activity will contract. Finally, if the injections are greater than the leakages, so that $I + G > S + T$, economic activity will expand. All of this is summarized at the top of Table 7-5.

We must now consider another leakage and another injection. The leakage, of course, is imports (M), and the injection is exports (E). As the bottom part of Table 7-5 shows, all three leakages—$S + T + M$—must be equal to all three injections—$I + G + E$—if the level of economic activity is to remain constant. However, if $S + T + M > I + G + E$, output and employment will contract. Finally, if $I + G + E > S + T + M$, the economy will expand.

E. SUMMARY

International trade is growing in proportion to our domestic economic activity, as well as in relation to world economic performance. Trade among nations extends the benefits of specialization beyond national borders and allows countries to consume beyond their domestic capabilities. The basis of trade and specialization rests on natural or acquired advantages as a result of resource endowments.

Nevertheless, and mainly for domestic political reasons, nations have traditionally attempted to restrict the free flow of international commerce. During the post–World War II period, however, there has been a concerted effort to reduce the tariff barriers to the flow of trade among countries. Significant other barriers remain.

United States transactions with the rest of the world are recorded in the balance of payments. Two main categories of transaction are included—goods and services and financial flows. Surpluses or deficits in goods and services, however, are offset by deficits or surpluses in financial flows, including official transactions of the U.S. government.

Foreign trade affects the level of domestic output and employment, as demonstrated through the circular flow. Net exports (exports minus imports) are part of aggregate demand. An increase in net exports has the effect of increasing domestic output and employment. A decrease has the opposite effect.

Terms and Concepts to Remember

Tariff	Balance of payments
Quota	Non-tariff barriers
Exchange rate	Infant industry
Absolute advantage	Foreign exchange market
Comparative advantage	Trade deficit and surpluses
Current account	Capital Account
Basic balance	

Questions for Review

1. The theories of *absolute* and *comparative advantage* show that all nations gain from trade. Yet nations have built barriers to free trade. What are some of these barriers?

2. The text lists four arguments in favor of trade barriers. Discuss and evaluate each of these.

3. How can a country have an absolute advantage in all commodities and still find it advantageous to trade?

4. A nation's overall balance of payments must balance. In what sense, then, can there be a deficit or surplus in the balance of payments?

5. "An exchange rate is the price of one currency in terms of another." Explain.

6. Suppose households increase their demand for foreign goods. What is likely to be the short-run effect on domestic output and employment? On the exchange rate?

Appendix: The Law
of Comparative Advantage

The law of comparative advantage can be stated as follows:

> Each country should specialize in producing products in which it has a comparative advantage, the lowest *relative* cost of production, exchanging through trade the surplus of these products for other products in

which it has a comparative disadvantage. The result will be mutually beneficial. As a result of trade, consumption possibilities will be higher in all countries.

We will illustrate by using the Texas-Labrador example discussed above. Refer to Table 7A-1 as we restate the problem. An hour of labor can produce 12 pounds of fish and 8 pounds of cotton in Texas, while in Labrador the same efforts produce 6 pounds of fish and 1 pound of cotton. Texas has an 8-to-1 advantage in cotton production and a 2-to-1 advantage in fish. In other words, Texas has an *absolute advantage* in both products. However, its greater advantage is in cotton (8 to 1), while its advantage in fish is smaller (2 to 1).

To see the significance of this, let's state the internal opportunity cost of producing each product in each country. In Texas, *1 pound of cotton costs 1 1/2 pounds of fish, while 1 pound of fish costs 2/3 pound of cotton.* In Labrador, on the other hand, *1 pound of cotton costs 6 pounds of fish, while 1 pound of fish costs 1/6 pound of cotton.* Restating in terms of products: It costs 1 1/2 pounds of fish to produce 1 pound of cotton in Texas, while it costs 6 pounds of fish to produce 1 pound of cotton in Labrador. Therefore, in terms of real opportunity costs, it is much cheaper to produce cotton in Texas; Texans have a comparative advantage in that product. Fish, of course, is cheaper in Labrador, where 1 pound of fish costs 1/6 pound of cotton. In Texas, 1 pound of fish costs 2/3 pound of cotton. As a result, Labrador has a comparative advantage in the production of fish even though it has an absolute disadvantage in both products.

Now, a basis of trade and mutual benefit exists. If Texas can trade 1 pound of cotton and get more than 1 1/2 pounds of fish in exchange, Texans will be better off. Labrador will be better off if its citizens can trade 1 pound of fish and get more than 1/6 pound of cotton. So, for both countries to gain cotton and fish, they must trade somewhere between the following limits:

1 pound cotton = 1 1/2 pounds of fish or more

1 pound cotton = 6 pounds of fish or less

Suppose the international exchange rate (terms of trade) is 1 pound cotton = 3 pounds of fish. Note that this is between the limits above. Can both countries benefit? Yes indeed! Texans can get 3 pounds of fish for 1 pound of cotton in trade,

TABLE 7A-1   Pounds of Output of One Hour of Labor

	Texas	Labrador
Fish	12	6
Cotton	8	1

but they could only get 1 1/2 pounds of fish if they produced at home. What about Labrador? Labradorians can get 1/3 pound of cotton for each pound of fish traded, but they could only get 1/6 pound of cotton for each pound of fish if they produced at home.

Therefore we conclude that Texas should specialize in cotton production and Labrador in fish production. International trade, with Texas exporting cotton and importing fish, and Labrador exporting fish and importing cotton, would be to the benefit of both countries. Remember, these gains exist, even though Texas has an absolute advantage in producing both products.

8

The Measurement of Economic Activity

chapter preview

- The national income and product accounts are the best available measurement of the economy's overall performance through time.

- The two product accounts are gross national product (GNP) and net national product (NNP).

- GNP can be measured in several ways: GNP = value of total output = value of total income = value of total spending.

- Viewed as total spending the major components of GNP are consumer spending (*C*), gross investment spending by business (*I*), spending by governments on goods and services (*G*), and net spending from the rest of the world (*E-M*).

- Depreciation measures the annual physical wear and tear on a nation's stock of capital. Replacement investment replaces the capital that wears out each year. GNP minus depreciation equals NNP. Only new capital formation is included in NNP.

- National income at factor cost is composed of the income payments

made to all the productive resources in the economy: wages and salaries, interest, rents, and profits.

- Personal income is a measure of gross household income. It measures total household income before personal taxes are deducted.

- Disposable personal income is what remains to households after personal taxes have been deducted. Households then divide this income into consumption and personal saving.

- The national income accounts have some shortcomings as measures of economic performance. Not all production gets measured—the services of housewives and activity in the underground economy, for example.

- The national income accounts make no provision for deducting the "bads" created by the production and consumption of things.

- The distorting effects of price inflation on the measurement of output is removed from the accounts by a process called deflation.

"The time has come," the Walrus said,
"To talk of many things;
Of shoes—and ships—and sealing-wax—
Of cabbages—and kings—
And why the sea is boiling hot—
And whether pigs have wings."[1]

The walrus mentions a number of things in this verse from Lewis Carroll's *Through the Looking Glass,* but they amount to very little compared with what we find in the gross national product (GNP). Just try to imagine counting all the goods and services produced in the United States every year. It boggles the mind. Yet we have to measure the total volume of all this output as best we can if we are to know how well or how poorly the economy is doing. Of course, we can't accurately measure everything that is produced. Also, a number of things that should be included in GNP aren't included. Overall, however, the U.S. Department of Commerce does an excellent job of calculating GNP and related accounts.

The main purpose of this chapter is to examine the national product and income accounts in some detail. In a very important sense, this chapter is simply a review of much that has been covered in the last three chapters, but it also serves as a steppingstone to the next five chapters. Thus it represents a crucial midpoint and deserves careful study.

Sections A and B use the circular flow model to define and explain how the gross national product is calculated. Then Section C discusses in some detail the four important components of GNP. Sections D and E discuss the net national product (NNP) and the other income accounts in the official form published by the Department of Commerce. The accounts are widely used by both government and business to keep track of economic conditions, and they become the basis on which forecasts are made. Finally, Section F considers some of the shortcomings and flaws of the accounts. Despite these defects, the national product and income accounts "stand as the jewel of U.S. statistics."[2]

[1]Lewis Carroll, *Through the Looking Glass and What Alice Found There* (New York: Random House, 1946), p. 59.

[2]A. T. Somers, *The U.S. Economy Demystified* (Lexington, MA: Heath, 1985) p. 2.

A. GROSS NATIONAL PRODUCT (GNP)

We need to begin with a definition.

Definition: GNP is the sum of the final values of all goods and services produced in the economy during the year.

Note that GNP is a *flow measure*—that is, it measures the flow of the nation's production through time. The figure is always cited as production at annual rates— e.g., $4,010 billion in 1985, $4,235 billion in 1986, $4,486 billion in 1987.

Actually, GNP is the sum of the total dollar values of the consumption flow, the investment flow, the government flow (but not transfer payments), and the foreign sector flow—all of those flows in the circular flow model. Recall from Chapter 5 that the *C* flow measures the total volume of physical consumer goods and services produced by business firms. Chapter 5 also pointed out that the *I* flow measures the real volume of capital goods being produced, including inventories. Then Chapter 6 showed that the *G* flow is the monetary measurement of goods and services produced for government. Finally, the $(E - M)$ flow of Chapter 7 measures the net flow of goods and services between the United States and the rest of the world. Thus we can write: $GNP = C + I + G + (E - M)$.

Note that GNP measures the *current* production of goods and services. Items produced in previous years but sold this year, such as used cars or old houses, are not included; they would of course have already been measured in the year in which they were produced. However, the value of agents and brokers involved in, say, the resale of a house would be included. These are newly produced services and hence should be counted in GNP. Also, any improvements on the used car that enhance its resale value would be included. The net values added in cases such as these are considered as current production.

But how do the people at the U.S. Department of Commerce go about adding up all the different things produced throughout the year—all those things ranging from apples, baseball gloves, and candy to X-rays, yarn, and zoo trips? Do they pull the trick that Lewis Carroll wrote about in *Alice in Wonderland?*

"Write that down," the King said to the jury, and the jury eagerly wrote down all three dates on their slates, and then added them up, and reduced the answer to shillings and pence.

Obviously that's not how it's done. There are no real mysteries in GNP accounting (although there are some serious flaws). There is a simple reason why all the different things produced every year can be added together, and that is that *they all possess a common denominator—namely, a money price.* Once the market prices of such products as apples, corn, tractors, books, shirts, trucks, haircuts, waitress services, and drill presses are known, they can all be added together in an appropriate way. And this, at base, is how GNP is calculated year in and out.

Note, however, that the Department of Commerce avoids double counting as best it can. Look again at the definition given above and observe that it refers to GNP as the sum of the *final values* of all goods and services produced. The emphasis is on the word *final:* Only the market value of the *final product* is included or counted in GNP. There is a good reason for this. If the values of all the "intermediate" goods and services used in producing the final product were also included, the resulting figure would definitely be misleading. GNP would be unrealistically magnified many times.

An example will make this clear. From the myriad goods and services being produced this year, we single out only one—a chair. Actually, this chair goes through a number of stages of production as it moves from the very early stages to the final product. These stages are shown in Table 8-1.

The process of production naturally begins with the raw materials and ends with the chair being bought by some consumer. At the first stage of production, the lumber cost $10. Or, to put it more precisely, the timber grower has added $10 (lumber) to the economy's output. In the next stage, the lumber is cut, trimmed, and finished so that it can be used for some other purpose (for example, a chair). Its market value (i.e., the price of the transformed lumber) has risen to $15; in other words, the second stage of production has added a *net value* (a *net output*) of $5 to the timber. The timber is then used by the furniture manufacturer to produce the chair itself: It is this final product that he sells to the retailer at a price of $30. The manufacturer has therefore added a *net* value (or *net* output) of $15 to the chair.

What do we have so far? The timber grower (Stage 1) added a new value of $10 to the economy's output. At Stage 2, the lumber company added another $5, bringing the total up to $15, and this is the price the chair manufacturer paid to get the wood. He then, at Stage 3, converted the material into a chair that is valued at $30, which means he has added $15 to the total value. Finally, we come to Stage 4, the retail stage, and the retailer adds a net value of $20 to the chair when he marks it up and sells it at the price of $50.

The end result of all these steps is summarized in Table 8-1, columns 1, 2, and 3. The important thing out of all this is as follows.

Conclusion: The value of the final product is *the sum of the net values added at each stage of production. It is not the sum of the prices at each level of production.*

TABLE 8-1

Stage of Production (1)	Net Value Added (2)	Cumulative Net Value Added (3)	Selling Price Next Stage (4)	Cumulative Selling Price (5)
1. Lumber	$10	$10	$10	$10
2. Cut and trim	5	15	15	25
3. Chair assembly	15	30	30	55
4. Retail	20	50	50	105

What would be the case if, for some unknown reason, GNP were calculated as the sum of all the selling prices involved in the production process? If the Commerce Department were to do this, it would have to sum up the successive selling prices in column 4 of Table 8-1. This is done in column 5. The result is seriously misleading, for this procedure says that the final value of the chair is $105. But this can't be so, for the consumer who finally bought the chair paid only $50 for it. So what Commerce does is to sum up the *net values* added, not the selling prices, and by thus counting only the final market value in GNP it avoids double counting.

B. GNP: PRODUCTION, INCOME, AND SPENDING

The circular flow model developed in the last three chapters gives us a good idea of how GNP is measured. Recall that business firms in the economy produce goods and services for households, government, and the rest of the world. Recall, too, that business firms themselves are customers for capital goods—that is, some firms produce capital goods for other firms.

Now, as business firms produce their varied outputs, they incur costs; and as the Expenditures-Income flow in many of the diagrams in Chapter 5 reveals, these expenditures by firms become incomes for households.

> **Conclusion:** GNP can be measured either as a flow of production of goods and services by business firms (the product accounts) or as income received by households (the income accounts). Either approach should add up to the same amount.

Accordingly, we can make the following statement:

$$\text{GNP} = \text{Total production} = \text{Total income}$$

Still another way of looking at GNP is in terms of the amounts spent on current output—that is, the *total spending* for goods and services. (In the next chapter, we will refer to this as *aggregate demand*.) In fact, this is how the Commerce Department measures total output. Instead of measuring the total value of all consumer goods produced by adding up the final values of each, the Commerce Department measures the dollar expenditures that households make in order to acquire them. The same procedure is used for the other types of output produced by business firms—that is, *they are all measured by the total spending for them.*

In a very important sense, then, total spending is the same as total production. This being the case, we can write:

$$\text{GNP} = \text{Total output} = \text{Total income} = \text{Total spending}$$

We have, therefore, three distinct, but compatible, ways of measuring the flow of GNP through time. In what follows, however, we will emphasize the role of total spending in determining the size of the GNP flow. That is, as total spending rises, so does GNP; and conversely, when total spending slumps, so does GNP.

C. THE COMPONENTS OF TOTAL PRODUCT (= TOTAL SPENDING)

Since aggregate (total) spending ultimately calls the tune as far as current production is concerned, it definitely needs closer study. There are, as we know, four major components of total spending. We have considered these before, but they now warrant more attention:

1. The spending by households on the output of final consumer goods and services. The official accounts refer to this as Personal Consumption Expenditures, but we will simplify and call it Consumption, or, still more simply, *C*.

2. The spending by business firms on the output of final investment goods and services. This is referred to as Gross Private Domestic Investment, or, more simply, Investment (*I*).

3. The spending by governments at all levels on the goods and services they are demanding. The official accounts label this as Government Purchases of Goods and Services; we abbreviate to *G*. Recall that this *G* figure *does not* include transfer payments.

4. Finally, there is the spending by foreigners on our output less our spending on things imported from abroad. This is labeled Net Exports of Goods and Services, or, as we put it, Exports minus Imports (*E − M*). This figure may be either positive or, as in recent years, negative.

Thus business firms provide different products (and services) that we label $C + I + G + (E − M)$, and these are each measured by the expenditures made to get them. This is why we can write:

$$\text{GNP} = C + I + G + (E − M) = \text{total spending}$$

All of this can be seen in Table 8–2 and Figure 8–1 for the year 1987. Let's now look at each component in more detail.

1. Consumer Spending (C)

Consumption is by far the largest component of total spending. In 1987, it amounted to $2,966 billion—that is, $2 trillion, $966 billion, (see the *C* arrow in Figure 8–1). That amounts to about two-thirds to three-fourths of GNP. It seems that the great bulk of the economy's activity is directed toward satisfying consumers' current needs and desires. Also, because of its lion's share of total spending, household behavior is very important in determining the level and course of production in the economy.

TABLE 8-2

The Major Components of GNP, 1987 (In Billions of $)	
Consumer Output (expenditures)	$2,966
Investment Output (expenditures)	716
Output for Government (expenditures)	924
Output for Foreigners, less imports from abroad (expenditures)	−120
TOTAL OR GROSS NATIONAL PRODUCT	$4,486

Source: Economic Report of the President, February 1988.

Note: Total is the result of rounding and doesn't match figures used in the text.

2. Investment Spending (*I*)

The investment spending part of GNP consists of three subparts: (1) the output of machinery, equipment, and tools; (2) *all* construction, both business plants and office buildings, as well as residential housing; and (3) inventory changes. In 1987, total investment was $716 billion.

As far as machinery, equipment, and tools are concerned, little needs to be said. These are obviously a form of private business investment. The same is true of the construction of plants—factories, stores, warehouses, and so on—that is, all nonresidential construction.

Apartment buildings and houses built to rent are also a type of private business investment. This should be clear enough. But what of the construction of houses for private families? Should this be considered as a form of private investment? Yes, because people rarely build their own houses anymore. Instead they turn to professional builders. In fact, the houses are often built before the contractor has

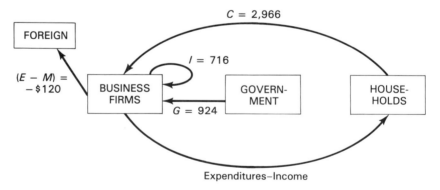

FIGURE 8-1   The Circular Flow Model and the Product Approach to Measuring GNP (in billions of dollars)

Source: Based on *Economic Report of the President,* 1988.

a buyer. Because of this, we can easily consider this type of construction as private business investment. The contractor, as it were, invests in housing with the hope of selling his output at a net profit.

The only thing remaining to consider in the *I* component is inventory changes. You may have raised the question earlier when we were discussing the *C* component—What if businesses produce consumer goods that aren't sold? The answer to this is that the unsold goods pile up as inventories; and since capital funds are tied up in these inventories, they are counted as investment. In 1987, the change in inventories was about $46 billion. Keep in mind, however, that the net change may be negative—that is, businesses may sell more during the year than they actually produce. In this case, they must draw down on their existing stock of goods—that is, there is inventory *dis*investment. In fact, it is inventory change that makes total output equal total spending.

Of all the components of GNP, investment is next to the smallest, and it is also the most changeable. It continually fluctuates—rising and falling in very short periods of time. As we will see in the next two chapters, this variability of *I* over time is a major source of economic instability in a market-oriented economy.

3. Output for Government (G)

A large amount of goods and services are produced for government (at all levels). In 1987, this amounted to $924 billion (see Figure 8-1). Since we explained government spending in Chapter 6, little needs to be added here. One thing, however, to keep in mind is that not all government spending is on goods and services; some takes the form of *transfer payments*. Recall that transfer payments do not represent expenditure on current production. Instead they are a reshuffling of funds from some parties to other parties—e.g., social security benefits, unemployment compensation, interest on the national debt, and so on. Since these don't represent current productive activity, they are excluded. Thus the *G* arrow in Figure 8-1 includes *only the outlays on goods and services bought by government in 1987.*

4. Net Exports or Imports (E − M)

As we noted in Chapter 7, the United States engages in international trade, and this must be taken into account when calculating GNP.

When foreigners buy goods and services from us, their spending stimulates current production here at home. *Exports,* in other words, create output and employment here. On the other hand, *imports* by Americans stimulate output and employment abroad. When we buy Volkswagens from Germany, stereos from Japan, coffee from Brazil, and wines from France—to mention only a few items that we import—we must deduct our expenditures abroad. Hence our (*E* − *M*) component of GNP may be either positive or negative. In recent years, since imports have far exceeded exports, our (*E* − *M*) figure is negative. Thus the (*E* − M) arrow in Figure 8-1 is shown as flowing out of the business firms box. In 1987, we imported $120 billion more than we exported.

5. Interim Summary

Figure 8-1 summarizes much of what has been said thus far. The figure concentrates on the business firms box. The *C* arrow, which flows into the box, measures all those things produced for and bought by households. Note that the *C* arrow stands for $2,966 billion of consumer goods produced and sold; it also measures revenue for business firms.

Similarly, the *G* arrow flowing into the business firms box measures the monetary value of all the goods and services produced by firms for government. The *G* arrow measures another $924 billion of revenue received by businesses in 1987.

Then there is the *I* arrow, which loops back to the business firms box because firms producing capital goods receive a revenue from the sales of these goods to other firms. In 1987, this arrow amounted to $716 billion.

Finally, the $(E - M)$ arrow for 1987 flowed out of the business firms box to the rest of the world. This is because imports exceeded exports by $120 billion.

Note that we have slipped in another way of viewing GNP, and that is as business firms' revenue from their total sales. Thus:

$$\text{GNP} = \text{Total output} = \text{Total income} = \text{Total spending}$$
$$= \text{Total business revenue}$$

D. NET NATIONAL PRODUCT (NNP)

Now that we know what GNP is, let's introduce a refinement—net national product (NNP), which provides a more accurate measurement of current production. The reason why NNP is more accurate than GNP is that, despite all that was said earlier about avoiding double counting, GNP still contains a particular type of double counting.

1. Replacement Investment

What is this double counting? And what causes it? It is due to what is called *replacement investment*. And just what is meant by replacement investment? An example will explain.

During 1987, business firms employed, bought, and hired many of the means of production to produce the GNP of $4,486 billion in that year. But they also made use of the capital goods they already possessed, and in the process of production, some of these capital goods were used up—that is, many machines and tools, and even some buildings, were worn out. Indeed, in 1987, business firms used up $479 billion of capital goods in producing GNP. And these had to be replaced, or at least the business firms that owned them felt that they had to be replaced. This, then, is what is meant by replacement investment.

> **Definition:** *Replacement investment* is investment in capital goods to replace the capital that has worn out in the production process.

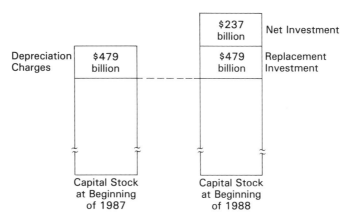

FIGURE 8-2   Change in the Capital Stock

An interesting thing about replacement investment is that it adds nothing to the total stock of capital goods. Indeed, it adds nothing to total output. As the term implies, it just simply replaces. Look at Figure 8-2. Let's assume that the 1987 rectangle represents the total private business stock of capital goods. Let's assume also that the only new capital goods produced in 1987 amounted to $479 billion, the amount of the worn-out capital shown at the top of the rectangle. In this event, then, all investment would be replacement investment, as shown in the 1988 rectangle; and we would have begun 1988 with the same capital stock that we had at the beginning of 1987. This being the case, we can hardly expect there to be much economic growth.

2. Net Investment

We have, however, experienced economic growth over the years; and in some part this is because year after year (with a few exceptions) we have produced more capital goods than needed to satisfy replacement investment. For 1987, in fact, our total investment (called gross private domestic investment) was $716 billion. Of this, $479 billion was used to satisfy replacement investment needs, leaving a remainder of $237 billion. In other words, the economy produced $237 billion capital goods over what was needed to maintain the stock of capital goods. This addition is called *net investment,* or *net capital formation.*

> **Definition:** *Private investment* is business spending on plant, equipment, and inventories. The expenditures that exceed replacement investment constitute *net investment* and measure additions to the productive capital capacity of the private sector of the economy.

Figure 8-2 shows the actual growth of the capital stock by the amount of net investment ($237 billion).

TABLE 8-3

The Product Approach to Measuring Gross
And Net National Product, 1987 (Billions of $)

Components of GNP			
C	=	consumption expenditures	$2,966
I	=	total investment expenditures	716
G	=	government expenditures	924
$(E - M)$	=	net exports of goods and services	−120
GNP	=	Gross National Product	$4,486
		Less: Replacement Investment	479
NNP	=	Net National Product	$4,007

Source: Economic Report of the President, February 1988.

Once replacement investment (which, remember, adds nothing new) has been deducted frm GNP, we have *net* national product (NNP). This is shown in Table 8–3. The NNP figure of $4,007 billion is a more accurate statement of the economy's performance for 1987, for NNP measures the *net, new* current output of the economy for the year.

As we will see in the following chapters, the behavior of *net investment* is crucial to the overall functioning of the economy. For one thing, small changes in it will likely cause much larger changes in NNP and employment. Fluctuations in net investment spending are a major cause of cyclical economic fluctuations. Also, as long as there is net investment over the long haul, the economy will continue growing. Net investment not only means that we have more plant and equipment to produce things, it is also an important route by which new knowledge in the form of technology is put to use. In short, new technological advances can be incorporated into the new net investment, making our capital stock more efficient. It is also possible to incorporate the new technology into replacement investment.

3. Interim Summary: Product Approach

Let's pause for a moment and summarize (see Figure 8-3 and Table 8-3). The total of consumer goods output (C), investment output (I), output for government (G), and output for foreigners ($E - M$) equals GNP. Recall that these outputs are measured in terms of the dollar expenditures made on them. Thus: GNP = C + I + G + ($E - M$), and this measures the market value of the total output of final goods and services for the year.

The I figure in GNP, however, includes replacement investment, which *adds nothing* to total output. Thus, in order to determine the economy's *net* new production for the year, replacement investment must be deducted from GNP. The resulting figure is NNP. All of this is summarized in Table 8-3 and Figure 8-3.

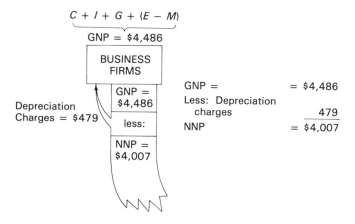

FIGURE 8-3   Another View of GNP and NNP (in billions of dollars)

E. THE NATIONAL INCOME ACCOUNTS

In all of our circular flow discussion, we have stressed that the expenditures made by business firms flow as income toward households. And earlier in this chapter we showed that output, income, and spending are the same thing. But then, in the preceding section, we saw that one expenditure—that for replacement investment—will never reach the households as income. It is true that replacement investment is a form of spending, but it must be treated as leakage from the Expenditures-Income flow.

1. From NNP to National Income at Factor Cost

However, not even all of NNP will flow to the households, for another important leakage—indirect business taxes—reduces the Expenditures-Income flow. Recall that Chapter 6 discussed this type of tax; indirect business taxes, such as sales taxes and excise taxes, are included in the actual final outlays consumers make. Moreover, the seller of the goods and services upon which these taxes are imposed collects the tax revenues and turns them over to the government. This is why they are called indirect taxes; the government doesn't collect them directly from households but rather indirectly through business firms. These taxes are of course included in the price of products sold (see Figure 8-4).

The reason why the Commerce Department deducts these taxes at this juncture is to avoid another form of double counting. This double counting arises because indirect business taxes are included in the C arrow (sales taxes for instance), the I arrow (excise taxes for instance), and the $(E - M)$ arrow (import duties). Thus they are included in GNP and NNP, for both of these are calculated in terms of expenditures on the goods and services. But then government, having collected them, spends the tax revenues, and hence they are included in the G arrow as government expendi-

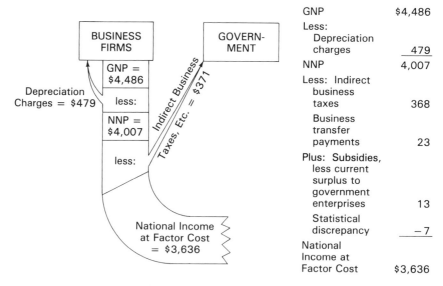

FIGURE 8-4 **From NNP to National Income at Factor Cost (in billions of dollars)**

tures. Accordingly, indirect business taxes are included twice in GNP and NNP, and it is for this reason that they are deducted here.

Some other minor adjustments are made, and we will simply add them to indirect business taxes. Once this amount has been deducted from NNP, we have National Income at Factor Cost, or, as it is usually called, National Income. This is shown in Figure 8-5 (see page 160; see also Exhibit 8-1). This account measures the amount of expenditures made by business firms for the use of productive resources. They consist of wages and salaries, rent, interest, and profits, the incomes received by the owners of the economy's productive resources.

2. From National Income to Personal Income

Not even all of national income, however, will arrive at households, even though they have earned it. There are still some important leakages to consider.

First, we must recognize that the board of directors of a corporation need not declare all (or any, for that matter) of the firm's profits as dividends to the stockholders. Rather, it may decide to hold some (or all) of the profits in order to "plow" them back into the firm in the form of capital investment. This major source of business saving is shown by the arrow labeled "Undistributed Corporate Profits" in Figure 8-5. It loops back to the business firms box, and in 1987 it amounted to $43 billion.

Government is directly responsible for the next two leakages in Figure 8-5— corporate income taxes and social security taxes. These were discussed in Chapter 6. Once these tax payments are deducted, the Expenditures-Income flow is narrowed

EXHIBIT 8-1
National Income at Factor Cost Equals Payments to Households

By the time we have allowed for both replacement investment and indirect business taxes, we end up with the account officially titled National Income at Factor Cost. The word *factor* needs a bit of explanation. Economists have for years called the different productive resources "factors of production." We have not used this term, preferring instead simply "productive resources." In any event, the account National Income at Factor Cost refers to the payments made by businesses to the households that own all the *factors of production.* Thus the cost expenditures by businesses amount to incomes for households, an idea we first met in Chapter 5.

If this is the case (and it is), then the incomes of households—in the form of wages and salaries, rent, interest, and profit—should add up to National Income at Factor Cost. Let's see if they do. The different types of income received by households in 1987 are shown in the accompanying table.

Types of Income	Amount (Billions of $)
Wages and salaries	$2,648
Rent	19
Interest	337
Proprietors' income	328
Corporate profits	305
National Income at Factor Cost	$3,636

This was how national income was allocated among the owners of the factors of production (households) in 1987. Of course, households did not receive this amount, for a number of tax leakages occurred before households received the income they could dispose of as they saw fit.

even more. However, the flow is swelled by the injection of transfer payments made by both business and government, but mainly by government.

The final result, then, after these three deductions and one injection, is Personal Income (see Figure 8–5). In 1987, Personal Income amounted to $3,746 billion.

3. From Personal Income to Disposable Income

There is only one more step to be taken and then we will be done with the national income accounts. This final step entails accounting for personal income taxes, for

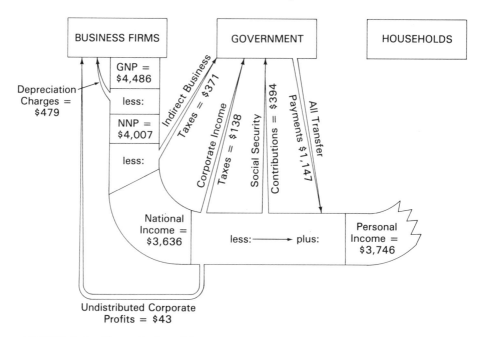

FIGURE 8-5   From National Income at Factor Cost to Personal Income (in billions of dollars)

these taxes are imposed on our personal incomes. Once we deduct personal income taxes, as we have done in Figure 8-6, we wind up with what is called Disposable Personal Income. These taxes ($565 billion in 1987) reduced personal income from $3,746 billion to a disposable income of $3,181 billion. Thus the arrow that originated at the business firms box as $4,486 billion (1987's GNP) was narrowed down to $3,181 billion (1987's disposable income). This was a reduction of $1,305 billion, or about 30 percent.

Disposable income is what households have left to do with as they see fit, and obviously the two important things they use it for are consumption and saving. Of these two, consumption takes the lion's share. During the past few years, households have saved a smaller and smaller percentage of disposable income. In 1987, they saved a mere 3.8 percent of disposable income. Since then, the savings rate has risen somewhat. As you might expect, this has a considerable impact on the general level of economic activity and may well have serious repercussions for the future.

F. SOME SHORTCOMINGS OF THE ACCOUNTS

Although GNP is very useful as an indicator of economic performance, it is not without its faults.

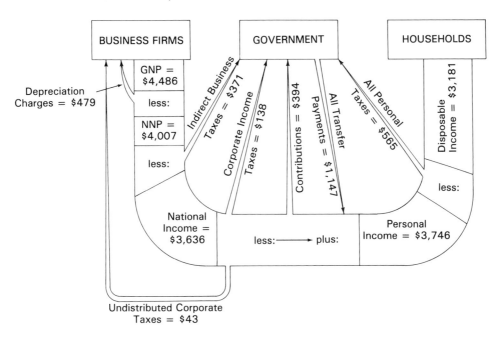

FIGURE 8-6   From Personal Income to Disposable Income (in billions of dollars)

1. Housewives, Househusbands, and Do-It-Yourselfers

One major weakness of the accounts is that not all goods and services produced are counted in GNP. For example, the services of housewives and househusbands aren't included, simply because there is no market exchange process through which they can be counted. Clearly, however, these services are important. As it is, when the houseperson washes clothes, cleans the house, prepares meals, mows lawns, and takes care of small children, these aren't counted in GNP. But if they were performed by a maid, a yardman, and a day-care center, they would indeed be included. In the former case, there is no market price for the services performed; in the latter case, there is. In this respect, then, GNP understates the actual production in the economy.

2. Pollution and Economic Welfare

Much of the production of goods that are a part of GNP also creates "bads" in some form or another. The firm that pollutes streams and the air with the byproducts of its production processes is a case in point. Toxic wastes are an increasingly severe problem for the United States. How are they safely disposed of? The same problem exists for less-dangerous refuse—i.e., garbage—for space is an increasingly relatively scarce resource. These toxic wastes and garbage are "bads" and require resources for their disposal, resources that could be used for other purposes. The same is true of the wastes emitted by automobiles and other gasoline-driven vehicles, since they pose a serious threat to the environment and our well-being.

The product accounts, as presently constructed, make no provision for deducting the "bads" created by the production and consumption of things. Yet they do indeed reduce our well-being. Good arguments can be made for making negative entries to reduce the amount of GNP by the amount of these "bads" if only such a figure could be devised.

3. The Underground Economy

The underground economy consists of a diversity of activities. For example, illegal activities such as gambling, prostitution, and illegal drugs are clearly exchanged through markets. There is a demand for them and there is a supply of them, and the interaction of demand and supply determines the prices of these services and things (e.g., cocaine). Yet these values aren't included in GNP because of the illegal status of the markets in which they are sold.

There is also a lot of personal swapping of services—for instance, "I'll help you build your bookcases if you help me with my plumbing"—which reflects values not included in GNP. Furthermore, some persons prefer to have their services paid for in cash. This type of payment is seldom included in GNP, since the payment isn't reported for tax purposes.

How large is the underground economy? No one knows. Studies vary considerably—some conclude that as much as 20 to 25 percent of GNP relates to these activities; others are much more conservative, arguing that the underground economy relates to only 3 to 5 percent of GNP.

4. Government Expenditures as Intermediate Goods

The treatment of government in the product accounts involves some major difficulties. Since the pricing mechanism rarely offers clues about the value of government's services, they are valued at cost. This may of course be quite misleading. There is also the problem of whether to treat many government expenditures—e.g., on education and highways—as intermediate goods. A good argument can be made for doing so, for these products and services are used by the private sector to increase the value of its output.

National defense poses a thorny problem. It doesn't provide any *direct* benefit to households or to the production of any product. This being the case, it should be treated as an intermediate good; it certainly helps to stabilize the environment in which private units operate. Accordingly, so this argument goes, national defense shouldn't be included in total output. The same holds true, as we saw above, for any other government output that serves an intermediate role.

G. FROM NOMINAL TO REAL GNP

A final point about the accounts: The national income accounts are published in both nominal (current dollar) and real (constant dollar) terms. Nominal GNP, for example, is simply the value of the nation's output at the average price level prevailing in that year. Problems in comparing the level of GNP from year to year arise whenever the price level changes over time. To illustrate, suppose that between two given years the nominal GNP doubles while the average level of prices also doubles. Clearly, the nation isn't twice as well off, for the entire rise in GNP is absorbed by price increases. In fact, the actual volume of (real) production hasn't changed at all.

Fortunately, a simple method exists to account for price level changes from period to period so that nominal values in the national income accounts can be converted to real values. The method is called *deflation* and requires the use of a measure of price change over time. This measure of price change is called a *price index*. A price index measures prices in any year relative to some base year, where in the base year prices are expressed as 100. Thus an index of 110 in 1988 would indicate that the average price level had risen 10 percent from the base year.

The formula for converting nominal GNP to real GNP is

$$\text{Real GNP} = \frac{\text{Nominal GNP}}{\text{Price index}} \times 100$$

In words, if the nominal GNP is divided by the price index and the result is multiplied by 100, the calculation yields real GNP. Table 8–4 shows the conversion of nominal GNP into real GNP for the 1982–87 period. Since 1982 is the base year for the price index, note that nominal and real GNP are the same. Note also that inflation has caused nominal GNP to rise faster than real GNP.

TABLE 8-4   Calculation of Real GNP from Nominal GNP, selected years

Year	Nominal GNP (billions)	Price Index	Real GNP (billions)
1982	3,166	100.0	3,166
1983	3,406	103.9	3,279
1984	3,772	107.7	3,508
1985	4,010	111.2	3,608
1986	4,235	114.1	3,713
1987	4,486	117.4	3,820

Source: Economic Report of the President, February 1988, pp. 248, 250.

H. SUMMARY

And so we are done with the national income and product accounts. Rather than attempt to summarize all the steps involved in moving from GNP to disposable income, we will let Figure 8-7 stand as our summary. Study it carefully; it is very pertinent to our discussion in the following chapters.

Terms and Concepts to Remember

Gross national product
(GNP)
Replacement investment
Net national product
(NNP)
Indirect business taxes
National income at
factor cost

Personal income
Disposable income
Nominal income
Real income

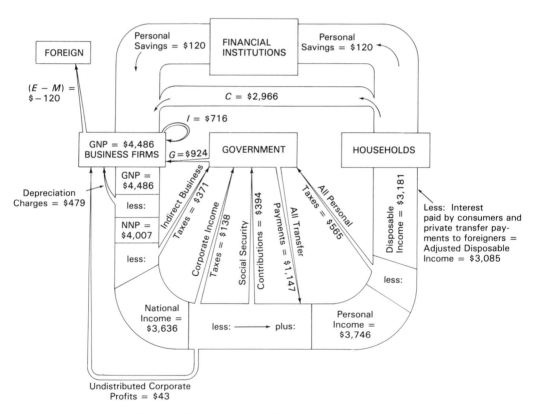

FIGURE 8-7 The Completed Circular Flow (in billions of dollars)

Questions for Review

1. Define what is meant by GNP and discuss all the elements of double counting that you think are included in it.

2. Why are intermediate values excluded from the calculation of GNP? What does this imply about a lot of government spending on goods and services?

3. Why must GNP, when calculated by the product approach, be equal to GNP calculated by the Expenditures-Income approach?

4. With reference to the Expenditures-Income flow in the circular flow model, list all the leakages as they take place sequentially moving from left to right. Now explain why these leakages are in fact treated as such.

5. Discuss why and how each of the following creates problems for national income and product accounting: (a) the do-it-yourself movement, (b) national defense, and (c) the underground economy.

6. Using data from the most recent year draw the complete circular flow model as shown in Figure 8-7.

9

The Roller Coaster Economy

chapter preview

- The growth path of the economy over time is characterized by ups and downs we call the business cycle.
- Potential GNP is the total real output of goods and services that could be produced if there were continuing full employment of the labor force.
- When actual GNP is below potential GNP, there are substantial opportunity costs in the form of output that could have been produced.
- The Employment Act of 1946 commits the government to three difficult goals—continuing full employment, price level stability, and a high rate of economic growth.
- Attempts to attain all three of these goals in the short run create trade-offs and opportunity costs.
- Full employment is said to exist when 94 to 95 percent of the labor force are holding jobs.
- The official unemployment figures can give a misleading picture of the status of the jobless.
- Inflation is a rise in the general level of prices over time—i.e., the inflation rate is the percentage increase in the average level of prices.
- The rate of inflation expected by the public becomes reflected in the money rate of interest.
- As a measure of price change, the Consumer Price Index (CPI) probably overstates the inflation rate by two or three percentage points.
- Economists believe that the main cause of inflation over the long run is excessive increases in the stock of money.
- Economic growth is measured by the rate of change of real per capita GNP over long periods of time.
- The growth performance of the U.S. relative to other industrialized nations has been poor in recent years.

We are now ready to embark on the study of *macroeconomics*. In a quite important sense, *macroeconomics* is the study of how efficiently the overall economy functions. For example, widespread unemployment of economic resources could hardly be called efficient. Indeed, idle workers unable to get jobs, and plants standing empty or only partly used, represent inefficiency in the use of the economy's resources.

This chapter explains this type of inefficiency; it also considers the record and potential of economic growth in the United States.

A. BUSINESS CYCLES

Look at Figure 9-1. It contains a fantastic record of the American economy. Real GNP has grown from $709 billion in 1929 to almost $4 trillion in 1987. This boils down to an annual average growth rate of 3 to 4 percent. This long-term upward sweep of real GNP is one way of depicting economic growth. A better, though still not completely satisfactory, way of measuring economic growth is to use *per capita* GNP—that is, real GNP divided by total population. The record clearly shows that per capita GNP has also undergone a long-term upward climb (see Figure 9-7).

A closer look, however, reveals that the long-run growth of GNP hasn't been smooth. To the contrary, it has continually been interrupted by recurring periods of booms and busts. These fluctuations, which we call the *business cycle,* have sometimes been severe (even catastrophic) for people in all walks of life. The historical record shown in Figure 9-1 clearly reveals that the business cycle has plagued the economy for quite a long time. Periods of unemployment and idle productive capacity being followed by periods of full employment and inflation have been commonplace, albeit undesirable in many respects. There is nothing static about our economy; indeed, *dynamic* seems to be the best way to describe it.

1. Recent Developments in Cyclical Fluctuations

Some other things about Figure 9-1 are important. Economists have observed that although all cyclical disturbances are similar, they aren't exactly alike. One early business-cycle theorist pointed out that all cycles belong to the same family, but no two are identical twins. How are they similar? In this sense: They each have four stages—the expansionary stage, the upper-turning point, the contractionary stage, and the lower-turning point. This similarity is what allows us to measure business

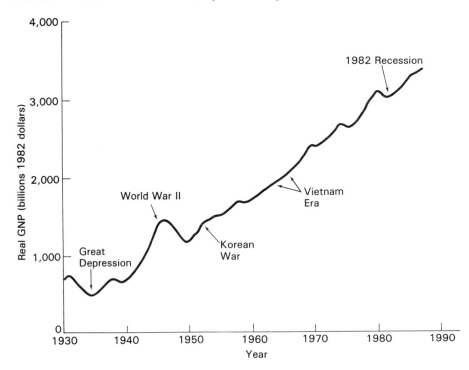

FIGURE 9-1   Real GNP 1929-87 (in 1982 dollars)   Since the 1930s,there has been a substantial rise in the economy's output of real goods and services. This rise has periodically been interrupted by recessions of varying degrees of severity.

Source: Economic Report of the President, February 1988, p. 250.

cycles and to search for a theoretical explanation of them. Thus, in our efforts to acquire a useful and appropriate theory of the business cycle, we must put the peculiarities and uniqueness of each cycle to one side. (But when we talk about a particular historical cycle, all these details must be brought into the discussion.)

However, the pattern of similarity has changed over time. Cyclical disturbances prior to World War II were much longer and certainly more severe than those that followed 1946. The earlier business cycle averaged from six to eight years, whereas the postwar cycles have averaged from three to four years. Not only are the postwar disturbances shorter, they are much milder than the prewar cycles.

What accounts for this changed pattern? A number of things, as we shall see, but the most important is that our society has acquired and used a tremendous body of knowledge about economic instability. We now know a lot more about what causes these fluctuations; and we know also a lot about what can be done to offset them. This doesn't mean that we have perfect knowledge about this matter. Far from that. What it does mean is that we have made tremendous strides in understanding and controlling the business cycle. The result is that cyclical disturbances in the postwar period are substantially different from those prior to World War II. Nonetheless, the cycle is far from tamed; it continues to present a recurring problem for the economy. The contraction of 1981–82 demonstrates this.

Figures 9-2 and 9-3 show two other dimensions of economic instability. The unemployment rate—that is, the percentage of the labor force without work and looking for work—behaves pretty much as expected. Whenever the economy goes into a contraction, the unemployment rate rises; then, as the economy recovers and output rises, the unemployment rate declines.

There is, however, another important thing about Figure 9-2. Observe how the unemployment rate has crept upward since 1945. Also observe that when the economy recovers from a contraction and passes through the expansionary stage, the unemployment rate drops, to be sure, but not so low as earlier. Thus there seems to be a ratchet effect built in to the economy, so that the unemployment rate continues to creep upward. More on this later.

Figure 9-3 tells us something about the inflation rate in the business cycle. The inflation rate is the percentage by which the price level changes over time. If, for example, the *annual* inflation rate is 5 percent, this means that prices in general are *rising* at the rate of 5 percent per year. We will have much more to say about inflation. What we want to stress here is that inflation now seems to be an integral part

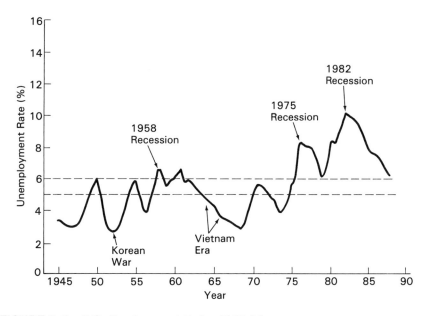

FIGURE 9-2   U.S. Employment Rate, 1945–88   The unemployment rate fluctuates with the business cycle, rising in recessions and falling in expansions. Over the period, there seems to be a trend of an upward drift in the unemployment rate.

Source: 1986 Historical Chart Book, Board of Governors of the Federal Reserve System, p. 20; and *The Economic Report of the President,* 1988.

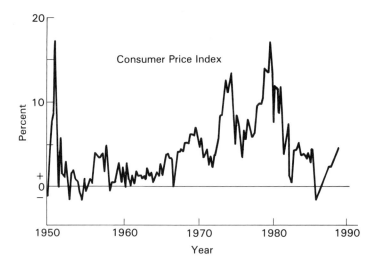

FIGURE 9-3   Rate of Inflation: Consumer Prices, 1950-87   Inflation tends to increase in the latter stages of a cyclical expansion and tends to fall late in recession periods.

Source: 1986 Historical Chart Book, Board of Governors of the Federal Reserve System, p. 37.

of our society. Prior to World War II—and even as late as 1947-48—whenever the economy went into a contraction, the price level actually fell. Put otherwise, the inflation rate went negative. But since the war, prices have continued to rise, even during contractions. It is true that the price level increased at a slower rate during the contractions than it did during the expansions, but nonetheless it went up. This phenomenon of inflation accompanying contraction is now called "inflated recession." This, along with the upward ratchet effect of the unemployment rate, is a new feature of the U.S. economy.

2. The Stages of the Cycle in More Detail

How do economists measure the business cycle? We have already noted that they divide it into four parts, but now we want to modify that a bit. Figure 9-4 shows these modified stages.

The expansionary stage, once it gets under way, is characterized by rising levels of output and employment. The economy seems to be getting healthier, as shown by a falling unemployment rate. However, the economic evil of inflation begins to rear its head. As the economy approaches full employment, price levels begin to rise—slowly at first, but then at a faster pace. Thus we can posit an important conclusion (yet to be established, of course).

> **Conclusion:**   Inflation and full employment tend to go hand in glove. Moreover, the inflation rate at full employment contributes strongly to the reversal of the expansion and its replacement by contraction.

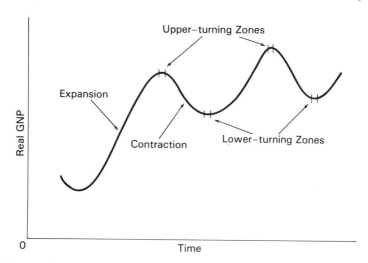

FIGURE 9-4   Stages of the Cycle   No two business cycles are identical, although they follow a similar course. The sequence of events is expansion, upper-turning zone, contraction into recession, lower-turning zone, and finally expansion once again.

This impact of the inflation rate is spelled out in the next chapter, but the role inflation plays in bringing on contraction is undeniable.

Earlier we referred to the upper-turning point as marking the change from expansion to contraction. A much better term is upper-turning *zone,* for the transition from expansion to contraction is not so abrupt as the word ''point'' implies but is instead a bit more gradual. Hence we will use the term *upper-turning zone.*

Once the contraction gets under way, both output and employment will decline. The price level, on the other hand, continues to rise, but at a slower rate—that is, the inflation rate has declined—and this is usually considered desirable. But now the evil of a rising unemployment rate rears its head. Indeed, as the contraction proceeds, the unemployment rate becomes higher and higher.

What causes the reversal from contraction to expansion? For years, economists strove to find a satisfactory theoretical explanation of the lower-turning zone, but with no great success. However, we don't need to concern ourselves with this problem, since the government will step in and provide measures to reverse the economy. What these measures may be and how they work are matters for chapters 10–14. But they can and do work, and so the expansion again gets under way.

This pattern of ebb and flow in the business cycle, to repeat, is clearly revealed in Figure 9–1. But the ebb and flow has been much milder in the period following World War II than it was before the war, when government didn't provide any measures to offset cyclical disturbances.

3. Actual GNP versus Potential GNP

Looking at the business cycle alone isn't enough; we need to put it in perspective. A useful way of doing this is to contrast the cyclical behavior of real GNP with what is called potential GNP.

Definition: *Potential* GNP is the total real output of goods and services that would be forthcoming if there were continuing full employment of the labor force.

Following current convention, we will assign the figure of 94 percent of the labor force as being full employment—that is, 6 percent of the labor force being unemployed is consistent with "full employment." But more on this in the next section of this chapter.

The smooth ascending curve in Figure 9-5 shows potential GNP. You may view this as a desirable goal to be reached and maintained. The jagged line lying beneath the potential GNP curve shows what has happened to real GNP over the same time period. The business cycle is evident in the real GNP curve; but we must also note how often and how long real GNP tends to lie beneath potential GNP.

We should also observe that occasionally the real GNP has risen above the potential. This occurred in 1950–52, 1965–68, and 1973. How can this be? This is the same as saying that the economy can produce at some point outside its production-possibilities curve, because the production-possibilities curve, like potential GNP,

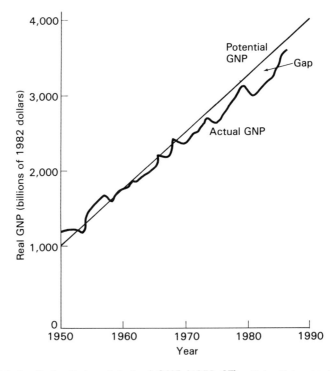

FIGURE 9-5   Potential and Actual GNP (1950-87)   Potential output represents the capacity of the economy to produce. Actual GNP moves toward potential in expansions and falls below potential during recessions.

Source: Economic Report of the President, February 1988, p. 250.

should reflect *potential, not maximum,* possible output. There are some valid reasons why maximum real output can exceed potential for short periods of time.

First, most business firms don't plan to operate their plants and other productive facilities at 100 percent of physical capacity. Instead they plan to operate on average at about 85 percent of capacity. Indeed, businesspeople sometimes refer to 85 percent operation as "full capacity." It isn't, of course, "full" in any physical sense, but that isn't the point. The main point is this: If there is some need to operate at higher rates of output than 85 percent, the plants have the capacity to do so. They aren't, however, designed to operate permanently at such high rates. In the short run, therefore, actual output can indeed exceed potential, and in this sense, the economy may for a short while lie beyond its production-possibilities curve. This, however, is like saying that the economy's actual GNP may exceed its potential GNP for a short while.

Another reason why this may happen is that if the economy is very strong in its expansion, business firms may offer higher wages in order to get the extra workers they need. These higher wages are needed to attract new workers into the labor force; but when the upper-turning zone occurs and real GNP falls, they tend to leave the labor force. For the moment, these two reasons are enough to explain why actual GNP may exceed the potential for rather short periods.

The great wastes occur, however, in the reverse case, when actual lies beneath potential GNP. This distance is often referred to as the *GNP Gap,* and the greater the gap, the greater the costs to society. As we have stressed in all the preceding chapters, the economy's resources are really scarce, and therefore there is need to use them as efficiently as possible. But when they are idle—when they aren't being used at all—the inefficiency is great indeed. There is, to be sure, an opportunity cost involved, and the greater the GNP Gap, the greater the opportunity cost to society in terms of forgone output.

This opportunity cost is the amount of goods and services that could have been produced but was not because of idle resources. Consider an example. There was an economic contraction in 1953–54, and the lost output—i.e., the GNP Gap—for 1954 was $16 billion. The *cumulative* opportunity cost from 1955 through 1964 was $237 billion, quite a sizable amount. However, for the short three-year span from 1970 through 1972, the GNP Gap amounted to $83.9 billion; and from 1974 through 1980, the lost output leaped to $500.5 billion. From 1980 on, the GNP Gap has been large, amounting to about $440 billion from 1980 through 1985.[1]

These costs are something we need to consider and that is the task of the next four chapters. In the meanwhile, we need to concentrate on some other matters.

4. Some Other Fluctuations

Two other types of economic fluctuations should be noted. First, there are *seasonal fluctuations.* By definition, these take place in less than a year's time. Examples:

[1]All the dollar figures in this paragraph are in terms of 1972 dollars. Hence they are comparable in real terms.

Department store sales rise at Christmas time; the labor force increases in the spring and declines in the fall as students leave and return to school; the demand for heating oil rises in the wintertime, whereas that for electrical power rises in the summertime.

Seasonal fluctuations are due to natural factors, such as the changing seasons, or to cultural and social factors, such as religious holidays and closing-starting dates for schools. As a general rule, seasonal fluctuations are predictable. Although they are important for the households and businesses affected by them, they are insignificant in the aggregate. In fact, nearly all the data we have used so far—GNP, NNP, unemployment, and disposable income, for example—have been statistically adjusted to remove the influence of these fluctuations.

Some fluctuations, however, are almost totally unpredictable. These are called *irregular fluctuations;* they are also said to be due to "exogenous" forces—that is, forces from the outside. Examples are earthquakes, floods, drought, political events, and that loose category that insurance companies call "acts of God." They appear sporadically and unpredictably; and while they may have severe economic repercussions, they are not necessarily caused by economic factors. For an example of their economic impact, refer again to Figure 9-1 to see how World War II affected GNP. Also consider how the Korean War and the Vietnam War both caused actual GNP to rise above potential GNP (Figure 9-5).

One major exogenous shock was the tremendous rise in prices in the middle and late 1970s due to the pricing policies of the Organization of Petroleum Exporting Countries (OPEC). The impact of OPEC can clearly be seen in Figure 9-3.

In all these cases, the causes of the economic changes were exogenous and largely unpredictable. This, however, doesn't minimize their importance.

B. EMPLOYMENT AND UNEMPLOYMENT

The fears of many, if not most, economists and the doubts and anxieties of most politicians as World War II came to an end resulted in a crucial piece of economic legislation. These fears and anxieties were based on the predictions that there would be a serious economic contraction immediately after the war. As it turned out, the postwar contraction did occur, but it was nowhere as severe and long as had been predicted.

Nonetheless, the economic situation seemed to call for a new outlook, a new attitude about government's role in the economy, and the result was the *Employment Act of 1946*. (Canada, Australia, and Great Britain have similar laws.) The act mandates three goals for government policy makers:

1. Price-level stability
2. Full employment
3. Economic growth

The act, however, doesn't tell us what is meant by price-level stability; nor does it reveal what constitutes full employment; nor does it divulge the meaning of economic growth. More important, it doesn't even hint at the possible conflicts among these goals. The preceding section on the stages of the cycle pointed out one basic, unavoidable conflict—namely, that as the economy moves closer and closer to full employment, inflation tends to rise; and as the economy moves into a contraction so that inflation is eased, unemployment in its turn rears *its* ugly head. These are the twin evils of our unstable economy, and their mutual exclusiveness wasn't considered by the drafters of the Employment Act of 1946.

As a result, we are left in something of a quandary. We need to provide some useful definitions. Let's begin with the idea of full employment.

1. The Idea of Full Employment

The majority of economists in the United States would define *full employment* as 94 to 95 percent of the labor force holding jobs. Thus they tend to go along with an *unemployment rate* of 5 to 6 percent as being consistent with full employment. Certainly most economists will complain if the unemployment rate rises above 6 percent; indeed, not a few will grumble when it is around 5 percent. For right now, we will simply go along with the majority and accept the following.

> **Definition:**   Full employment prevails when 94 to 95 percent of the labor force hold jobs. From the employment side, this means that 5 to 6 percent of the work force are unemployed when there is full employment.

Still another way of viewing this would be to say that if the unemployment rate were in the 5 to 6 percent range, the economy would be producing at roughly potential GNP.

But just how has this figure been decided? Why not higher (say, 8 percent) or lower (say, 3 percent)? There are some good reasons for the 5 to 6 percent unemployment rate being acceptable; to get to them, however, we need to have some idea of what constitutes the labor force and how it is measured. Also, we need to distinguish between different kinds of unemployment.

2. The Labor Force and Voluntary Unemployment

Obviously the labor force is smaller than the country's total population. Not everyone needs to work, is able to work, or wants to work. In fact, there are some who don't even qualify to be members of the work force. In the first place, everyone under the age of sixteen isn't counted (although some of them may be working and others may be looking for work). In the second place, those who are "institutionalized" aren't included—that is, people in prison, mental institutions, and so on, aren't counted in the civilian labor force. Then there are those who voluntarily decide, for whatever reason, not to be in the work force.

The armed forces are another matter. Labor force data may or may not include them. For our purposes, we will exclude the people in the armed forces and place them with all the groups listed in the preceding paragraph. Once we exclude all these people, we have the civilian labor force. In 1987, the labor force consisted of about 120 million persons, or nearly two-thirds of the civilian, noninstitutionalized population.

We now come to the important task of defining and measuring unemployment. At first glance, defining unemployment seems simple enough. After all, anyone who is out of work is obviously unemployed. But it really isn't all that simple because different people may be out of work for different reasons. Put otherwise, there are several types of unemployment.

The first type to be considered is *voluntary unemployment.* These are the people sixteen years of age and older who are able to work but aren't actively seeking employment. Most of these people are housewives (who, of course, insist that they work hard); but many others are out of work and not actively seeking a job. These may range from the idler living off of his inheritance to the college student who is home for the summer and decides to take it easy.

Since these people are voluntarily unemployed, there is no need to be concerned with them in the definition of full employment. We should point out, however, that in times of economic distress—such as a period of rapid inflation when the husband's take-home pay buys less and less—the wife may choose to enter the work force and work part time in order to help meet the bills. Also, many formerly voluntarily unemployed mothers decide to enter the labor force once the children are out of the house and on their own. In other words, there is a lot of movement into and out of the ranks of the voluntarily unemployed.

3. Frictional Unemployment and Full Employment

The second type of unemployment is called *frictional unemployment.* Every day, some people quit their jobs to look for better jobs; and every day, other people get laid off. Maybe either or both of these things have happened to you. They certainly happen to thousands of people daily. Also, there are always people who are entering the labor force for the very first time.

Now, all these people must spend some time searching for jobs. They usually don't take the first opening offered to them. Instead they search for positions they feel are best suited for them.

At the same time, employers with work openings are searching for people to fill the vacant slots. They, too, aren't apt to hire the first person to come along, for they want the ones best suited for the available positions.

After a period of time (search), however, the job seekers will take the best job offered, and the employers will hire the best applicants. Most will have successfully concluded their searches in two or three weeks. But, in the meantime, other people are beginning their searches for jobs for any of the reasons given above, and although they will conclude the search process in, say, three weeks, still others are entering the work force for the first time, or have been fired, or have quit to look for greener pastures—and so it goes. There is a steady turnover of people in the unemployment pool, most of whom are employed within short periods of time. These we call the *frictionally unemployed.*

Economists have always argued that this type of unemployment is a healthy thing. As long as workers are free to choose among jobs, and as long as employers are free to choose among workers, there will be a more efficient use of labor resources than if these freedoms were denied. Note, however, that these freedoms also mean that frictional unemployment is virtually unavoidable. Thus it is ever present, and it is desirable. It simply means that workers are looking for the best jobs, and employers are looking for the best workers.

We are now ready to define *full employment.* Certainly "full" employment can't mean employment of 100 percent of the workers in the labor force because it must take frictional unemployment into account. Remember, frictional unemployment is both desirable and unavoidable. Thus full employment is calculated as follows:

Labor Force   = 100%
    Less: Frictional unemployment   = 5% to 6%
    Full employment   = 94% to 95%

Note that we have assigned the figures of 5 to 6 percent to frictional unemployment in order to get to full employment. Most economists have also relabeled frictional unemployment as the *natural rate* of unemployment.

The natural rate of unemployment has drifted upward over the years (see Figure 9-2). In the 1960s, for example, most experts would have considered the 3 to 4 percent range accurate rather than the 5 to 6 percent used today.

Why, then, is there this rise in the natural rate? The main reason has been the dramatic changes in the age composition of our population. Another reason has been the participation rates of certain groups in the labor force. We have already mentioned the large increase in the number of women desiring or needing to work. This swelled the labor force. At the same time, the labor force was increased even more by the earlier war and postwar "baby boom"; many of these babies became adults and entered the labor force in the 1960s and 1970s.

Thus the labor force has a higher percentage of both young people and women today than in earlier years. These two factors alone can largely account for the increase in the frictional rate of unemployment. The reason boils down to the work habits of these workers who are entering the labor force for the first time. Consider first the plight of the young people. They are inexperienced and unskilled. They also typically change jobs frequently, and this means that they are usually unemployed for longer periods of time than are older workers. We might say that new entrants in the workplace are apt to spend some period of time sampling different jobs and gaining different experiences and knowledge as they seek the best "niche in life" for themselves. Consequently, they spend far more time than older workers do being frictionally unemployed. And since there are so many more of them, the frictional unemployment rate has been pushed up. And what is true of young entrants also seems true of women at any age. When women enter the workplace for the first time, they seem to go through roughly the same process as young adults. And since there are now many more women in the labor force, it is not surprising that the natural rate of unemployment moved upward in the 1970s and early 1980s. Many economists also feel that the frictional unemployment rate is increased somewhat by the nation's comprehensive unemployment insurance program. This program allows workers to have longer search periods while looking for employment.

On the reverse side, many economists are now predicting that the frictional rate will fall in the near future. That is, it will occur when the percentage of women desiring to work levels off (or, perhaps, drops) and the war babies pass into the relatively stable work habits of middle age.

4. Involuntary (Cyclical) Unemployment

Once we have accounted for voluntary and frictional unemployment, what we have left is *involuntary unemployment*. These are the workers who are sixteen years of age and older and are able to work, are willing to work, are seeking jobs, but can't find employment. Seek as they will, employment eludes them.

This type of unemployment is in excess of frictional unemployment. In the early 1980s, for example, the unemployment rate reached as high as 10 percent of the labor force. If we take 5 percent as the accepted figure for frictional unemployment, we can say that 5 percent of the labor force were involuntarily unemployed.

This type of unemployment is also called *cyclical unemployment* because it varies over the course of a business cycle. During the contractionary period, involuntary unemployment rises; there simply are fewer jobs when the economy is operating at low levels. On the other hand, involuntary unemployment declines during the expansionary stage of the cycle. Refer again to Figure 9–2 to see this cyclical behavior of involuntary unemployment. The unemployment rate tends to rise above 5 percent during contractions and tends to fall during expansion.

5. Other Dimensions of Unemployment

Four final aspects of unemployment are very important because each one of them isn't considered by the Bureau of Labor Statistics when it announces the unemployment rate each month.

First, suppose a friend of yours graduates from college with a degree in clinical psychology but can't find a job in any clinic, hospital, or research organization. In fact, suppose economic times are so bad that the only "decent" job he can find is driving a taxi full time. Is your friend employed in the usual sense of the word? He is indeed working a full-time eight-hour day, and most people would therefore say that he is employed.

Many, however, would disagree because he isn't working in a job that suits his skills. His case represents what is called *disguised unemployment*. Any time someone is working at a job that demands fewer skills than he or she has, there is disguised unemployment. What, for instance, about the NASA engineer who, because of cutbacks in the space program, ended up working in a McDonald's? He also represents disguised unemployment. Sure, it is perhaps better for him to be working there cooking hamburgers than not to be working at all; and it is perhaps better for your friend to be driving a cab than to be involuntarily unemployed. Nonetheless, there is disguised unemployment in both cases. And this type of unemployment increases when cyclical unemployment increases. Moreover, there may be much disguised unemployment, even in good times, because of racial and sexual discrimination in the labor market. All too frequently, women and blacks, Hispanics, and other ethnic minorities are placed in jobs with skill requirements far below their ability. This of course means that there is an inefficient use of our labor resources; the opportunity cost is in the amount that the disguised unemployed could produce if these people were placed in jobs suited to their skills.

Second, there is *partial unemployment*. There is nothing tricky or difficult about defining this: It means exactly what it says. A person who is only working part time isn't fully employed. However, and this is the main point, the Bureau of Labor Statistics counts everyone who is only working part time (even only one hour a week) as employed, and this clearly understates the actual unemployment rate.

Third, there is *discouraged worker unemployment*. These workers have been out of a job and have looked so long for a job without finding one that they become "discouraged" and drop out of the labor force. In the official statistics, they are counted as voluntarily unemployed. Many economists, however, argue that these workers dropped out of the labor force because of prolonged involuntary unemployment and lack of jobs available, and hence they should be counted as unemployed. The Bureau of Labor Statistics has recognized the merit of this argument and now estimates the unemployment rate of these discouraged workers; yet it isn't included in the reported unemployment rate.

Finally, there is the issue of structural unemployment. Here a problem of definition arises. *Structural unemployment* is defined by economists as a situation in which the skills of the unemployed don't match the skills needed in job vacancies. In other words, jobs exist, perhaps in abundance, but the unemployed can't be hired because they lack the skills required to do the job.

Such labor market mismatches can be created by changes in consumer demand and changes in technology. In recent years, upheavals in the steel and auto industries have displaced hundreds of thousands of high-paid, low-skilled workers nationwide. At the same time, new job openings have been created in information processing. The skills required in the latter don't match the skills of those released from the former. Some of the displaced workers have found employment elsewhere, albeit at much lower wages, while others work part time. Still others, frustrated by lack of opportunity, have dropped out of the labor force altogether. Thus our classifications of *partial unemployment* and *discouraged worker unemployment* contain most of the structural type.

Enough has been said about full employment and the various types of unemployment. Let's now turn to the second goal posited by the Employment Act of 1946—the goal of price stability.

C. PRICES AND INFLATION

The earlier discussion in this chapter about the stages of the business cycle argued that inflation seems to have become a permanent part of the American economy. The deflation (i.e., falling prices) that used to accompany the contractionary stage of the pre–World War II business cycle has been replaced by a *fall in the rate* of inflation. This means that the price level continues to rise, but less rapidly than it did during the expansionary stage of the cycle. "Inflated recession," "stagflation"— whatever it is called—inflation as a way of life seems to be with us.

We therefore need to take a closer look at this economic phenomenon. Exactly how is inflation defined? Is inflation acceptable over long periods? What groups are hurt by inflation? Who is helped? These important questions deserve satisfactory answers.

1. What Is Price Stability?

As we have seen, the Employment Act of 1946 failed to define what is meant by price-level stability. What this really means is that the act failed to define inflation. Here is a generally accepted definition.

> **Definition:** *Inflation* is a rise in the general level of prices over time. It is usually measured as the percentage change in the cost-of-living index.

This cost-of-living index is also known as the consumer price index (CPI).

Note that we say that inflation is a *rise* in prices, not high prices. It's quite possible for prices in 1986 to be higher than prices in, say, 1980 and still have no inflation in 1986. If the CPI had remained constant (which it did not) throughout 1986, then there would have been high prices but no inflation. Thus, to repeat ourselves, inflation is a rise in prices. And the faster prices in general rise, the higher the rate of inflation. Look back to Figure 9–3, which shows how the rate of inflation has varied over time. In some periods (e.g., the late 1970s), it was much higher than in other periods (e.g., the middle 1980s).

Another important point is this: If the price of gasoline were to rise by 50 percent, that by itself wouldn't be inflation. Inflation is a rise in the *general level of prices,* not just one or a few items. In other words, prices on average must rise if there is inflation. This doesn't mean, however, that all prices rise at the same rate or, for that matter, all prices rise. During periods of inflation, some prices may be stable and some may actually fall; some prices rise at various rates close to the inflation rate; and still other prices (e.g., medical services) jump ahead at double or triple the increase in the general price level. Still, it is true that most prices do rise during a period of inflation. Figure 9–6 shows how the prices of different categories of goods and services have risen since 1910.

The question remains: What is price-level stability? In a very strict sense, it would mean no rise in the price level (i.e., the CPI). This would mean zero inflation. Such a goal is much too rigid.

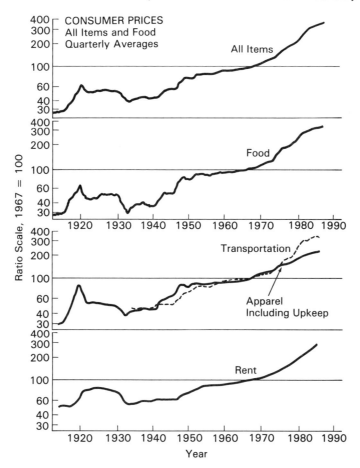

FIGURE 9-6   Consumer Price Index and Component Items (1910-87)   The separate items composing the consumer price index tend to move in the same general direction over time but at different rates in the short run.

Source: 1986 Historical Chart Book, Board of Governors of the Federal Reserve System, pp. 40 and 41.

The consensus of economists is that, given the way that the CPI is calculated, a rise in the CPI of 1 to 2 percent per year is the same thing as price-level stability. The feeling is that the CPI overstates the true rate of inflation by about 2 percent. There are three basic reasons why this is so.

First, the CPI measures prices based on a fixed "market basket" of goods and services purchased by some "typical household." In this market basket there are so many pounds of beef, so many cans of fruit, a certain amount of medical care, transportation, housing, and so on, up to a total of about four hundred different items. A basic assumption underlying the calculations of the CPI is that households buy the same market basket year after year no matter what. For example, let's suppose that the market basket contains five pounds of beef per week per family, and then let's allow the price of beef to jump from $5 per pound to $20 per pound. Obviously, the average family, if it were to continue buying the five pounds of beef, would have to lay out $100 per week instead of $25. Most households won't do this, however, for they will purchase less beef and more less-expensive substitutes, such as chicken, pork, and fish. Consumers do respond to price changes such as this and substitute the relatively cheaper for the more expensive items in the market basket. Insofar as they do, then the CPI overstates the true rise in the cost of living—it continues to record the typical family buying $100 worth of beef when it may be purchasing only $30 worth.

The second and even more serious reason why the actual inflation rate is overstated is that the CPI doesn't include any allowance for improvements in the quality of goods and services. Thus a $400 refrigerator that will last twenty years with minimal repairs is really worth more than a $400 lemon of a refrigerator. Put otherwise, both items cost the consumer the same amount of dollars, but the first one costs the consumer far less per unit of service than the second one. However, this difference isn't recorded in the CPI; and yet it is obvious that improved quality lowers the cost of using many goods and services. For these items, then, the CPI overstates the rate of inflation.

The third reason why the CPI overstates price increases is that it doesn't take into account the presence of new products. The only way to avoid this problem would be to change the composition of the market basket whenever new products were introduced in the market. The major drawback to doing this is that the changed market basket can't be compared with earlier market baskets, or, put otherwise, the price level between periods can't be compared in a satisfactory way.

Therefore it seems that the best we can do is to continue using the CPI but also recognize that it is an imperfect measure of price changes, probably overstating actual inflation by about 2 percent. If we keep this qualification in mind, we can appropriately use the CPI as a measurement of the rate of inflation over time.

2. Benefits and Costs of Inflation

Inflation has an uneven impact on the members of society, hurting some and helping others. For example, families whose money incomes are fixed and thus can't adjust to a general rise in prices are obviously hurt by inflation. Their real income (purchasing power) falls as prices rise, and they must therefore experience a reduced level of living. These households—usually consisting of retired people—are obviously hurt by inflation, and the greater the rate of inflation, the greater the hurt. However, the social security part of a retiree's income is indexed to changes in the CPI.

On the other hand, many households have incomes that are flexible and that may therefore rise as fast as, perhaps even faster than, the price increases. In the recent past, medical doctors and executives in expanding industries have had their money incomes rise faster than the price level. They have therefore experienced an increased real (purchasing power) income. Others, whose money incomes rise proportionately with the price rise, hold the line with their real incomes.

Can we draw any generalizations from all of this? Certainly, and a very important one indeed:

> **Conclusion:** Generally speaking, inflation redistributes real income away from those whose money incomes (for whatever reason) fail to keep pace with inflation to those whose money incomes (again, for whatever reason) rise faster than prices.

Indeed, in periods of strong inflation, the rise in prices can be a savage redistributor of real income.

Let's turn to another impact that inflation has on society. Debtors and creditors are also unequally affected by rising prices, but in spelling this out we have to distinguish between *anticipated* and *unanticipated* inflation. When inflation isn't anticipated, it tends to benefit debtors and harm creditors. An example will show why. Suppose you receive a student loan for $1,000, which must be paid off following graduation. Suppose also that the lender is so gratuitous as to charge you no interest on the loan. Finally, suppose the price level rises by 3 percent per year over the five-year period between the time you took out the loan and the time you pay it back. Therefore, when you actually do repay the loan, you hand over the $1,000. But because of inflation, the amount of real dollars you pay back is only $850. How do we get this figure of $850? Simply by performing three steps. First, multiply the annual inflation rate by the number of years of the loan. Doing this, we get 3% × 5 years = 15%. This gives us the amount of inflation over the five-year period. Second, multiply this figure (15%) by the amount of the loan. Doing this, we get 15% × $1,000 = $150. This tells us how much the $1,000 lost in purchasing power for the period. Finally, subtract this figure ($150) from the amount of the loan, and we get $1,000 − $150 = $850, which is the real income that the lender receives from you five years later. Clearly, the lender has been harmed by inflation: $1,000 of purchasing power was loaned out but only $850 was paid back.

Is is possible for the lender (i.e., the creditor) to protect himself from such a loss of purchasing power? Yes, and that is to charge a rate of interest on the loan at least equal to the anticipated amount of inflation. If the lender is still gratuitous and doesn't want to charge you an interest rate but only wants to protect himself from the erosion of purchasing power caused by inflation, he must charge you a rate of interest equal to 3 percent per year.

On a more realistic level, we must admit that whoever lends money does so in the fond hope of receiving a net income. Thus, if the lender desires a 4 percent real return on his loan and the expected rate of inflation is 3 percent, he will try to charge the borrower an interest rate of 7 percent. If the price level, then, does rise by the anticipated 3 percent, the creditor receives his hoped-for real interest rate of 4 percent.

But suppose there is some unforeseen event (an exogenous shock) that drives the price level up by 10 percent. The unexpected inflation then hurts the lender and helps the borrower. In effect, the creditor has loaned out money at a minus 3 percent rate while the borrower has gained a like amount. The reverse, of course, is also true. If the actual rate of inflation is less than the expected rate, the borrower is hurt and the lender benefited.

Let's move away from hypothetical examples to the real world. A clearly observable phenomenon in the economy is this: During periods of inflation, money rates of interest also rise. Now we know why these money rates of interest rise. If at first prices are stable, lenders may be quite satisfied with a 4 percent rate of interest. But if inflation rises to, say, 3 percent, then to keep the same real interest rate, they must charge a money rate of 7 percent. Should inflation continue to, say, 6 percent, then in order to keep a real rate of 4 percent, they raise the rate they charge to 10 percent. And so it goes, with accelerating inflation driving the money rate of interest higher.

From this we can draw another important conclusion. This can be stated in either of two ways:

$$\begin{matrix} \text{Money rate} \\ \text{of interest} \end{matrix} = \begin{matrix} \text{Real rate} \\ \text{of interest} \end{matrix} + \begin{matrix} \text{Expected rate} \\ \text{of inflation} \end{matrix}$$

$$\begin{matrix} \text{Real rate} \\ \text{of interest} \end{matrix} = \begin{matrix} \text{Money rate} \\ \text{of interest} \end{matrix} - \begin{matrix} \text{Expected rate} \\ \text{of inflation} \end{matrix}$$

The important rate to consider is the real rate, but of course we can't calculate it until we know the expected rate of inflation and the money rate. Much more on this in Chapters 11 and 12.

3. Concluding Comments on Inflation

Is inflation ever good or desirable? Perhaps. Some economists believe that major benefits flow from mild inflation of around 3 percent per year. Mild inflation, they contend, is conducive to high-level spending. Profits, and the expectation of still more profits, tend to stimulate optimism and the willingness of businesses to expand investment spending and, therefore, output and employment. These economists argue, in other words, that a little inflation will help keep the level of actual GNP closer to potential GNP than it would otherwise be.

All economists, however, would agree that when inflation passes the "mild range," all the benefits of inflation disappear. In the environment of rising inflation, all groups—workers, businesses, unions, etc.—battle to increase, or just maintain, their share of purchasing power. And if government provides enough money, inflation can turn into runaway inflation (i.e., hyperinflation) in which all are hurt. The end result of hyperinflation is usually economic collapse.

Finally, most economists believe that the main cause of inflation that prevails over long periods is too much money in circulation. For shorter periods, inflation may be caused by other factors as well. But all of this is covered in Chapters 11 and 12.

D. ECONOMIC GROWTH

In macroeconomics, business cycles are said to occur over short-run periods—say, three to five years. At times, however, we need to take a much longer view, for economic growth takes place over a more extended period. Recall that Figure 9–1 shows the long-run upward sweep of GNP. It is true that this growth pattern was periodically interrupted by economic contractions, but nevertheless there has been much growth in the American economy.

There is, however, no generally acceptable definition of economic growth. Should we define it as simply increases in real GNP? Most economists wouldn't accept such a simple definition. Another approach is to calculate GNP per capita— i.e., divide real GNP by population. While this shows how much output there is per person, it overlooks how that output may be distributed. In reality, some persons receive far more real GNP than do others. Nonetheless, we will tentatively define economic growth in terms of real GNP per capita. Using this measure, Figure 9–7 shows that the American economy has performed quite well.

1. The Recent Slowdown

As great as the economy's growth has been, the 1960s, 1970s, and early 1980s witnessed a significant slowdown in the growth rate. Indeed, many nations grew much more rapidly than the United States in these two and one-half decades. For example, during the 1960s and 1970s, the major industrial nations of Europe and Japan had per capita growth rates of output significantly above those of the United States. Per capita output in the United States grew at roughly 2.5 percent over the period while Japan averaged about 6 percent and the industrialized nations of Europe almost 4 to 5 percent. Although some of the superior performance of these other nations can be accounted for as a kind of "catch up" from World War II, the trends remain worrisome to many Americans.

Because of this poor performance, much debate rages about what should and could be done to restore America's growth rate. Some argue that we need to restore the "competitiveness" of American industry, both here and abroad. Others argue that we should apply Japanese business management techniques. Still others fall back on the argument that tariff protection is needed; but there are those, too, who argue that we should have a truly free international market that would in turn exert competitive discipline on our business firms. And so the arguments go, diverse and contradictory. Chapter 14 concentrates on our recent slowdown and on many of these arguments.

2. Is Too Much Bad for Us?

We must not overlook the arguments of those who contend that the economic growth of the past has had undesirable side effects on society and the environment. These economists (and others) argue that we should have slow growth or even per-

FIGURE 9-7   Per Capita GNP (1982 dollars) 1900-87   Per capita GNP in the United States has increased dramatically since 1900. The long-term upward movement has been interrupted by short-term downturns associated with periods of recession.

Source: 1986 Historical Chart Book, Board of Governors of the Federal Reserve System, p. 11, and update by authors.

haps no growth. The slow or no growth advocates, to put it simply, fear future global environmental disaster. Rapidly growing societies demand prodigious amounts of exhaustible resources—i.e., resources that are present in only finite amounts and can't be replaced when once consumed. Thus, it is alleged that the world will soon run out of these resources.

Meanwhile, industrialization has created, and is creating, health-damaging levels of air and water pollution, as well as enormous amounts of waste (some toxic) to be disposed of. World population growth has induced (required?) extensive clearing of forests, which are essential in the production of oxygen in the life cycle. This process of deforestation, however, is considered necessary to provide the land to produce food for the increasing number of hungry people.

The end result, some believe, will be an unlivable planet. Many environmentalists argue, therefore, that we would be far better off if we slowed or stopped population growth and used more of the available resources to clean up the mess we have already made, rather than producing more of a mess. Yet these arguments run up against the hard fact that, at present, a majority of the world's population live in abject poverty. Besides, even here at home there is a poverty problem. Therefore, further economic growth seems to be necessary if we are serious about improving the lot of the people at the bottom of the economic ladder.

E. SUMMARY

The long-sustained upward sweep of gross national product has frequently been interrupted by economic disturbances, but most disturbances take the form of the business cycle.

The business cycle can be divided into four stages: expansion, upper-turning zone, contraction, and lower-turning zone. Although no two cycles are alike, they all have basic resemblances.

Cyclical disturbances have been fewer and less severe in the post–World War II period, largely because of the increased use of monetary and fiscal policy. This improved record, however, doesn't mean that the cycle has been completely eliminated. Rather, it implies that the cycle has been tamed somewhat by the reasonably effective use of policy programs.

Despite the improved postwar record, the cyclical performance of the economy is disturbing when we consider that actual GNP went through its cyclical fluctuations at levels below potential GNP. By viewing the cycle as deviations of actual versus potential GNP, we obtain a better perspective on the true performance of the economy.

As the expansionary stage of the business cycle continues, the economy first experiences little or no inflation and then accelerating price increases as full employment is reached. Inflation has several effects, on both the distribution of income and the overall performance of the economy.

Until the post–World War II period, contractions were accompanied by deflation (that is, a decline in the general price level), but since the 1953–54 economic setback, the price level has continued to rise during periods of contraction. This is called "inflated recession."

Full employment is defined as about 94 percent of the labor force; the other 6 percent is considered frictional unemployment. Involuntary unemployment exists when there are more workers seeking jobs than there are jobs available. However, the official unemployment figures tend to ignore disguised and part-time unemployment, as well as the unemployment of discouraged workers. The actual unemployment rate is usually higher than the reported rate.

Economic growth is considered important because it gives us the means for reducing poverty. However, growth also raises the issues about present and future environmental problems.

Terms and Concepts to Remember

Business cycle	Money rate of interest
Potential GNP	Real rate of interest
GNP Gap	Employment Act of 1946

Voluntary unemployment
Frictional unemployment
Natural rate of unem-
    ployment
Involuntary unemploy-
    ment
Discouraged workers
Inflation

Disguised unemployment
Full employment
Structural unemployment
Partial unemployment
Price stability
Consumer price index
    (CPI)
Economic growth

Questions for Review

1. Sketch the circular flow diagram and use it to explain how a fall in household consumption expenditures can lead to a rise in involuntary unemployment.

2. Why is it necessary to define several types of unemployment in order to define full employment?

3. How does full employment relate to potential GNP? Can employment rise enough so that actual GNP exceeds potential GNP? How?

4. Distinguish between the level of prices and the rate of inflation. What means are used to record the cost-of-living changes for the typical household?

5. It is said that changes in the CPI overstate the effects of inflation on the buying power of income. What are the reasons?

6. If there is an increase in the rate of inflation, what will happen to the money (nominal) rate of interest?

10

The Process of Economic Change: Aggregate Supply and Aggregate Demand

chapter preview

• Interactions between aggregate supply and aggregate demand determine the course of total output and the general level of prices.

• The aggregate demand curve is derived by allowing only the general price level to change and holding the following constant: (1) disposable income, (2) wealth, (3) income distribution, (4) taxes, (5) the rate of interest, and (6) expectations of future income and price changes. If any of these were to change, the aggregate demand curve would shift.

• The aggregate supply curve is derived by allowing only the general price level to change. The things held constant in this case are (1) the interest rate, (2) the size of the capital stock, (3) changes in technology, (4) taxes, and (5) expectations.

• The most important determinant of a change in aggregate demand is disposable income. We refer to this as a "fundamental psychological law"—i.e., when disposable income changes, consumption changes in the same direction but by a lesser amount.

• The marginal propensity to consume (MPC) measures how much consumption changes when disposable income changes. It is written as MPC $= \triangle C / \triangle DI$.

• The MPC determines in large part how great the multiplier will be. A given change in, say, investment spending will result in a magnified change in the level of total output, and the MPC is important in determining how much total output will change.

• The shape of the aggregate supply curve is the other major factor determining how much real total output will change. Given the initial change in spending, the flatter the aggregate supply curve, the greater the change in real output and the smaller the change in the price level. On the other hand, the steeper the aggregate supply curve, the smaller the change in total output and the greater the variation in the general price level.

• Changes in aggregate demand can occur for any of a number of reasons (e.g., a change in investment or government spending sets the economy off on the roller coaster of the business cycle).

This chapter starts out in a somewhat different way. First, there are some questions. What determines the overall level of output, employment, and prices in the economy? What causes these levels to change, sometimes rising, sometimes falling? Indeed, what causes them at times to move in opposite directions?

The answers to these questions shouldn't be too difficult because we have most of the tools needed to deal with them. Much earlier we developed basic supply and demand analysis (see Chapter 4). There we saw that demand and supply curves are powerful weapons in understanding how markets work. In that chapter, however, we limited the analysis to particular commodities. Now we want to use the same analysis, but not talk about the demand for and supply of particular products; rather, we want to consider the demand for and supply of all goods and services together. We are, in other words, concerned with *aggregate* supply and *aggregate* demand.

Chapters 5, 6, and 7 proceeded to develop the circular flow model. This model shows how each sector of the economy—households, business firms, government, and the rest of the world—is influenced by the flow of economic activity and in turn influences that flow. Then, in Chapter 8, we showed how the various flows of activity are measured in terms of the national income and product accounts. Chapter 9 provided some important definitions of employment, unemployment, inflation, and the business cycle.

It is now time to put all this material together and explain how the levels of output, employment, and prices are determined. It is also time to explain how these important magnitudes behave over the course of the business cycle.

A. AGGREGATE DEMAND, AGGREGATE SUPPLY, AND THE CIRCULAR FLOW

As we pointed out above, this chapter is concerned with aggregate demand and aggregate supply.

> *Aggregate* means summed up, combined. *Aggregate demand* is the sum total of all planned expenditures by consumers, businesses, governments, and foreign buyers on real goods and services at each general price level.
>
> *Aggregate supply* is the sum total of the output of real goods and services forthcoming from producers at each general price level.

Thus we will continue to rely on the useful tools of supply and demand, but we will now use them at the economywide level, the macroeconomic level. And we will also continue to use the circular flow model. In fact, we will begin with the very simplistic circular flow in Figure 10-1. Note that in this basic version of the circular flow of economic activity, there is no government and there is no foreign trade. The only new thing about it is that we have placed the aggregate supply and aggregate demand curves at the top of the diagram. Our job now is to explain the relationships between the circular flow and the aggregate demand and supply curves.

The very act of producing goods and services means that business firms must employ productive services (land, labor, and capital). In other words, production generates a flow of costs or expenses that must be covered; and as the circular flow model shows, these expenses become incomes for households. Here we have the basis of the aggregate demand curve. Households receive their incomes and then use them to demand goods and services. Of course, households may save part of their income, but by far the greater part of it (about 97 percent) is used for consumption. Thus the production process generates two things—an output of goods and services and the income of households to buy that output. We might also say that the consumption process generates two things—the supply of productive services needed to produce output and the demand for that output.

To derive the aggregate demand curve in Figure 10-1, we must hold all other determinants of aggregate demand constant. These other things are discussed below

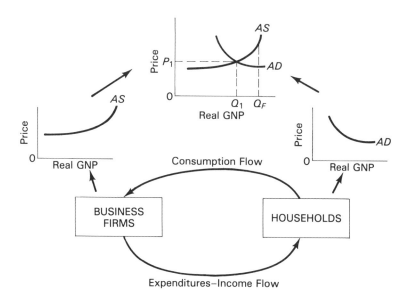

FIGURE 10-1   Aggregate Demand and Aggregate Supply in the Circular Flow   The act of production by businesses generates an aggregate supply (*AS*) and at the same time generates expenses that become income for households. Households use that income as the basis for aggregate demand (*AD*). The interaction of *AS* and *AD* determines both the general price level and the total real output.

when we consider each of the major components of aggregate demand—*C, I, G,* and *(E - M).* But as long as they are given, we can derive an aggregate demand curve that shows that a greater aggregate output will be demanded at a lower general price level.

What about the aggregate supply curve? Again, we must hold constant all those other things that influence supply and allow only the general price level to change. The resulting aggregate supply curve is shown in Figure 10–1. The other things that affect aggregate supply curve are discussed below.

However, note the following about the aggregate supply curve as we have drawn it in Figure 10–1: At some low level of prices, the curve is more or less flat. This means that rather small increases in the price level will trigger large changes in aggregate output. This segment of the curve prevails in a depression economy.

However, as the economy moves toward full employment, the aggregate supply curve becomes steeper. We will have much to say about why this happens, but right now we merely want to stress that as the economy's total output pushes up against full employment, further increases in output are associated with relatively large increases in prices. Inflation, it seems, is the inevitable price of continued high levels of employment.

Now let's put aggregate demand and aggregate supply together in the top part of Figure 10–1. There is, as we can see, only one general price level (P_1), which equates the aggregate quantity demanded with the aggregate quantity supplied (Q_1). Note that this equilibrium intersection of the two curves may occur at any level of output (and hence employment). Indeed, in Figure 10–1 we have the equilibrium level of real GNP occurring at less than full employment (which we show as Q_F).

There is no reason, of course, to assume that the equilibrium GNP will stay at Q_1 for long. To the contrary! As the preceding chapter has emphasized, ours is a dynamic, ever-changing economy. Hence we may expect the equilibrium price level and real GNP to be altered as either (or both) aggregate demand or aggregate supply changes or shifts.

These changes in supply and demand are so important in determining the state of the economy that we must examine both aggregate supply and aggregate demand in some detail. We begin with aggregate demand.

B. AGGREGATE DEMAND

Aggregate demand really measures the willingness and ability of people and organizations to buy what the economy is producing.

There are two ways of viewing aggregate demand. First, we may look at it as *the flow of total money demand* through the economy. Second, we may look at it as *the flows of different types of spending*—that is, the spending for different basic classes or categories of goods and services. Both ways of looking at aggregate demand amount to the same thing. The only difference is that they view the flows in different ways.

1. Aggregate Demand as Money Flow

If we are to consider aggregate demand as the flow of total *money* demand, we must stress the importance of the money supply as a factor determining the total volume of spending. In Chapter 3, we defined *money* as anything that is generally accepted as a medium of exchange, and the *money supply* as the total amount of these means of payments. (We will have much more to say about money in Chapter 11; for our present purposes, let's just use the common-sense idea of money being what people use to buy things.)

When people spend money for the goods and services they buy, the money they spend is, of course, passed on to the sellers. Put otherwise, the money spent by buyers becomes *money income* for the sellers; and the sellers can now act as buyers and spend their incomes. Their spending in turn becomes income for still other people. Therefore it is the flow of money spending throughout the economic society that generates incomes and allows people to purchase the nation's output. It also allows business firms to buy the resources they need for producing the output they sell.

All of this should sound familiar; it is merely a restatement of the circular flow model. Here, however, we must recognize a new dimension of the circular flow—the role of the money supply and the turnover (or velocity) of the money supply. The money supply flows round and round the circular flow of economic activity, but at times it makes its rounds quickly and at other times it makes them slowly. This can be stated as follows:

$$\text{Money supply} \times \text{Velocity} = \text{Money GNP}$$

or, alternatively:

$$M \times V = P \times Q$$

in which M = money supply, V = velocity or turnover of M, P = general price level, and Q = real GNP. $P \times Q$, therefore, is money GNP. Thus the two equations say the same thing. Let's look at the second equation more closely to see what it might tell us.

In the first place, the left-hand side of the equation states that the money supply (M) is spent (or turned over) some number of times (V). If, for example, the money supply is $300 billion and is turned over (or spent) twice during the year, then MV = $300 billion $\times$ 2 = $600 billion. This is really a statement of the total dollar value of aggregate demand. (We will hold off discussion of the $P \times Q$ side of the equation until we get to Section F of this chapter, but we can point out now that $P \times Q$ is another statement of aggregate supply.)

The idea of velocity needs a closer look. It is, as we saw above, the number of times the money supply is spent during the year. The same amount of money may sometimes be spent faster and at other times slower. A good way of viewing turnover is to think of "money at rest" and "money on the wing." Money at rest has a velocity of zero; it is not being spent but is being held as idle balances by the public. In Chapter 5 we saw what would happen if households decided to hoard part of their savings in the form of idle balances buried in the backyard. Hoarded money, in other words, has a turnover of zero.[1]

But, of course, money is not at rest; it is, instead, on the wing, moving around through the economy financing all sorts of economic activity and generating demand, output, and income. Let's define velocity this way:

Definition: *Velocity* measures the number of times an average dollar circulates through the circular flow of economic activity in a given time period.

Now, the same typical dollar may circulate a number of times, that is, velocity is high. Or it may be very lethargic, that is, velocity is low. If the public is willing and able to spend its "typical" dollars at a high rate of turnover, then aggregate demand will be high. If, on the other hand, the public is timid and less able to spend its dollars, aggregate demand will be low. Exhibit 10-1 shows that velocity has indeed changed over time.

Let's see what we have now. Clearly, the amount of money in the economy, as well as the speed at which it is spent, determines the strength or level of aggregate demand. Both the money supply *and* velocity are important in determining the output and price levels. For instance, if the money supply increases and velocity remains constant, then aggregate demand will rise, pushing output, employment, and prices higher. Conversely, if the money supply decreases and velocity still remains constant, output, employment, and prices will fall.

Let's turn it around and look at it from velocity's point of view. If the money supply remains constant and velocity rises, then aggregate demand will rise. On the other hand, if the supply of money still remains constant and turnover falls, then aggregate demand will also fall. These changes in velocity plus an imponderable, are discussed in Exhibit 10-1.

2. The Components of Aggregate Demand

When we view aggregate demand from the other perspective, we need to move beyond the simple circular flow model and include both government and the rest of the world in the analysis. This is the approach that the majority of economists use. It has the advantage of concentrating on the spending by each of the major groups in the economy—households, businesses, government, and the international sector—and allowing us to examine the spending behavior of each. The money flow

---

[1]See pages 84–85 for a refresher. There we had *all* saving taking the form of hoarding, and thus the amount saved (hoarded) did not reenter the spending-income stream and the circular flow of economic activity contracted. This, however, is the same as saying that when saving was hoarded, velocity fell. Most of the money supply was still used for consumption, but that part held out reduced V.

EXHIBIT 10-1
Changes in Velocity

In 1987, the U.S. economy churned out a fantastic GNP of $4,486.2 billion. But for the same year, the money supply was only $753.2 billion. This means that the money supply had to be used a number of times to finance so large a GNP. How many times did it, in fact, turn over? Our formula allows us to calculate velocity. Since

$$MV = PQ,$$

then

$$V = \frac{PQ}{M}$$

We know the PQ for 1987—it was the GNP of $4,486.2 billion. And we know the M—it was $753.2 billion. Therefore:

$$V = \frac{4,486.2}{753.2}$$

$$= 5.9$$

Thus the money supply was turned over 5.9 times or, put otherwise, had a velocity of 5.9.

In an important sense, velocity measures how efficiently the money supply is being used. If, for example, the same dollar can finance twice as many expenditures in one year as opposed to the last, then it is being used twice as efficiently.

The accompanying chart on page 196 shows what has happened to velocity since 1934. There are three distinct periods. From 1930 to the end of World War II, velocity consistently declined from about 4 to 2. During this period, then, the efficient use of the typical dollar declined. Much of this was due to uncertainty and a tendency to hoard. Then, during World War II, there was simply less for households to spend on.

However, from 1946 to 1982, velocity rose consistently from about 2 to 7. The greater use of credit cards, the improved financial management techniques by corporations, and the growing availability of short-term credit contributed to this rise. The money supply, in short, was being used more efficiently from year to year.

The year 1982 seems to have marked another turning point. Velocity declined from 7 to 5.9 in 1987. Does this mean that a new period of decline has set in? Who knows?

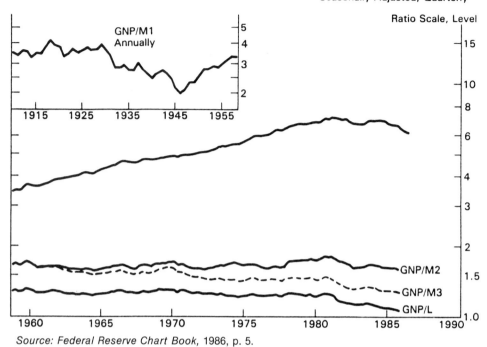

Source: *Federal Reserve Chart Book,* 1986, p. 5.

method discussed above doesn't allow this, since it simply lumps all spending groups together. Yet the factors that affect consumer spending are definitely not the same as those that influence government spending. The spending by each group warrants separate discussion. In what follows, we look at households, then businesses, then government, and finally the foreign sector.

C. CONSUMER DEMAND BY HOUSEHOLDS

From what has been said so far in this book, it is clear that everyone is a consumer. Therefore, consumption expenditures by households make up by far the largest part of aggregate demand. In 1987, for example, they were $2,966 billion, which amounted to 65 percent of GNP.

Earlier, when we drew the aggregate demand curve in Figure 10-1, we mentioned that the other things that influence consumer behavior are held constant. We are now interested in seeing what each of these will do to aggregate demand as we relax the *ceteris paribus* assumption. These other factors are (1) disposable income, (2) wealth, (3) the rate of interest, (4) personal income taxes, (5) income distribution, and (6) expectations. The most important of these is disposable income. Nevertheless, the others are important enough to call for some discussion, and we will cover them first.

1. Wealth

The amount of wealth that a family owns in the form of stocks, bonds, and similar assets will influence the family's consumption behavior. Generally speaking, the greater the family's wealth, the more willing the family is to consume out of current income. If, for example, your income is $25,000 per year and you have no accumulated savings, you may want to save some of your income, say, 5 percent. You may want to do this in order to build up enough savings to make a down payment later on for a house or automobile, or it may be that you simply want to save for that "rainy day" that everyone talks about.

But if you have the same income and, say, $50,000 in stocks and bonds, your motive to save out of current income might well be less. Therefore families with large amounts of wealth are apt to spend a larger percentage of their income—in other words, these families are apt to save a smaller percentage of their income.

Our major conclusion is that a general increase in wealth will shift the aggregate demand curve to the right because of its effect in increasing aggregate consumer demand. A decline in wealth, on the other hand, will reduce consumption expenditures and shift aggregate demand to the left. This is the reason why economists were so concerned about the stock market crash of October 1987.

2. Income Distribution

The distribution of income also affects the level of consumption. The more equally income is distributed among families, the higher the level of consumption. Families in the lower-income levels tend to spend a much larger percentage of their income than do families in the upper levels. So, if we take a dollar away from a wealthy family and transfer it to a poor family that spends all of its income, total consumption will rise. A number of government transfer payments programs achieve just this result.

All things considered, a more equal distribution of income will sustain aggregate consumption, and a movement toward even more equality may increase this component of aggregate demand.

3. The Rate of Interest

The level of interest rates can also affect the level of aggregate consumer demand. The reason for this is that households in general do save a portion of their income and consequently receive an interest income. A rise in interest rates increases the reward for saving and may well induce people to save a larger portion of their given income. This of course means that, out of the same income, they consume less.

Interest rates affect consumption in yet another way. Most households need to borrow from time to time in order to purchase such things as automobiles, houses, and washers. The interest rate they pay on these loans is a large part of the total costs of the items. Accordingly, a rise in interest rates is viewed as an increase in the total cost of borrowing, making purchases such as these more expensive.

Higher costs, in turn, make the consumer less willing to buy and hence more willing to make do with the old house and the old car. The conclusion, then, is that higher rates of interest tend to reduce consumption, and lower rates tend to raise it.

4. Income and a Fundamental Psychological Law

Of all the things that influence how much households spend and save, the dominant one is disposable income.

> **Definition:** *Disposable income* is the income households have to spend or save, or both, but only after all taxes have been paid.

The fact that disposable income affects consumption may sound obvious, but it has major implications.

The great British economist John Maynard Keynes was the first to give a satisfactory explanation of the relationship between consumption and income (see Exhibit 10-2). He called it a "fundamental psychological law" and put it this way:

> The fundamental psychological law . . . is that men are disposed, as a rule and on the average, to increase their consumption as their income increases, but not by as much as the increase in their income.[2]

We can rephrase this more simply as follows:

> Whenever disposable income changes, consumption changes in the same direction, but not by as much.

Thus, if disposable income rises, people in general will spend most, but not all, of this increase on goods and services. What isn't spent is added to personal savings. Conversely, if disposable income falls, so will both consumption and saving, but consumption will fall much more than saving.

Many studies of household spending and saving have been conducted, and they generally support this "psychological law." This doesn't mean, of course, that every household behaves this way, but enough do to make the "law" a good, sound, general description of consumption and saving behavior.

This relationship between consumption and income is important in explaining how high or low the levels of output, prices, and employment may be. Let's play around with a hypothetical example to see why this is so. In this example, we are also going to introduce a major concept—the *marginal propensity to consume.*

Suppose there is a rise in aggregate demand because of an increase in investment spending by business firms. We will later explain why and how this rise in business spending takes place. What matters for now is that businesses are spending

---

[2]J. M. Keynes, *The General Theory of Employment, Interest, and Money* (New York: Harcourt Brace Jovanovich, 1964), p. 96. First published in 1936.

EXHIBIT 10-2
J. M. Keynes and the Keynesian Revolution

On Thursday, October 24, 1929, a panic shook Wall Street and then the rest of the nation. This day, known as Black Thursday, foreshadowed the worst and the longest economic depression in the history of the United States. Although the financial panic was, for all practical purposes, over by noon, the aftermath lingered for the rest of the decade. By 1933, about 25 percent of the labor force was unemployed, many business firms had failed, and surviving firms had much excess capacity. Farmers were dumping milk, burning crops, and shooting livestock because the markets for these goods had almost completely collapsed. Prices were low, and so indeed was the general state of confidence. In short, the circular flow of spending-income had contracted to historically low levels.

What caused this economic catastrophe? The economists of the time did not know, nor do economists today agree on the cause. And without knowledge of how the economy got into such straits, the economists of the 1930s had no serious recommendations on how to bring about the needed economic recovery.

In 1936, however, John Maynard Keynes (pronounced Kaynes) published his pathbreaking *General Theory of Employment, Interest, and Money,* in which he provided a new analysis of how the economy got to where it did, and thus he could propose how to get the economy back on its feet. *The General Theory* was preceded in 1934 by a pamphlet entitled *The Means to Prosperity*.

Keynes's major argument was that there was a seriously deficient aggregate demand. Moreover, he pointed out that there are two major components of *private* aggregate demand—consumption and investment. However, he wasn't very optimistic about either of these having a resurgence so that the economy could start expanding toward full employment. Consumption depends mainly on disposable income, he argued, and until income rose, consumers were stuck. Nor, he argued further, could we count on a rise in private investment spending. The state of confidence was too low, and rightly so, to expect businesses to build new plants and equipment.

What was needed, of course, was an increase in spending. As he put it in an earlier writing, "one man's expenditure is another man's income."* But as long as private spending couldn't be expected, then we should look elsewhere. Keynes looked elsewhere and found government as a source of spending. Remember, private spending—both consumption and investment—couldn't be counted on.

*From the essay by Keynes in *The World's Economic Crisis and the Way to Escape* (Port Washington, NY: Kennikat Press, 1971), p. 74. First published in 1932.

If this proves to be so, there will be no means of escape from prolonged and perhaps interminable depression except by direct state intervention to promote and subsidize new investment.[†]

Thus was born the idea of fiscal policy in modern times—that is, government acting in such a way as to stimulate private investment and, perhaps, even providing its own public investment. Government could thus encourage private spending. It could even do so by cutting personal income taxes to increase disposable income, hence consumption, hence aggregate demand.

Keynes didn't live long enough to see how his ideas had resulted in new policies, nor did he live long enough to see that his ideas had generated a new revolution in economic thought. That revolution has perhaps run its course, for Keynesian economics generated in its turn some counter-Keynesian ideas.

[†]*Ibid.*, p. 85.

more in order to build their new plant and equipment, and what they spend becomes income for the workers and for the suppliers of the materials going into the new plants and machines. Note how this rise in aggregate demand raises both income and employment.

However, we can't stop here, for Keynes's "law" tells us that as income rises, so too will consumption rise, although not by as much. The workers and suppliers mentioned above will, in other words, spend a part—in fact, most—of their new income on consumer goods and services. This increase in their spending, however, becomes income for other households, which will in turn spend most of their new income. And so it goes, round after round after round. Every time someone spends, it becomes income, of which most (not all) is spent, and that in turn becomes income. Time after time income rises. When an initial increase in aggregate demand occurs, it causes income and aggregate demand to increase again and again.

This whole process of income-demand creation is called the *multiplier*. What it means is this:

> **Conclusion:**   An initial increase in *any* component part of aggregate demand sets off a chain reaction that ends up causing income to rise by some *multiple* amount.

As might be expected, the process also works in reverse. A fall in any component of aggregate demand will trigger a multiple reduction in income. Again the relationships and interactions are the same. A fall in income reduces consumption, which reduces income, which reduces consumption, and so on, only now in a downhill direction. This is a *negative multiplier*.

By how much will income and consumption change once a multiplier gets under way? A number of factors may be important, but one factor is dominant, namely, the marginal propensity to consume.

Definition: The *marginal propensity to consume* measures how much of a change in disposable income is devoted to a change in consumption. It is written as

$$\text{MPC} = \frac{\Delta C}{\Delta DI}$$

in which ΔC is the change in consumption resulting from ΔDI, the change in disposable income.

For instance, suppose there is a $100 billion increase in disposable income, and out of this, households spend $95 billion. The marginal propensity to consume would be .95. That is:

$$\text{MPC} = \frac{\Delta C}{\Delta DI}$$

$$= \frac{95}{100}$$

$$= .95$$

If, on the other hand, extra spending had only been $80 billion out of the additional $100 billion, the MPC = .80. Whatever the MPC actually is depends on how much consumers spend out of their changed disposable income. It is, of course, their choice.[3]

The significance of the marginal propensity to consume is that the higher it is, the greater the multiplier. The first MPC above gives us a multiplier stream of income change like this:

$$\Delta I \;+\; \Delta C_1 \;+\; \Delta C_2 \;+\; \Delta C_3 \;+\; \Delta C_4 \ldots$$

$$100 \;+\; 95 \;+\; 90.25 \;+\; 85.74 \;+\; 81.45 \ldots$$

and the second (lower one) gives us this multiplier stream:

$$\Delta I \;+\; \Delta C_1 \;+\; \Delta C_2 \;+\; \Delta C_3 \;+\; \Delta C_4 \ldots$$

$$100 \;+\; 80.00 \;+\; 64.00 \;+\; 51.20 \;+\; 40.1 \ldots$$

Clearly, the first of these two flows generates more added economic activity. The importance of the marginal propensity to consume and the multiplier is elaborated in the appendix to this chapter.

---

[3]Not every household's MPC will be the same as the MPC for *all households taken together.* Some may have an MPC as high as 1.00. What does this imply? What is *your own* MPC? Is it the same as your family's?

The major conclusion to be drawn from all of this is twofold. First, anything that changes disposable income will have a direct immediate impact on aggregate consumer demand, although we must always keep the "fundamental psychological law" in mind. Thus an increase in disposable income, no matter what the source, will increase aggregate consumer demand by a somewhat lesser amount. Yet, and this is the second point, the "law" tells us that the increase in consumer spending sets off further rounds of increases in aggregate consumer demand—that is, there is a multiplier effect.

5. Taxes

One particular source of a change in disposable income must be identified here, that is, changes in taxes and transfer payments. Government has the power to affect the level of consumption through its powers to tax and to enact transfer payments programs. If, for example, government were to raise the personal income tax or reduce transfer payments, disposable income would fall; and therefore households would cut back on their consumption spending. But remember the "fundamental psychological law"—the cut in spending would probably be less than the cut in disposable income. Saving would also be reduced.

If, on the other hand, government were to reduce taxes or raise transfer payments, exactly the opposite results would occur. A cut in taxes would mean higher disposable income, out of which households would increase both consumption and saving. As we shall see, especially in Chapter 12, the power of government to affect consumption and therefore aggregate demand through taxes and transfer payments is considerable.

6. Expectations

Household expectations of future income and prices also affect current consumption spending. A rise in expected future income or price levels stimulates higher levels of consumption out of current income. The reverse would lead to decreases in current consumption and aggregate demand. Expectations are much more important in determining investment demand.

7. A Preliminary Summary

Earlier we pointed out that the aggregate demand curve has a negative slope. Thus changes in the general price level cause changes in the total quantity demanded of *all* goods and services. The aggregate demand curve, however, was drawn on the assumption that all the other major factors affecting aggregate consumer behavior were constant. We then showed how a change in each of these would cause a change in aggregate consumer demand and hence a shift in the aggregate demand curve.

To repeat: An increase in general holdings of wealth, a more equal distribution of income, a fall in the rate of interest, a cut in personal taxes, and any increase in disposable income would cause consumption to rise and hence the aggregate demand curve to shift to the right. The reverse of all these changes would cause the aggregate demand curve to shift to the left.

Also, once a change in disposable income does occur, the multiplier will generate further changes in the same direction. The size of the marginal propensity to consume plays a major role in determining the strength of the multiplier.

D. INVESTMENT DEMAND BY BUSINESSES

Business demand for new capital goods, including inventories, is by far the most unstable component of aggregate demand. This instability is in turn responsible for most of the fluctuations in aggregate demand. And, as we discussed above, these fluctuations cause multiple changes in the levels of output, employment, and prices through the multiplier process.

Economists are generally agreed that six major factors can influence investment decisions: (1) the rate of interest, (2) the level of GNP, (3) the size of the existing capital stock, (4) advances in technology, (5) corporate tax rates, and especially (6) expectations. All of these were held constant by the *ceteris paribus* assumption when we drew the Figure 10-1 aggregate demand curve. Thus if any one of them changes, it will cause the aggregate demand curve to shift.

With regard to this component of aggregate demand, note that all investment is future oriented. Plants and shops and machines are built and purchased today for operation over a period of time stretching perhaps far into the future. The future, as we know, is uncertain, and therefore visions of things to come are based on expectations about the future. But these expectations are precarious because our knowledge of the future is so uncertain.

Look at some of the questions that must be "answered" before an investment decision can be made and the plans can be implemented. For instance, what will be the rate of interest, say, one year from now? Should we borrow to invest now? Or should we wait until the rate is lower (if it does, indeed, go lower)? What about the demand for our product? Will it remain strong? Or will disposable income maybe slump next year, forcing us into a loss situation? Is it possible that we shouldn't invest at all because there are rumors that government is going to raise corporate tax rates? In that case, maybe we shouldn't start the new venture. But what if government doesn't raise taxes after all, and some other firm makes its investment and beats us to the punch in our market? What then?

Just these questions alone show how tenuous investment decisions are. They have to be based on estimates of what is going to happen in the uncertain future. Our *state of confidence* depends mainly on these estimates. If business confidence is strong, then investment spending is also likely to be strong, increasing aggregate demand and setting off a positive multiplier. On the other hand, confidence may slump, causing a cutback in investment spending and setting off a negative multiplier.

There is nothing solid and lasting about the state of confidence, based as it is on expectations. As noted above, expectations are precarious, and hence "they are subject to sudden and violent changes.''[4] This is probably the main reason for the volatility of the investment component of aggregate demand. If this is so, small wonder that our economy is as unstable as it is.

We now need to look at each of the factors affecting investment decisions. In doing so, we will invoke the *ceteris paribus* assumption, but keep in mind, too, that throughout we are holding expectations constant. For the moment this is justifiable. We certainly relax this assumption when we take our trip through the business cycle in Section G of this chapter.

1. The Interest Rate Again

Investment in capital goods usually requires large outlays of money so that the business can purchase its new plant and equipment. On the other hand, the revenue coming in from the operation of the new plant doesn't appear today or even tomorrow. Instead, it will come in over a long period in the future.

Still, the plant must be built today, and to obtain the funds to finance the venture, businesspeople must often borrow funds in the financial market. The cost of acquiring funds in this way is, of course, the interest rate. Higher rates of interest make it more expensive to get the funds and hence make businesses less willing to borrow. Lower rates, on the other hand, make borrowing cheaper and tend to stimulate new investment spending.

In many cases, however, businesses don't have to borrow from outside sources; instead they can use the profits they have accumulated from past operations. Will the interest rate be a factor influencing investment in such cases? The answer is definitely yes. Why? Because the firm incurs an opportunity cost if it uses its own funds. In other words, the firm could follow the alternative of lending its own money out to others and receive an interest income. This forgone interest income, therefore, is the opportunity cost of the firm when it uses its own funds.

Our conclusion, then, is that a reduction in the interest rate will, all other things equal, stimulate new investment, and therefore the aggregate demand curve will shift to the right. Conversely, an increase in the interest rate will stifle investment demand, and accordingly the aggregate demand curve will fall.

2. The Level of GNP

Let's turn to the second factor that affects investment spending—namely, changes in total output and income. There is a direct impact on investment when the levels of output and employment change. Rising levels, for example, push business operations toward full capacity. This is accompanied by a rise in prices, and all of this may improve business expectations as businesspeople tend to anticipate still higher levels of sales in the future. Thus businesses may want to enlarge productive capacity in order to meet the anticipated higher sales. This occurs in the expansionary stage of the business cycle. In the contractionary stage, on the other hand, falling sales

---

[4]Keynes, *General Theory*, p. 315.

seem to breed a more pessimistic state of confidence, and thus investment demand also slumps. This factor illustrates very effectively the impact of changing expectations on investment spending.

3. The Size of the Capital Stock

Investment is also influenced by the size of the already existing capital stock. All other things equal, the larger the size of the capital stock, the smaller the incentive to invest in new plants and equipment. The reason is simple. The more capital a firm already has, the better able it is to serve current consumer demand. Therefore there is less need for new capital.

4. Technological Change

Advances in technology can also affect investment by making new capital more profitable. This by itself should encourage new investment. There is, however, another side to this, for the new capital goods may make some of the existing capital goods obsolete. The historical record indicates that, on net balance, technological advances stimulate new investment spending, causing the aggregate demand curve to shift to the right.

5. Taxes

Finally, corporate and business taxes can affect aggregate investment spending. Cuts in these taxes tend to stimulate new investment spending, although the linkage is not always clear. Nonetheless, government has in the past used this technique quite often to stimulate new investment and set off a multiplier. Tax increases, on the other hand, tend to discourage investment spending.

6. Another Interim Summary

The investment component of aggregate demand is responsive to changes in a number of factors. The following tend to increase investment spending and hence aggregate demand: a fall in interest rates, a rising GNP, a cut in corporate taxes, and technological advances. All of these will encourage new investment spending, however, only if the state of confidence is supportive. Investment spending, on the other hand, is dampened under the following circumstances: a rising rate of interest, a falling GNP, increases in taxes, and an already large capital stock. All of these don't have to appear together in order for investment to be discouraged. Any one or a combination of them can do the trick, especially if expectations are pessimistic.

E. GOVERNMENT AND NET EXPORTS

The two remaining components of aggregate demand are government purchases of goods and services and exports minus imports.

1. Government Purchases

Government (at all levels) buys enormous quantities of goods and services every year. These purchases must eventually be paid out of tax revenues, although, as Chapter 6 pointed out, government frequently resorts to borrowing to pay for what it purchases.

The governmental decisions to buy labor services, national defense, highways, and the like, are largely made as a part of the political process. The attitudes of the voters, as reflected in Congress and the administration, determine the amount of defense, the size of our welfare programs, and all the other things government spends money on.

Only government purchases of goods and services are included in aggregate demand (transfer payments aren't; remember, they don't represent productive activity). The government component of aggregate demand affects the levels of output, prices, and employment directly. But on the other side of the coin, changes in this component are unpredictable. This is because government spending is subject to sudden changes in political outlook, and these cannot be foreseen very accurately. Nonetheless, we conclude that increases in government spending on goods and services will shift the aggregate demand curve to the right. Conversely, a cutback in these spending programs induces a slump in aggregate demand.

2. Exports Minus Imports

We know from Chapter 7 that foreign trade is crucial for the United States. More and more we find that we rely on foreign sources for some products needed to maintain our standard of living. Imports mean that we demand foreign output, whereas exports mean that foreigners are demanding our output; and when we subtract imports from exports, we get the *net demand*. Thus, if exports exceed imports, the rest of the world is, on net balance, demanding more of our output than we are demanding from abroad. In this event, *net exports* are a *positive* figure. On the other hand, when we demand more from other countries than they demand from us, *net exports* are a *negative* figure.

Whether net exports—i.e., net foreign demand—are positive or negative depends mainly on two things. First, the prices of goods at home relative to prices abroad are important. The lower the prices are here at home, the more the foreigners will buy from us and the less we will buy from abroad. Lower prices at home, therefore, tend to increase our exports and dampen our imports. So, whenever we have an increase in our net exports, aggregate demand rises.

The reverse, however, may also be true, that is, we may become a net importer. This has indeed occurred for a number of years. Higher prices here at home relative to prices abroad have led to an increase in our imports and a decrease in our exports. As a consequence, there is a leftward pressure on the aggregate demand curve.

Exchange rates also affect relative prices between the United States and other countries. When the value of the dollar falls in the foreign exchange market, U.S. goods become cheaper and the goods in other countries tend to become more expensive. Therefore, falling dollar exchange rates stimulate our exports, dampen imports, and thus add to aggregate demand. On the contrary, a rise in the international value of the dollar means that our prices tend to be higher and foreign prices lower. In this event, then, exports are dampened, imports are stimulated, and aggregate demand tends to fall.

Clearly, therefore, we can't afford to ignore the foreign sector in any discussion of aggregate demand. It is for this reason that we add it to consumer demand, investment demand, and government demand to get to aggregate demand.

F. AGGREGATE SUPPLY

It is now time to turn to the supply side of the analysis and examine aggregate supply. The aggregate supply curve reflects the ability and willingness of the economy to produce goods and services at different price levels.

The aggregate supply curve in Figure 10-2 is drawn on the assumption that the general price level is the only thing influencing total output. Thus the higher the price level, the greater the quantity supplied. The factors that will cause the aggregate supply curve to shift are held constant by the *ceteris paribus* assumption. These other factors are (1) prices of productive services, especially wages; (2) technology; and (3) changes in the size of the capital stock and the size of the labor force.

But note also the shape of the aggregate supply curve in Figure 10-2. This, along with the shifts of the curve, needs to be explained, and we discuss it first.

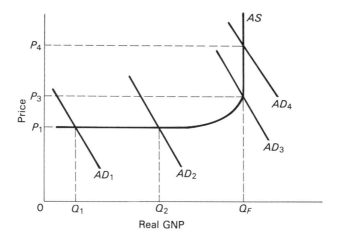

FIGURE 10-2   Aggregate Demand and the Price Level   As aggregate demand shifts to the right in the flat range of the *AS* curve, real output rises but not the price level. As aggregate demand closes in on full-employment GNP (i.e., from AD_2 to AD_3), the general price level rises because of bottlenecks and the use of less-efficient resources. Once full-employment GNP is reached, further increases in aggregate demand have no effect on output, but only on prices.

1. The Shape of the Aggregate Supply Curve

To understand why the aggregate supply curve is at first relatively flat, then rises gently, and finally rises sharply and becomes vertical, let's follow the behavior of prices and output through the stages of the business cycle. In doing this, we will hold all input prices constant. We also assume that productivity is static and that there are no changes in the amount of resources in the economy.

Let's begin with output at Q_1. Aggregate demand (AD_1) in this case is very anemic, resulting in a large pool of unemployed labor and a lot of idle plant capacity. Thus there are many resources that can be drawn on to provide increases in output. (Q_F in Figure 10–2 designates the full-employment rate of total output.)

Now suppose that somehow or other an expansion gets under way, as shown by the shift of the aggregate demand curve from AD_1 to AD_2. In response to the rise in demand, total output also rises from Q_1 to Q_2 by means of the multiplier process. Note, however, that this increased economic activity takes place in the flat range of the aggregate supply curve, and this tells us that output has increased, *but with no increase in prices.* The reason for this zero inflation is perhaps simple enough. The involuntarily unemployed workers are more than happy to work at the prevailing wage; they want jobs and incomes and will not jeopardize them by asking for higher wages. In consequence, employment increases without any rise in labor costs of production.

Nor will prices rise, for businesspeople are happy to increase their output and sell it at the prevailing price level. By doing this, they will add to their total revenue, and they too will not want to jeopardize their new gains by raising prices. Moreover, as long as wages remain constant, there is less need to raise prices. Thus, as long as aggregate demand remains in the flat segment of the aggregate supply curve, total output can be increased *with no inflation.*

However, as aggregate demand continues to rise, it will push into the positively sloped range of the aggregate supply curve. As the expansion continues, aggregate output begins to approach potential GNP—i.e., Q_F, as shown by the AD_3 curve. Note that in this range of the aggregate supply curve, further rises in GNP are accompanied by some inflation.

Why does the supply curve begin to rise and slope upward sharply in this range? Two reasons are pertinent. First, "bottlenecks" begin to crop up here and there. These are sectors or industries that reach full capacity before the economy as a whole reaches Q_F. For example, the steel industry may reach full operation while aggregate demand is still rising from AD_2 to AD_3. Thus the steel firms are operating at full capacity while the demand for steel by, say, the automobile and construction industries continues to expand. The result is obviously a rise in the price of steel, and as long as a lot of buyers continue to scramble for the scarce supply, prices will be bid up even more. Accordingly, the prices of all the products using steel as a basic ingredient will also rise as the higher costs are passed on.

There may be many such bottlenecks, and even more will develop and emerge as the economy nears full employment. At any event, further increases in output are accompanied by rising prices. The closer the output comes to potential GNP, the sharper the price increases and the smaller the increases in output.

Figure 10–2 shows us two equal increases in GNP. The first one, from Q_1 to Q_2, was carried out with no inflation: the price level remained at P_1. The second one, however, from Q_2 to Q_F, was achieved only at the cost of the rise in the price level from P_1 to P_3.

Bottlenecks aren't the only cause of the upward slope of the aggregate supply curve. Another reason why prices rise as the economy nears full employment is that business firms must make use of less-efficient workers and less-efficient capital. Earlier, when output grew from Q_1 to Q_2 and even beyond, business firms employed the most-efficient laborers and used the most-efficient capital. However, as full employment is approached, less-efficient means of production must be used. Older and slower-operating machinery is used, and workers with lower skills are hired. This results in a declining efficiency, and declining efficiency means higher costs and therefore higher prices.

Once the economy is at full employment (Q_F in Figure 10–2), any further increases in aggregate demand (as to AD_4) *may* result in some minor and temporary increases in output beyond Q_F, but they *will certainly* create substantial upward pressure on prices. Thus when aggregate demand rises to AD_4, there are, for all practical purposes, only temporary increases in total output, but the price level rises from P_3 to P_4. The major difference between this inflation and the earlier one (when prices rose from P_1 to P_3) is that this one is accompanied by no increase in output. The only thing that increases once aggregate demand passes into the vertical range of the aggregate supply curve is the price level.[5]

2. Shifts in the Aggregate Supply Curve

The aggregate supply curve will shift whenever the factors other than price change. These factors are (1) the prices of inputs, particularly wages; (2) technology; and (3) the size of both the labor force and the capital stock.

Let's look first at wages. They amount to about two-thirds of total costs of production, and therefore changes in the level of money wages have a decided impact on the aggregate supply curve.

Two kinds of wage changes should be noted. As the economy expands beyond output Q_2 in Figure 10–2, the aggregate supply curve begins to rise because of bottlenecks in production. There may also be shortages of certain types of skilled labor, and as demand continues to rise, these workers demand higher wages. The impact of these *selective* wage increases on aggregate supply is the same as the bottlenecks

---

[5]All of this can also be explained by means of the quantity theory presented in Section B-1 of this chapter. Remember: $MV = PQ$. Now if we are at full employment, so that total real output, Q, cannot rise, then any increase in aggregate demand, MV, must cause the price level, P, to rise proportionately. Thus, if MV rises by, say, 8 percent, then P must also rise by 8 percent. But this would occur only in the vertical range.

In the horizontal range, in which P is assumed to be constant, any increase in MV must result in a proportionate rise in total output Q. Finally, in the intermediate range of the aggregate supply curve, increases in MV result in PQ rising proportionately, but we can't tell how much each increases without further information.

we have just discussed. Thus the change in aggregate supply is shown as a movement up the *AS* curve, such as from Q_2 to Q_F back in Figure 10-2.

The other change, however, is more *general* and is shown as shifting the *entire* aggregate supply curve upward. As the economy continues through the expansionary stage, the demand for labor rises across the board and, accordingly, wages tend to rise economywide. The *general* increases in the wage rate will shift the entire aggregate supply curve up (selective wage increases do not shift the curve). The upward shift is shown by the AS_2 curve in Figure 10-3. High levels of activity that create a general shortage of labor also create rising wages and expectations of more of the same.

Downward shifts of the aggregate supply curve are also possible as money wages fall. Sustained periods of widespread unemployment, such as in a severe and drawn-out depression, could lead to a general fall in wages. If this were to occur, the aggregate supply curve would also fall. Something like this happened during the Great Depression of the 1930s. Also, in the contraction of 1981–82, the general wage level didn't fall, but wage increases went from double-digit annual percentage increases to virtually no change by the time the recession came to an end. This downward shift is shown by AS_3 in Figure 10-3.

The two other causes of shifts in the aggregate supply curve can quickly be covered; they belong more properly in the Chapter 13 discussion of economic growth. The first of these is changes in productivity due to technological advances. The changes in technology that we consider here are cost reducing. Thus, once they

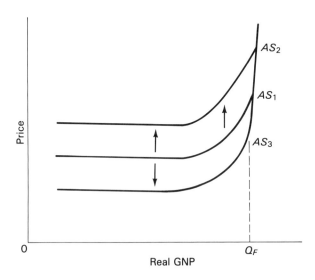

FIGURE 10-3   Impact of Changing Input Prices on the Aggregate Supply Curve   A general increase in input prices will shift the *AS* curve *vertically upward,* since potential GNP (Q_F) hasn't changed. A general decrease in input prices will shift the *AS* curve *vertically downward.*

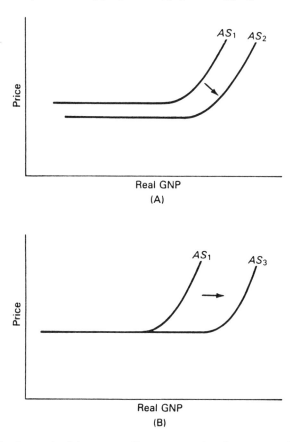

FIGURE 10-4 Impact of Long-run Factors on the Aggregate Supply Curve
Panel (A) shows the result of a cost-reducing technological change. The curve shifts
downward because of the now lower costs of production; it shifts to the right because
the technological advance increases the economy's resource base.

Panel (B) shows the result of an increase in the labor force or the capital stock (or
both). Note that the curve doesn't shift down in this case because costs of production
haven't been affected. It shifts right because the economy's resource base has been
expanded.

materialize, the aggregate supply curve shifts down and to the right. This is shown
by the AS_2 curve in Figure 10-4(A).

The final cause of a shift in the aggregate supply curve is an increase in the
size of the labor force and capital stock. The new aggregate supply curve resulting
from this sort of change is shown as AS_3 in Figure 10-4(B). Note that this curve
shifts to the right, but not down. This is because there has, by assumption, been no
change in wage rates and no change in productivity. Therefore the flat segment of
the new curve is at the same height as the flat part of AS_1.

G. THE DETERMINATION OF OUTPUT, EMPLOYMENT, AND PRICES

We have now come full circle. We started out with the basic idea of aggregate supply and aggregate demand interacting to determine the levels of output, employment, and prices. Next we examined the different components of aggregate demand. We then discussed the forces underlying the aggregate supply curve. It is now time to put both demand and supply together and see how they interact to determine the general level of economic activity.

1. The Equilibrium Level of GNP

Figure 10-5 shows that the aggregate supply curve (AS_1) intersects the aggregate demand curve (AD_1) at the output level of Q_1. The corresponding price level is P_1. The letter E_1 at the point of intersection indicates that this is an equilibrium level of output and prices.

But why is this an equilibrium? For the very same reason that we discussed back in Chapter 4. Recall that if the amount demanded is greater than the amount supplied, both output and price will rise until the two quantities become equal. Conversely, if quantity supplied exceeds quantity demanded, output will fall, and price will also fall until the equilibrium is reached.

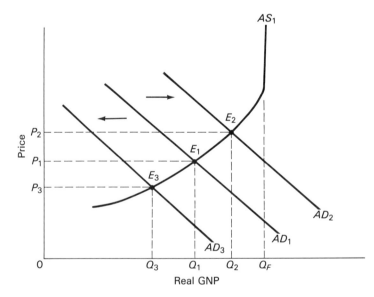

FIGURE 10-5   Effects on Output and Prices of Changes in Aggregate Demand   In this case, a rise in aggregate demand causes both real output and the general level of prices to rise. Conversely, a fall in aggregate demand causes both real output and the general level of prices to fall. These results occur because the changes in aggregate demand are in the upward-sloping range of the aggregate supply curve.

One final thing about Figure 10-5. Note that the equilibrium level of Q_1 is at less than full-capacity, full-employment Q_F. In order for Q_F to be reached, aggregate demand must rise. But note also that in an unstable economy, aggregate demand may fall, and this will create more unemployment. Also, it is quite conceivable that aggregate supply may also change—that is, the whole curve may shift, say, to the right for any of several reasons. In fact, as you already know, there are all sorts of possible changes.

Let's examine three of these possibilities. In doing this, we will follow the procedure of allowing only one thing—either aggregate supply *or* aggregate demand—to change and then see how the change affects both GNP and the price level *(P)*.

2. A Rise in Investment Demand

Suppose that, because of some change in business expectations, there is a rise in investment demand by business firms in general. This shifts the aggregate demand curve to the right from AD_1 to AD_2. The additional demand raises production and employment closer to full employment—that is, from Q_1 to Q_2. In the process, costs rise, and so do prices, from P_1 to P_2. So, expanding demand in this case is accompanied by both increasing output and employment and some inflation. The new equilibrium is at point E_2.

3. A Fall in Government Spending

Now let's consider the case in which government spending falls. In this event, aggregate demand shifts to the left from, say, AD_1 to AD_3. The result is that the levels of output, employment, and prices all fall. Another equilibrium is established at E_3 with prices at P_3 and output and employment at Q_3. Thus, if there is no offsetting increase in aggregate demand, a recession results.

4. An Increase in the Money Supply

Consider now the case of an increase in the money supply. As the money supply increases, and supposing velocity remains the same, aggregate demand will rise (again we use Figure 10-5) from AD_1 to AD_2. The increase in the money supply will also, of course, be recorded as a rise in consumption, investment, government expenditure, or net exports; that is, the new money will be spent on any or a combination of these major types of spending. In any event, the higher aggregate demand will raise output, employment, and prices as the new equilibrium at E_2 is approached.

5. The Anatomy of a Business Cycle

We now have enough tools at our command to examine what happens in the economy over the course of a typical business cycle. A few words, however, before we do this.

First, not so many years ago, economists had come to believe that the business cycle had been banished—had become a thing of the past. They indeed believed that the economy could and would grow with hardly any ups and downs—and that when there were ups and downs, policy measures could be used to offset them.

Unfortunately, events of the early 1980s showed that the business cycle was very much alive. So it was still necessary to discover the causes of booms and busts, inflation and unemployment, and so on. The cycle was not dead, at least not yet!

Second, the aggregate supply and demand analysis we have used so far must be interpreted very carefully. We must read the curves and changes in them in a dynamic way. That is, the supply and demand curves are actually always on the move, and this means that equilibrium is never reached. Yet, at the same time, the equilibrium concept is important because it allows us to reorganize our thoughts. Thus, what we must realize is that although an equilibrium is never established, the economy is always tending toward equilibrium in response to any shock. But as it nears this equilibrium, something in a system as dynamic and complex as ours is bound to change, creating movement toward a new equilibrium. This is how the business cycle unfolds, like a series of ever-shifting equilibrium positions.

Let's begin our description of the business cycle by supposing that our economy is suffering from a deep recession. Figure 10–6 shows that the economy is in a rough equilibrium at point E_1. The price level is temporarily stable at P_1, and output and employment are far short of full employment—that is, Q_1 versus Q_F.

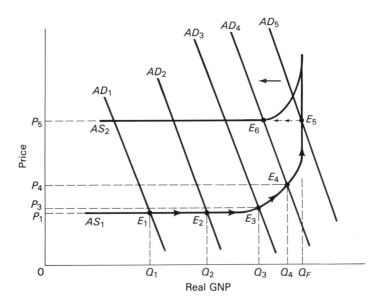

FIGURE 10-6   Aggregate Demand over the Business Cycle   As the business cycle runs its course, the upper turning point occurs and aggregate demand slumps (from AD_5 to AD_4). In the later stages of the expansion, however, rising input prices cause the aggregate supply curve to shift up from AS_1 to AS_2.

Under these conditions, there is likely to be a public outcry for the government to do something, and as we have already seen, the government can take some definite actions. For one thing, it can cut taxes; for another, it can raise spending; and, finally, it can increase the money supply. So, for our purposes, let's suppose that government responds to the public outcry by cutting taxes, increasing spending, and inducing an increase in the money supply. The increase in government expenditures raises aggregate demand directly and immediately while the cut in taxes leads indirectly to an increase in aggregate demand by raising disposable income and hence spending by households. At the same time, the added money also contributes directly to aggregate demand. Thus the aggregate demand curve shifts to the right to, say, AD_2.

This higher demand will bring forth more output, and some of the unemployed people will begin to return to work. And as the incomes of households rise even higher, consumption expenditures will also continue to expand. Aggregate demand, therefore, rises even higher to AD_3. The result is a more intense use of productive capacity and even greater increases in employment. The unemployment rate begins to fall rapidly, but because of the bottlenecks and shortages, the price level begins to rise as output continues to increase.

By now, however, a strong interaction will begin. The rising sales and demand mean that a lot of plant and equipment is working at full capacity. Moreover, the rising demand and price levels make businesspeople much more optimistic. Under these circumstances, it is understandable that businesses will want to expand their production facilities in anticipation of a still higher level of sales. As a result, the rising business investment in plant and equipment will add further to the rightward shift of aggregate demand to AD_4.

However, since the economy is by now very close to potential GNP, any *further* increase in aggregate demand won't increase total output by very much. In fact, the rise from AD_4 to AD_5 increases total output only from Q_4 to Q_F. However, prices take a very sharp jump from P_4 to P_5 because of sharply rising costs. At this point, therefore, increases in aggregate demand have minimal effects on production and substantial effects on the price level. Inflation thus becomes stronger and stronger as the economy approaches full employment. Finally, and very important, the tight labor market causes the *general level* of wages to rise, shifting the aggregate supply curve up to AS_2, adding further to inflation.

For various reasons, the high level of aggregate demand isn't likely to be sustained. In fact, there are a number of reasons why it is apt to fall. For example, once businesses have completed their investment plans, they will cut back spending on new plant and equipment, and this will cause aggregate demand to slump. Also, government may decide to trim expenditures or, perhaps, even to raise taxes as the inflation continues. Rising prices have another depressing impact—they reduce our competitive position with respect to that of the rest of the world. In other words, our imports will tend to rise and our exports will tend to fall, and this will also cause aggregate demand to slump even more.

Suppose that, as a result of these events, aggregate demand shifts back to AD_4. What will happen now? Will the economy simply slide back down the aggregate supply curve (AS_1) to lower levels of output and prices? The answer is no! Once higher prices and wages have been established, they don't easily fall, as shown by the higher level of aggregate supply (AS_2). There are several reasons for this. For instance, major labor union contracts set wages for long periods of time, such as two and three years. Thus, when aggregate demand slumps, wages don't fall right away. Moreover, since wages don't fall, and since wages make up the greater part of the costs of production, prices also don't fall. Instead business firms hold prices at the same level and cut back on production, hence leading to increasing unemployment.

However, more than union contracts prevent wages from falling in a recession. Even if there were no such contracts, employers would be reluctant to cut wages. Even without unions, workers resist wage cuts, for the workers feel that their economic value as human beings has been downgraded. Deep morale problems arise, and this could have an adverse effect on production, both now and in the future. Management therefore tends to avoid these morale problems by maintaining wages as best it can during the recessions. As we mentioned above, only in severe sustained recessions would the general level of wages fall.

Another major factor causing downward rigidity of wages and prices is the expectations of both management and labor with respect to government policy. Since the end of World War II (1945), our government has responded to most slumps in aggregate demand by raising spending or cutting taxes (or both). Sometimes government has lagged in doing this, but generally it has responded in order to increase aggregate demand to reverse the recession. Since management and labor expect this to occur, they see no reason to cut wages and prices. Instead they sit back and wait for government to help move the economy back toward full employment. The major exception to this was the deep recession of the early 1980s where wage pressures substantially weakened as the recession continued.

The result of all of these things is that prices tend to remain high in the short run even though aggregate demand is falling and the economy is entering a recession. This is shown in Figure 10-6 by the arrows pointing leftward from E_5 to E_6. What happens, therefore, is that output and employment, not prices, fall as the recession initially deepens. Indeed, the situation could be worse than this. If there has been a long boom period with attendant inflation and expectations for more of the same, then the general level of wages may continue to rise and the aggregate supply curve shifts up even as aggregate demand falls. In other words, as a result of past price increases and expectations of more inflation, forces build up such a momentum that prices continue to rise in the face of slumping demand. In this case, we have the worst possible situation—*inflated recession.*

One final comment: The explanation of the aggregate supply curve given in this chapter, and the events of recent history, suggest that at least in the short run, it is difficult to achieve high levels of output and employment without inflation. Indeed, the period ranging from the early 1970s to the early 1980s witnessed an almost continuing escalation of price inflation. The deep recession of the 1981–82 period did, with a lag, cause the inflation rate to drop substantially. The cost in terms of lost output and employment was enormous, however. Perhaps the lesson to be learned is that recessions are necessary to reduce inflation—the more severe the inflation, the more severe the recession required for the cure. At this point, it becomes obvious that government has a role to play in maintaining stable aggregate demand at close to potential GNP. The federal government has taken upon itself the responsibility for stabilizing output at or near potential GNP and maintaining stable prices at the same time. Can the task be done? Stabilization policy is the subject of the next three chapters.

H. SUMMARY

The level of economic activity is determined by the interaction of aggregate demand and aggregate supply. Fluctuations in the levels of output and prices are caused by fluctuations of aggregate demand, and we show this by movements along the aggregate supply curve. When aggregate demand rises, expansions occur; when aggregate demand falls, contractions occur.

Aggregate demand can be looked at in either of two ways; as total money demand (i.e., *MV)*, or as a flow of different kinds of spending. When aggregate demand is viewed as the flow of total money demand, changes in money supply (*M)* and its velocity (*V)* are emphasized as the basic causes of changes in real GNP, prices, and employment. When viewed as the sum total of the different kinds of spending (consumption, investment, government, and net exports), changes in any one or more of these components cause changes in the general level of economic activity.

Aggregate supply, in essence, reflects the unit costs of production of total output. As aggregate demand rises, increased quantities of output first occur at no price-level changes, then at rising prices, and finally further increases in demand result only in price inflation.

In the business cycle, the expansion gets under way by some rise in aggregate demand. At first, output rises at constant or only gently rising prices. Then two things may occur. First, the rise in demand will improve expectations and thus fuel further rise in demand and output. Second, because of bottlenecks and growing inefficiency, inflation sets in. In the latter stages of the expansion, prices rise sharply and output little or not at all. The upper-turning zone is brought about by a slump in aggregate demand. Although output and employment fall during the ensuing contraction, prices don't fall. There seems to be a short-run downward rigidity in wage rates.

As for the lower-turning zone, that is usually brought on by government policy. This is the topic of the next two chapters.

Terms and Concepts to Remember

Aggregate supply
Aggregate demand
Velocity (turnover)
Marginal propensity to
    consume

Multiplier
Keynes's fundamental
    psychological law

Questions for Review

1. What happens to aggregate demand if
   a. Money supply doubles and velocity is constant?
   b. Money supply doubles and velocity is halved?
   c. Money supply is constant and velocity doubles?

2. What effects will the following changes have on household consumption and aggregate demand?
   a. A rise in interest rates
   b. A cut in personal taxes
   c. A rise in disposable income

3. What effects will the following changes have on business investment expenditure and aggregate demand?
   a. A collapse in stock market prices
   b. A fall in interest rates
   c. A rapid rise in real GNP

4. Suppose that aggregate demand is stable and that there is a huge increase in oil prices. What happens to aggregate supply, output, and the price level as a result?

5. What happens to output and general prices as aggregate demand
   a. Expands in the flat range of the aggregate supply curve?
   b. Expands into the upward-sloping portion of the aggregate supply curve?
   c. Rises into the vertical segment of aggregate supply?
   d. Slumps from cycle peak into recession?

Appendix: Another Look at the Multiplier

This chapter has stressed how a change in aggregate demand will lead to a multiple change in output (and employment). The chapter also emphasized the multiplier process as a part of the business cycle. Indeed, the multiplier was treated as a disequilibrium process. We can, however, also examine it from the equilibrium point of view, and that is the purpose of this appendix.

In our discussion of the circular flow model, we have demonstrated that an equilibrium level of income exists (i.e., $AD = AS$) when leakages from the income stream equal injections into the stream. In the simplest form of the circular flow, this occurs when household saving (S) equals business investment (I), or $S = I$. If $I > S$, then $AD > AS$, and output and income rise until S and I are once again in equality. If $S > I$, then $AD < AS$, and output and income fall until leakages and injections are equal again. Note that *once in a state of disequilibrium, it is the change in income and output itself that reestablishes equilibrium* between S and I and hence AD and AS. The amount of that income change depends, in turn, on the size of the marginal propensity to consume (MPC).

The means by which a disequilibrium causes income to change is called the income multiplier process. Below we describe the effect on GNP over time of a rise in investment expenditures. As we know, each dollar of added investment gives us more than a dollar of added income.

Suppose GNP is in initial equilibrium at $100 billion with $I = S = \$50$ billion. Further suppose that the collective MPC is 50 percent—that is, households consume half and save half of each additional dollar of income. Finally suppose that because of an improved business climate, firms raise investment spending by $10 billion ($\triangle I = 10$). As a result, $AD > AS$ and $I > S$, so that GNP begins to rise. The time sequence of events is described in Table 10A–1. (Note that Table 10A–1 records only the changes involved.)

In time period one, the rise in I of $10 billion increases capital goods production, and through the circular flow this $10 billion ends up as additional household income. With an MPC of 50 percent, households save $5 billion and increase consumption by $5 billion. The added household demand increases production of consumer goods, and the spending flows to still other households as added income of $5 billion. Thus GNP rises again in period two, but only by $5 billion. These other households now have $5 billion more income, which they divide as follows: $2.5 billion to more consumption and $2.5 billion extra savings. Again the added consumption becomes increased production and income of $2.5 billion to still other households. Note that by the end of period three, the original $10 billion rise in

TABLE 10A–1   The Income Multiplier (in billions of dollars)

Time Period	Change in Investment	Change in GNP	Change in Consumption	Change in Saving
1	10	10	5	5
2	0	5	2.5	2.5
3	0	2.5	1.25	1.25
4	0	1.25	.625	.625
5	0	.625	.313	.313
6	0	.313	.156	.156
Total 6 Rounds	10 0 0	19.69	9.84	9.84
Total Change	10	20	10	10

investment has generated a $17.5 billion rise in GNP. Income continues to rise, however, because the added income of $2.5 billion in period three increases household consumption demand by $1.25 billion, which becomes still more income in period four. And so it goes. Each time income is increased, half of it is spent on additional consumption that becomes additional income, the amounts ever diminishing toward zero as time passes. After a large number of time periods, the total change in GNP approaches $20 billion, and the added annual savings accumulate to $10 billion. At this point we can say that once again equilibrium has been established, since GNP, or income, has risen by enough to generate the added savings needed to match the original increase in investment of $10 billion. Specifically, GNP rose by $2 for each $1 increase in investment—that is, the income multiplier is two. GNP is now at $120 billion, savings and investment are equal at $60 billion, and $AD = AS$ once again. Three final points should be noted.

First, the size of the multiplier varies directly with the marginal propensity to consume. In our example, an MPC of .5 led to a first-round increase in consumption of $5 billion. If the MPC were .8, however, the first-round increase in consumption would be $8 billion; and if the MPC were .9, consumption would rise by $9 billion. Clearly, then, the amount of income change rises with the MPC.

Second, the multiplier effect takes place over time. How long might the time period be? The time sequence of the income multiplier is related to the velocity of circulation of the money supply. Each time period (as in Table 10A–1) would correspond to a single turnover of the money stock. For example, if velocity were 6 per year, then the income multiplier through three periods would take six months. In our example, GNP would have risen by $17.5 billion from $100 billion to $117.5 billion six months after the rise in investment. Clearly, as velocity changes, so does the speed of the income multiplier.

Finally, we have implied that each rise in income in the multiplier process represents an increase in real output or GNP. This is only true as long as the economy is operating along the flat portion of the aggregate supply curve. If instead aggregate supply is upward sloping, the increase in dollar income will be the same, but some part of it will be dissipated in higher prices instead of real output. In the vertical range of aggregate supply, all income increases take the form of higher prices—that is, there are no increases in real output.

11

The Role of Money and Banking in the Economy

chapter preview

- Money performs three functions in society: (1) it serves as a unit of account (i.e., measurement), (2) as a medium of exchange, and (3) as a store of value.

- In the United States a number of things serve as money—coins, paper currency, demand deposits, other checkable deposits, and traveler's checks. The total of these make up the money supply ($M1$).

- Demand deposits are by far the most important form of money in our society.

- Because of the fractional reserve banking system, banks create money as they make loans.

- The ability of banks to make new loans depends on the excess of their actual reserves over the required reserves. These are appropriately called excess reserves.

- The money-creating power of the commercial banking system depends upon the legal reserve ratio, the cash drain, and desired excess reserves.

- The central bank controls the legal reserve ratio, the general public controls the cash drain, and individual banks determine desired excess reserves.

- Changes in the cash drain and desired excess reserves can cause changes in the money supply.

- The banking system, given an injection of new reserves into the system, can create an amount of money that is a multiple of the amount of new reserves.

- This relationship is called the money multiplier.

- Gold has played an important role in our monetary system in the past and may again in the future.

This chapter is about money in our economy; it gets very specific about money—what it is, and where it comes from. It also asks (and answers) the important question, How does the commercial banking system create and destroy money? The logical next question of how the banks and money supply can be controlled is left for the next chapter.

We have some good background for this discussion. Chapter 3, for example, defined *money* as *anything that is generally accepted as a medium of exchange.* That chapter also explained how money allows us to avoid the clumsiness of barter. Money, in fact, is as important as it is because it allows the exchange process to function smoothly. In this way, then, we obtain the great benefits of division of labor and enjoy a higher standard of living.

At a different level, Chapter 10 showed how the stock of money multiplied by its velocity constitutes the economy's annual aggregate demand for goods and services. Aggregate demand, in turn, along with aggregate supply, determines the levels of output, employment, and prices. There is, in other words, a direct link between the money supply and the general level of economic activity.

So much for background. This chapter elaborates on the role of money in our economy. Sections A and B review the functions of money and provide a more-detailed definition of money. Section C takes a look at some of the unique features of banking in the United States. Section D then concentrates on an important economic phenomenon, that is, the ability of the banking system to create and destroy money.

A. THE VARIOUS FUNCTIONS OF MONEY

A good way to get a better idea of the role of money is to highlight the different jobs it does. As we shall see, money, if it is to be money and do its job well, must perform three basic functions. Money must serve as a unit of account, a medium of exchange, and a store of value.

1. Unit of Account

First of all, whatever is used as money must serve as a *unit of account*—that is, the basic unit of economic measurement. In our society, the unit of account is the *dollar,* and as we saw in Chapter 8, the economic value of the hundreds of thousands of things produced in the economy can be added up to give us the gross national product because all of these things are stated in dollar amounts.

We could conceivably express the economic value of things in terms of any commodity we chose to use—bushels of corn, pounds of oranges, packages of jellybeans. Thus we might say that the value of last year's GNP was so many nonillion packages of jellybeans.[1] The problem, however, is that jellybeans—or for that matter any other commodity—don't serve the other functions of money very well.

It is for this reason that we have settled on an *abstract unit* of account; and if we hadn't chosen the dollar as the unit of account, we would have had to devise some other abstract measure.

The United States has opted for the dollar as the basic unit of account in which economic values are calculated. Gross national product, therefore, is stated in terms of the dollar, and so are the prices of coffee, bulldozers, ice cream, and pictures. Similarly, the national debt is stated in dollar terms, and so is your personal debt. *The dollar as the basic unit of account is used everywhere in the United States.* Other countries, of course, have different units of account: In Great Britain it is the pound, in France it is the franc, in Japan it is the yen, and so on. (You may want to refer again to Exhibit 7–2 for a list of many of the units of account used throughout the world.)

2. Medium of Exchange

Money also, as we know, functions as a *medium of exchange.* We will merely summarize our earlier discussion by saying that money, as generalized purchasing power, permits us to acquire more easily all the goods and services that make up our material standards of living. In a money economy, the exchange sequence may be said to be

$$\text{Commodities} \;\rightarrow\; \text{Money} \;\rightarrow\; \text{Commodities}$$

Money allows the process of trade to occur with relative ease. (Think about how difficult exchange would be if we used bushels of wheat, pounds of oranges, or any other commodity as money.)

3. Store of Value

Finally, money serves as a *store of value (wealth)*—that is, we can hold part or all of our wealth in the form of money (although it is unlikely that we would hold all of it this way).

> **Definition:**   *Wealth* is the stock of monetary and nonmonetary assets that is owned by an economic unit, say, a business or a household.

---

[1]A *nonillion* is any number, say, 1, with thirty zeros behind it.

In some cases, wealth is obviously monetary—e.g., the household's checking account. In many other cases, however, wealth takes obviously nonmonetary forms—e.g., houses, automobiles, furniture, and so on. But in some cases, wealth may take nonmonetary forms and yet be very close to being money. Examples of this would be savings accounts and high-grade stocks and bonds; these are not money (you cannot buy anything with them), but they can easily be converted into money. (Think again of how difficult it would be to hold some of your wealth in the form of pounds of oranges, packages of jellybeans, or most other commodities.)

Most of us (including businesses and governments) hold some of our wealth in the form of money. But why do we? There must be some reasons for doing so. Yet we now know enough about economics to recognize that there must also be some costs in doing so. Let's look at these advantages and costs.

There is only one reason for holding any of our wealth as money, and that is because, unlike any other asset, money is *perfectly liquid.*

> **Definition:** *Liquidity* measures the ease and speed with which an asset may be converted into money. This definition can be turned around as follows: *Liquidity* measures the ease and speed with which money can be exchanged for other things.

Clearly, according to this definition, money is highly liquid because it is generally accepted as a medium of exchange. It exchanges easily and quickly for other assets. We may also say, in a roundabout way, that money has perfect liquidity because it can always be easily and quickly converted into money.

Other assets do not have perfect liquidity, but some are very liquid. Above we mentioned that savings accounts are close to money but yet are not money. They can easily and rather quickly be converted into money. The same is true of high-grade corporate stocks and bonds, and especially federal government securities. All of these can easily and rather quickly be turned into money.

There are of course a host of assets that are much less liquid. Some, in fact, are very illiquid, such as a small plot of land in a rural, underdeveloped area. The owner may, to be sure, get some money by selling it, but when and for how much are very questionable.

The reason why we want to hold some of our wealth as money is that there are always some items we want to buy, and since money is perfectly liquid, we can always find someone to take it off our hands. In other words, nearly all of our purchases are made with money.

There is, however, a serious disadvantage (cost) of holding wealth as money. Wealth in the form of stocks, bonds, capital, and land yields a rate of return in some form or another (dividends, interest, profit, rent). Money, on the other hand, yields no such return, and therefore there is a cost of holding money, and that cost takes the form of an old acquaintance—*opportunity cost.* The cost of holding money as such is the rate of return that could have been received if the wealth had been held in some other form, such as bonds.

There is an important conclusion to be reached here, and there are two important points also to be made.

Conclusion: Holding wealth as money carries with it an important opportunity cost, but it provides the advantages of liquidity. On the other hand, holding wealth in nonmonetary forms allows a rate of return, but at the cost of forgone liquidity. Here, then, is an important trade-off.

The first of the two points to be made is this: Changes in the interest rate (or any other rate of return) affect people's inclination to hold money as a store of value. A rise in the rate of interest increases the opportunity cost of holding money. When this happens, people tend to switch out of money into, say, bonds; that is, they buy higher-yielding assets, but only by sacrificing some of their liquidity. If, on the other hand, the rate of interest were to fall, the opportunity cost of holding money would also fall. People would thus be inclined to hold money as wealth and, in fact, might sell some low-yielding assets to get more money. The opportunity cost of holding money is lower at lower interest rates.

The second point has to do with inflation. Inflation also imposes a cost on holding money as a store of value. Chapter 9 showed us that inflation reduces the purchasing power of money. This by itself is a cost of holding wealth as money. If, for example, prices were to rise by 10 percent per year, then each year any dollar you held as money would have 10 percent lower purchasing power than in the preceding year. This is truly a cost of holding money, and therefore people tend to hold less money during periods of inflation and to buy assets whose values rise along with the price level. Shifts out of money into other assets are a common phenomenon during inflationary periods.

4. Money in Hyperinflation

In the introductory paragraphs to this chapter we stated that "money, in fact, is as important as it is because it allows the exchange process to function smoothly." This is true, but only if the supply of money is kept under control. For example, if there is too much money around so that inflation occurs, money may not perform its functions very well. This is particularly true in periods of runaway inflation (hyperinflation). In this case, the price level races upward so rapidly that no one wants to hold money as wealth. When hyperinflation persists, money disappears as a form of wealth and also as a medium of exchange, and the society slips back into barter exchange.

You might object that inflation of this sort is unrealistic, that such periods of runaway inflation are merely imaginary. Not so! A number of historical instances clearly show how inflation can destroy the economic significance of money and drive money from the scene. Consider an example from here at home: During the revolutionary period, the method of financing the war increased the money supply by prodigious amounts, and as a result, prices rose four times between 1775 and

1780. Consider now a much more drastic example: Prices in Germany rose 34 billion times between 1921 and 1923—that is, an item priced at one mark in 1921 cost 34,000,000,000 marks in 1923. Consider this final case: In Hungary after World War II, an item that cost one pengö in 1946 cost 1.4 *nonillion* pengös only one year later.[2]

These are pathological situations in which the authorities allowed the money supply to get completely out of control. While we agree that such a situation is unlikely to happen in the United States today, we should keep in mind that strong, short-run spurts in inflation (as in the late 1970s) put a lot of pressure on the ability of money to perform its functions very well. For this reason, we will devote a lot of attention later to monetary policy—that is, control of the money supply.

B. MONEY DEFINED

Now that we have seen what money does, let's find out what money is—that is, what serves as money.

It may surprise you (or maybe it doesn't) to discover that economists are far from agreeing about what money is. There is, however, a good reason for this state of confusion, and that is that today more assets than ever are highly liquid. While these "near monies" can't be used as money, they certainly influence what we do with the money that we do have. We discussed this in part in the preceding section (also see Exhibit 11–1).

Rather than review all this controversy, important as it is, we will simply rely on the generally used definition.

Definition: The *money supply* (*M*1) is made up of coins, paper currency, demand deposits at commercial banks, traveler's checks, and other checkable deposits at banks and thrift institutions.

A few points need to be made about this rather clumsy definition. First, the notation *M*1 implies that there are other definitions of the money supply, and so there are. Exhibit 11–1 reviews several alternative definitions.

Second, it is easy to see why coins and paper currency are a part of our money supply. However, we should stress that these aren't all that important in our economy. Coins and paper money are used mainly as convenience money—that is, to finance small transactions. Usually we pay for an ice-cream cone or a candy bar or notebook paper with this kind of money.

Third, what actually dominates the money supply in the United States is money in the form of checking (checkable) deposits. We usually refer to these simply

[2]These examples are from L. S. Ritter and W. L. Silber, *Money* (New York: Basic Books, 1981), pp. 69–70.

EXHIBIT 11-1
Definitions of Money Aggregates

$M1$ = Coins, paper currency, demand deposits at commercial banks, traveler's checks, and other checkable deposits at banks and thrift institutions.

$M2$ = $M1$ plus noncheckable saving and small time deposits, shares at retail money market funds, and money market deposit time accounts.

$M3$ = $M2$ plus large time deposits, shares at institutional money market funds, and large repurchase agreements.

L = $M3$ plus savings bonds, short-term Treasury securities, and commercial paper. The letter L stands for liquidity.

as *demand deposits*.[3] These are deposits that households and businesses have in commercial banks and some thrift institutions, and against which checks are written to finance transactions. It is estimated that more than 90 percent of the total dollar *value* of transactions every year are paid by check. Therefore, if we are interested in how money affects the economy, we must pay a lot of attention to this kind of money. Demand deposits make up nearly three-fourths of our money supply.

A final word about our definition. You may have noticed that nowhere have we referred to gold or silver or anything else as "backing" for our money. The reason is simple enough; there is no backing of this sort for our money. There used to be. We have had both gold and silver as backing, but that was some time ago.[4]

Today all of our money is really nothing more than debt, debt that is backed by the stability of the issuing institutions. Coins, for example, are liabilities (debt) of the U.S. Treasury, which mints all of our coins. Paper money is debt of the Federal Reserve System, which issues all of our paper money. Finally, demand deposits are liabilities and hence debt of the commercial banks and thrift institutions that hold them for their depositor customers.

Thus, all money is debt, although not all debt is money. Economists often refer to money in this form as *fiat money*. Fiat money is money because the government has stated that it is money. Therefore coins and paper money are fiat money. But are demand deposits also fiat money? Not really, but the government itself accepts checks as payments, makes payments in the form of checks, and generally

---

[3]*Demand* deposits are our checking deposits at commercial banks; *checkable* deposits are similar deposits held at such thrift institutions as credit unions and savings and loan associations. These latter institutions usually carry restrictions on the amount of checks that may be written during a given time period without penalty. However, demand deposits and checkable deposits are both "checkable," since both are used as a medium of exchange.

[4]Gold and silver as money were discussed in Chapter 3. See also the appendix to this chapter.

stands behind our banking system. If not fiat money, demand deposits are close to it.

C. THE BUSINESS OF COMMERCIAL BANKING

Commercial banks, savings and loan associations, credit unions, life insurance companies, investment banks, and pension funds—all of these financial institutions occupy a strategic place in the circular flow of economic activity. Earlier we introduced these institutions as middleman firms that stand between household savers and business firm borrowers. (You may want to refer again to Figure 5–3 and the accompanying discussion.)

Back then, however, we simplified a great deal by assuming that only households save and only businesses borrow these savings. In reality, any economic unit, be it business firm, government, foreigner, or household, may be a saver; *as long as it spends less than its income, it is a saver.* Furthermore, borrowers may be any economic unit, whether household, firm, government, or foreigner. *Any unit that spends more than its income is a borrower* (or a thief).

Using these more general concepts of savers and borrowers, we can expand our views of the role of financial institutions in the economy.

> **Conclusion:**   The economic function of financial institutions is to channel funds from business firms, households, governments, and foreigners that are currently spending less than their incomes to other business firms, households, governments, and foreigners that are currently spending more than their incomes.

Actually, the role of financial institutions is the same as that in Chapter 5; we have simply added more actors to the scene. Figure 11–1 contains a close-up of that part of the circular flow model.

Commercial banks, however, are unique and have a major role to play beyond channeling savings to borrowers. As we asserted above, they can (and do) create and destroy money. And, in recent years, savings and loan associations and credit

FIGURE 11–1   Financial Institutions and the Transfer of Savings into Investment   Financial institutions channel the leakages from the circular flow back into the circular flow as injections by moving funds from those groups that save to those that wish to borrow.

unions have been allowed to perform certain functions that were historically restricted to commercial banks. These functions mean that they too participate in the process of money creation and money destruction. For sake of simplicity, we will lump them all together under the heading of "commercial banks."

1. Demand Deposit as Asset and Liability

One of the basic functions of commercial banks is that they hold demand deposits (checkable accounts) for their customers. This is obvious; most of us have checking accounts, and we consider these to be assets. Here is an important definition.

> **Definition:** An *asset* is anything that the economic unit owns or has owed to it by any other economic unit.

Clearly, the demand deposit that you have at your bank is an asset to you. In fact, it is payable to you on demand; and the bank must honor the checks you write against it in order to purchase goods and services.

But note that what is an asset to you, in this case, is a liability to your bank. Time for another definition.

> **Definition:** A *liability* is anything owed by the economic unit to any other economic unit.

The bank holds your demand deposit, but since it must make that deposit available to you at your demand, it considers the deposit a liability. If, for example, you have a $700 checking account at your bank, that is an asset to you; but the same $700 deposit is a liability to the bank. (See Exhibit 11–2 for more discussion of the commercial bank's assets and liabilities.)

2. The Matter of Required Reserves

Since commercial banks work with other people's money, we have felt that there must be some safeguard for the depositors. In our money and banking system, that safeguard takes the form of *required reserves*. The amount of *legally* required reserves is usually stated as a percentage of demand deposit and is set by the Federal Reserve System.[5] As we shall see, the Federal Reserve can and does use the required reserve ratio as a means of controlling the money supply.

> **Definition:** *Required reserves* are the percentage of the bank's demand deposits that *must be held as reserves*. These reserves are kept on deposit in the Federal Reserve banks.

---

[5]Other safeguards are present, notably the Federal Deposit Insurance Corporation, which insures deposits up to $100,000 per depositor in a covered bank.

EXHIBIT 11–2
The Commercial Bank's Balance Sheet

A commercial bank is like any other business in that it has a balance sheet. A *balance sheet* is simply a snapshot picture of the assets and liabilities of the bank at some point in time. Actually, it is a still-life picture of the bank's financial status.

Clearly, if a bank (or, for that matter, any other business) is to be a continuing, ongoing firm, its assets had better be greater than its liabilities. If the reverse were true—if its liabilities exceeded its assets—it would be declared bankrupt.

Why is a balance sheet called a balance sheet? Simply because we term the difference between assets and liabilities *net worth*. This is also an entry on the right-hand side of the balance sheet, and it is this entry that keeps the balance sheet in balance. The accompanying table shows a greatly oversimplified balance sheet for Commercial Bank A. This bank has assets amounting to $500,000—that is, its *total worth* is $500,000. However, it has liabilities of $400,000; put otherwise, it owes $400,000 to various other parties. When we deduct what the bank owes to others ($400,000) from its total worth ($500,000) we get the bank's *net worth* ($100,000). This is the claim that the owners have against the bank's total assets.

Assets		Bank A	Liabilities + Net Worth	
			Liabilities	$400,000
Assets	$500,000		Net worth	100,000
Total	$500,000		Total	$500,000

Net worth is always a residual figure; by definition, it is always equal to total assets minus total liabilities. Thus:

$$\text{Net worth} = \text{Total assets} - \text{Total liabilities}$$

Put otherwise:

$$\text{Total assets} = \text{Total liabilities} + \text{net worth}$$

If, for example, assets rise and liabilities remain constant, net worth rises. Conversely, if assets remain constant and liabilities rise, net worth declines. (If both assets and liabilities rise or fall, what happens to net worth?)

Definition: The legally required reserve *ratio* is the percentage of demand deposits that must be held as required reserves. It is set by the Federal Reserve.

Thus, if you were to deposit, say, $1,000 in your bank and if the required reserve ratio were 20 percent, your bank would have to hold $200 at the Federal Reserve as required reserves. The law stipulates that required reserves be held at the Federal Reserve.[6]

The bank considers these required reserves an asset—they are something the bank owns. However, the Federal Reserve treats these as a liability, something they owe to the bank.

Now that we have seen what required reserves are, we must point out that there is another type of reserves—namely, *excess reserves*. When, in our example directly above, you deposited $1,000 in your bank, the bank had to put $200 in its required reserves account at the Federal Reserve. This, however, left $800, and it is this amount that we call excess reserves.

Definition: *Excess reserves* are the amount in the bank's reserves over what must be held as required reserves.

In our example, the bank added $1,000 to its reserves account, of which $200 was required and the remainder of $800 was excess. Excess reserves allow banks to make loans. Indeed, excess reserves are the lifeblood, as it were, of commercial banks, for it is by lending them out that banks receive an interest income, their major type of revenue.

3. The Depository and Lending Functions

A commercial bank earns its profits by performing two important and related functions. First, it accepts demand deposits from its customers. We will call this the *depository function*. In performing this function, the bank accepts a liability equal to the amount of the deposit. Remember, a demand deposit is a liability to the bank.

However, the bank is quite happy to accept this liability, for, by doing so, it also accepts an asset—that is, the bank increases its reserve account by the amount of the deposit. Part of this will go into required reserves, leaving the remainder as excess reserves.

Once the bank has acquired excess reserves, it can perform the *lending function*. It is by performing this function that the commercial bank makes its income and thus makes a profit, for it lends its excess reserves out at an interest rate.

---

[6]There is a minor exception to this. The bank's "vault cash"—i.e., the amount of paper money and coins that the bank keeps on hand—is counted as part of the bank's required reserves. This is, however, such a small amount that we will ignore it and stipulate that *all* required reserves must be held at the Federal Reserve.

4. A Quick Summary

Banks acquire funds in the form of deposits. These deposits are treated as liabilities by the banks. The banks set aside, as an asset, some specified amount as required reserves, leaving the remainder of the funds as excess reserves. It is these excess reserves that the banks lend out at interest. Thus, by performing the depository function, the commercial banks can follow up with the lending function.

D. MONEY CREATED; MONEY DESTROYED

We now turn to one of the most fascinating (and often misunderstood) aspects of commercial banking, the fact that the banking system can, and does, create and destroy money. It can do this because, as we have seen, commercial banks operate on the basis of fractional required reserves—that is, banks are required to hold only a fraction of their demand deposits in the form of required reserves.

1. The Model

A simple, but very useful, model will show how banks create and destroy money. This model is based on the following assumptions:

a. First, we assume that demand deposits are the only type of money used—that is, all payments, no matter how small, are made by check. The reason for this assumption is to make sure that all money ends up being deposited in some commercial bank or other. It also means that there is no hoarding.

b. The Federal Reserve has, at its own discretion, set the required reserve ratio at 10 percent. Thus banks must hold $0.10 behind every $1.00 of demand deposits.

c. We also assume that banks are always willing and able to lend out all of their excess reserves. This makes sense, for this is how the commercial banks make a profit.

d. Initially, all the banks are fully loaned up—that is, they have loaned out all of their excess reserves. No bank, therefore, is able to make any further loans.

e. Finally, we assume that the banks keep all of their *excess reserves,* if they have any, on deposit at the Federal Reserve. We know that they must keep their required reserves there; now we assume that they keep their excess reserves there too.

A final point: We will make extensive use of the balance sheet accounts discussed in Exhibit 11-2. Recall that demand deposits are liabilities, and they therefore appear on the right-hand side of the bank's balance sheet, as shown in Table 11-1. Reserves, however, are an asset, and they therefore appear on the left-hand side of the balance sheet. Note that we have broken the reserves account into its two component parts—required reserves and excess reserves.

TABLE 11-1   The Commercial Bank's Balance Sheet

Assets	Liabilities and Net Worth*
Reserves	Demand Deposits
Required	
Excess	
Loans	Net Worth*

*From now on we will omit this entry, although we know that it exists.

Note also that another account is included on the asset side—loans. This appears as an asset for good reason. If you decide to borrow, say, $8,500 from your bank in order to purchase an automobile, the bank, when it extends the loan, will have you sign a *promissory note*. This piece of paper states that you have promised to pay the bank the $8,500 plus interest by a specified time. This promissory note, therefore, is an asset to the bank, and since it represents a loan, the bank includes it in its Loans account. Surely it represents an asset to the bank (and, just as surely, it represents a liability to you).

This, then, is our basic model. The commercial banking system is all loaned up—that is, no bank has any excess reserves (and if they were to get any, they would lend them out as soon as possible). All balance sheets are in balance. In the next section, we are going to disturb this equilibrium situation and trace out what will happen to the money supply. In that analysis, we will be concerned only with measuring changes that will take place in the banks' balance sheets. Increases will be recorded with a " + " and decreases will be shown by a " − ". Keep in mind, however, that after all the +'s and −'s have been recorded, each balance sheet must remain in balance.

2. Money Creation

To get things started, suppose a miserly uncle of mine has given me $1,000 in cash as a reward for my not smoking for a full year. The first thing I do with this money is to deposit it in my bank, which we will simply call Bank A. (Note that this deposit doesn't change the money supply; it merely substitutes one form of money for another.) The bank will, as we now know, happily accept this deposit as a liability, for by doing so it acquires an asset of the same amount. The relevant entries are shown in Bank A's balance sheet in Table 11-2. These entries are labeled "depository function."

Bank A has, of course, now obtained $900 of excess reserves, and thus it is ready to perform the lending function. It can now lend out its excess reserves of $900.

A point made earlier (assumption *e* above) should be stressed here. We know that banks must keep their legally required reserves on deposit at the Federal Reserve. Our model also assumes that banks keep their excess reserves on deposit there

TABLE 11-2   Bank A's Balance Sheet

	Assets		Liabilities	
Depository Function	Reserves Required Excess	+1,000 100 900	Demand Deposits	+1,000
Lending Function	Loans	+900	Demand Deposits	+900
Clearing Function	Reserves Required Excess	−900 100 0	Demand Deposits	−900

as well. The reason for this is that economic activity is spread far and wide across the face of the country, and it is therefore quite likely that when Bank A makes a loan, and when the borrower spends it, *the money will end up in some other bank.* When this happens, Bank A owes that amount to the bank in which the money is deposited. It is for this reason that we assume that Bank A (and all other banks) keep their excess reserves on deposit at the Federal Reserve. The Federal Reserve serves as the clearinghouse for the banks in the banking system.

But this is getting ahead of ourselves. Let's see how all of this transpires as we carry the example further. Remember that Bank A's balance sheet looks like the one in the top part of Table 11-2—that is, it has performed the depository function. Both its assets and its liabilities have increased by $1,000; and in the process the bank has acquired $900 of excess reserves.

Let's suppose now that a good customer comes to the bank and asks for a loan of $900, and since he is indeed a good and regular customer, the loan officer extends the loan to him. The customer signs a promissory note, and hence the Loans account on the asset side is increased by $900. At the same time, the bank increases the customer's checking account, as shown by the increase in demand deposits of $900. After all, the customer borrowed the $900 so that he could spend it. Let's also suppose that he has had some home repairs completed and has borrowed the money to pay the contractor. All of this is described as the "lending function" in Table 11-2.

We now need to leave Bank A's balance sheet for a short while; we will return to it soon enough. Once the contractor receives the $900 check for his services rendered, he deposits it in his bank, Bank B. In terms with which we are all now familiar, Bank B performs the depository function. This is shown in Table 11-3. Once Bank B accepts the contractor's deposit, it increases both the demand deposit liability and the reserves asset by the same amount ($900).

Then Bank B will send the $900 check (written against Bank A, remember) for deposit in its reserves account at the Federal Reserve. Part of it ($90) must be held as required reserves; the remainder ($810) is excess reserves. The Federal Reserve will now increase Bank B's reserves account by the amount of the check ($900) and

TABLE 11-3 Bank B's Balance Sheet

	Assets		Liabilities	
Depository Function	Reserves Required Excess	+900 90 810	Demand Deposits	+900
Lending Function	Loans	+810	Demand Deposits	+810
Clearing Function	Reserves Required Excess	−810 90 0	Demand Deposits	−810

will, at the same time, reduce Bank A's reserves by $900. As far as the Federal Reserve is concerned, Bank A owes Bank B $900, and it accordingly transfers the $900 from A's account to B's account.

The Federal Reserve then cancels the check and sends it back to Bank A, which now knows that two things have occurred: (a) demand deposits have been reduced by $900, and (b) it has lost $900 of reserves to some other bank. Accordingly, it reduces the borrower's demand deposit by $900 (and sends the canceled check to him), and it also reduces its reserves account at the Federal Reserve by $900. All of this is described as the "clearing function" back in Table 11-2.

We now come to four important conclusions. First, note that (in Table 11-2) Bank A's balance sheet is still in balance: That is, all the +'s and −'s cancel out on each side so that balance persists. Second, Bank A now has only $100 in reserves, which is all right because that $100 is 10 percent of the additional demand deposit of $1,000. The bank is therefore meeting the 10 percent legal reserve requirement. Third, observe that the composition of the asset side of the bank's balance sheet has been altered, and the reason for this is that the bank has exchanged its $900 of excess reserves for a $900 interest-bearing asset. At the same time, however, and this is our fourth conclusion, Bank A has generated a $900 increase in the money supply—that is, it created a brand new $900 demand deposit for its borrowing customer. Although this $900 ended up in some other bank (Bank B, in our case), it was in the form of a new $900 demand deposit. Here we arrive at another important conclusion.

> **Conclusion:** Whenever a commercial bank lends out its excess reserves, these reserves take the form of new money in the economy. The excess reserves have become monetized, turned into money via the lending function.

The process, however, doesn't stop here, for now that Bank B has performed the depository function, it is in a position to carry out the lending function. This is shown in Table 11-3. In this case, the bank has excess reserves of $810 ($90 having gone into required reserves). By our assumption, Bank B will lend out its excess reserves of $810, and in doing so, it creates a new demand deposit and acquires a new asset, both equal to $810. This is shown as the "lending function" in Table 11–3.

In this case, we will assume that the owner of an ice-cream shop needs to borrow the $810 in order to acquire some new inventory. Since the $810 will end up in some other bank, say, Bank C (Table 11–4), when the shopowner pays the dairy for her purchases, the check must once again be cleared. This clearing function is shown by the bottom entries in Table 11–3. Recall that when a check is cleared, the Federal Reserve will transfer reserves from the bank against which the check is written over to the bank accepting the deposit. Thus $810 is transferred from B's reserves over to C's reserves; the check is then canceled and sent back to Bank B. Bank B will thus reduce both its demand deposits and its reserves by $810.

Again, note that the bank's balance sheet remains in balance. Also Bank B has acquired an interest-bearing asset (Loans) by having lent out its excess reserves. The bank is still meeting the legal reserve requirement, for it has $90 in its reserves behind the new demand deposit of $900. Finally, and quite important, the money supply has been increased again, this time by $810 (i.e., the amount of excess reserves created by the deposit of $900 in Bank B).

So far, then, Bank A has increased the money supply by $900 and Bank B by $810; and now the ball is in Bank C's court, for it has received the new deposit of $810. Table 11–4 shows that it has performed the depository function and is now able to lend out $729 (its excess reserves) to some of its customers. When it does, it too increases the money supply further, this time by $729. Suppose the loan is made, and a check for $729 is written and deposited in Bank D. In short, Bank C has performed both the depository and lending functions, and when the check is deposited in Bank D, the clearing function will be performed; the Federal Reserve will see to that.

Although Bank C is now all loaned up—i.e., has no excess reserves—Bank D is capable of increasing the money supply by $656. The process can, and under our

TABLE 11-4   Bank C's Balance Sheet

	Assets		Liabilities	
Depository Function	Reserves Required Excess	+800 81 729	Demand Deposits	+810
Lending Function	Loans	+729	Demand Deposits	+729
Clearing Function	Reserves Required Excess	−729 81 0	Demand Deposits	−729

assumptions will, continue through Banks E, F, G, and so on. The amount each bank can lend out, however, gets smaller and smaller. So far, we have the following:

A creates $900.

B creates $810.

C creates $729.

D creates $656.

Note that each increase is 90 percent of the preceding increase. The reason for this is that each time a bank accepts a new demand deposit, it must hold out 10 percent (in our example) in the form of required reserves. Thus, once Bank E has acquired the new deposit of $656, the amount of money created by Bank D, it can lend out 90 percent of $656, or $590. Bank F, then, can lend out 90 percent of the $590; and so on and on, from bank to bank.

3. The Money Multiplier

The process described above is the *multiple expansion of the money supply*. Clearly, the money supply is expanded by some multiple amount. We started out with a $1,000 deposit of cash and traced the process through just the first four banks. These loans can create new money in the amount of $3,095, and there is still more to come.

It should be clear by now that the amount of demand deposits that the banking system can create depends on two things: first, the original dollar amount of excess reserves; second, the legal reserve requirement. In our example, I deposited $1,000 of cash, and given the legal reserve requirement of 10 percent, this means that Bank A acquired $1,000 of new reserves, $900 of which is excess reserves. Note: These reserves didn't exist prior to the deposit of cash; they are brand new in the banking system.

Now, given the fact that there is $900 of new excess reserves, the question

TABLE 11-5   Bank D's Balance Sheet

	Assets		Liabilities	
Depository Function	Reserves Required Excess	+729 73 656	Demand Deposits	+729
Lending Function	Loans	+656	Demand Deposits	+656
Clearing Function	Reserves Required Excess	−656 73 0	Demand Deposits	−656

arises, How much new money can be created? Remember, the legal reserve requirement has been assumed to be 10 percent. Thus the $900 of excess reserves is 10 percent of $9,000, and that is by how much the money supply can be expanded. In the process, the $900 of excess reserves becomes required reserves. This whole process is summarized in Table 11–6.

All of this can be summarized in a different way. The following formula tells us by how much the money supply can be increased when I deposit my $1,000 of cash in Bank A and when the legal reserve requirement is 10 percent:

$$\Delta DD = \Delta XR \cdot \frac{1}{RRR}$$

Here $\triangle$, as usual, stands for "change in" and DD stands for demand deposits. Also, $\triangle XR$ is the original change in excess reserves, and RRR is the required reserve ratio. Since we have assumed that $RRR = 10$ percent, then my cash deposit of $1,000 means that $XR = $900. So:

$$\Delta DD = \Delta XR \cdot \frac{1}{RRR}$$

$$= \$900 \cdot \frac{1}{.10}$$

$$= \$900 \cdot 10$$

$$= \$9,000$$

TABLE 11-6 Deposit Multiplier

Bank	Change in Deposits	Required Reserves	New Loans
A	$ 1,000*	$100	$900
B	900	90	810
C	810	81	729
D	729	72.90	656.10
E	656.10	65.61	590.49
F	590.49	59.05	531.44
G	531.44	53.14	478.30
H	478.30	47.83	430.47
I–N th Bank	4,304.67	430.47	3,874.20
Total	$10,000	$1,000	9,000

*This particular change in deposits is due to the original deposit of cash; it, and of itself, does not constitute a change in the money supply.

Note, however, how the results will differ if the required reserve ratio is different. If, for example, the required reserve ratio is 20 percent, then

$$\Delta DD = \Delta XR \cdot \frac{1}{RRR}$$

$$= \$800 \cdot \frac{1}{.20}$$

$$= \$800 \cdot 5$$

$$= \$4,000$$

In this case, since $RRR = 20$ percent, my \$1,000 cash deposit means that only \$800 of new excess reserves is created. Since $RRR = 20$ percent, then \$200 of the \$1,000 must be held as required reserves.

Let's look at a final example and then draw an important conclusion. Suppose the required reserve ratio is 25 percent. If so, then by how much can M1 increase when I deposit my \$1,000 cash? In this case, the required reserves will be \$250, and thus the excess reserves will be \$750. So:

$$\Delta DD = \Delta XR \cdot \frac{1}{RRR}$$

$$= \$750 \cdot \frac{1}{.25}$$

$$= \$750 \cdot 4$$

$$= \$3,000$$

Our important conclusion is drawn from the preceding examples.

Conclusion: The higher the legal reserve requirement, the lower the multiple expansion of the money supply. The converse is also true: The lower the required reserve ratio, the greater the multiple expansion of M1.

The next chapter shows how important this conclusion actually is.

4. Some Qualifications

The model we introduced above has proved very useful in explaining how the commercial banking system creates multiple expansion of the money supply. We also saw that changes in the legally required reserve ratio affects this ability of the banking system because it determines the amount of excess reserves that can be lent out. Indeed, we can restate the important conclusion above as follows:

Conclusion: Anything that affects the amount of excess reserves held by banks also directly affects the money-creating ability of the banks.

Here we want to qualify our model, useful as it has been, to take into account two things that influence the amount of excess reserves.

First, households and businesses obviously do not make all payments by check. To the contrary, they also use coins and currency for most of their minor purchases. Thus we want to modify assumption *a,* above and take this fact into account. In actuality, experience has taught bankers that the public desires to hold a certain fraction of its money in the form of cash, the rest going into demand deposits. Suppose, for purposes of illustration, that the public wants to hold 25 percent of income as cash. This means that whenever a household or business gets some extra money, it will deposit only 75 percent of it, keeping the rest as cash. Note what this does to the banks' ability to create new money. In our original example, when I made my deposit, I put the entire $1,000 in my checking account. Now, however, I hold out $250 in cash and deposit the remaining $750. This means that Bank A has new excess reserves of only $675 (i.e., $750 − $75 = $675). Thus it can create only $675 of new money. Moreover, when someone gets this $675, he holds back $169 as cash, depositing in Bank B the remaining $506. This in turn gives Bank B only $455 of excess reserves that it can monetize. Clearly, as the public holds out some of the newly created money as cash, the banking system's ability to create new money is restricted. The multiple expansion is less than what we saw above. The banks must always hold 25 percent of their reserves over the legal required limit to meet these cash demands.

Second, commercial banks often desire to hold reserves over what is legally required. There are many reasons for doing so, and usually the percentage of reserves held for these reasons amounts to about 2 percent or less.[7] This too has the effect of reducing the commercial banks' ability to increase the money supply.

So far we have two reasons why the excess reserves of banks are lower than our simple model allowed—the desire of the public to hold part of its income as cash, and the desire of banks to hold reserves above the required level. And, as we saw above, anything that reduces the amount of excess reserves of the banks (and these two do), the money-creating ability of the banking system is restricted. The formula we used earlier, therefore, should be rewritten as

$$\Delta DD = \Delta XR \cdot \cfrac{1}{\underset{\substack{\text{reserve} \\ \text{required}}}{RRR + \text{Cash}} + \underset{\substack{\text{extra} \\ \text{reserves}}}{\text{Desired}}}$$

[7]The actual percentage held will vary for a number of reasons, usually being higher at the first of the month or week (whatever the pay period may be). It is also higher during the Christmas season. Our 25 percent figure is thus a simplification.

If *RRR* is 10 percent, the cash reserve requirement is 25 percent, and the desired extra reserves are 2 percent, then we must rewrite our formula as

$$\Delta DD = \Delta XR \cdot \frac{1}{.10 + .25 + .02}$$

$$= \Delta XR \cdot \frac{1}{.37}$$

$$= \Delta XR \cdot 2.7$$

My deposit of $1,000 thus allows the money supply to rise by only $1,782, not the $9,000 we had in our first example. This modified formula is much more realistic.

5. Money Destruction and the FDIC

A final point for this chapter. Just as there can be multiple expansions of the money supply, so can there be multiple contractions. In the event of a multiple contraction, demand deposits are reduced simply by loans being paid off and not replaced by new loans. For instance, if you pay back a loan you have made at your bank, you do so by writing a check against your demand deposit. That portion of your demand deposit has therefore disappeared, and if the bank makes no new loan to replace it, the money supply falls. If this happens on a wide scale, there can be a multiple contraction of the money supply.

More important, a multiple contraction may occur if there is a general "run" on the banks by depositors who want their money in the form of cash instead of demand deposits. In this event, the banks won't have enough cash to satisfy their customers. To obtain more cash, they won't grant new loans as old ones are paid off. The result could well be a multiple contraction, such as the one we had during the early 1930s.

The monetary and economic catastrophe of the 1930s led to some major changes in our monetary and banking system. One of the most significant of these was the establishment of the Federal Deposit Insurance Corporation in 1933. The FDIC insures customer deposits up to $100,000 in insured banks, thereby eliminating in large part the threat of a general run on the banks. Indeed, this turns out to be the main objective of the FDIC, although two other objectives are also important:

a. To protect depositors, especially small ones, against loss in the event of bank failure.

b. To provide better supervision of banks that have joined the FDIC. (Nearly all commercial banks are members.)

An outstanding feature of the operation of the FDIC is that when a bank is near failure, the corporation will strive to merge that bank with some successful bank. In this way, as many depositors as possible are protected. However, in cases where insolvency is unavoidable, the FDIC will liquidate the bank.

Has the FDIC been successful? It appears to have been, although the challenges it faces in the 1990s may raise some doubt.

E. SUMMARY

Money, to do its job, must perform three basic functions. It must serve as a unit of account or basic unit of economic measurement; it must be a medium of exchange; and it must be a store of value. The cost of holding money as a store of value is the next-best rate of return that could be earned if it were invested in another asset. Inflation, caused by an excessive amount of money in circulation, imposes a tax on those who hold money.

For purposes of analysis, we define the money supply (M1) as being composed of coins, paper currency, demand deposits at commercial banks, traveler's checks, and other checkable deposits at banks and thrift institutions. Most of the dollar volume of transactions in our society are paid for by check.

The major economic function of financial institutions is to channel funds from business firms, households, governments, and foreigners that currently spend less than their incomes to other firms, households, governments, and foreigners that currently spend more than their incomes.

Commercial banks are strategic financial institutions because they can "create" money as loans are being made. Banks acquire funds in the form of deposits. Some fraction of these deposits is set aside as reserves. The remainder or excess reserves can then be lent out at interest. These loans of excess reserves take the form of new money in circulation.

As the banking system lends its excess reserves, a process of multiple expansion of deposits takes place. This multiple expansion of deposit money depends on the legal reserve requirement imposed by the monetary authorities. The higher the legal reserve requirement, the lower the money multiplier of the banking system, and vice versa.

The money supply is expanded as the banking system makes new loans, and it contracts as old loans are being paid off. The amount by which the banking system can change the volume of deposit money in circulation depends on the legal reserve requirement and the dollar amount of excess reserves.

Terms and Concepts to Remember

Medium of exchange	Demand deposits
Unit of account	Required reserves
Store of value	Excess reserves
Liquidity	Money multiplier
M1, M2	FDIC
Fiat money	Checkable deposits

Questions for Review

1. What does it mean when we say that money is a store of value? What factors are important in determining the amount of money held as a store of value?

2. Differentiate between the definitions of money—*M*1, *M*2, and *M*3.

3. When a commercial bank makes a loan, how is the bank's balance sheet affected?

4. Based on a reserve requirement of 20 percent, and on injection of $5,000 in excess reserves, explain the process by which and the amount by which the banking system can expand the money supply.

5. What is the money multiplier, and what three things determine its size?

6. What role does the FDIC play in our banking system?

Appendix: The Historical Role of Gold in the Monetary System

An aura of mysticism has persistently surrounded the relationship of gold to money. For many years, people insisted that gold "back" our money 100 percent; in fact, they insisted that gold circulate as money in the form of full-bodied coins. Today, however, gold no longer serves any domestic monetary function: The last tenuous link between gold and our domestic money supply was severed in March 1968. Yet some people continue to believe that our money must have at least some gold backing; otherwise, so the argument goes, the public will lose confidence in the dollar. Thus the mystique of gold continues, although its importance is rapidly dwindling.

This appendix presents a brief historical account of the role of gold in our monetary system. The major conclusion is that the complete abandonment of gold backing of our domestic money supply in 1968 didn't cause a significant loss of confidence in our monetary system. Since 1968, the role of gold in international monetary affairs has evolved into a somewhat ambiguous state.

A. THE "PURE" GOLD STANDARD

About sixty years ago, gold coins circulated freely as money in this country (along with paper money that was convertible into gold coins or bullion on a dollar-for-dollar basis). At that time, we were on the "pure" gold standard and had been since the Gold Standard Act of 1900. This meant that every dollar in circulation had a gold reserve behind it. Of course, a "dollar's worth" of gold was defined arbitrarily by 1900 federal legislation as 13.71 grains of pure gold. Thus a $20 gold piece had 274.20 grains of pure gold in it, just as a $20 paper bill had 274.20 grains of pure gold behind it. Under the pure gold standard, the possessor of $20 of money could demand, and receive, 274.20 grains of pure gold from the U.S. Treasury. Furthermore, he could sell the 274.20 grains of gold to the Treasury for $20. Gold coins, gold bullion, and paper money, in other words, were freely convertible.

Presumably people felt safe with this monetary arrangement, although the pure gold standard didn't always function very well. It was modified in 1914, abandoned in 1917, reinstated in 1919, and supplemented by discretionary Federal Reserve action in the 1921–24 period. Clearly, there was nothing sacrosanct or immutable about this particular monetary standard. And yet the mystique about gold and its relationship to money was perpetuated by both the public and governmental officials. Now, however, we can clear the air and see exactly what the monetary significance of gold is.

1. The Monetary Characteristics of Gold

The discussion in Chapter 3 of various types of money points out that virtually anything can serve as money. In fact, some rather strange (to us) commodities (wampum, oxen, tobacco, stones) have served, and still do serve, as money. Historically, however, gold has dominated all other commodities in this respect, primarily because it has certain characteristics that other goods do not have. It is durable, fairly easily transportable, and divisible into monetary units of different denominations. Moreover, gold has generally been revered in many societies because of its nonmonetary uses, such as jewelry. Because of the general demand for gold, it became the generally accepted medium of exchange in international transactions. Consequently, gold flowed between countries as payment for goods and services. In fact, this was the main reason why we used gold as money: It facilitated the international exchange process.

Finally, and very important, gold is limited in supply. Even today, after centuries of search for the yellow stuff, there are only slightly more than forty thousand tons in stock. The limited supply of the gold stock is important in that it puts some upper limit on how much the money supply of a country may expand, thus imposing an effective constraint on inflation (at least, so the theory of the pure gold standard concludes). For example, if prices in the United States were to rise relative to prices in other countries also on the gold standard, the following would occur: (1) foreigners would reduce their demand for American goods, and thus the inflow of gold from abroad would diminish; (2) Americans would presumably reduce their demand for the relatively higher priced domestic goods and increase their demand for the relatively lower priced foreign-made goods, thus causing gold to flow out of the country.[8] These results would reduce both the money supply and the aggregate de-

---

[8]This argument, of course, assumes that there are no artificial barriers to the flow of goods among countries. It also assumes that the economic systems engaged in trade are very competitive, so that prices move easily and quickly in response to changes in demand.

mand here at home and would therefore cause the price level to fall. Voilà! Inflation is automatically "cured." (Can you complete the analysis of the reverse case—how unemployment and deflation here at home could be "cured" under the pure gold standard?)

2. The Breakdown of the Pure Gold Standard

A certain aesthetic quality about the pure gold standard has appealed to many people. There is also the attraction that it (theoretically, at least) minimizes economic instability with a minimum of government intervention. As indicated above, under the pure gold standard an inflationary situation automatically corrects itself because the inflation causes money to leave the country. Thus government (or the Fed) doesn't have to intervene in the economy in order to control inflation, nor does it have to intervene to correct a contraction.

However, the pure gold standard encountered some very rough going in the early 1930s. The Depression resulted in a tremendous net outflow of gold, and since gold was money, this meant that the money supply was reduced at a time when the economy desperately needed an expanding stock of money (or at least a stable one). Congress and the president reacted to this adverse situation by passing the Gold Reserve Act of 1934, which took us off the pure gold standard and replaced it with a modified gold standard. Under the new monetary arrangement, gold continued to play a role, albeit a more limited one than before, in our domestic monetary affairs. The dollar was still defined in terms of gold, but gold was no longer allowed to circulate as money.[9] In other words, the new gold standard placed discretionary control of the money supply in the hands of the Federal Reserve so that the monetary authorities could use monetary policy as an anticontractionary weapon. This was precisely the major purpose of the act: to divorce the money supply from changes in the amount of gold in the country, and to vest control of it in the hands of a centralized control agency.

3. Partial Backing: Gold Certificates

However, Congress was reluctant to drop the gold backing completely, so the Gold Reserve Act stipulated that the Federal Reserve must hold 40 percent required reserves behind its outstanding Federal Reserve notes and 35 percent behind member bank reserve deposits. Moreover, these required reserves had to be held in the form of gold certificates. Finally, the new law allowed the Treasury to sell gold to any buyer, foreign or otherwise, at the same price. Until 1968, the Treasury followed the intent of the act and stood ready to buy and sell at $35 an ounce.

B. GOLD SINCE THE 1960s

Despite the fact that there was only partial backing for gold (in the form of gold certificates that couldn't be used as money), and despite the fact that the Reserve

---

[9]It was still being used in international transactions. It was also being used for private business purposes—for example, by jewelry manufacturers and dentists.

Act of 1934 made it illegal to use gold as money, we still persisted with the idea of gold backing of our money—at least until the 1960s. During that decade, however, problems began to develop. When the sixties opened, we had $18 billion in gold and $50 billion in Federal Reserve notes and reserve deposits. Thus the 25 percent required reserve ratio was easily met, leaving the Fed with a substantial amount of excess reserves in its gold certificates account. But then large deficits in the basic international accounts created a net gold outflow, so that by 1963 our gold stock was reduced to $16 billion while Federal Reserve notes and reserve deposits had increased to $55 billion. Gold was only 29 percent of notes and reserve deposits. We were clearly approaching the limit imposed by the required reserve ratio. Our gold backing was being stretched to the hilt. Something obviously had to be done.

Something was done. In 1965, Congress very quietly removed the reserve requirements behind reserve deposits, thereby leaving gold backing behind only Federal Reserve notes. This freed enough gold so that we again had excess reserves. However, things continued to get worse. Gold still flowed out of the country while the amount of Federal Reserve notes continued to increase. By the end of 1967, our gold stock had declined to $12 billion, and our Federal Reserve notes outstanding had increased to $42 billion. The problem of inadequate gold reserves had to be faced once again.

Congress faced the issue, and in March 1968 it eliminated the required reserve behind Federal Reserve notes. The action aroused very little public interest; in fact, it was barely noticed in the news that we had finally divorced our monetary system from gold. At present, there is no gold backing of our money.

Although the link between the money supply and gold was severed in 1968, it continued to play an international role for several years. Annual large trade deficits increased the amount of dollars held by foreign central banks. These dollar balances built up until early 1971 when an international flight from the dollar took place. Foreign central banks redeemed their dollar balances into U.S. gold, and the gold outflow became a flood. In response, President Nixon in August of that year announced that the United States would no longer redeem dollars with gold. With that action began a series of events that led in 1973 to a collapse of the post–World War II international monetary system known as Bretton Woods. The essentially fixed exchange rate system of Bretton Woods gave way to the type of fluctuating exchange rate system we have today.

Under the present international monetary system, gold no longer serves much of a role as an international reserve asset or medium of exchange. The U.S. gold stock has remained roughly the same since that time, with its value fluctuating widely with the world market price of the metal.

What does the future hold? Volatile exchange rates of recent years have led many to propose a return to some type of fixed exchange rate system like Bretton Woods. If such occurs, perhaps gold will once again play the role of an international medium of exchange. Almost certainly, however, it will never again be linked to the domestic money supply.

12

The Federal Reserve and Monetary Control

chapter preview

• The Federal Reserve, our central bank, is the source of monetary policy.

• The policy of the Federal Reserve is carried out by the Board of Governors located in Washington, D.C.

• The two main functions of the Federal Reserve are to control the money supply and interest rates, and to provide aid to banks in financial distress.

• The Federal Reserve also clears and collects checks, transfers funds, supervises banks, and acts as a fiscal agent for the U.S. Treasurer.

• The Federal Reserve carries out monetary policy by indirectly manipulating the money supply.

• The Federal Reserve exercises its control over the money supply through three tools—legal reserve requirements, the discount rate, and open-market operations.

• The legal reserve requirement is the percentage of deposits that banks must hold at the Federal Reserve. A change in the legal reserve ratio changes the money multiplier.

• The discount rate is the rate the Federal Reserve system charges banks when they borrow money in order to augment reserves or to cover their losses.

• The most powerful of the three is open-market operations, which are purchases or sales of U.S. government securities by the Federal Reserve in the open market.

• An open-market sale by the Federal Reserve drains bank reserves and eventually reduces the money supply.

• An open-market purchase by the Federal Reserve increases bank reserves and eventually increases the money supply.

• Open-market purchases also lower interest rates, while open-market sales push interest rates up.

• Changes in the interest rate affect general output and employment through changes in investment spending.

Monetary panics racked the American economy throughout the nineteenth century in a more or less recurring pattern. There were crises in 1819, 1837, 1873, 1884, and 1893, and this instability continued into the twentieth century with the panic of 1907. The money supply seemed to have been on a roller coaster, racing uphill, then down, creating all sorts of economic discomfort and uncertainty. There was finally a response to all of this when, in 1913, Congress passed the Federal Reserve Act, and President Wilson signed it into law during the waning days of the year.[1]

The Federal Reserve System is the central bank of the United States. All industrially advanced nations have a central bank, although the Federal Reserve is somewhat different from the others. There are, for example, the Bank of France, the Deutsche Bundesbank of Germany, the Netherlands Bank, and the bank of England.

> **Definition:** A *central bank* is a financial institution that has control over the size of the money supply of the economy. It is usually directly responsible to the nation's government, although in some countries it is somewhat independent of the government.

The notion of centralized control over the money supply is quite in keeping with the whole idea of money. Remember, money is an artificial institution. In fact, it has been ranked by some serious thinkers along with fire, the wheel, and the printing press as one of the human race's greatest achievements. There is therefore nothing sacrosanct or untouchable about money itself; it is simply a device that human beings have developed to aid in and facilitate the economic process. As long as there is exchange, there will likely be money in some form or other.

All central banks perform essentially the same functions, although here we are concerned only with the Federal Reserve. Section A of this chapter examines the rather unique structure of our central bank. Section B explains the basic functions and services performed by the Federal Reserve. Section C finally gets to the heart of the chapter; it concentrates on how the Federal Reserve controls the money supply and the rate of interest.

---

[1]This is one of the few pieces of legislation that both houses of Congress passed with only one dissenting vote. For a very readable history of money and of the Federal Reserve System, see J. K. Galbraith, *Money: Whence It Came, Where It Went* (Boston: Houghton Mifflin, 1973). Also available as a Bantam paperback.

A. THE STRUCTURE OF THE FEDERAL RESERVE

At its very inception, the Federal Reserve was the outcome of a series of compromises among various interest groups—agriculture, the states, business, the federal government, and banking itself. Each of these groups was fearful that one or more of the others would gain control of the Fed and thus be able to exert tremendous control over the economy (in its own interests, of course).

The result of this was that the Federal Reserve Act divided the country into twelve districts, each with its own Federal Reserve Bank (an anachronism that still persists today—see Figure 12-1). This geographical dispersion was intended to prevent any particular geographic, economic, or financial body from dominating the central bank.

The same reasoning underlies the peculiar ownership arrangement of the Federal Reserve banks. The act requires that all commercial banks that receive their corporate charters from the national government be members of the Federal Reserve System. But those banks that receive their charters from state governments may opt to be member banks. Most, in fact, decide not to, but this has little or no impact on monetary policy (see Exhibit 12-1).

Yet, control of the Fed is not lodged in the stockholding member banks. Instead it resides with the seven-member Board of Governors, and each member of the Board is appointed by the president, with the advice and consent of the Senate. Moreover, each member serves a term of fourteen years, thus (presumably) relieving him or her of the political pressures that usually accompany changes in administration every four years. The Chairman of the Board is named by the president, again with the advice and consent of the Senate.

To sum up, although the member banks own the Federal Reserve banks, the Board of Governors leads a life quite independent of the pressures and demands of

---

EXHIBIT 12-1
Extension of Federal Reserve Control

In recent years, there have been many important changes in banking and financial institutions and also in their relationship to the Federal Reserve. The Depository Institutions Deregulation and Monetary Act of 1980 has, among many other things, extended Federal Reserve monetary control over all commercial banks and several types of nonbank financial institutions.

Specifically, all commercial banks, whether members of the Federal Reserve or not, plus all savings and loan associations, credit unions, and mutual savings banks that accept checkable accounts, are bound by the legal reserve requirements set by the Fed. Thus the monetary authorities are able to control the limits of loan and deposit expansion of the entire financial system.

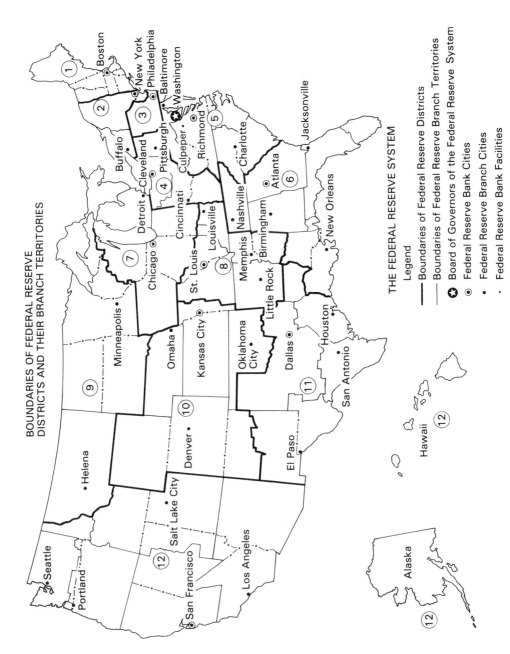

BOUNDARIES OF FEDERAL RESERVE
DISTRICTS AND THEIR BRANCH TERRITORIES

THE FEDERAL RESERVE SYSTEM

Legend

— Boundaries of Federal Reserve Districts
— Boundaries of Federal Reserve Branch Territories
✪ Board of Governors of the Federal Reserve System
⊙ Federal Reserve Bank Cities
• Federal Reserve Branch Cities
· Federal Reserve Bank Facilities

FIGURE 12-1 The Federal Reserve System

the owners. At the same time, the length of the staggered terms of the Board members makes the Board of Governors more or less independent of the government. Thus the Federal Reserve is a unique organization—it is, at one and the same time, private and public. But its actions are always oriented toward the public welfare, not for the benefit of its owners or the administration. Its basic charge is to contribute to the stability and growth of the economy.

B. FUNCTIONS AND SERVICES OF THE FEDERAL RESERVE

The two foremost functions of the Federal Reserve—(a) controlling the money supply and the interest rate and (b) providing aid to banks in periods of general financial distress—are considered at length in the next section of this chapter. They deserve special emphasis and examination.

However, a number of other functions also deserve attention. These are the more or less routine services provided by the Federal Reserve. They make up the lion's share of the physical work done by the Fed and are vitally important to the smooth operations of the commercial banking system. They include the clearing and collection of checks, the wire transfer of funds, the supervision of member banks, and acting as the fiscal agent for the U.S. Treasury.

1. Clearing and Collection of checks

Because of the overwhelming importance and widespread use of demand deposits as a medium of exchange, an enormous volume of checks must be cleared every day. The Federal Reserve plays a crucial role here. During a typical year, several trillions of dollars worth of checks are cleared through the Fed. The last chapter showed how the clearing function is performed, and although some checks are cleared without the Federal Reserve, this service nonetheless reduces uncertainties and delays in economic transactions.

2. Transfer of Funds

Another service of the Federal Reserve is that it provides for a quick transfer of funds by wire. An example will show how this service works. Suppose I am in Chicago and I need $50,000 from you *now* to carry out a fast land deal. But you are in Houston! After a telephone conversation between us, you go to your bank and present a $50,000 check written on your account. Your bank then telegraphs the Dallas Federal Reserve Bank to transfer $50,000 to the Chicago Federal Reserve Bank. The Dallas Federal Reserve Bank does this: It deducts $50,000 from your bank's reserve deposit, and it instructs the Chicago Federal Reserve Bank to add $50,000 to my bank's reserve deposit. The Chicago Federal Reserve Bank then wires my bank, telling it to add $50,000 to my checking account. All of this can take place in a matter of minutes, and thus it is very helpful in speeding up money transactions over great distances.

3. Bank Supervision

The Federal Reserve System is also empowered to examine and supervise the books of the commercial banks that are "member banks." The reason for this is to protect depositors from shoddy or dishonest management and thus to keep the monetary system as "healthy" as possible. Each Federal Reserve Bank has a staff of bank examiners; also, the member banks must present periodic reports to the Federal Reserve.

4. Fiscal Agent

The Federal Reserve serves as the fiscal agent for the U.S. Treasury, and, at the same time, it performs a number of important services for the U.S. government. For example, it holds deposits for the Treasury, and it clears all the checks written against these accounts. The Federal Reserve also handles most of the mechanical details involved when the Treasury sells government securities, just as it handles all the details when government securities are redeemed. Finally, the Federal Reserve acts as agent of the Treasury in all foreign exchange transactions.

C. MONETARY CONTROL

Although the Board of Governors has many different tasks, by far the most important is deciding on and carrying out monetary policy.

> **Definition:** *Monetary policy* involves deliberate control of the money supply and the rate of interest for the purpose of keeping actual GNP on a noninflationary track at potential GNP.

The Federal Reserve has three tools that it uses to carry out its monetary policy:

a. *Changes in the legal reserve requirement*—that is, the percentage of demand deposits that must kept on deposit as required reserves.[2] These changes are

---

[2]There are legal restrictions to which the Board of Governors is subject in setting the required reserve ratio. These are 3 percent on all net transaction (checking) accounts of $30 million or less; 12 percent on net transactions accounts over $30 million, with the limits set at 8 percent minimum and 14 percent maximum. An added 4 percent will be required on accounts over $30 million by the Fed in emergencies. Personal savings as annual time deposits have no reserve requirements, while short-term business or corporate time deposits have a 3 percent reserve requirement and a legal maximum of 9 percent. Long-term time deposits by business have no reserve requirement, although the Fed has legal authority to set them at 9 percent.

determined by the Board of Governors, and they directly affect both the amount of excess reserves held by banks and the deposit, or money, multipliers.

b. *Changes in the discount rate*—the discount rate is the interest rate at which the Federal Reserve lends reserves to member banks. Although each district can set its own discount rate, the Board of Governors must grant its approval. In effect, therefore, the Board controls the rate.

c. *Open-market operations*—these are the most powerful tool of the Federal Reserve. They are really nothing more than the purchase and/or sale of outstanding U.S. government securities for its own account. Actually, the open-market operations are performed by the Federal Open Market Committee (FOMC). This committee has twelve members: the seven members of the Board of Governors plus five of the presidents of the Federal Reserve banks.[3] As we shall see, open-market operations are a formidable weapon.

Let's look at these policy tools in more detail, beginning with changes in the legal reserve requirement. In the following discussion, however, it is important to keep this point in mind: The Federal Reserve doesn't actually control demand deposits directly. It cannot push a button or wave a wand and cause the money supply or the interest rate to increase or decrease as it would like. Instead it controls the process of deposit creation by banks, and it does this by manipulating the amount of excess reserves in the banking system. It may also, at times, control the deposit multiplier.

Put otherwise, Federal Reserve monetary policy controls money supply (ΔM) by affecting the amount of excess reserves in the banking system (ΔXR) and/or the deposit multiplier ($1/RRR$). In our formula:

$$\Delta M1 = \Delta XR \cdot 1/RRR$$

Also, by controlling excess reserves in the banking system, it exerts an indirect influence on the rate of interest. All things equal, an increase in the amount of reserves will cause the interest rate to fall, while a decrease in reserves will cause the interest rate to rise. Thus the Federal Reserve affects both money supply and the interest rate as it exercises its control over the amount of reserves in the banking system.

Let's now look at each of the three monetary weapons in more detail.

1. Changes in the Reserve Requirement

Changes in the legally required reserve ratio can be a potent method of monetary control. The following example shows how. Suppose the legal reserve requirement is at present 10 percent and that commercial banks also have reserves of $20 billion, loans of $180 billion, and demand deposits of $200 billion. The banks, in other

---

[3]The Reserve Bank presidents rotate these positions, with the exception of the New York Federal Reserve president, who has a permanent position on the FOMC.

words, are all loaned up and have no excess reserves. The balance sheet of the banking system is shown in Table 12–1(A).

In this condition, there can be no further increase in the money supply. Yet, what if the Board of Governors decided that there was need for some expansion of the amount of money in the economy? The Board might also feel that the rate of interest should be reduced in order to stimulate more investment spending by business. In short, they have decided that the general level of economic activity should rise, generating more output and jobs.

One way to help bring about expansion is for the Board to lower the required reserve ratio, and we assume that they do so by cutting the required reserve ratio from 10 percent to 5 percent. What this does is to reduce the amount that banks must hold as required reserves behind the original $200 billion of demand deposits from $20 billion to $10 billion. This action, therefore, frees up $10 billion of excess reserves, as shown in Table 12–1(B).

Now that the commercial banks have $10 billion of new excess reserves, two things can happen. First, the rate of interest will be reduced. This result is shown in Figure 12–2. The demand curve for loans is shown as the downward-sloping *D* curve

TABLE 12-1

(A)

Assets		Liabilities	
Reserves	$20b	Demand deposits	$200b
{required	$20b		
excess	0}		
Loans	$180b		

(B)

Assets		Liabilities	
Reserves	$20b	Demand deposits	$200b
{required	$10b		
excess	$10b}		
Loans	$180b		

(C)

Assets		Liabilities	
Reserves	$20b	Demand deposits	$400b
{required	$20b		
excess	0}		
Loans	$380b		

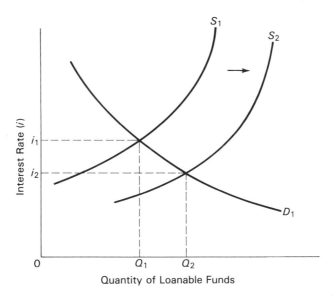

FIGURE 12-2   The Supply of and Demand for Loanable Funds   The lowering of reserve requirements creates excess reserves for the banking system, which increases the supply of loanable funds and lowers interest rates.

and is assumed to remain constant. The amount of funds now available for loans, however, has risen, as illustrated by the rightward shift of the supply curve from S to S_1. As a result, the price of loans—that is, the rate of interest—will fall from i to i_1.

At the same time, the money supply can be expanded by as much as $200 billion. Why? Because the $10 billion of new reserves stand as required reserves (at the 5 percent ratio) behind $400 billion of demand deposits. Or, relying on our formula, we can say that the $\Delta XR = \$10$ billion and the money multiplier $= 1/RRR = 1/.05 = 20$. Thus:

$$\Delta M_1 = \Delta XR \cdot 1/RRR$$
$$= \$10 \text{ billion} \cdot 1/.05$$
$$= \$10 \text{ billion} \cdot 20$$
$$= \$200 \text{ billion}$$

This newly created $200 billion, when added to the original $200 billion of demand deposits, brings the total money supply to $400 billion. After the multiple expansion has taken place, the balance sheet will look like the one in Table 12-1(C).

Note that in all of this, the total reserves account remains constant at $20 billion. The amount of demand deposits, however, has doubled from $200 billion to $400 billion. The reason is that the reserve requirement was cut from 10 percent to 5 percent. When it was 10 percent, the $20 billion of reserves stood as required reserves behind $200 billion of deposits. When it was cut to 5 percent, the $20 billion stood as required reserves behind $400 billion of deposits.

Note also that when the reserve requirement was cut, two things happened in our formula. First, the amount of excess reserves rose; second, the deposit multiplier was increased (from 10 at 10 percent to 20 at 5 percent).

Conclusion: When the legal reserve requirement is reduced, both the amount of excess reserves and the deposit multiplier rise. To this we must add the further conclusion that the rate of interest will fall.

Let's return to our original condition, shown now in Table 12–2(A), but let's also suppose that the Board of Governors feels that there is too much money in circulation and thus wants to reduce the money supply. In this event, they could raise the required reserve ratio from, say, 10 percent to 20 percent. Since 20 percent of $200 billion (the existing demand deposits) is $40 billion of required reserves, the

TABLE 12-2

(A)

Assets		Liabilities	
Reserves	$20b	Demand deposits	$200b
{required	$20		
excess	0}		
Loans	$180b		

(B)

Assets		Liabilities	
Reserves	$20b	Demand deposits	$200b
{required	$40b		
deficiency	$20b}		
Loans	$180b		

(C)

Assets		Liabilities	
Reserves	$20b	Demand deposits	$100b
{required	$20b		
excess	0}		
Loans	$80b		

banks find themselves short; they have only $20 billion in reserves. This reserve *deficiency* is shown in Table 12-2(B). The banks now find themselves in the position of having to reduce demand deposits down to the level of $100 billion. They do this by not extending new loans when or as old loans are paid off. Thus both the demand deposits account and the loans account are reduced by $100 billion, and the final balance sheet will be like that in Table 12-2(C).

> **Conclusion:**   When the legal reserve requirement is raised, the money supply is reduced. So also is the money multiplier reduced. To this we must add the further conclusion that the interest rate will tend to rise.

It would seem, then, that changes in the legal reserve requirement are a formidable monetary weapon, and yet they have rarely been used. There are two reasons for this. First, the Board of Governors seems to feel that if care were not taken, an increase in the reserve requirement could cause a *general* reserve deficiency, and this would in turn result in a multiple contraction of the money supply. Such an event could, in its own turn, cause a general contraction of economic activity. Second, other tools of monetary control are much more efficient, and consequently they are used more often.

Nonetheless, when reserve requirements were changed in the past, they were lowered to induce expansions in the money supply and a fall in the interest rate in recessions and were raised to dampen aggregate demand in periods of inflation by reducing the money supply and raising the rate of interest.

2. Changes in the Discount Rate

Recall that the discount rate is the rate of interest paid by member banks when they borrow reserves from the Federal Reserve. Banks would want to borrow reserves from the system for either of two reasons: First, they may have reserve deficiencies and must borrow to make them up; second, they may want to acquire new excess reserves in order to lend them out at a rate of interest greater than the discount rate.

In periods of recession, then, the Federal Reserve will lower the discount rate relative to the rate of interest that banks are charging on loans. The purpose here is to induce banks to borrow excess reserves at a low rate (say, 7 percent) and lend them out at a higher rate (say, 8 percent). If the banks do in fact respond this way, then there could be a multiple expansion of the money supply, and this can be good antirecessionary medicine.

On the other hand, during periods of actual or threatened inflation, the medicine requires an increase in the discount rate relative to the rate charged by the banks. This of course makes it more costly for member banks to borrow excess reserves and then lend these out. The economy doesn't need more money when inflation is already a real thing or a potential threat.

Are changes in the discount rate very effective? Hardly, although their impact should not be minimized. In the first place, commercial banks have traditionally been very reluctant to borrow from the Federal Reserve. They usually borrow from the central bank only as a last resort—that is, when they have an actual or a threatened reserve deficiency that can't be covered in some other way. But there is another side to this matter, which is that the Federal Reserve doesn't encourage banks to borrow. The central bank's position is that borrowing by member banks is a privilege, not a right, and it is a privilege not to be abused.

If this is the case, of what significance is discount policy? For one thing, financial markets, both here and abroad, tend to respond quickly (and at times drastically) to changes in the discount rate. When the Federal Reserve raises the discount rate, the financial markets interpret this action as a clue that further restrictive actions will soon be taken. Furthermore, a cut in the rate is taken as a warning that further easing in monetary policy will soon follow. There is, in short, an "announcement effect" that accompanies changes in the discount rate. Financial markets tend to read subsequent Federal Reserve actions into this change and will often respond before the subsequent actions are taken.

The Federal Reserve authorities frequently reinforce the announcement effects of changes in the discount rate with *moral suasion*—that is, talk. The purpose is to convince bankers to move in the direction that the Federal Reserve desires (more loans or fewer loans). While moral suasion alone can hardly be considered an important weapon of monetary policy, it can be useful indeed in conjunction with the announced changes in the discount rate.

All in all, however, changes in the discount rate in and of themselves do not have a strong impact on the money supply. Still, the announcement dimensions must be considered important.

3. Open-Market Operations

We now come to the most effective instrument of the Federal Reserve for controlling the amount of reserves, the amount of money, and the level of the interest rate—namely, open-market operations. The basic procedure of this powerful policy tool is quite straightforward. It is simply the exchange of government securities back and forth in the market between the Federal Reserve on the one hand and the public and the banking system on the other.

Here at the outset we can set forth two basic rules of thumb. First, if the Federal Reserve authorities want to reduce inflationary forces, they will *sell* government securities in the open market. Second, if, on the contrary, they want to combat recessionary forces, they will *purchase* government securities in the open market.

But where do these government securities that are sold back and forth in the market come from? They are present because of current and past federal budget deficits. To finance deficits, the government must borrow funds, and the Treasury Department does this by issuing and selling different types of securities: There are treasury bills (short-term debt), treasury notes (intermediate-term debt; and treasury bonds (long-term debt). Most of us are familiar with such long-term government securities as savings bonds—i.e., Series E and Series EE bonds. Most of the federal debt, however, is financed by the sale of treasury bills; and nearly all the Federal Reserve open-market operations use treasury bills.

The open-market decisions are made by the Federal Open Market Committee (FOMC). The committee meets about every four weeks in Washington, D.C., in the greatest of secrecy. At that time, after careful examination of the current economic scene and likely future events, they may decide either to buy or sell securities or to hold the line. Whatever they decide to do will affect the economy in general.

Once the FOMC makes its decision, it notifies the manager of the Open-Market Account (located at the New York Federal Reserve Bank), who then carries out the decision by contacting a group of "dealers" in government securities. These dealers are located mainly in New York; they are specialized financial intermediaries who deal only in government securities, both for their own account and for the accounts of others. Their position is shown in Figure 12–3. However (and this is important), since the dealers directly link the FOMC with the rest of the market, we will act as if the Federal Reserve deals directly with the commercial banking system and the public.

Now let's examine how the open-market operations affect reserves, the money supply, and the rate of interest.

4. Open-Market Sales

Suppose the economy is booming and inflation has broken out. In this event, the FOMC is quite likely to take anti-inflationary measures and tighten up the money supply and will do so by *selling* securities in the open market. Suppose also that they decide on the figure of $2 billion to be sold to the public.

The public buys these securities and pays the Federal Reserve by writing checks in the total amount of $2 billion on their demand deposits. The Federal Reserve now holds $2 billion of checks as claims against various commercial banks, and it collects on these checks by reducing the reserve balances of the banks. Once the checks have been cleared, the banks reduce the demand deposits of the people who bought the securities, reduce their reserve account and send the canceled checks to their customers. All of these actions are summarized in Table 12–3. When the Federal Reserve sells the $2 billion of securities, its assets are reduced by this amount, as shown in the Federal Reserve balance sheet in Table 12–3(A). The asset side of the public's balance sheet will therefore increase by $2 billion as the public obtains

FIGURE 12–3   The Open Market in Government Securities   Open-market operations are carried out through a handful of security dealers who act as a conduit to the general public in the purchase or sale of securities.

TABLE 12-3   **Open-Market Sale of Securities: Effects on Balance Sheets**

(A)
Federal Reserve

Assets	Liabilities
−$2b Securities	−$2b Reserves

(B)
Public

Assets	Liabilities
+$2b Securities −$2b Demand deposits	

(C)
Commercial Banks

Assets	Liabilities
−$2b Reserves	−$2b Demand deposits

the securities. But, at the same time, the public's assets will fall by $2 billion as people write checks to pay for the securities. These steps are summarized in Table 12-3(B). The Federal Reserve, collecting these checks, will reduce the liabilities side of its balance sheet, for the banks now owe the Fed $2 billion, and it simply collects the $2 billion by reducing what it owes (reserves) to the banks, as shown in Table 12-3(A). Having canceled the checks, the Federal Reserve sends them to the commercial banks, which now realize that they have lost $2 billion of demand deposits and $2 billion of reserves. These two minuses are shown in the banks' balance sheet in Table 12-3(C).

The result of all this is threefold. First, the open-market sale has reduced the money supply by $2 billion (verify this by looking at what happens to the public's demand deposits in Table 12-3). Second, the reserves of the banking system are also reduced by $2 billion. If all of this was in the form of excess reserves, then the banks' ability to create more new money has been wiped out. If, on the other hand, the loss of $2 billion of reserves creates a reserve deficiency, there could be a potential multiple contraction of demand deposits. The third conclusion is shown in Figure 12-4, in which the supply curve of loanable funds shifts to the left because of the $2 billion reduction of reserves. Accordingly, all things equal, the rate of interest will rise. This could in turn reduce investment expenditures and hence aggregate demand. This will dampen inflationary pressures, which is what the Federal Reserve set out to do.

Conclusion: An *open-market sale* has the consequences of (a) reducing demand deposits directly, (b) reducing reserves and hence potential demand deposits, and (c) raising the rate of interest.

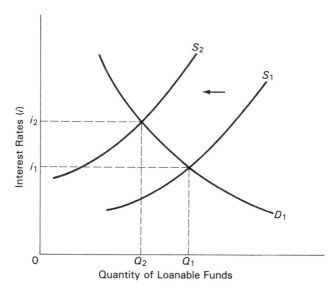

FIGURE 12-4   Open-Market Sale of Securities—Effect on Interest Rates   A sale of $2 billion of securities in the open market drains $2 billion of reserves from the banking system, reducing the supply of loanable funds and raising interest rates.

5. Open-Market Purchases

Let's turn the situation around and have the economy already in a recession. In this situation, the FOMC will decide to buy government securities, say $2 billion, from the public. When the public sells these securities, it is paid in the form of checks from the Federal Reserve.

The public deposits its checks in the banks, and thus demand deposits are increased by $2 billion. These two transactions are shown in the public's balance sheet in Table 12-4(B). The commercial banks also increase their reserve account by $2 billion and send the checks for deposit to the Federal Reserve. Thus they increase their reserve account by $2 billion, as in Table 12-4(C). The Federal Reserve also increases the banks' reserve account by $2 billion, so that in its balance sheet in Table 12-4(A), both assets and liabilities rise by $2 billion.

Now, only a fraction of the new reserves is required; the rest is excess. Thus the commercial banking system is in a position to bring about a multiple expansion of the money supply. In fact, there is again a threefold result.

> **Conclusion:**   (a) The money supply increases directly when the Federal Reserve buys government securities from the public; (b) the open-market purchase increases reserves and, in fact, generates new excess reserves and hence a potential monetary expansion; and (c) the new excess reserves will cause the rate of interest to fall, all things equal.

This completes our discussion of what money is, how it is created and destroyed, and what kind of mechanics are used for its control. The next chapter

**TABLE 12-4   Open-Market Purchase of Securities:
Effects on Balance Sheets**

(A)
Federal Reserve

Assets	Liabilities
+$2b Securities	+$2b Reserves

(B)
Public

Assets	Liabilities
+$2b Demand deposits −$2b Securities	

(C)
Commercial Banks

Assets	Liabilities
+$2b Reserves	+$2b Demand deposits

brings all these ideas together and combines them with what we have learned about fiscal policy.

D. SUMMARY

The Federal Reserve, our central bank, is a unique institution, being neither completely private nor completely public. It is the main source of monetary policy.

The Federal Reserve exercises its control over the money supply mainly through three tools—legal reserve requirements, the discount rate, and open-market operations. A change in the required reserve ratio affects both the money multiplier and the volume of reserves. A change in the discount rate doesn't affect either the money multiplier or the amount of reserves, although it influences the *availability* of borrowed reserves. Open-market operations are the most powerful tool. They affect the quantity of reserves, but they also have a direct impact on the money supply and interest rate.

Terms and Concepts to Remember

Central bank
Check clearing
Fiscal agent
Discount rate
Open-market operations

Moral suasion
Federal Open Market Committee
Board of Governors
Legal reserve requirements
Announcement effect

Questions for Review

1. What body controls the monetary policy of the Federal Reserve System?

2. What are the two major functions of the Federal Reserve?

3. Define *monetary policy* and explain its purpose in terms of aggregate supply and aggregate demand.

4. Explain the mechanism through which a lowering of legal reserve requirements would lead to an increase in the money supply.

5. What function does the discount rate play in monetary policy?

6. What are open-market operations? How are they carried out?

7. The Federal Reserve sells U.S. government securities in the open market. What would be the effect of this transaction on bank reserves, the money supply, and interest rates?

13

Monetary, Fiscal and Other Policies

chapter preview

- Countercyclical policy is composed of fiscal and monetary policy.
- Discretionary fiscal policy is how the government softens the fluctuations of aggregate demand by changing taxes and government spending.
- Deficit financing is appropriate antirecessionary discretionary fiscal policy. The proper anti-inflationary policy is surplus financing.
- Deficit and surplus financing of fiscal policy has major effects on financial markets.
- Pure fiscal policy has no impact on the money supply but does affect interest rates and private spending.
- Discretionary fiscal policy carried out through the Federal Reserve has effects on the money supply. Deficit financing increases the money supply, whereas surplus financing reduces the

money supply.

- A possible consequence of deficit financing is that it may crowd out spending for private investment and consumer durable goods.
- Automatic fiscal policy tends to moderate the severity of cyclical swings.
- Monetary policy is purposeful control of bank reserves by the central bank, for the purpose of controlling aggregate demand and the business cycle.
- The effectiveness of discretionary fiscal and monetary policy is affected by the recognition lag, the action lag, and the impact lag.
- Monetary and fiscal policy should be coordinated for best results, although in practice this is difficult to do.

This chapter is very important. It does two things. First, it pulls together the basic ideas and concepts of the preceding four chapters, and in this respect, it serves somewhat as a summary. Second, it provides an answer to a critical question—namely, How can the federal government *and* the Federal Reserve stabilize the level of total production at full employment and, at the same time, stabilize the general level of prices?[1]

Chapters 9 and 10 have pointed out that the levels of employment and output (real GNP) fluctuate over time. These chapters, and particularly Chapter 10, also pointed out that these fluctuations are due mainly to the instability of aggregate demand: That is, (a) when aggregate demand falls, output and employment also fall, but by some larger amount via the multiplier process; and (b) when aggregate demand rises, output, employment, and prices also rise, but again by some magnified amount due to the multiplier.

All of this discussion about fluctuations probably makes the broad objective or goal of stabilization policy quite clear to you. It is to eliminate (as best as possible) the ups and downs in aggregate demand and thus hold the economy's total output as close to potential GNP as it can. This should be done, however, in a manner consistent with price-level stability. If the policies were, for some weird reason, completely successful, then actual GNP would settle on and stay on the growth path of potential GNP in a noninflationary way.

There is, however, a much more realistic goal, and that is to iron out as much as possible the inevitable fluctuations in aggregate output. Even so, as we shall see, this goal is difficult to fulfill. At the very least, policies should prevent such extremes of the business cycle as deep and prolonged depression and runaway inflation.

The policies that are used to strive for this more realistic goal are, first, *fiscal control* (as determined by the federal government), and second, *monetary control* (as exercised by the Federal Reserve). Chapter 10 introduced fiscal policy, although in a rather loose way, when it included government spending *(G)* in our statement of aggregate demand as $AD = C + I + G$. Then Chapter 12 introduced monetary policy, also rather loosely, when it showed how the Federal Reserve authorities can control the money supply and interest rates.

This chapter elaborates on monetary and fiscal policy, and as might be sus-

---

[1]Remember that "full" employment *does not* mean that 100 percent of the labor force have jobs. Remember, too, that "stability" of the price level allows some upward drift of prices in general. You may want to refer to Chapter 9 for a refresher of what the terms *full employment* and *price-level stability* mean to most economists.

pected, the two types of policy don't always operate in tandem. Indeed, sometimes they can (and do) work at cross purposes. Nor do they always do what they are supposed to do. Nonetheless, monetary and fiscal controls are the traditional stabilization policies used in our society, and therefore we need to look at them in some detail. Sections A through D of this chapter concentrate on fiscal policy—what it is, how it may be used, and what are some of its flaws and shortcomings. Section E does the same things for monetary policy. Finally, Section F looks briefly at problems of coordinating fiscal and monetary controls.[2]

A. DISCRETIONARY FISCAL POLICY

Our government taxes and spends for a variety of reasons, and these reasons have increased tremendously over the past half-century (see Chapter 6). Here, however, we are concerned only with taxing and spending by the federal government as they take the form of fiscal policy. Perhaps a general definition will be helpful.

> **Definition:** *Fiscal policy* is how the government softens the ups and downs of aggregate demand (and hence the business cycle) by changing taxes and government spending programs.

For example, suppose the economy pushes up along the aggregate supply curve into a period of high-employment inflation. In this situation, the fiscal authorities (that is, Congress and the executive branch) can introduce changes in tax legislation and government spending programs to reduce the inflationary pressures. They could, for instance, raise taxes or cut spending, or both. On the other hand, if the economy slides back down the aggregate supply curve into a recession, the fiscal authorities can initiate a different set of actions, in this case to stimulate aggregate demand. They would presumably do the reverse of the steps above; that is, they would cut taxes or increase government spending, or both.

These are examples of what is called *discretionary fiscal policy,* in which the government officials decide on the "best" or "proper" course of action for a particular economic situation and then act on that decision. There is, however, nothing irrevocable about the action taken—in fact, any discretionary fiscal policy decided upon can be reversed, continued, or even stopped and then taken up again at some later date.

> **Definition:** *Discretionary fiscal policy* consists of deliberate changes in taxes and government spending for the purpose of correcting a particular economic situation and directing the economy toward full employment without inflation.

---

[2]It may seem that the amount of discussion in this chapter is lopsided in favor of fiscal policy. Not so; remember that we have already devoted two full chapters (11 and 12) as background for monetary policy. A goodly portion of this chapter must now lay the groundwork for fiscal policy.

We must stress here that the government spending we are talking about is *spending on goods and services,* that the G in $AD = C + I + G$ is government's demand for currently produced goods and services. Discretionary fiscal spending, in other words, *does not include spending via transfer payments,* such as social security, unemployment compensation, and welfare programs. These transfers are indeed a part of fiscal policy, but not discretionary fiscal policy. We will examine them later when we discuss automatic fiscal policy.

1. Two Transmission Mechanisms and Two Budgetary Rules

There are two routes that discretionary fiscal policy can take to affect aggregate demand. One is *direct*—namely, changes in government spending *(G).* Since G is a component of aggregate demand, any change in it *directly* affects the total demand for goods and services. The chain of events here is from a change in G to a change in aggregate demand to some magnified change in GNP through the multiplier.

The other route is a bit *indirect*—namely, changes in consumption resulting from a change in taxes. Recall from Chapter 10 that consumption is a function of disposable income and that it is through this functional relationship that the second transmission mechanism works. For example, if taxes were raised, households' disposable income would fall by the same amount. Then, since consumption is a function of disposable income, households would respond by reducing both consumption spending *and* saving. It is, of course, this fall in consumption that lowers aggregate demand.[3] The chain of events, then, is from a change in taxes to a change in disposable income to a change in consumption to a change in aggregate demand and, finally, to some magnified change in GNP. This is more indirect than the transmission mechanism for a change in government spending.

Since the purpose of discretionary fiscal policy is to stabilize aggregate demand as close as possible to potential GNP, the following two statements apply.

> **Definition:** In a period of high-employment inflation, raise taxes, or cut spending, or do both. This is known as *surplus financing.*
> **Definition:** In a period of low output and much unemployment, cut taxes or raise spending, or do both. This is known as *deficit financing.*

Figure 13-1 illustrates the applications of both of these policies. Panel (A) shows that when aggregate demand is at AD_1, the price level is at P_1. Note also that the economy is at full employment—that is, AD_1 intersects AS at Q_F (on the horizontal axis). Figure 13-1(A) thus describes the high-employment inflation situation to which our first policy statement applies. The policy response here is to reduce aggregate demand and hence ease the inflationary pressures. The fiscal authorities, there-

---

[3]Remember, however, that a dollar increase in taxes won't reduce consumption by the same amount, for a part of the higher tax is paid out of what would have been saved. A reduction of taxes, on the other hand, raises disposable income so that *both* consumption and saving will increase.

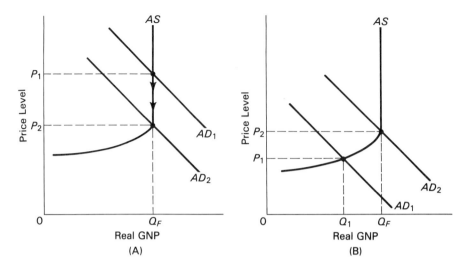

FIGURE 13-1   Countercyclical Discretionary Fiscal Policy   Panel (A) shows
how fiscal policy can reduce inflationary pressure by lowering aggregate demand. However, recall from Chapter 10 that there is an upward ratchet effect for the aggregate
supply curve, showing that the price level continues to creep up over the stages of the
business cycle. The *AS* curve here includes the inflationary effect.

fore, should either raise taxes or cut spending, or both. Remember, the cut in spending reduces aggregate demand directly, while the increase in taxes reduces it
indirectly. In any event, there will be a negative multiplier effect, reducing aggregate
demand even more. In Figure 13-1(A), we have assumed that aggregate demand
settles at AD_2 and hence the price level falls to P_2.[4]

This policy has a budgetary impact that we cannot ignore. The scene in Figure
13-1(A) calls for *surplus financing* as the appropriate fiscal action—that is, have
the government collect more in tax revenues than it spends. In this event, the circular
flow of inflationary spending will fall. The reason is simple enough: The government is taking more out of the spending stream in the form of taxes than it is return-
ing. This could be a potent anti-inflationary weapon.

Figure 13-1(B) depicts the low-employment recession situation to which our
second policy statement applies. The aggregate demand AD_1 cuts the *AS* curve to
the left of Q_F. The desirable fiscal policy here is to increase aggregate demand and
hence create more job opportunities. The fiscal authorities, therefore, should either
increase government spending or cut taxes, or both. Again, there will be a multiplier
effect, only this time a positive one that, we assume, pushes aggregate demand up
to AD_2 where full employment prevails. But note also that the price level rises from
P_1 to P_2.[5]

---

[4]You might see a possible and potent problem here. If the fiscal authorities reduce aggregate
demand too far, the economy may end up somewhere to the left of Q_F. That is, they could "correct"
the inflation by bringing on a recession. This possibility is discussed below.

[5]Again, there is the bothersome problem that the authorities may push aggregate demand too far,
so that now inflation may result.

This rule of fiscal response means that the government must engage in *deficit financing*—that is, the government is committed to spending more than it collects in tax revenues. Deficit financing, in other words, means that the government is putting more into the spending stream than it is taking out. This, therefore, is a powerful antirecessionary control.[6]

2. Some Important Consequences

In both of the above cases, the discretionary fiscal policy will have a significant impact on both aggregate demand and the federal budget. But the policy makers should also take into account two further matters—first, how the policy will affect the money supply, and second, how the method of financing will affect interest rates.

It doesn't matter what fiscal policy is put into effect; both surplus and deficit financing have these further financial repercussions. However, as we saw much earlier, the federal government has more often than not engaged in deficit financing—indeed, so much so, that deficit piled on deficit has resulted in a national debt of over $3 trillion (for more on the national debt, see the appendix to this chapter). Because of the prevalence of deficit financing, we will concentrate on it in the following discussion.

Clearly, when the government spends more than it collects in tax revenues, it must borrow to make up the difference. It does this by selling government securities to anyone who is willing to buy them, that is, anyone who is willing to lend money to the government. Let's distinguish between two situations here.

First, there is what we may call *pure fiscal policy*. This occurs when the government borrows exclusively from the private sector of the economy (i.e., not from the Federal Reserve). In this case, then, the government securities are sold to private buyers; put otherwise, households and private businesses lend money by purchasing securities from the government.

Of course, the private sector must part with some of its money as it pays for the government securities. This means that the money supply in the hands of the public has been reduced by the amount of the deficit. But then the government turns around and spends what it has borrowed; and since it makes all of its purchases from private businesses and households, the money ends up back in the private sector.

What, then, are the results (so far) of pure fiscal policy? They are twofold: First, the private sector has the same amount of money as before; but second, it now has something more—it has the government securities that it has purchased. The thing to be stressed, however, is that under pure fiscal policy, there is no change

---

[6]Actually, it's a bit more complicated. In the case of surplus financing, if the budget were initially in balance, the actions taken would create a surplus. On the other hand, if there were already a surplus in the budget, that surplus would get larger. Finally, if the budget initially showed a deficit, the surplus financing would make the deficit smaller.

In the case of deficit financing, if the budget were initially in balance, a deficit would result. If, on the other hand, the budget showed a surplus, the surplus would shrink. Finally, if there already is a deficit, the deficit financing would make it larger.

in the money supply. This is crucial, for if the economy is already on an inflationary track and there is, at the same time, deficit financing, pure fiscal policy adds less to the inflation than the other method of financing the deficit. Let's look at the other method now.

The consequences are quite different when the government circumvents the private sector and borrows exclusively from the Federal Reserve. In this procedure, *new money is created by the deficit financing.* The central bank pays for the securities it buys by simply increasing the federal government's checking account at the Federal Reserve. Recall from Chapter 12 that the federal government holds its funds on deposit at the Federal Reserve, and it is this account that the Federal Reserve increases when buying the securities from the government. This is essentially how the Federal Reserve lends to the government.

When the government spends what it has borrowed from the Federal Reserve, the amount spent becomes new money. At least, the people and businesses that receive the government checks treat them as money. They deposit them in their demand deposit accounts and then proceed to write checks against them.

In this case, the Federal Reserve holds the newly sold securities, but the private sector has the newly created money. This method of financing the deficit is quite different from pure fiscal policy. Under pure fiscal policy, there is no change in the money supply; but under this method, there is a monetary effect—that is, the money supply is increased—and this smacks of monetary policy as well as fiscal policy. In a very real sense, the deficit has been monetized, and thus the fiscal action laps over into monetary policy. Certainly this increase in the money supply must be taken into account by the Federal Reserve when it is deliberating what course of monetary action it should take.

It is rather unlikely that the federal government can pursue a course of pure fiscal policy, for when it engages in deficit financing, it borrows from whomever it can. Thus it is apt to borrow from both the private sector and from the Federal Reserve, and the consequences would be a mix of those above. The private sector will end up with *some* of the *securities* as well as the new money created when the Federal Reserve lends to the government.

3. Deficit Budgets and "Crowding Out"

Let's return for a moment to pure fiscal policy and trace out a further impact it has—this time, on the interest rate. We have already seen that there is no change in the money supply when the government follows pure deficit fiscal policy, although the private sector now owns more government securities. But there is also the additional consequence that interest rates will tend to rise, and those who propose the use of deficit financing must take this into account.

To see why there is an upward pressure on interest rates, let's suppose that at the time of the financing there is a given amount of private funds available for both private and public borrowing. This is shown by the S_1 supply curve in Figure 13-2. Let's suppose also that the original demand curve for these funds is D_1. This is the

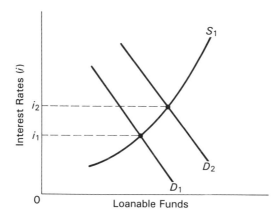

FIGURE 13-2   **Effect of Fiscal Policy on Interest Rates**   Deficit financing carried out by selling bonds to the public increases the demand for loanable funds, thus driving up the rate of interest. Buying bonds from the public has the reverse effect.

demand curve for loanable funds to *finance deficit spending both private and public.* Thus the equilibrium market rate of interest is i_1.

The deficit financing, however, alters all of this, for it means that government has increased its demand for loanable funds, and we show this by shifting the demand curve to the right to D_2. The result, then, is a rise in the rate of interest to i_2.

This result is important. As we saw in Chapter 10, an increase in the interest rate tends to reduce the demand for funds by businesses to finance the purchases of new capital goods. Rising äinterest rates are also apt to slow down household spending on such consumer durable goods as automobiles, washers, and dryers. The reason is that households usually have to borrow in order to buy these items, and higher rates of interest make it more expensive to purchase these goods on credit.

A possible consequence of deficit financing, therefore, is that it runs the risk of "crowding out," or reducing, private spending on capital goods and consumer durables because of the higher interest rates. This in turn lessens the positive impact on output and employment that flows through the multiplier process triggered by the discretionary deficit financing.

None of this, however, means that the "crowding out" effect always occurs whenever there is deficit financing by the government, nor does it mean that the deficit financing is unwarranted. As for the first point, the extent of any crowding out depends on where the economy is on the aggregate supply curve. Conceivably, we could be in such a depressionary state that there is little if any private spending on consumer durables and capital goods to be crowded out by the higher interest rates. Of course, if we are already at full employment, then any increase in deficit financing will do some crowding out, and this may be undesirable.

As for the second point, the government deficit financing may well be on projects that generally benefit society and the economy, both now and in the future. This would be true of highways, dams, bridges, and similar public works projects.

Indeed, these tend to make business more efficient and may help to stimulate some private investment spending.

4. Some Comments on Surplus Financing

Let's turn the coin around and ask now about the financial impacts of surplus financing. If the federal budget were actually in surplus, then the government would be saving—that is, its tax revenues would exceed its expenditures. This in and of itself is contractionary, for the government is taking more out of the spending stream of the circular flow than it is putting back.

For example, if tax revenues are $900 billion, of which the government spends only $800 billion, the surplus is $100 billion. What this also means is that the money supply is reduced by $100 billion. Why? Because when the private sector paid its taxes its demand deposits fell by $900 billion, but it got back only $800 billion when the government did its spending.

The government, therefore, has the residual $100 billion in its account at the Federal Reserve. This is what we mean by the money supply being reduced by the amount of the surplus. The private sector no longer has this money. And this is precisely the sort of fiscal policy needed if the economy is experiencing full-employment inflation. It would not, however, be appropriate if the economy were in a recession.

Yet, much depends on what the government does with its surplus. If it simply keeps it, then the anti-inflationary impact of the surplus is preserved. On the other hand, if the surplus is all spent, then the impact is completely wiped out. But there is also the possibility that the government will use the surplus to retire a part of the national debt. There are two alternatives here.

First, the government may retire debt held by the Federal Reserve. In this event, the tax surplus doesn't find its way back into the private sector as money. The Federal Reserve simply parts with some of the securities it holds and gets paid for them by reducing the government's checking account. Thus the anti-inflationary impact is preserved. Again, this laps over into monetary policy.

The second alternative is *pure fiscal policy*. This occurs when the government retires some of the debt held by the private sector. As it does this, it simply channels the money it had been holding as a tax surplus back to the private sector. Thus when all is said and done, the money supply remains constant.

Therefore, the way the government uses its tax surplus matters a great deal.

B. AUTOMATIC FISCAL POLICY

Fiscal policy in this country isn't limited solely to discretionary actions by the authorities. As it turns out, several pieces of legislation also act as fiscal policy. Although these laws weren't designed for this purpose (instead they were passed for other reasons), their fiscal impact is important to the continued health of the economy. Most of them take the form of transfer payments, which were discussed in Chapters 6 and 8.

1. Definition

These *automatic stabilizers,* as they are called, are characterized by the automatic (or built-in) responses of government tax revenues and spending to changes in GNP. They therefore differ drastically from discretionary fiscal policy in that no deliberate, direct action by Congress is needed for them to begin operating in a counter-cyclical manner.

> **Definition:** *Automatic stabilizers* are features (usually legal) of the economy that automatically respond countercyclically to changes in GNP; no discretionary human action is required for them to act to smooth out the peaks and troughs of the business cycle.

Thus, as the economy moves into a contraction, fiscal stimulus occurs automatically. It takes the form of deficit financing, which, as we have seen, works against recessionary forces. Conversely, when the economy pushes into a period of high-employment inflation, the automatic stabilizers trigger a tendency toward a surplus in the federal budget.

This doesn't mean that the automatic stabilizers can prevent or cure a recession or inflation. As pointed out below, they are responses to changes that in turn prevent these changes from getting worse.

2. The Stabilizers in Action

One of the major automatic stabilizers is the unemployment compensation program. This built-in stabilizer traces back to the 1930s when Congress enacted legislation to help the masses of unemployed people. Under this program, when workers become involuntarily unemployed, they receive some payment from the unemployment compensation funds.[7]

Note how the law operates as an automatic stabilizer. When real GNP falls and unemployment rises, there is a built-in tendency for government spending to rise, and the greater the amount of unemployment, the greater the amount of spending. This means that the unemployed, although their standard of living must fall, can maintain their spending on goods and services at some minimum level. It also means that there is a floor to the fall in total consumption spending by households. Thus aggregate demand won't, as far as this component is concerned, continue to fall, and this eases the burden placed on discretionary fiscal policy and monetary policy.

In the opposite situation, when the recession has been reversed and the economy is climbing back to full employment, then government expenditures on unemployment compensation will fall.

At the same time that these expenditures are changing against the flow of the cycle, so too are tax revenues. Recall from Chapter 6 that the personal income tax

---

[7]Unemployment compensation is actually a part of the social security legislation of the 1930s. The program covers nearly 90 percent of civilian employees and is administered on a state-by-state basis.

is the main source of tax revenues for the federal government, and therefore tax revenues change in the same direction as personal income. There is an important consequence of this: When the economy enters a recessionary period, not only do expenditures on unemployment consumption rise but tax revenues fall. Accordingly, a tendency toward a deficit is unavoidable. Even if Congress undertook no discretionary fiscal action, deficit financing would still emerge and have its impact.

Furthermore, as the economy moves into the reverse situation and nears full employment and experiences some inflation, two things will automatically happen: Tax revenues will rise as more households earn higher taxable incomes, and government spending on unemployment compensation will fall. Thus, and again unavoidably, a built-in budget response occurs, only this time it is a tendency toward a surplus.

Welfare programs also act as automatic stabilizers. In a full-employment boom period, many people who would otherwise be on welfare relief are able to obtain jobs. Hence expenditures on these programs decline. On the other hand, when real GNP begins to drop, these people are among the first to be laid off and join the welfare rolls. Thus, spending of this sort tends to behave countercyclically, rising as the economy falls into a recession, and falling as full employment is approached.

Two other, but less important, stabilizers are the corporate income tax and the agricultural price-support program. These don't have nearly the stabilizing powers of the personal income tax, unemployment compensation, and welfare programs.

3. A Graphic Illustration and Major Limitations

Figure 13–3 shows how the automatic stabilizers work. The *TT* curve reflects what happens to tax revenues as GNP changes, *given the prevailing tax structure.* As GNP rises, tax revenues also rise, as shown by the upward sweep of the *TT* curve. The *GG* curve, on the other hand, reveals what happens to government expenditures, *given the existing spending programs.* Thus, as GNP rises, government expenditures automatically fall. The *GG* curve, therefore, has a negative slope.[8] The point at which the two curves intersect is important, for it is here that the budget is balanced (again, given the existing tax and spending programs). This is shown by point *B*.

Let's suppose that the best of all possible macroeconomic worlds exists—that is, the budget is balanced when the economy is at Q_F (at which real GNP is equal to potential GNP), and there is no inflation. We won't allow this idyllic condition to continue for long, for we also assume that there is a slump in private investment spending, pulling the economy (via the multiplier) to Q_1. Note that when this happens, the automatic stabilizers create a deficit (shown to the left of *B* in Figure 13–3).

[8]We must stress that both curves assume that the relevant legislation is in place and not changing. But if, on the other hand, the tax laws are altered, then the *TT* curve would shift either up or down, depending on the nature of the change. A change in spending programs would shift the *GG* curve.

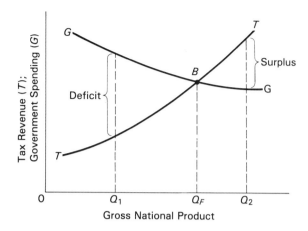

FIGURE 13-3   The Automatic Stabilizers at Work   The budget is in balance at point *B*. At the only level of GNP below full employment, the automatic stabilizers create a tendency toward a deficit. On the other hand, inflationary pressures create a tendency toward a surplus.

To be sure, this deficit is not sufficient to reverse the recession and create an expansionary upsurge. It can't do this; it is, after all, a *response* to the recessionary behavior of the economy. But, and this is important, it reduces the recessionary slump and thus makes the task of restoring the economy to full employment all that much easier for discretionary fiscal and monetary policy.

In the opposite situation, if the economy were to move beyond Q_F, so that inflationary forces dominate the scene, the automatic stabilizers would work to reduce the pressure of these forces. In this case, as shown at Q_2 in Figure 13–3, the stabilizers would automatically create a surplus in the budget.

Again, however, this surplus isn't enough to whip the inflation. It, too, is simply a response to the inflationary forces already at play in the economy, but as such it eases the anti-inflationary job for discretionary fiscal and monetary policy.

Conclusion: The surpluses and deficits resulting from the behavior of the automatic stabilizers are responses to economic forces already in place. They are not, therefore, corrective in their impacts. But they do soften the tasks of monetary policy and discretionary fiscal policy by creating appropriate budgetary imbalances.

The stabilizers are thus a significant part of any countercyclical policy program.

Let's now take a look at a recent experiment in fiscal policy, namely, the "supply-side" fiscal program of the Reagan administration (1980–88).

C. SUPPLY-SIDE FISCAL POLICY

Monetary and fiscal policies have traditionally been oriented toward controlling aggregate demand and have tended, therefore, to ignore the aggregate supply side of economic activity. Under the Reagan administration, however, a new approach was used, an approach that was designed to increase aggregate supply. These policies were pointed toward influencing the decisions of economic agents to work, save, and invest in new capital goods, and hence to encourage increases in the aggregate supply of goods and services.

1. The Argument

The basic argument of supply-side economics was essentially that the progressive tax system of the 1970s, coupled with the rapid inflation of the 1970s, pushed people and businesses into higher tax brackets. It also assumed that businesses and households were motivated mainly by after-tax income. Therefore the then high tax rates and inflation had seriously eroded economic incentives, and this in turn had restricted the total amount of resources they put on the market.

The proper policy in this event would be to cut tax rates (both personal and business) in order to motivate people to work more and save more and, similarly, to encourage businesses to invest more in capital goods. This increase in the availability of resources would lead to an increase in aggregate supply. Moreover, supply-side advocates argued also that the resulting rise in GNP would be in greater proportion than the drop in tax rates; accordingly, government tax revenues would rise.

An illustration, albeit an extreme one, will help us understand the supply-side arguments. We consider, in the example, the economic effects of a marginal tax rate of 50 percent. In this case, an investment of money capital (savings) in a corporate bond that yields 10 percent results only in a 5 percent return after taxes. This, then, results in a diminution of private savings available for investment. As for investment, consider what would happen to a risky, new investment proposal that might be expected to yield a 20 percent rate of return. The high marginal tax rate, however, means that the rate of return would be halved, and this might not be sufficient to trigger the risky expenditure.

In both cases, it was argued, the high marginal tax rates discourage productive activity—in the one case, they reduce saving; in the other, they stifle investment spending. Supply-siders also assume that labor effort is affected in the same way, and that high marginal tax rates reduce the total amount of labor that is made available. Thus labor supply is also restricted.

The "remedy," as noted above, is a tax cut, and indeed supply-side tax cuts were enacted in 1981—especially the rates for the higher-income brackets. Further modifications in rates were made in the Tax Reform Act of 1986, although these were not explicitly for supply-side reasons. After the 1981 cuts, government tax revenues fell sharply, but this was due as much (probably more) to the 1981–82 recession's pulling revenues down.

Then, with the recovery that commenced in 1983, tax receipts rose until by

1987 they were approximately the same percentage of GNP as they had been in 1980 (20 percent). In other words, the tax cuts didn't cause revenues to fall as a percentage of GNP. However, federal spending continued to expand during the same period, but at a faster rate. Consequently, very large annual deficits emerged and remained consistently high during the Reagan years (see the appendix to this chapter).

2. The Critique

It is perhaps too early to pass judgment on supply-side fiscal policy. Certainly the tax cuts didn't stimulate any significant increases in aggregate supply—at least, not as much as hoped for by the original proponents of the policy. Some advocates of the policy, however, have argued that the actions taken may have set the stage for faster economic growth over the long haul. Even so, our rate of growth has been somewhat low relative to historical standards (see Chapter 14).

Also, as we observed, our illustration using a 50 percent marginal tax rate is quite extreme. At the time of the 1981 tax cuts, that rate was relevant only for households receiving an adjusted family income of over $100,000 per year, an income bracket beyond the reach of nearly all American families.[9] The relevant effective marginal tax rates for the bulk of households were around 15 percent, and this wouldn't have the same negative impact as the much higher rates. Of course, an integral part of the supply-side position was that, since most personal saving is provided by the higher-income families, it is the higher marginal rates that must be cut. This is why the personal income tax cuts were more beneficial for these households.

However, neither savings nor investment responded as the supply-siders thought they would. Yet, despite the very large deficits (or maybe because of them?), the economy continued its slow, but steady, recovery until by 1987 there was essential full employment and quite acceptable rises in the general price level. The two ominous blots in the picture were the tremendous budget shortfalls and the large deficits in the international balance of trade.

One final point, a point that stresses once again the interrelatedness of economic phenomena—supply-side tax cuts also have a significant impact on aggregate demand. Cuts in marginal tax rates on personal income have the effect of increasing disposable income and therefore aggregate consumer demand. And tax cuts for businesses do indeed increase after tax returns and thus stimulate business investment demand. Thus the policies oriented toward increasing aggregate supply also have the beneficial results of increasing aggregate demand.

D. SOME PROBLEMS OF FISCAL POLICY

Up to now we have been discussing discretionary fiscal policy as if it could be applied with no problems. This is far from being true, however. Anyone familiar with

[9]The relevant adjusted income for single taxpayers was over $85,000 per year, again beyond the reach of most single households.

the cumbersome method of reaching legislative-executive consensus knows better. The main problem is that of timing.

For one thing, there is the *recognition lag*—that is, the period of time that elapses between the actual need for action and the recognition of this need. Our economy is extremely complex; and not only is it difficult to predict where it is headed, it is almost as difficult to know just where it actually is at *any* moment of time. Thus, quite a few months (probably around six) may slip by before whatever the problem may be is recognized; and all the while it continues festering.

Then there is the *action lag,* which is the time lapse between the recognition of the problem and the taking of action. It is this that is so disturbing for discretionary fiscal policy. Example: Suppose a tax increase is proposed (as it was in late 1965) because of serious inflation, and Congress then debates the matter for a couple of years (as it did in 1966 and 1967) before enacting the tax change (which was passed in 1968). During this period, the inflationary forces may gather strength (as was also true), so that when the tax increase comes it is too little and too late (and it certainly was in 1968–69).

Finally, there is the *impact lag,* which for discretionary fiscal policy is rather short. A change in income taxes is felt almost immediately (because of our tax-withholding system), and, similarly, a change in government spending makes itself felt directly.

In sum, the recognition and action lags serve to reduce the effectiveness and use of discretionary fiscal policy considerably. As a result, it has been used sparingly. This, however, shouldn't be construed as a criticism of discretionary fiscal policy as such; instead, it indicates the complexity of decision making in the democratic process. It is, on the other hand, quite possible for new methods to emerge which could greatly enhance the use of this policy approach.

E. MONETARY POLICY

Let's now turn to monetary policy as a means of controlling aggregate demand and hence the business cycle.

> **Definition:** *Monetary policy* is purposeful control of total bank reserves by the central bank in order to control the money supply and interest rates and thus to smooth out the peaks and troughs of the business cycle.

1. The Transmission Mechanism

Economists generally agree that the relevant transmission mechanism for monetary policy is as follows:

$$\Delta R \rightarrow \Delta M \rightarrow \Delta i \rightarrow \Delta I \rightarrow \Delta AD \rightarrow \Delta \text{GNP}$$

This can easily be deciphered. Read it as: A change in commercial bank reserves (ΔR) engineered by the Federal Reserve leads to a change in the money supply (ΔM); this in turn leads to a change in the rate of interest (Δi), which in its own turn results in a change in private investment spending (ΔI); and since investment spending is part of aggregate demand, a change in it leads to a change in aggregate demand (ΔAD), and this generates a change in the general level of economic activity (ΔGNP).

However, just because economists may agree on the transmission mechanism is no reason to believe that they agree on the effectiveness of monetary policy. They don't, and there is actually a lot of room for disagreement. There is no overwhelming consensus, for example, about the magnitude and timing of monetary policy. Moreover, the lags we discussed above also plague monetary policy.

2. Two Scenarios

Let's suppose, first, that the economy is in a recession, with real GNP below potential. The proper response here, we now know, is to increase aggregate demand. But how can the Federal Reserve authorities do this? Chapter 12 showed us that they have three weapons at their disposal: (a) changes in the required reserve ratio, (b) changes in the discount rate, and (c) open-market operations. Of these, the Federal Reserve relies almost exclusively on open-market operations. Therefore, in the recessionary scenario we are now concerned with, the Federal Reserve will *buy securities in the open market.*

The immediate result of this is to pump new reserves (by the same dollar amount as the purchase) into the commercial banking system. This is the ΔR in our statement of the transmission mechanism above. Now that they have more excess reserves, the profit motive induces commercial banks to make more loans, and as Chapter 11 pointed out, these loans lead to a multiple expansion of the money supply. This is our ΔM.

At the same time, the rate of interest will fall (our Δi), and this induces more capital investment (ΔI) by business firms. This investment spending is a part of aggregate demand, which therefore also increases (ΔAD). Finally, the increase in aggregate demand will, because of the multiplier process, lead to a further magnified increase in the total output of goods and services (ΔGNP).

It is quite conceivable that another multiplier could be unfolding at the same time if the fall in the interest rate encouraged more household spending on consumer durables (ΔC). In this event, the transmission mechanism must be enlarged to include our ΔC along with the ΔI, and therefore the ΔAD and ΔGNP would each be larger.

In the second scenario—one of high-employment inflation—the proper monetary response would be the opposite of what should be done in a recession. The major steps taken by the Federal Reserve would be to *sell securities in the open market,* thus draining excess reserves from commercial banks. This loss of reserves (ΔR) would cause banks to contract loans. As a result, the money supply would fall

(ΔM) and interest rates would rise (Δi). The higher interest rates would in turn reduce investment spending by business (ΔI) and spending on consumer durables by households (ΔC). This would in turn contract aggregate demand and, as a result, would eventually diminish inflationary pressure.

3. The Magnitude of Monetary Policy

The sequence of events making up the transmission mechanism raises an important question. Will a given change in bank reserves produce a weak or a strong change in aggregate demand? Whatever the change in aggregate demand will be depends on the behavior of the major actors in the picture, that is, commercial bankers, businesspeople, and households.

Suppose the economy is in a recession and the Federal Reserve has reacted to this by having purchased securities. The banks thus have some newly created excess reserves.

Now, unless bankers are willing to lend out their new reserves, there will be no expansion of the money supply and therefore no stimulus to aggregate demand and GNP.

But let's assume that bankers *are* willing to make loans; thus there will be a downward pressure on interest rates. What is important now is how households and businesses respond to the lower rate of interest. On the one hand, if their demand isn't very responsive to changes in rates, then there will be little borrowing to finance new investments and purchase of consumer durables. Accordingly, aggregate demand won't rise by much and monetary policy will have been ineffective. On the other hand, if household and business demands for funds are sensitive to changes in the interest rates, they will increase their borrowing substantially. In this event, aggregate demand will rise significantly and this monetary policy will have been effective.

We can only conclude, therefore, that there is much uncertainty about the effectiveness of monetary policy. It is effective only if household and business demands for funds are sensitive to changes in the interest rates.

4. Those Lags Again

The uncertainty about the effectiveness of monetary policy is compounded by the same lags that plague fiscal policy. This is especially true of the recognition and impact lags. The action lag, however, is quite a different matter, for the Board of Governors and the Federal Open Market Committee (FOMC) can quickly take action once the problem has been recognized.

The recognition lag, on the other hand, is the same as that for fiscal policy.[10]

[10]This may not be quite correct, for the Federal Reserve authorities are much more aware of and knowledgeable about economic and financial matters than most congressional members are. Thus the recognition lag may be longer for fiscal policy than it is for monetary policy as lawmakers persist in arguing along political lines and with eyes and ears closed to the real economy.

It is the impact lag that is particularly bothersome for monetary policy. Historical evidence indicates that a change in monetary policy has its impacts from about three months to one year later. Moreover, the price level is affected up to two years following the change. In other words, the impact lag varies considerably over a rather long period.

Look at the problems these lags can create. If the economy slips into a recession, it may be there for up to six months before the monetary authorities recognize the fact. And a lot can happen during these six months. Once recognized, the Federal Reserve can take quick action. The real problems now arise with respect to the impact lag, which is drawn out over a long period. During this rather protracted period, the economy may have recovered and be at (or near) full employment just as the impact on the price level makes itself felt. The result, then, would be a tardy monetary stimulus occurring just when it isn't needed, pushing the economy into full inflation.

Once the Federal Reserve recognizes its past error, it may slam on the monetary brakes, and this could conceivably throw the economy into a recession. This is hardly an appropriate cure for cyclical instability.

5. Monetarism

The difficulties we have described above have prompted a group of economists (known as "monetarists") to advocate that the Federal Reserve give up its discretionary controls and instead follow a "monetary rule." This rule, in its simplest form, would require the Federal Reserve to increase the money supply at some constant rate, say, 3 to 4 percent per year, and *this is to be done regardless of what is happening to the levels of GNP, prices, and employment.*

The basic idea underlying this is that the money supply should increase at roughly the same rate as potential GNP increases over long periods of time. Historically, this has been 3 to 4 percent per year *on the average.* The added money would provide additional purchasing power at the same rate at which additional goods and services are produced.

The monetarists contend that, with the money supply expanding at a constant (and hence predicted) rate, the business cycle would moderate. In periods of inflation, the money supply would become relatively tight—that is, people would increase their demand for it (because of higher prices) more rapidly than the supply would increase (say, 4 percent per year). In consequence, interest rates would rise, and this would moderate the inflation by reducing business spending on investment goods and household spending on consumer durables.

During recessions, on the other hand, the steadily increasing money supply means that more money would be available, and therefore interest rates would fall. This could encourage spending on consumer durables and capital goods.

Compared with the way that monetary policy has traditionally been practiced in this country, the monetarists' proposal is quite drastic. Moreover, in order for it to be effective, several important and far-reaching changes in the banking system would have to be made. The most notable of these would be that commercial banks would have to operate under the constraint of 100 percent required reserves. This, of course, would virtually eliminate the banks' lending function.

F. THE COORDINATION OF POLICIES

Ideally, since they both have the same objective of controlling the business cycle, monetary and discretionary fiscal policy should be coordinated and work in tandem. Figure 13-4(A) shows what would be the result of such coordinated efforts. The solid wavelike line shows the behavior of actual GNP over the course of the business cycle in the absence of any countercyclical policy. The dashed line, on the other hand, reveals how actual GNP fluctuates when there is both proper monetary policy and proper fiscal policy, and when these two policies are coordinated. Here proper and coordinated policies significantly reduce cyclical fluctuations.

Much of our discussion, however, has stressed the importance of timing and magnitude of policy changes. All too often, both discretionary fiscal and monetary policy act perversely because of the lags. When this happens, particularly if the two types of policies are not coordinated, the cyclical fluctuations of real GNP may be magnified. Panel (B) of Figure 13-4 shows the result. The solid line in panel (B) is the same as that in panel (A). The dashed line now swings more widely around

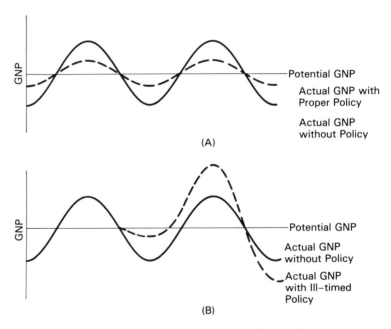

FIGURE 13-4 Two Possible Macroeconomic Policy Scenarios   Panel (A) shows the proper goal of macroeconomic policy—namely, to mitigate the fluctuations in GNP. Panel (B), on the other hand, shows how ill-timed policy can aggravate the swings in GNP.

potential GNP because policies are acting to aggravate cyclical disturbances. Here the lags in both types of policies are creating procyclical, not countercyclical, forces. We have already given several examples of this possibility. Consider what would happen if lags were affecting both types at the same time and in the same direction. The result would be greater instability.

Does this mean that policy doesn't work and in fact makes things worse? Our response to this is that monetary policy doesn't work as perversely as we may have implied. Federal Reserve authorities are, of course, aware of the lags. They are also in continuous contact with the course of the economy, and once they realize a potential mistake they can take steps to correct it. Certainly this doesn't mean that mistakes can't be made. For example, many economists believe that the inflation of the 1970s was "cured" by the severe recession of the early 1980s, a recession engineered by excessively tight monetary policy. Nevertheless, most observers agree that in recent years the monetary policy makers have been able to avoid serious mistakes.

Prospects for better timing in discretionary fiscal policy, on the other hand, aren't likely. Congressional members make their spending and taxing decisions based on a variety of factors, among which the general health of the economy may rank very low. Indeed, it is often the rather narrow point of view derived from representing only a small part of the economy that prevents the broader view. And there are other problems. As we observed above, members of Congress do not like to vote for tax increases, and thus surplus financing, when needed, is hard to come by.

One proposal that has been advanced is to give the executive branch broader fiscal powers than it now has. More particularly, allow the president to change taxes when needed in a countercyclical manner, for the executive branch takes a broader view of the economy than individual congressional members tend to do. Such a change from the present reality in our government, however, is unlikely.

G. SUMMARY

Fiscal policy is how the government moderates the swings in aggregate demand (the business cycle) by changes in taxes and government spending programs. Discretionary fiscal policy involves deliberate changes in taxes and government spending for directing the economy toward full employment without price inflation.

Proper fiscal policy in high-employment inflation is to cut spending or raise taxes, or some of both. In recession, spending increases or tax cuts, or both, are the proper medicine.

Fiscal policy has significant financial consequences. Deficit financing, as in recession, requires the sale of bonds. The sale of bonds to the general public tends to drive up interest rates, reducing private investment spending and consumption of consumer durables by households. A sale of bonds to the Federal Reserve, on the other hand, increases the money supply but not interest rates. Surplus financing tends to operate the opposite way.

Automatic fiscal policy is a built-in feature of the economy. As a result of specific tax and spending programs, tax receipts and outlays respond automatically to movements in the business cycle. Recessions automatically reduce tax receipts and increase spending, which cushions the income fall. High-employment inflation automatically increases tax receipts and reduces spending, restraining but not eliminating the inflation.

Supply-side fiscal policy focuses on the effect of tax rates on aggregate supply or productive capacity of the economy to produce. The effectiveness of supply-side policies has been hotly debated in recent years.

The effective use of discretionary fiscal policy for countercyclical purposes suffers from the problem of lags. The recognition, action, and impact lags create a difficulty in timing discretionary fiscal policy.

Monetary policy is the purposeful control of total bank reserves by the Federal Reserve for the purpose of controlling the money supply, interest rates, and ultimately the business cycle. The transmission mechanism of monetary policy moves from bank reserves to money supply to interest rates and on to investment spending, aggregate demand, and GNP.

Monetary policy suffers from the same lag problem as fiscal policy. One advantage of monetary policy is that the action lag is very short when compared with fiscal policy. However, uncertainty exists about the length of the impact lag.

Monetarists, a group of economists who emphasize the importance of the money supply in aggregate demand, believe that monetary policy should be carried out by "rule," that is, steady growth of the money stock over time is preferable to countercyclical movement. Steady growth in the money supply would minimize many of the problems created by the lags.

Although difficult for political and other reasons, it is clear that fiscal and monetary policies should be coordinated for best results.

Terms and Concepts to Remember

Discretionary fiscal policy	Recognition lag
Automatic fiscal policy	Action lag
Pure fiscal policy	Impact lag
Crowding out	Supply-side economics
Automatic stabilizers	Monetarism
Transmission mechanism	

Questions for Review

1. Differentiate between *discretionary* and *automatic* fiscal policies.

2. What would be the proper *pure* fiscal policy in a recession? Would it be as effective as fiscal policy carried out with the cooperation of the central bank? Why?

3. How does automatic fiscal policy cushion a recession?

4. How can fiscal policy crowd out private spending? Is this inevitably the case? Explain.

5. What is the transmission mechanism for monetary policy? What are the potential weak links in this mechanism? Discuss each.

6. Are the recognition, action, and impact lags the same for both monetary and fiscal policy? If not, how do they differ?

7. Discuss each of the following: (a) supply-side economics; (b) monetarism.

Appendix: The Public (National) Debt

A topic that has confused and bothered many people for a long time is the size of the national debt. As we have seen, deficits in the federal budget have occurred much more frequently than surpluses. Moreover, these deficits have assumed huge proportions in recent years. Consequently, the federal debt now exceeds $3 trillion and continues to increase at a rapid pace. The result is a great deal of consternation and even fear about the financial "soundness" of the federal government. Is it possible that the government is spending itself into bankruptcy? Is there no limit to the public debt? The answer, as usual in economics, is that "it all depends."

Consider first the question of whether debt is bad in and of itself. To answer this question, let's look at the typical household and business firm. From time to time households have budget deficits—that is, their spending exceeds income for a period. To finance these deficits, households may draw on previously accumulated savings or they may more typically borrow. Households borrow to buy homes, automobiles, and other durable goods. When they purchase these items, their personal balance sheets change. They acquire a new asset, say a home, and a new liability, a mortgage debt. Thus the debt is offset by an asset of at least equal value. As long as household income is sufficient to service the debt, it is no burden to the household. And under these conditions, borrowing is a rational act. In early 1987, total household installment and mortgage debt was about $3 trillion. Business firms are also prodigious borrowers of funds for purposes of investment for new capital. Businesses acquire new capital assets with the expectation that the added income from the investment will be enough to repay all debt plus interest and still have some left over as profits. This is possible because new capital is productive. When businesses borrow, we do not normally consider it deficit spending, but that is exactly what it is. In 1986 alone, American corporations had collective deficits, or had borrowed, about $232 billion through bond issues.

Should household and business debt be feared? Not necessarily. As long as the household has enough income after basic expenses to cover principal and interest, there is no problem. Of course, the amount of debt that households can carry depends on income—so there are limits, and certainly households would want to be clear of debt by retirement. For the business firm, debt is no burden if the actual income from the assets acquired is sufficient to service the debt. The conclusion is that for the private sector, debt is no burden if it is offset or backed by a productive asset.

Essentially the same rule should apply to government. Governments are responsible for investment in public capital such as highways, water projects, bridges, and harbors. Public capital of this type is productive in the sense that it can complement private capital. For example, a new bridge may shorten the distance from farm to market, thus increasing the efficiency and lowering the cost of food to local buyers. Therefore it seems reasonable to conclude that if government borrows to finance productive public capital, then that debt would be no burden. The improved performance of the economy should generate enough added tax revenue to service the debt.

At this point, we have a problem in assessing whether the federal deficit was accounted for by new public capital. The problem is that the federal budget isn't broken down into current and capital items, and as a result it is difficult to assess. Various estimates show that public capital investment in several years has been a substantial part of the deficit. Usually, however, public capital has been rather broadly defined. Yet it is probably true that in most recent years, a substantial amount of deficit spending has been for current expense items. Therefore we conclude that deficit financing is bad if used to cover current expenses, whether the economic unit is public or private.

A change in economic circumstances can create debt burdens where none existed before. For example, a severe recession can create burdens for households that lose jobs and incomes and thus the capacity to repay debt. People in these circumstances often become bankrupt and lose houses, autos, and so on. The same is true of business. A recession-induced loss of income can force private businesses into bankruptcy. The federal government, however, can technically never become bankrupt. The reason is that it has, unlike the rest of us, the power to tax and print money. However, this doesn't mean that federal debt can't become too large. Certainly a debt large in relation to tax revenues creates problems in that large fractions of those receipts would be necessary to pay interest. Furthermore, all debt must eventually be serviced by taxes, so in that sense the burden will be on future generations. Perhaps these constraints are why governments are often tempted to inflate the debt away by money creation.

To sum up, let's say that federal debt is no burden to society if it is used to acquire productive public capital and if over the long haul it grows roughly at the same rate as the GNP.

14

Economic Growth: The Long View

chapter preview

- The rate of economic growth has become a high-priority goal since World War II. This is true for most countries.

- The best measure of economic growth is the percentage change in capita real GNP over long periods of time.

- Per capita real GNP is calculated by dividing real GNP by population.

- Economic growth stems from both an increased quantity and an improved quality of resources—land, labor, capital, and entrepreneurship.

- New natural resources are constantly being discovered and destroyed.

- Capital is increased by saving and investment.

- Demographic forces such as changes in the age-structure of the population determine the long-run supply of labor.

- Entrepreneurship is the crucial catalyst in the growth process.

- Political stability is also necessary for economic growth.

- In the absence of technological change, the growth rate of real GNP will drop and become equal to the growth rate of the labor force due to diminishing returns to capital.

- Changes in technology, however, can offset diminishing returns to capital and raise the growth rate.

- Changes in technology depend largely upon research and development, which in turn depend upon the quality of education.

- Government tax and spending policies can encourage or discourage economic growth.

- A stable economic environment—the goal of monetary and fiscal policy—creates a climate conducive to economic growth.

A powerful new force has worked its way into recent international economic and political debate—namely, nations vying with one another over high rates of growth. The turning point in this respect was World War II. Prior to the war, the United States took growth pretty much for granted; we acted as if it were a process that naturally took place. This rather lackadaisical attitude continued for a decade or so following the war. Now, however, it is quite another matter; we have made economic growth a prime target and the subject of a lot of discussion, both analytical and political. Hence, this chapter.

Interestingly, the growth race seems to be much more keen among the already industrially advanced nations, such as the United States, Japan, West Germany, and the Soviet Union. Each of the rich countries strives to increase—or at least maintain—its relative position in this race. Thus the contest seems to be mainly among the economic giants, with each trying to become even more gigantic.

This doesn't mean, however, that the wealthy nations are the only ones concerned with growth. Poor countries want desperately to break out of their economic backwardness and to achieve a high-level growth track. In recent years, some of these countries—e.g., South Korea, Taiwan, and Brazil—have made astounding progress. Other countries also hold out promises of future improvement.

This chapter, however, is restricted solely to the growth of the already advanced countries. This means that we must now shift our attention from the short-run analysis in the past five chapters to the long-run analysis of economic growth.

Let's go back to the production-possibilities curve in Chapter 2 to help us make this transition. The production-possibilities curve in panel (A) of Figure 14–1 is drawn on the twin assumptions of (a) a given amount of resources and (b) a given static technology. Indeed, this is how we define the short run in macroeconomics— a fixed supply of resources and an unchanging technology. The last few chapters have explained how the economy can be at some point U beneath the curve. Point U represents the fact that real GNP is below potential. These chapters also discussed policies that could get us back on, or close to, the curve at, say, point F with minimum inflation.

We now move to the long run by relaxing the assumptions of a fixed supply of resources and a static technology and asking what happens to GNP as a result. Panel (B) of Figure 14–1 illustrates what we mean. The rightward shifts of the production-possibilities curve occur as more and more resources become available and as new technologies make these resources more efficient.

What are the nuts and bolts of economic growth? Section A of this chapter discusses some general ideas about growth, including how it is measured. Section B

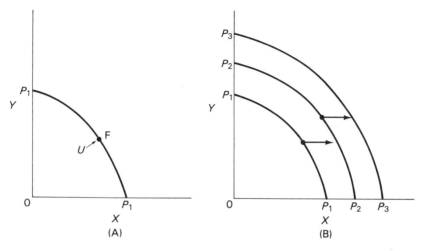

FIGURE 14-1   Production-Possibilities Curve Over Time   Panel (A) shows the production choices available to society in the short run. Panel (B) shows how an increase in the quantity and quality of the resource base and technological improvement can affect the ability to produce output.

then considers the sources of economic growth. The process, or pattern, of growth is the subject of Section C. Section D analyzes the policies that may be used to stimulate and maintain growth.

A. DIMENSIONS OF ECONOMIC GROWTH

We are concerned here with two general questions. First, why all the recent emphasis on growth? Second, how is economic growth measured? Let's answer these questions in turn.

1. The Emphasis on Growth

Of the several reasons that underlie the recent discussion, three stand out (at least in the United States) as vitally important.

In the first place, growth has become a part of the ideological dispute between the Communist and non-Communist parts of the world. Immediately after World War II, the Soviet Union (a command-type economy) experienced a very rapid rate of growth. In fact, its growth rate, which was as high as 7 percent in some years, was much higher than ours. This accomplishment was taken up as a serious challenge to the market-oriented economies of the West, and the growth race was on. Each side strove to show that its type of economic society was more conducive to growth than the other side's.

This conflict spread over into the third-world nations. At first, the less-developed countries tended to embrace the command model as the best approach to generating economic expansion and development. In recent years, however, the obvious stagnation in the centrally planned economies, coupled with the success of the Pacific Rim nations using the market model, has led to a growing interest in the private market approach to economic growth among the developed nations.[1]

"More is better" is the second reason for the emphasis on growth. If we measure economic welfare in terms of per capita GNP (of which, more below), and if per capita GNP is rising, then presumably the populace is better off. The argument runs as follows: Economic growth means that people can consume more than before, and it allows people at the lower rungs of the income ladder to have their circumstances improved with no necessary sacrifice on the part of others. Therefore economic growth is desirable in itself, but particularly if our per capita GNP is higher than anyone else's. For years that was true; now, however, some countries approach the United States in per capita value of production.

However, the "more is better" argument isn't completely persuasive. Economic growth may create goods and services, but it also generates negative goods—that is, "bads"—and these bads reduce the quality of life for many people. Examples: pollution of the air, earth, and water; less time for the pursuit of the noneconomic aims of life; increased crowding (see Exhibit 14–1). Economic growth, in other words, creates "illfare" along with "welfare," and this must be considered in any assessment of growth.

Finally, both the Employment Act of 1946 and the Humphrey-Hawkins Act of 1978 impose on government the *continuing commitment* to full employment—that is, not just full employment for now, but full employment through time. The idea, then, would be for the economy to be at some preferred point on each curve in Figure 14–1(B) as it shifts to the right. The last chapter, however, revealed the difficulty involved in maintaining a noninflationary, full-employment situation through time.

2. The Measurement of Growth

How do we measure economic growth? Just above we used *per capita GNP,* and while this isn't an ideal measurement, it is much better than using *total GNP.*

Total real GNP, as we know, has risen consistently over time (of course, given the ups and downs of the business cycle). In this respect, we can say that the United States has experienced sustained economic growth. But this method of measurement is seriously flawed. It doesn't tell us what is happening to "economic welfare." For instance, it is quite possible for the total real GNP of a country to grow from one generation to another and still experience a decline in standards of living. How can this be? Simply because total population has grown faster than total GNP (see Exhibit 14–1).

[1]The Pacific Rim nations are Korea, Japan, Taiwan, Singapore, and Malaysia.

EXHIBIT 14-1
Thomas Robert Malthus on Population and Economic Growth

One of Adam Smith's followers was Thomas Robert Malthus, an English parson turned economist and demographer. Malthus (1766-1834) is best known for his population theory. In its simplest form, this story asserts that *if* population were to increase at a *geometric rate* from generation to generation and the output of foodstuffs were to grow at an *arithmetical rate,* overpopulation would undoubtedly occur. Illustration: Suppose that there is no technical progress, that the subsistence income is the equivalent of 500 bushels of grain per year, that population initially is 100 persons, and that output is 100,000 bushels of grain. Per capita real income, therefore, is 100,000 ÷ 100 = 1,000 bushels of grain. This is far above the assumed basic subsistence.

Malthus argued that when real income exceeds the subsistence level, population naturally increases. Now, a geometric rate of increase means that population will double from one generation to the next *if unchecked.* Thus we would have population growing at 100—200—400—800—, etc.

Clearly, under these circumstances, population will outstrip the growth of foodstuffs; indeed, in this simple model, this is bound to occur. We can see why in the accompanying table. The first row lists the total output of bushels of grain; reading from left to right we see that grain production grows at an arithmetical rate. The second row tells us that total population grows geometrically. Finally, the third row shows per capita grain income; it is calculated by dividing the numbers in the first row by the corresponding numbers in the second.

Note that our assumed per capita real subsistence income is reached in the fourth generation. Up to then, per capita income is greater than the subsistence level, and so families continue to be formed and to propagate. But the inevitable occurs, and population pushes beyond the point at which per capita income falls below the subsistence level; thus, population will fall. This is, *ceteris paribus,* unavoidable. Look at the situation in the fifth and sixth generations. There is no way that persons beyond the number 800 can survive.

			Generations			
	1	2	3	4	5	6
Grain output	100,000	200,000	300,000	400,000	500,000	600,000
Population	100	200	400	800	1,600	3,200
Grain per capita	1,000	1,000	750	500	312.5	187.5

As a result, there will be what Malthus called "positive checks," such as starvation, disease, and epidemics. These will of course reduce populations to, say 200. And then the cycle is ready to resume; for at 200, per capita income is once again greater than subsistence, families propagate, and overpopulation eventually occurs again. The positive checks occur, reducing population to the point at which real income exceeds subsistence; and so it goes.

Is all of this inevitable? Malthus argued that it was not, that families could make use of what he termed the "preventative checks." These, if used properly, could reduce the birthrate so that population growth would be brought more in line with the growth rate of foodstuffs. What are these preventative checks? Malthus again, in his simplest model, argued in favor of late marriage and abstinence until marriage occurs. At a far more realistic and practical level, however, he suggested the use of birth control methods other than abstinence. Malthus also recommended technological progress in both agriculture and manufacturing. This would of course raise the growth rate productivity of foodstuffs.

Many have criticized Malthus as being too unrealistic. To this we respond by saying that in the more sophisticated versions of his model, he stressed factors that would influence both the birthrate and the rate of growth of foodstuffs to postpone the day of reckoning. Also, it may be worthwhile for us to bear in mind that currently the world's population is just about doubling from generation to generation. What does this imply about our future?

Per capita income, therefore, is more useful as measurement than total income. It is calculated as

$$\text{Per capita real GNP} = \frac{\text{Total real GNP}}{\text{Population}}$$

This formula tells us that there are two possible ways for per capita real GNP to change. The first occurs when population grows faster than real GNP; in this case, per capita income falls. Second, if total real GNP grows faster than population, per capita real income will rise. If the two values change proportionally, real GNP per capita will remain constant.

Table 14-1 reveals which of these two possibilities has been relevant for the United States since 1950. Aside from an occasional dip, per capita real GNP has displayed a consistently upward trend. However, we must be very careful in using this particular method of measuring growth as a proxy for economic welfare. It must be qualified, and for a number of reasons.

First, as Chapter 8 reveals, GNP doesn't include all the goods and services that contribute directly and positively to people's welfare. Ranking very high on this list are leisure, shorter workweeks, earlier retirements, and more vacations—all of which add a dimension to life that GNP doesn't record. (Yet we should also remember that, as more of our time is spent in consumption of material things, less is left for other pursuits.)

On the other side of the coin, many things included in GNP should perhaps be omitted when it is used to measure economic growth. Maybe military expenditures

TABLE 14-1   Real Per Capital GNP: U.S. 1945–86

Year	Per Capita GNP (1982) dollars
1950	—
1955	$ 8,819
1960	$ 9,080
1965	$10,644
1970	$11,781
1971	$11,905
1972	$12,473
1973	$13,178
1974	$12,970
1975	$12,478
1976	$13,250
1977	$13,840
1978	$13,993
1979	$14,182
1980	$13,994
1981	$14,114
1982	$13,614
1983	$13,964
1984	$14,721
1985	$14,981
1986	$15,359
1987	$15,672

Source: Economic Report of the President, February 1988; and *Federal Reserve Bulletin;* June 1988, Table A-52.

shouldn't be included when we try to assess economic welfare. The argument here is that these expenditures contribute to welfare, but only indirectly; therefore their impact is difficult to quantify. Indeed, some people argue that much of military spending is unnecessary and wasteful, and these expenditures should actually be deducted from total GNP when we use per capita GNP as a proxy for economic welfare. These resources could have been used in other more productive ways had they been made available to the private sector of the economy.

Another qualification is that per capita real GNP isn't a useful measurement over long periods of time. The reason for this is that the composition of GNP has changed drastically over the years, so that comparisons between now and much earlier years are meaningless. Examples abound. The automobile has replaced the horse and buggy, and tractors have superseded the horse-drawn plow; electric lights have done away with kerosene lamps; zippers have been substituted for buttons; and plastics are now being used instead of glass and metal in many items. However, plastic items are harder to dispose of and thus add to our illfare. The list goes on and on. These changes raise serious questions about using GNP for purposes of comparison. How can we appropriately contrast a per capita GNP of $13,000 today with the same income of, say, fifty years ago? The one buys such a different configuration of goods than the other could have bought that the contrast boils down to comparing apples and oranges with diesel trucks. It just doesn't make much sense.

Still another shortcoming of per capita income as a measurement is that it ignores the importance of income distribution. A rising per capita income may gloss over the fact that the benefits of growth may be going to only a small part of the population. For instance, a country may have per capita income of, say, $15,000, but nearly all its members are poor farmers or tradesmen. The remaining members are multi-millionaires, and it is they who pull up the average income. If GNP were to continue to rise, and if all of this increase were to go to the already wealthy families, the per capita GNP would rise, but this would hardly measure an increase in economic welfare for most of the population.

Finally, and quite important, too much concentration on GNP as measurement tends to lure us into the trap of ignoring the noneconomic dimensions of life. Love and beauty, peace and inner harmony aren't counted in GNP, nor are the richness of spiritual values and the pleasures derived from nature. Yet, these are far more important than the automobiles and the hair sprays, liquor, designer jeans, and antiperspirants that are included.

All told, then, there are many major qualifications to using GNP (either total or per capita) as a measure of economic growth. Per capita GNP is, at best, a poor measurement; nonetheless, it seems to be the most suitable that we have. It will serve so long as we are aware of its limitations.

B. SOURCES OF ECONOMIC GROWTH

As we noted above, the change in emphasis from short-run to long-run analysis calls for a new view of things. The past few chapters have considered the business cycle as fluctuations of the aggregate demand around a fixed and stable aggregate supply. This chapter considers what happens to aggregate supply as part of economic growth.

One view is given in Figure 14–1(B), which shows the production-possibilities curve shifting to the right when we relax the assumptions of a given supply of resources and a fixed technology. Another view is given in Figure 14–2. The top part of the figure is very much like Figure 14–1(B)—that is, the production-possibilities curve shifts continuously to the right as more resources become available and as technological changes occur. Note how we have labeled these curves with dates— 1970, 1980, and 1990. Because of the changed supplies of resources and increased technology, the *P–P* curve of 1990 lies to the right of *P–P* of 1980, which in turn lies to the right of 1970.

The same pattern of growth is shown in the bottom part of Figure 14–2. Here we have the aggregate supply curve shifting to the right because of more resources and technology. Note that we have assumed that the aggregate demand curve has also shifted to the right proportionally, so that the price level remains constant at P_0. This, however, hasn't occurred. Throughout the second half of the nineteenth century, aggregate supply increased more than aggregate demand, and thus the price

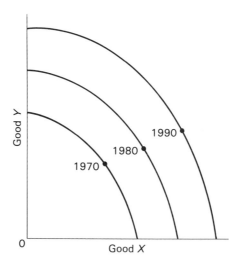

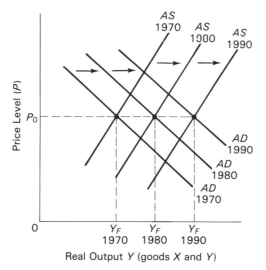

FIGURE 14-2 Aggregate Supply, Aggregate Demand, and Economic Growth As economic growth unfolds, both aggregate demand and aggregate supply curves shift to the right. In this case, we have them rising proportionately so that the price level remains constant. Throughout the nineteenth century, however, aggregate supply increased more than aggregate demand; therefore the price level fell. During the twentieth century, on the other hand, the reverse occurred—aggregate demand started to rise more than aggregate supply, causing the price level to rise.

level tended to fall. The second half of the twentieth century, however, has been another story. Aggregate demand has tended to expand more than aggregate supply, so that the price level has tended upward.

It is reasonable to conclude that as the economy acquires more resources and has advancing technologies, the production-possibilities curve will naturally shift to the right. This is correct, but much more is involved than simply having more plants, more machines, and more mineral deposits. Technical change is also important; indeed, anything that enhances technology (such as education and research) stimulates economic growth more than the mere growth of the labor force and the amount of real physical capital. The powerful role of education crops up time and again throughout the rest of this chapter.

1. Labor

Clearly, the more hands there are for work, the more work that can be done; and in the United States there are more hands year after year. Currently, the labor force is growing by about 2 million workers per year. However, the decline in birthrates in recent years means that we can expect the labor force to grow more slowly in the future. Increased immigration (relative to emigration) may slow down this trend, however.

Important as the quantity of labor may be, possibly more important is the *quality* of the work force. More years of high-quality education expand the knowledge base of the labor force, making it more skillful and hence more productive.

Once again we refer to that great economist Adam Smith, for it was he who first recognized the tremendous importance of division of labor for economic growth. His argument, moreover, is as relevant today as it was in 1776. Technical schools train people in very specific, highly productive skills that are crucial to expanding new industries. Also, the time spent on specialized jobs, such as machine tool operator, stone masonry, X-ray technician, and auto mechanic, builds skill levels through on-the-job training. Finally, improved management skills and techniques can increase the efficiency with which all resources are used.

Then, too, the quality of the work force depends to a great extent on the broader aspects of society. The healthier and more vigorous the members of society are, the greater their productivity. The same holds true for protection from potential threats to health and body. Thus better and more available medical care, improved nutrition, and efficient police and fire forces make positive contributions to the growth process. On the other hand, poverty, ignorance, malnutrition, alcoholism and other drug addictions, and high crime rates are obviously detrimental. However, more on this below.

2. Capital

Capital, although not necessarily owned by the workers, is essentially the tool of the work force. Historically, the capital stock in the United States has grown faster than the labor force, so that the amount of capital per worker has increased. This in turn has been a significant source of the long-term rise in labor productivity in this country.

We already have some good background for discussing the role of capital in economic growth. If there is to be economic growth, there must be an increase in the economy's stock of capital; and if the capital stock is to grow, there must be net business investment in new plants and equipment. In other words, if business firms annually acquire more new capital goods than their old capital wears out in the production process, then the capital stock will increase over time.

We know that the new capital is made possible by society's savings. Saving means that not all of the economy's resources are being used to produce consumer goods and services; therefore, some resources are available for the production of capital goods. Moreover, a society that saves a large percentage of its annual income will, all other things equal, be able to accumulate more capital over time than a society that saves a small percentage of its income. In this case, the former society will sustain a higher growth *rate* than the latter (see Exhibit 14–2).

On this matter, recall that the current savings rate in the United States is about 5 percent. In Japan, on the other hand, it is about 14 percent, and in West Germany it is about 9 percent. Perhaps, then, this helps to explain the high rates of growth in these two countries and our rather lagging performance in recent years. More on this in Section E.

The quality of the capital stock is also an important determinant of economic growth. In other words, technological advances improve the productivity of capital. For instance, more-advanced computers increase the amount of work that can be done in a given period of time. Robot welders have reduced both the time and the cost of producing automobiles. Genetic engineering and more-sophisticated equipment promise dramatic increases in agricultural productivity. These and many other changes in technology, when embodied in new plants and productive processes, raise the average quality of the capital stock and hence increase the aggregate capacity of the economy to produce.

Technological change, however, isn't automatic. It is itself dependent on basic and applied research and development, as well as on the willingness of management to put the new (and maybe risky) ideas into operation. Expenditures on research and development are crucial in the growth process; and of course education underlies research and development. Not only do educational advances directly improve the productivity of labor, but they are also important for advances in technology—in fact, probably more important. More on this at the end of Section C in this chapter.

A final point: We must also keep in mind that technological advances are a mixed bag of blessings. In fact, they can be downright harmful to some; and, in more than a few instances, they have imposed harm on society. Technological changes, for example, may force some business firms to close down. A good example of this is American agriculture, in which technology has spelled a continuing decline of small farms until they are virtually a thing of the past. Also, there is the cost of unemployment as capital displaces labor—e.g., robots displacing the blue-collar assembly-line workers in the automobile industry. Too, the chemical-plastic industry has the problem of toxic waste disposal.

Granted, technology has its costs; but it still remains a powerful force for growth and change.

EXHIBIT 14-2
Capital Formation and Economic Growth

The role of saving and investment in economic growth can be illustrated by the production-possibilities curve. Panel (A) of the accompanying diagram has capital goods *(K)* on the vertical axis and consumer goods *(C)* on the horizontal axis. Let's suppose the economy is at point *G* on the production-possibilities curve P_1P_1. This means, and we know this applies to all countries, that the bulk of the economy's resources is devoted to the production of consumer goods. Only a small portion is used to produce *K* goods.

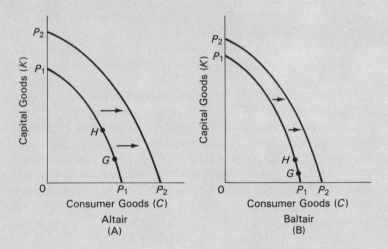

Altair
(A)

Baltair
(B)

Let's introduce a change here and have the economy in panel (A) increase the amount of resources devoted to *K* goods, so that the economy slides up the curve to point *H*. Note that this is a rather large reallocation of resources away from *C* goods over to *K* goods. We know that this change creates an immediate opportunity cost—that is, fewer *C* goods are being produced in order for there to be more *K* goods. This is the same as saying that the economy has increased its savings by reducing consumption.

The cost, however, is short run in nature; for once the new capital formation has been completed, the labor force will be more efficient because it now has more capital to work with. This will especially occur if new technology is incorporated into the new *K* goods. In this event, the work force becomes even more productive. Consequence? The production-possibilities curve will shift to the right; we have drawn it as moving to P_2P_2.

Let's summarize: The households in society experienced a short-run opportunity cost as consumption was cut back to facilitate new capital goods production. This reduction in consumption means that households have increased their savings. The end result, then, was a shift of the economy's production-possibilities curve to the right, that is, economic growth.

But all of this is true only for the country in panel (A), the country we name Altair. As a result of the increased saving, Altair experienced rather good growth, at least as compared with Baltair, as shown in panel (B). Baltair's initial production-possibilities curve P_1P_1, and its original position on the curve at G, are the same as for Altair. The major difference between the two societies is shown in how little Baltair saves compared with Altair. In consequence, there is much less new capital formation, so that Baltair experiences much less growth; its production-possibilities curve shifts only to P_2P_2 in panel (B).

Is there a moral to be drawn from this example?

3. Land: Natural Resources

Will Rogers is supposed to have said that the best investment is in land "because they don't make no more of that." He was right. The quantity of land is, for all practical purposes, fixed. True, swamps can be drained, some arid regions can be irrigated, and, as the Dutch have shown, some lands can even be reclaimed from the seas. Still, it remains true that the total amount of land can't be appreciably increased.

Remember that when economists speak of "land" they also mean forests, minerals, and all the other natural resources. Many (maybe most) of these are irreplaceable; that is, once they have been consumed and used up, they cannot be replaced. Coal, once burned, is gone; so is natural gas, and so is petroleum. Forests, of course, can be replaced, but topsoil lost due to poor farming techniques and erosion can't be.

Hence, over time economic growth tends to deplete the economy's natural resources, and this calls for more efficient use of those we have, greater emphasis on discovering more, and development of new technologies that increase the efficiency of resource use. Thus the fertility of land can be enhanced by the use of proper farming techniques. Also, more efficient ways can be found to recover the remaining supplies of minerals from the earth. The sea holds promise for additional supplies of minerals once technology has been developed to obtain access to remote underwater locations. Nor should the use of solar energy be overlooked, let alone the potential advantages of nuclear energy. All in all, there are many sources of energy and resources available in the future, but this is no guarantee that there will be a sufficient amount to accommodate a growing population.

4. Entrepreneurship

A final important point needs to be made: Our description of the sources of economic growth makes it sound as if it is more or less a mechanical process that brings all these changes into being. This is hardly the case. It is something more than, say, following a recipe to bake a cake. Someone must of course bring all the ingredients together and in the proper proportions. In the real world, however, the recipe is constantly changing, and it must be a daring cook indeed who tries to bake a cake. There will definitely be a final product, but will it be any good? Here is where the challenge comes. Who, indeed, is enterprising enough to try to produce a good product under ever-changing conditions?

What our example is leading up to is that there must be people of enterprising spirit if the process of economic growth is to materialize. This spirit is sometimes called "entrepreneurship," but no matter what it is called, there must be those who are willing to risk time, effort, and money on new ideas, new products, and new ways of doing things. Growth, therefore, isn't an automatic process. There must be those who seek out the challenges of change and, in the hope of profit, put these changes into effect.

We must further recognize that the process of growth within a nation is strongly affected by the institutional and cultural factors found in that society. These have a direct impact on what the people think, want, and are willing to risk. Many societies possess the resources necessary for substantial economic growth but remain at low levels of living. They don't possess the institutional and cultural factors necessary for substantial growth. On the other hand, some few nations possess very few natural resources but seem to have an abundance of entrepreneurship and institutions conducive to growth. Japan is the outstanding example in this respect.

5. Interactions

So far, this part of the chapter has shown how change in technology and increases in the quantity of resources will shift the economy's aggregate supply curve to the right. In doing so, however, it rather ignored the demand side. Yet, in an important sense, the aggregate demand side can't be neglected, for changes in resource supplies will often affect both the supply and the demand sides. So, too, will technological changes.

Consider this example. A change in the capital stock *(I)* has a twofold effect. First, it represents an increase in aggregate supply, a point made above. But, second, an increase in the capital stock also leads to an increase in aggregate demand, especially through the multiplier. This is a major point made in Chapters 10 and 13. Accordingly, any analysis of growth must take this interaction into account.

Similarly, an increase in population affects both aggregate demand and aggregate supply (a point stressed in Exhibit 14-1). Aggregate demand rises because there are more mouths to feed; aggregate supply rises because there are more hands available for production.

These interactions lead us to an important question: Will the increased aggregate demand be sufficient to absorb the increased aggregate supply resulting from the larger labor force and greater capital stock and still yield satisfactory profits to businesses, or will aggregate demand expand faster than aggregate supply leading to long-run inflation? Let's turn to these problems now.

C. THE GROWTH PROCESS

Earlier in this chapter, we observed that while both the labor force and the capital stock are growing, the stock of capital is growing at a faster rate than the work force. Some studies, in fact, conclude that capital is growing about twice as fast as labor. Clearly, then, the amount of capital per worker is increasing, and this is very important.

To see why it is so important, let's suppose that capital is growing faster than labor and there are no technological advances. Two results occur. The first is that the increased amount of capital improves worker productivity. Remember, one farmer with a tractor is far more efficient than several farmers with only horses and plows. Yet, second, this increase in productivity has certain and clear limits. The reason for this is that an old friend comes back to haunt us—the law of diminishing returns. In this case, we have diminishing returns to capital; and this occurs simply because the capital stock is growing faster than the labor force. Therefore, at some time the productivity of capital will fall.

The fact that both inputs are increasing doesn't invalidate the law of diminishing returns; the only difference is that one input is relatively fixed while the other remains variable. Instead one is "fixed" only in comparison with the other—i.e., labor is increasing at a slower rate than capital. Hence, without technical change, diminishing returns to capital will eventually set in.

This means that eventually the profitability of capital will fall; and this in turn reduces the growth rate of capital. After all, if the anticipated profits of new capital become lower and lower (due to diminishing returns), the rate of capital formation must fall. This will of course reduce the growth rate of real GNP. But note that the rate of growth can't fall below the rate of growth of output caused by the changing labor force. If, in other words, the growth rate of the labor force accounts for 1 percent growth in real GNP, and if capital formation falls to the rate just necessary to accommodate the changing work force, we can reach an important conclusion.

> **Conclusion:** In the absence of technical change, the rate of growth of the capital stock will fall and match the growth of the labor force. The growth rate of real GNP, therefore, will be the same as the growth rate of the labor force.

Per capita GNP will remain constant if the labor force grows at the same rate as the population.

Actually, the analysis spelled out above doesn't fit the facts for most of the post–World War II period. In other words, for this period as a whole, there have been enough offsets to diminishing returns to capital to prevent stagnation in our economy. Studies show that growth in total output has averaged about 3 percent per year; the same studies point out that the labor force has grown at the rate of 1 percent per year. Thus output per worker (i.e., labor productivity) has grown at the rate of 2 percent per year.

Since the increased number of workers can account for only one-third of the rate of growth of real GNP, the remaining two-thirds must be due to technical change. This technical change, therefore, plays a crucial role in the growth process; indeed, it is essential.

Several major empirical studies show the relevance of technical change. R. M. Solow of the Massachusetts Institute of Technology concludes that technical change has accounted for more than one-half the growth rate of total output in the United States. J. W. Kendrick of the National Bureau of Economic Research arrives at essentially the same conclusion; his studies, however, show that technical progress has become more important over time. The same conclusion is reached by Edward Denison in his study for the Committee for Economic Development. A number of other studies conclude that technical progress has been as important in other advanced economies as in the United States.

This means that we can no longer be content with emphasizing the growth of the labor force and the capital stock as the basic sources of economic growth. They are important, of course, but without increasing education, knowledge, and research, our growth rate would have petered out long ago.

D. GROWTH POLICIES

What can be done to increase the rate of economic growth, assuming that we consider it desirable to do so? We have dropped a number of hints in the last few chapters, particularly Chapter 13.

First, the general atmosphere must be conducive to the types of actions that stimulate growth. We noted above that necessary prerequisites would include a stable government, a strong work ethic, and a positive attitude toward risk taking. Second, and very important, members of society should be oriented toward improvement of future conditions and not simply to maintaining the status quo.

History has shown that when these conditions aren't present, economies tend to stagnate despite large infusions of money capital. Where these conditions do exist, policy measures can be taken to enhance the growth process.

1. Tax and Spending Policies

First, tax and spending policies of the government should, in general, encourage and complement the actions of the private sector that lead to growth. Aside from the obvious provision of police and fire protection and an efficient system of courts, an adequate amount of government spending (at all levels) should be devoted to the improvement and maintenance of public capital, such as highways, streets, harbors, bridges, and water and sewer systems. All of these types of spending improve the productivity of private capital. Certainly an inadequate stock of public capital can stifle private incentives for investment. Just think of what would happen to private investment if the interstate highway system fell into such a state of disrepair that it became unusable.

Second, education also ranks extremely high on the list of priorities. We have already seen how education is crucial to the growth process. A better-educated public is important in that the "knowledge content" of job openings has been rising quite rapidly. The increasing technical sophistication of production processes requires that new entrants in the labor force have a sound, general education as well as the requisite skills. Recent studies of the educational system in this country conclude that we are probably falling far short of what is needed for us to hold our own in the growth race. Since knowledge is the prime mover of economic growth, and if we want to maintain a growth of 3 percent or more per year, then perhaps more resources need to be devoted to education, particularly at the state and local levels.

Third, the structure of taxes is important. As we have observed elsewhere, taxes should be simple, easy to administer, and perceived as fair by a majority of citizens. Just as important, tax rates shouldn't stifle incentives. Many economists believe that low marginal tax rates on income from labor, saving, and investment can increase work effort and capital formation. The tax rate reductions in 1981, and the very significant reduction of marginal rates on high incomes built into the Tax Reform Act of 1986, reflect this type of thinking.

2. Proper Monetary and Fiscal Policy

A stable economy provides a far more conducive environment for economic growth than one in which there are wide, unpredictable swings in business activity. For example, severe recessions interrupt the flow of saving into investment, while inflation makes it difficult to make sound investment decisions. Therefore proper anticyclical monetary and fiscal policies are important for growth.

E. RECENT GROWTH PERFORMANCE IN THE UNITED STATES

In the late 1970s and early 1980s, a dramatic slowdown of economic growth occurred in the United States. From 1929 to 1976, average annual output growth was about 3 percent. Between 1978 and 1982, however, nonfarm output grew at less than half that rate, and output per hour of work (labor productivity) barely changed at all. There have been many attempts to account for this disappointing performance, with no single cause emerging as the dominant one.

The data show a decline of investment as a percentage of the GNP and a large decline in the increase of capital per worker during the 1970s. Investment as a percentage of the GNP fell from a high of over 4 percent in the late 1960s to less than 3 percent in the 1976–77 period, while the change in capital per worker was nil during the same period. Since we know that the ultimate source of real capital is saving, it is instructive to note that private savings as a percentage of the GNP fell from over 6.0 percent to about 3.5 percent in the early 1980s. Thus a deficiency of money capital would certainly be part of the explanation of the slow growth over the period. What factors could in turn account for the savings shortfall?

Some believe that the shortage of saving is at least partially the result of a tax system that during the period encouraged consumption and discouraged saving. Interest has been fully deductible, whereas saving and the income from past saving have been fully taxed. This tax structure could account for a low saving rate, but not the significant drop that actually occurred. Since 1981, changes in the tax laws have restored part of the reward for saving.

More likely causes of the poor saving and investment performance are rooted in the general economic conditions of the period. The late 1970s were a period of escalating inflation and rising budget deficits. Inflation, in addition to pushing people into higher income-tax brackets, induces households to speed up consumption at the expense of saving, while rising government deficits absorb larger amounts of money capital, otherwise available for private capital formation. Crowding out, therefore, can have long-term effects on growth. In recent years, inflation has slowed down dramatically, but deficits are still enormous.

Other analysts argue that government has had a further impact on growth through regulation of industry. Regulation, whatever its other benefits to society, can reduce the willingness and ability of business to expand. An example would be the mandated expenditures to reduce pollution as the result of the environmental legislation of the 1970s.

There have also been a host of other partial explanations offered. A rising percentage of young, unskilled workers in the labor force during the 1970s could partly account for the low growth of productivity. During the same period, business research and development expenditures declined, which could have adversely affected technical progress. Finally, many believe that the traditional American "work ethic" has declined, bringing relatively poor economic performance in its wake.

Since the early 1980s, U.S. economic performance has improved, but many problems of the 1970s remain. Only time will tell if our recent troubles are temporary or the beginning of relative economic decline.

F. SUMMARY

Economic growth can't be taken for granted. It is the consequence of increases in the physical supplies of resources and, especially, of technical progress. This more important determinant of growth, however, is difficult to quantify because of its underpinnings—i.e., research and development, social and cultural factors, and, above all, education at every level.

In the absence of technical progress, the economy would experience stagnation. Growth of real GNP would be proportional to the growth of the work force; hence, real GNP per capita would stabilize.

Technical progress, however, has occurred enough to offset diminishing returns to capital, so that throughout the postwar period real GNP per capita has grown at about 2 percent per year. Most of this change is attributable to education and knowledge as embodied in technical progress.

The basic policies for stimulating growth are rather indirect. They include sufficient expenditures by government at all levels to provide and maintain the public capital that enhances productivity of privately owned resources. Also, government growth policies should encourage private saving and investment. Probably more important, they should provide as much short-run stability as possible, thus creating the sort of environment conducive to sound, rational decisions that result in economic growth. Finally, there is need—a strong need, at that—for government at all levels to encourage education both quantitatively and, especially, qualitatively. In the long run, economic growth flows mainly from knowledge put to use in economic affairs.

Terms and Concepts to Remember

Per capita real GNP   Technical change
Entrepreneurship   Research and development

Questions for Review

1. Define *per capita real GNP.* Why is it the best available measure of economic growth? What are its shortcomings as a measurement?

2. If the labor force grows faster than the capital stock, what will happen to the profitability of new capital investment and to the rate of growth of real GNP?

3. Why is entrepreneurship such a vital factor in the growth process?

4. What categories of government spending contribute most to economic growth?

5. What are the major reasons cited for the recent slowdown of growth in the United States?

15

Markets in the Circular Flow

chapter preview

- Microeconomics studies individual consumer and business behavior.

- The major emphasis of microeconomics is on allocative efficiency—that is, on how efficiently an economy uses its scarce resources.

- *Allocative efficiency* means that the mix of goods and services produced should match consumer demand. These goods and services should also be produced at their least cost.

- The market system sends out signals when allocative efficiency is not being realized. Economic units then respond to these signals.

- When competition prevails, the response of economic units—both households and businesses—restores allocative efficiency.

- Most economists agree that the more competitive the economy, the more likely efficiency will be achieved. On the other hand, monopoly elements drive the economy into inefficient use of resources.

- Competition prevails at different levels—between sellers and buyers, among buyers, and among sellers.

- The characteristics of a competitive industry are (1) a large number of small firms, (2) a homogeneous product, and (3) no barriers to the entry and exit of firms in and out of the market.

- The firms in a competitive industry focus their attention on price competition and on achieving maximum efficiency in production.

- A pure monopoly, however, yields a less efficient allocation of resources. By barring the entry of rival firms into the market, a monopoly thwarts competition and thus ends up charging a higher price and selling a smaller quantity.

- An oligopoly—like a monopoly—yields an inefficient allocation of resources. An oligopolistic industry is characterized by a few large, dominant firms. Hence it, too, thwarts competition.

In Chapters 9–14, we have been concerned with the idea of efficiency at the macroeconomic level. *Aggregate efficiency* exists when there is full employment of the economy's resources. Put otherwise, aggregate inefficiency prevails when there is general unemployment of resources. We now turn to the concept of efficiency at the *microeconomic* level. *Micro* means small, little, minute; and accordingly microeconomics focuses on the smaller units of the economy. These are the individual households and business firms as they make and carry out their decisions in the numerous markets that constitute the economy.

We must examine these markets—both product and resource—in detail, and our focal point will be the sort of efficiency that is relevant at the microeconomic level. This is the concept of allocative efficiency, and it is discussed and defined in Section A. Then Section B introduces two types of market structures—competition and monopoly—which have a definite bearing on how efficiently or inefficiently the economy's scarce resources are used. Sections C and D look at these two product market structures in more detail. Section E provides a brief examination of competition in resource markets. Section F closes the chapter with a final look at competition.

A. THE CONCEPT OF ALLOCATIVE EFFICIENCY

In Chapter 1, we stated that there are certain unavoidable questions that every economic society must answer. We also observed that in the United States, we rely predominantly on the market mechanism as the means of dealing with these problems. The questions are: (1) What goods and services should our scarce resources be used to produce? (2) How much of them should be made available? (3) What methods of production should be used to provide them? and (4) For whom should they be produced?

1. The Proper Mixture of Goods and Services

Let's look at the first two of these questions, the *what* and *how much* questions. Put together they indicate that some proper mixture of goods and services should be forthcoming in proper quantities if consumer demands are to be satisfied. Any other mixture will leave some demands unsatisfied—that is, some goods will be produced in deficient amounts while other goods will be produced in excess amounts. In this event, the economy's resources aren't being used efficiently. This would be shown by persistent shortages of some products and surpluses of others. In other words, our scarce resources are being "wasted."

From this we can derive a partial definition of an important concept. *Allocative efficiency,* in part, requires that the variety and quantities of goods and services produced match the configuration of demands for these goods and services. In this respect, it would seem that if there were no market surpluses and shortages, then allocative efficiency would prevail. This, however, is not quite correct. The concept of allocative efficiency must be broadened to include the question of what methods of production should be used in producing what consumers are demanding and the last question—For whom are the goods and services produced?

2. The Proper Resource Mixture

Once the proper mixture of goods and services has been given, allocative efficiency requires that they be produced at the lowest possible costs of production. This means that the producing firms must use the correct kinds and amounts of resources. That is, the resources must be used as efficiently as possible in producing the desired output. For example, if a specific product can be produced at a lower cost using four workers and one machine than it can with two workers and two machines, then that mixture of resources should be used. This leads to the other part of the definition of allocative efficiency: The producing firms should use the proper (least-cost) mix of resources.

But this isn't all. Firms desiring to use the proper resource mix establish a demand pattern for the scarce resources—labor, capital, and land. Resource demands in conjunction with the available supplies of these resources determine their prices and hence the income flows to households. Household income then provides the means for consumer demand and thus answers the final question—For whom is the output produced? Thus we come full circle back to our original questions of *what* and *how much* to produce. Clearly the questions *what, how much, how,* and *for whom* are interrelated. But this is what is implied by the circular flow.

3. A Definition

The full definition of allocative efficiency, therefore, would read as follows.

> **Definition:** *Allocative efficiency* requires that the mixture of goods and services supplied match the structure of households' demands for these goods and services. Also, this proper mix of goods and services should be produced at the least possible cost. That is, the proper mix of goods and services requires a corresponding proper mix of productive resources. This in turn sets resource demand, which together with supply determines household income.

Clearly, this concept of allocative efficiency means that a tremendous number of decisions must be made. For one thing, households must choose among the thousands of goods and services available to them, and their demands play the crucial role of determining which and how much of these will be produced. Business firms too must determine which of the goods and services they wish to produce and in what quantities. They must also make choices of which methods to use to produce, and this means that they must choose which productive services to use and in what combination they are to be used. How are all these choices made? How is the necessary information imparted to both households and business firms as they participate in product and resource decisions? What mechanism exists to coordinate the millions of independent decisions made by households and business firms?

4. Markets and Information

Markets and the price signals they emit are the mechanism through which all these plans and decisions are harmonized and by which allocative efficiency may or may not be achieved. Prices revealed in markets by supply and demand constitute the information necessary for the proper allocation of resources. To be sure, good information involves more than just price signals. Locations and qualities of products and resources, for example, are also important information. Nevertheless, market prices are the primary form of information needed for the coordination of separate markets. To illustrate, suppose that at some point in time, an excess demand for blue jeans exists and simultaneously there is an excess supply of shoes. Clearly, markets are *not* in equilibrium, and allocative efficiency does *not* exist. How is equilibrium restored? Price changes provide the informational signals that will do the trick. The price of blue jeans rises to reduce the excess amount demanded to the available supply while shoe prices fall, eliminating the excess supply by increasing quantity demanded.

Even though these price changes restore equilibrium, they are likely to be temporary, for they provide further information to blue jeans and shoe producers that will alter production and resource demand. Because of higher prices, business firms anticipate increased profit opportunities for blue jeans, whereas lower shoe prices have the opposite effect in that industry. The high potential profits lure new firms into blue jeans production and also induce existing firms to expand capacity. The demand for land, labor, and capital needed to produce blue jeans therefore increases, causing their prices to rise. Additional resources are thus drawn into blue jeans production. The end result is eventually an increase in the supply, which causes prices to fall.

Essentially the opposite happens in the shoe industry. Existing producers, depressed by the prospect of losses, leave the industry. This releases resources for other uses, among which is the increased production of blue jeans. After the shakeout, the supply of shoes falls and shoe prices rise.

What is the final result of all this? Changing prices initially signaled that markets were out of equilibrium—that is, the mix of outputs didn't match the structure of consumer demand. However, as firms responded to these signals, the mixture of products was brought into line with consumer demands. In this case, and in conformance with consumer wants, more blue jeans and fewer shoes are produced. Allocative efficiency is once again achieved.

However, things don't always work out as smoothly as our example may imply. How markets will actually work in providing allocative efficiency varies with the degree of competition. Economists are generally inclined to argue that allocative efficiency and competition go hand in glove and that resources are less efficiently used in monopolistic settings. Thus we need to look at these two types of industries (or market structures, as they are often called).

B. THE IDEA OF MARKET STRUCTURES

We begin by looking at the idea of competitive market structure; then we will look at monopoly.

1. Competition

Some industries are made up of a very large number of very small firms; these industries are usually referred to as *competitive*. Agricultural markets are a good example. Although they produce for a multitude of different product markets, there are over 2 million farms in the United States. With these numbers, it is likely that there is no one dominant firm, or even a few dominant firms, in any single agricultural market. The firms are, so to speak, *atomistic*—so much so that no one firm has any direct influence on the price of the product. Market price is, in this case, set by the interaction of supply (of a large number of small firms) and demand (of a large number of small households).

Note what is involved here. Competition is not a simple one-way flow of events. Nor does competition occur at only one level in the economy. Instead it takes place at several levels. First, there is the competition referred to above—that is, the competition between the two sides of the market. Buyers, of course, are always looking for the best price, and so are the sellers. The catch is that what is the best price for buyers isn't always the best price for sellers. There is thus competition between buyers and sellers as each side vies to get the "best" price. This is the sort of competition dealt with in Chapter 4.

Second, there is competition among the sellers on their own side of the market, and this level of competition is guaranteed if there are a large number of small sellers. Each seller competes by trying to produce in the most efficient manner possible. Put otherwise: It wouldn't be a very competitive market, would it, if there were thousands of small, independent buyers and only one huge seller? No, if there is to be effective competition, there must be a large number of small, independent sellers, all vying for the consumers' dollars (see Chapter 17).

Third, there is also competition among the households on the demand side of the market. We take this more or less for granted because no one or few consumers can exert much (if any) power in the market (see Chapter 16).

Two final dimensions of competition need to be covered. The sort of competition we have discussed so far is *price* competition, in which the main focus is on the price of the product. Indeed, price competition in competitive industries is quite vigorous. But another kind of competitive activity occupies a lot of attention and uses a lot of resources, and that is *nonprice competition* such as advertising and product style changes. This type of competition, however, is typically found in noncompetitive industries (see Chapter 20).

Finally, as we know from the circular flow model, competition need not be restricted to product markets alone. A glance back to Figure 5–2 shows that both households and business firms interact in resource markets as well. This is shown in the bottom part of the diagram. Competition may also prevail in these markets, again at the three levels we discussed above—(a) between suppliers and demanders, (b) among sellers, and (c) among buyers. Chapter 18 discusses competition in resource markets.

Nothing, however, guarantees that competition necessarily prevails in all the dimensions discussed above. To the contrary, monopoly may intrude at any level or levels, and we now turn to this market structure.

2. Monopoly

Some of our major industries are far removed from the type of competition described earlier. In fact, a *pure monopoly* exists when there is but *one firm* on the supply side of the market. Examples: the local waterworks, the power company from which you buy electricity, the local telephone company, and the natural gas company in your state or locality.

Also, many major industries are not really pure monopolies but at the same time are far from being purely competitive. A few large firms account for the lion's share of the sales in each of these industries. A good example is the chewing gum industry, in which the four largest firms account for 95 percent of the total sales of that industry. Another example is the electric light bulb industry; here the four largest firms produce 90 percent of the industry's output. Quite a number of major industries fall into this category—coffee, automobiles, textbooks, flat glass, aluminum, petroleum, pharmaceuticals, and typewriters, to mention only a few. For the moment, we have included this type of market structure under the heading of monopoly; Chapter 20 focuses on it.

3. Market Structures and Efficiency

Economists have paid a lot of attention to these different market structures because the pattern of resource allocation is greatly affected by the structure of industry using the resources. By and large they agree that resources are used much more efficiently under competitive conditions than they are under monopoly. This holds true for both product markets and resource markets. Thus, so the argument goes, consumers fare better when the goods and services they consume are produced by competitive industries. Why and how they fare better is a matter for the next five chapters to demonstrate.

C. THE CONDITIONS OF COMPETITION IN PRODUCT MARKETS

Four conditions are important in setting industries apart from one another in product markets: (a) the number of firms in the industry, (b) the size of these firms, (c) the nature of the product they produce, and (d) whether there are barriers to entry by new firms into the industry. How these conditions are met determines whether an industry or market is competitive or monopolistic.

1. The Number and Size of Firms

We have already discussed the conditions of number and size of firms, and so we may be brief here. There must be a large number of relatively small firms if the industry is to be competitive. Indeed, each firm must be so small that it has no direct, perceptible influence on market price; its output amounts to, say, 1/1,000 of the total industry output. A firm this small is unable to affect the market price as it changes its output.

2. The Product

In a purely competitive industry, each firm produces a product so similar to those produced by all other firms in the industry that we call them *homogeneous*. (This word comes from the Greek *homo* = same, and *genus* = race or kind.) In the cotton industry, for example, the cotton produced äby farmer Jones is essentially the same as the cotton produced by farmer Smith, whose cotton, in turn, is the same as farmer Brown's and so on from one farm to the next. Whatever the differences may be between the cottons produced by different farmers, they are so small that they are swamped by the similarities. Thus we say that the product is homogeneous. Since each seller produces essentially the same product, buyers don't care about whose output they purchase. Instead they are only concerned with buying at the lowest possible price.

We can draw an important conclusion at this point—namely, *the competition in competitive industries centers on price.* Since the products are identical (or close to it), and since numerous sellers are competing for the market demand, buyers are quite indifferent between sellers. The consequence of all this is significant.

> **Conclusion:**   In competitive industries (or markets), all producers sell their products at the same price.

If, for example, any seller were to charge a price even a fraction above the prevailing market price, his sales would fall to zero. On the other hand, it would be foolish for him to sell at any lower price, for he could dispose of all of his output at the prevailing market price. This leads us to another important conclusion: There is no nonprice competition, such as advertising and style changes, in a competitive industry. This sort of competitive activity belongs to other market structures. The point to stress here is that price competition in a competitive industry keeps the prices of all the sellers the same.

3. No Barriers to Entry

So far, we have stressed three outstanding features of competition: (a) a large number of firms, (b) each of which is relatively small, and (c) the fact that firms produce identical products. Two other features must now be considered. One of these— unrestricted entry of new firms into the industry—is very basic to competition. Without it, competition fails and withers away. It is that important. The other condition is also important; it is that firms already in the industry are free to exit, seeking better profit opportunities elsewhere if they so desire.

Let's look at entry first. What this really means is that there are no serious barriers (legal or otherwise) to new firms entering the industry and competing directly with the already established firms. Indeed, without this condition, consumers wouldn't gain the benefits of competition. Freedom of entry, to repeat, is essential to the survival of competition.

For example, suppose there is a rise in the demand for tea as consumers voluntarily shift their preferences from coffee to tea. As shown in Figure 15-1, this means that consumers are willing to pay a higher price to satisfy their newly discovered tastes. To keep matters simple, suppose also that as tea prices rise, so do the profits of the supplying firms already in the industry. So far, then, the market is doing what it is supposed to do: It has sent out the necessary signals—a higher price and larger

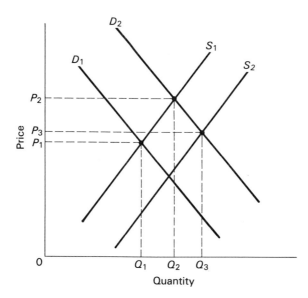

FIGURE 15-1 Changes in Demand and Supply When demand increased to D_2, it caused the market price to rise to P_2. This induced new firms to enter the industry, shifting the supply curve to S_2 and lowering the market price to P_3.

profits are to be had in the industry. Yet, if competition is to benefit consumers to the fullest, new firms must be allowed to enter the industry and begin supplying tea in the hope of obtaining some of the higher profits. This hope, however, can't be completely realized, for the entry of new firms means that the supply increases, and therefore price will be driven back down. How far will price fall? It depends.

Let's trace out this sequence of events, using Figure 15-1. At first, the equilibrium price was P_1 and the equilibrium quantity was Q_1. Then demand rose, as shown by the demand curve shifting to the right from D_1 to D_2. Accordingly, equilibrium price rose from P_1 to P_2, and equilibrium sales and output to Q_2. This signaled to outsiders what had taken place, and new firms were thus induced to enter the industry. The lure of higher profits was what attracted them. But note that this entry of new firms shifted the supply curve to the right (from S_1 to S_2). Price and quantity then sought their new equilibrium levels—price at P_3 and quantity at Q_3—at which quantity demanded once again equaled quantity supplied.

Observe that, in this case, the final equilibrium price P_3 is somewhat above the original equilibrium price P_1. The reason for this rather slight price increase is that supply didn't shift as far to the right as demand. But what would have happened to price if supply had increased more than demand? Finally, note that however much supply increases, the equilibrium quantity rises. And so we reach still another important conclusion.

> **Conclusion:** With the passage of time, the competitive industry gives the consumers what they want. Consumers behaving collectively determine what and how much will be produced under highly competitive conditions.

This will hold true, however, only if there are no barriers to entry. If a competitive market is to function smoothly and for the benefit of the consumer, there must be unrestricted entry of new firms into the industry. Put otherwise, the market position of a firm in a competitive industry is never safe. It is, to the contrary, always being contested by firms already in the industry *and* by new firms entering the industry.

Let's be clear on one point. "Unrestricted" doesn't mean "free." Far from that, because if for no other reason, the new firm must incur capital and other costs in starting up. What this condition of competition does mean is that no artificial barriers to entry are imposed by government. It also means that the firms already in the industry can't exert any pressure to keep potential entrants out. What it really means, therefore, is that there must always be enough firms, both existing and potential, to keep the competitive industry competitive.

4. Freedom of Exit

Another important point: There is also the condition of freedom of exit by firms already in the industry. In a dynamic, volatile market economy, in which demand, costs, and prices are everchanging, it is quite possible that some (maybe all) of the firms in the industry are experiencing losses. In this event, some at least will want to exit and move (they hope) to greener pastures where there are better potential profits. There should be no restrictions on such movements if competition is to exist. Therefore this condition is also necessary for a competitive industry to remain competitive and for resources to flow from worse to better employments and in response to consumer demand.

5. Competition as a Yardstick

Unfortunately, few industries in the United States economy—or anywhere for that matter—meet the conditions of pure competition. The best examples are found in unregulated agriculture and the securities markets.

   If this is so, why then should we spend any time on the study of this particular market structure? There is one major reason for doing so. As we pointed out above, economists are prone to argue that the economy's scarce resources are used more efficiently under pure competition than they are under the various types of monopoly. We have a long way to go before we can see why this is so, but until then, we will accept the purely competitive model as a yardstick with which we can measure the performance of the other market structures. For example, the traditional comparison of the purely competitive market structure with pure monopoly shows that (a) output is lower when the market is dominated by monopoly and (b) the price is higher. Put otherwise, output is greater and price is lower when competition prevails in the market. This is hardly a meaningless conclusion. It might even give us some incentive to make some markets more competitive than they are.

D. AND NOW ABOUT MONOPOLIES

Let's look now at the counterpart of competition—monopoly. In the strict sense of the word, *monopoly* means "one seller." (The Greek word for "alone" is *mono*, and *polein* means "to sell." Hence monopoly means one seller alone in the market.)

1. Monopoly I: Pure Monopoly

Since it is the only seller in the market, a pure monopoly by definition is "large"; after all, it accounts for 100 percent of the sales in the market. This is true even if the firm appears to be quite small—say, the only grocery store in a small, isolated town. No matter how small this store may appear to an outsider, it is still the only store in town, and therefore it is large relative to the market. In fact, it accounts for 100 percent of the grocery sales in town. Another example, one nearer to home, is the bookstore on campus. There may be other bookstores, but this is the only one selling textbooks. Again, a case of pure monopoly.

   What we are concerned with here is the meaning of size. In economics, we always measure size in *relative terms*. A competitive firm, for example, may appear to be quite large in terms of its total assets; but, if competitive, it nonetheless is small relative to the total market in which it operates. Similarly, a monopoly firm, no matter how small it may appear to be, is large relative to *its* market. As noted above, a *pure* monopoly is so "large" that it accounts for 100 percent of the sales in its market.

Definition: A *pure monopoly* is the only seller in its market; it faces no direct competition from other firms. Thus the firm is the industry, and the industry is the firm, for the market in question.

2. Sources of Monopoly Power and Barriers to Entry

Some final observations are in order about pure monopoly. When we say that the monopolist faces no competition, we must remember that every seller is in competition with every other seller for the consumer's dollar. In this respect, no firm is, or ever can be, a pure monopolist. Now, while this may be true, it doesn't mean a great deal. What is important is that the pure monopolist faces *no direct competition* from other firms in its market. It also *does not face any potential competition* from new firms entering the industry.

How does a monopoly acquire its dominating position? A number of things may give rise to monopoly power. For example, if a firm completely controls a unique resource, it has a monopoly position. For many years, the Aluminum Company of America controlled the bauxite deposits from which aluminum is derived, and this gave it a monopoly position in the aluminum industry. Also, DeBeers controls nearly all the diamond sales in the world. This source of monopoly power, however, tends to be very fragile over long periods of time (see Exhibit 15–1).

Another source of monopoly power stems in large part from what are called *economies of scale*. Economies of scale are advantages of large size that push costs down. Once a firm has taken advantage of these economies, other firms that are smaller (and hence have higher costs) can't compete effectively. Thus the firm that has grown by taking advantage of its economies of scale may well end up being the sole seller in the market. Other firms can't compete with it on a cost-price basis. This sort of monopoly is called *natural monopoly*. It is called "natural" because it doesn't use illegal or predatory measures to prevent competition with it (and this holds true, as well, for potential competition). Instead it eliminates competition by naturally charging lower prices than others can bear because of its lower costs. Examples are the firms we call public utilities (see Chapter 19).

Government, however, is probably the major source of monopoly power. It is government that grants patents and copyrights. A patent grants its holder seventeen years of exclusive right to do with the product as he or she sees fit. The important thing is that no one can infringe on the patent, and thus the firm has a virtual seventeen-year monopoly. Copyrights (of books, films, and articles) also provide a monopoly position for a period of fifty years beyond the death of the writer for the benefit of his or her heirs.

Government may also restrict competition by issuing permits and licenses to operate. The license to operate the only concession stand at a sports complex, for

EXHIBIT 15-1
A Gale of Creative Destruction

Joseph A. Schumpeter, the Austrian-born economist who migrated to the United States to avoid the ravages of Nazism, questioned the praises heaped on pure competition. What we should do, he cautioned, is take a much longer view than we are accustomed to take. Once we do that, we will see that monopoly is really a transient thing, that *innovations* come along and sweep away what appears to be well-established monopoly positions.

An innovation is a new way of doing something. Schumpeter listed five types of innovations that are relevant in economics: (a) a new product, (b) a new method of production, (c) the discovery of new resources, (d) a new method of marketing, and (e) a new method of organization.

Schumpeter argued that in the early stages of capitalism—say, prior to World War II—major innovations occurred because there were *entrepreneurs*. These were men and women of vision who were able and willing to assume risks, and they were the fountainhead of innovations. Indeed, the entrepreneurial function was a viable, integral part of early capitalism. Yet it could hardly be expected that the entrepreneur would risk all without some sort of protection; and that protection took the form of monopoly. In this event, the innovator could expect to reap an adequate (perhaps more than adequate) return on investment. These monopolies are, however, in the longer view, swept away by other innovations. Schumpeter pointed out that the automobiles and airplanes had replaced the monopoly railroads. This is a prime example of what he termed the gale of creative destruction—that is, innovations are destructive of old ways but are creative of new ways.

But he also argued that, in the later stages of capitalism, the entrepreneurial (i.e., innovative) function has withered. In Schumpeter's view, large-scale monopolistic enterprises have tended to stifle the individual entrepreneurs. These firms fear that the entrepreneur, if left unchecked, will innovate the firm out of existence. Thus they have bought up inventions and patents that threaten them, and they make it difficult for an innovation to get started. This is why our discussion of barriers to entry is so important (see Chapters 20 and 21).

example, is a grant of monopoly power; and so are the food and vending operations at, say, universities and other public institutions.

Finally, and very important, states grant monopoly power to the so-called public utilities. These firms experience substantial economies of scale—they are natural monopolies—and governments have recognized this. Accordingly, they have granted franchises for these firms to operate within the state, and the franchise also guarantees the utility that no new firms will enter and share the market with it. In return, the monopoly utility is subject to regulatory commissions that try to ensure that the lower costs are passed on to consumers in lower rates.

All of these sources of monopoly power also constitute serious barriers to entry once a monopoly has attained its power position. And therefore, unlike the purely competitive firm, the pure monopolist faces no direct competition and very little indirect (but see Exhibit 15–1).

3. Monopoly II: Oligopoly, or Shared Monopoly

Some industries are neither purely monopolistic nor highly competitive. They reside someplace in between. Some of these tend to resemble competition (see Exhibit 15–2), but the ones we want to concentrate on here are those that more closely resemble monopoly. These are the industries that are dominated by a few large firms; examples are automobiles, breakfast cereals, photographic equipment, cigarettes, tires,

EXHIBIT 15-2
A Blending of Competition and Monopoly

Schumpeter has not been the only economist to criticize conventional microeconomic analysis. Another critic was Harvard economist Edward H. Chamberlin, who developed the theory of monopolistic competition. His argument is that numerous industries are neither purely competitive nor purely monopolistic but rather are mixtures of the two. One example is the oligopolistic (shared monopoly) industry discussed in this chapter.

Another example is the type of industry in which all the conditions of pure competition are present save one, but this one is enough to allow some monopolistic elements to creep in. An industry of this sort is called *monopolistic competition*. Examples: the men's shoe industry, the ladies' garment industry, and the paperback book publishing industry. In all these examples, there are a large number of small firms, as well as freedom of entry and exit. They differ, however, from pure competition in that the firms in each industry produce *heterogeneous* products. (This word, too, comes from the Greek *hetero* = other, different; *genus* = race, kind.) The firms in a purely competitive industry, on the other hand, produce homogeneous products.

Why this emphasis on the nature of the product? Just this: The firms in a monopolistically competitive industry compete, to be sure, over price, but they also compete vigorously with advertising, style changes, product variation, and so on. This sort of nonprice competition is very important in industries other than the purely competitive and purely monopolistic. Each firm strives to create brand preference and loyalty for its product or products—that is, to create a little monopoly for its output. Yet all of its rivals are striving for the same goal, and thus the monopoly position of each is tenuous indeed.

detergents, and aircraft. In all these industries, only a few firms (sometimes just one or two) account for the lion's share of the total industry sales or assets. If there are any smaller firms in the industry, they are dominated by the large ones.

This sort of industry is often called "oligopoly" to signify the dominance by a few firms *(oligoi =* few; *polein =* to sell; hence a few sellers). A major characteristic of oligopolistic industries is that the dominant few usually tend to act as one by entering into agreement over price. Put more bluntly, they agree not to compete with each other over price. Thus they behave somewhat like a pure monopoly firm.

The agreements they enter into in order to remove price competition are varied. One type of agreement is price leadership, in which the dominant firm sets price and the others follow suit. Another type is the territorial cartel; still another is the price-quota cartel in which the firms agree on both the price to be charged and the amount each firm is to produce. In all these instances, the firms in the oligopolistic industry strive to act as one large, coordinated firm. This is what is called *shared monopoly.*

> **Definition:**   In a *shared monopoly,* all the firms in an oligopolistic industry collude over price in the attempt to act as a single firm in setting prices.

A few words about this idea of shared monopoly. First, it doesn't mean that the firms in the industry don't compete at all. They do, and quite fiercely, but most of the competition is *nonprice competition.* These firms have large advertising budgets, and they usually regularly change their products some way or another in order to keep or enlarge their respective shares of the market. Second, just because there is a shared monopoly is no sign that it is "writ in stone"—i.e., will last for a long time. To the contrary, these agreements are often tenuous and tend to break apart. However, once this happens, the firms soon reach another agreement. Oligopolistic firms deplore price competition, and the reasons why are given in Chapter 20.

4. Barriers to Entry Again

A significant feature of oligopolistic industries is that the existing firms are protected by some barriers to entry, and these are often quite large. Let's look at three of these. First, the mere magnitude of the capital needed to enter an industry and compete effectively on a cost basis is often sufficient to deter entry. Second, and more important, advertising and selling costs provide substantial barriers. Since the firms in the industry don't compete with price, they direct large amounts of resources into nonprice competition. This significantly raises the amount of money capital a firm needs to enter and compete efficiently. Finally, many firms have special skills and knowledge that potential rivals don't have. Thus specialized research, and technical and administrative expertise, can confer protective advantages on existing firms.

Let's switch away from product markets and examine competition in the markets for factors of production.

E. COMPETITION IN RESOURCE MARKETS

Competition also takes place in resource markets, and again there are three dimensions. First, there is competition between both sides of the market where supply and demand meet; second, there is competition among the participants on the seller's side; and third, there is rivalry among the demanders of productive services. In these markets—labor, capital, etc.—the buyers are the business firms and the sellers are the households.

If competition prevails in all three of these dimensions, resources will be used (or allocated) in their most efficient employments. In labor markets, for example, competition assures us that higher wages will be offered where workers are most needed, and workers attracted by these high wages will move to these more productive employments. The same type of signals and responses will occur in other competitive resource markets.

However, just as in product markets, there are substantial deviations from competition in resource markets. Labor unions, monopolistic employer practices, and government interventions cause many resource markets to be less than competitive; and when this occurs, resources aren't being used at their peak efficiency (see Chapter 18).

F. A FINAL WORD ON COMPETITION

The price competition in which competitive firms participate is very beneficial to consumers. Figure 15-2 shows, in a very preliminary way, why this is so. Monopolies always behave as monopolies—that is, they always tend to restrict output in order to charge a higher price. This is essentially how they make their monopoly profits—by charging a price higher than the price that would prevail if the industry were competitive. Thus, in Figure 15-2, the monopoly price is P_M, and it is higher than the competitive price P_C. At the same time, the output of the monopoly (Q_M) is less then the output of the competitive industry (Q_C). It is for this reason (and others as well) that most economists tend to favor competitive markets over monopolistic ones.

G. SUMMARY

The degree of efficiency with which the economy's scarce resources are used depends on the extent of competition in the industries using them. If industries are competitive in both product and resource markets, then the economy operates in the most

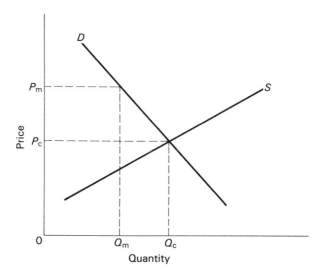

FIGURE 15-2   Monopoly and Competitive Prices and Outputs   Microeconomic analysis concludes that monopoly price is usually higher than competitive price, and therefore monopoly output is lower than competitive output. Accordingly, allocative efficiency is lacking.

efficient manner. The degree of competition envisaged here is pure competition, and the conditions of purely competitive markets are as follows: (a) a large number of small sellers, (b) a large number of small buyers, (c) an homogeneous product or service, (d) freedom of entry of new rivals, and (e) freedom of exit of participants.

Monopoly, either pure or shared, on the other hand, interferes with maximum resource efficiency. Pure monopoly exists when there is but one firm in the industry. Shared monopoly (that is, oligopoly) exists when the industry is dominated by a few large firms that collude over price. In the case of monopoly, significant barriers to entry prevent the entry of rivals and hence allow monopoly to persist over time.

Finally, the conventional comparison of the two types of market structures concludes that price is higher and output is lower under monopoly than under competition.

Terms and Concepts to Remember

Allocative efficiency
Competition
Monopoly

Nonprice competition
Oligopoly (shared monopoly)
Barriers to entry

Questions for Review

1. Differentiate between *aggregate efficiency* and *allocative efficiency*.

2. How do markets send out signals when there is a departure from allocative efficiency? How do competitive markets operate to restore allocative efficiency?

3. What conditions must be present in order for an industry to be competitive?

4. List and discuss the sources of monopoly power.

5. What is a "natural monopoly"? Why is it acceptable to economists?

6. Why are economists generally supportive of competition and opposed to monopoly?

16

Consumer Behavior and Demand

chapter preview

• The law of demand states that there is an inverse relationship between price and quantity demanded. Hence demand curves are downward sloping.

• The negative slope is attributed to diminishing marginal utility. As successive units of good are consumed, the consumer's total utility increases at a decreasing rate—that is, marginal utility diminishes.

• Because of diminishing marginal utility, consumers must be persuaded by lower prices to buy larger quantities of goods.

• The market demand curve for a good is downward sloping because it represents the sum of every individual consumer's demand curves for a particular good.

• The demand curve is constructed by holding constant all other factors that affect consumers—that is, the only thing allowed to vary is the price of a product.

• These other factors are (1) tastes, (2) income, (3) prices of other goods and services, and (4) expectations. A change in any one of these will, all other things being equal, cause demand to change.

• A change in demand is shown by a shift of the entire demand curve either to the right (an increase) or to the left (a decrease).

• Goods can be classified in different ways. Two important classifications are (1) substitutes and complements, and (2) normal and inferior.

• The demand for a normal good increases when consumer income rises; the reverse is also true. The demand for an inferior good falls when consumer income rises; the reverse is also true.

• Whenever the price of a substitute good changes, the demand for other substitute goods changes in the same direction. Whenever the price of a complementary good changes, the demand for other complementary goods changes in the opposite direction.

• The purely competitive firm views the demand for *its* product as perfectly elastic. The firm behaves as a price taker—that is, it takes the market price as given, utterly beyond its control.

• Marginal revenue is the amount that the last unit sold adds to the firm's total revenue. For a purely competitive firm, marginal revenue and price are identical.

We began Chapter 5 by saying, "We all consume." That is obviously correct. All of us are consumers, both as individuals and as members of households. As such, we play a powerful role in the market economy. And rightly so! As Adam Smith put it over two hundred years ago, the end purpose of all economic activity is consumption.[1] That is also what the economic theory of competition postulates and concludes—that consumer satisfaction is greatest in a competitive economic society.

Chapter 4 told us why this is so. Consumer spending guides business decisions about what to produce and when to produce it, as well as what prices to charge. But prices, as we also know from Chapter 4, are determined by more than demand alone; supply, too, must be considered. Now, however, we need to go beyond the basic supply and demand analysis of that chapter, and we begin our search by looking behind the demand side of the product market.

Figure 16–1 shows the place of consumer demand in the circular flow of economic activity. The demand curve there (drawn in above the households box) represents the demand curves of consumers for the myriad of goods and services flowing through product markets. Our task in this chapter is severalfold. First, Section A discusses the basic problem that any and all consumers face. Then Section B shows how to derive demand curves that are negatively sloped; this section of the chapter is very important. Section C considers how consumers respond to major changes, such as a change in income or a change in expectations. The remainder of the chapter deals with how the firm in a competitive industry views the demand for its product.

A. THE PROBLEM FACING THE CONSUMER

All of us have had experiences as consumers, and therefore we all have some ideas about how prices, income, advertising, and the like affect us. We all, too, are aware that many goods and services that we would like to have are beyond our means and are therefore only daydreams. These daydreams may become realities later on, but until then we have to limit our consumption to the realistic alternatives before us.

---

[1] What he really said was: "Consumption is the sole end and purpose of all production; and the interest of the producer ought to be attended to, only so far as it may be necessary for promoting that of the consumer. The maxim is so perfectly self-evident, that it would be absurd to attempt to prove it." *The Wealth of Nations* (New York: Modern Library, 1937), p. 625.

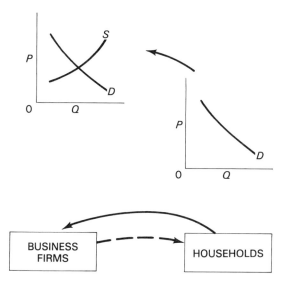

FIGURE 16-1   Consumer Demand in the Circular Flow Model   The demand curve shown here is the demand curve for, say, colas. It is then put up against the supply curve at the top of the diagram. This chapter's major task is to explain why this demand curve (like all other demand curves) has a negative slope.

1. The Concept of Utility

We purchase goods and services, of course, because of the satisfaction we get from consuming them. Clearly, that's why people consume—to obtain satisfaction, or as economists like to call it, utility.

> **Definition:**   *Utility* is an intrinsic aspect of a product or service that provides satisfaction or pleasure to the person who consumes it.

Utility, therefore, is a purely subjective, psychological quality that exists only in the consumer's mind. This is why economists use the word "good" so often in place of "product" or "commodity." A good is a good because the consumer views it as possessing some utility that is good for him or her. There is one thing for certain, however—if a product holds no promise of utility to a person (consumer), it will not be demanded by that person (consumer). More generally, a product must provide utility to at least some consumers if it is to be marketable. If it were to provide no utility to anyone, it wouldn't be demanded at all (and hence it wouldn't be produced).

2. The Goal and Limits of the Consumer

The economist carries the idea of utility a step further and attributes to the consumer one overriding goal, and that is to achieve as much total utility as possible. To put it in economic jargon: Economics assumes that the individual consumer behaves as a *utility maximizer*—that is, under given constraints, the consumer strives to attain *maximum total utility* derived from consumption.

Which of the constraints mentioned above does the consumer face as he or she pursues the goal of maximum total utility? Since we are going to use a fellow named Fred in our discussion below, let's introduce him now and consider the constraints he faces as a consumer.

For one thing, Fred's income is fixed for the time period in question (whether it be a year, a month, a week, or even a day). Fred is therefore already limited in his search for maximum total utility. If he had more income, he could undoubtedly buy more goods and services and thus experience a greater total utility. But, as it is, he has only so much to spend (even if he uses his credit cards). A restatement seems to be in order: The goal of the consumer is to get the largest possible total utility that his or her income allows.

Another constraint is that, in nearly all the purchases he makes, Fred has no control over the prices he pays. In short, he acts as a *price taker* and doesn't even consider bargaining over price when he makes most of his purchases. Prices certainly are a barrier to nearly all consumers; they impose a constraint on our behavior. "Like" is one thing; "can" is quite another. And prices determine in large part what Fred (and we) *can* buy.

There are other constraints—namely, fixed expectations and given tastes and habits—which we must take into account when we explain Fred's behavior as a consumer. But they come later. For now we need to stress another major assumption that underlies consumer demand theory: The economist assumes that the *consumer behaves rationally as he or she allocates his or her given income among different goods and services in the search for maximum total utility.*

Since Fred has a fixed income, he certainly doesn't want to waste any of it on foolish spending. This doesn't mean that he won't make mistakes as he spends his money, but it does mean that he won't continue to make the same mistake over and over. After all, we do learn from our mistakes (or at least we should). The assumption of rationality also means that Fred won't buy the same product at a higher price when he can get it at a lower price.

Finally, the assumption contends that Fed will rank his needs and then spend according to this ordering. In other words, he spends on his more urgent needs first, and then on down the line. For example, a hungry person is more apt to buy a meal than to buy a movie ticket at the same price.[2]

B. GETTING THE DEMAND CURVE

Let's now specify the five constraints facing the rational consumer in the pursuit of maximum utility: (a) the price of the good itself—that is, the one for which we want

---

[2]However, what is a matter of "urgency" for one person may be an "extravagance" for another. Remember, utility is highly subjective and is a matter of one's view of things and circumstances of the moment.

to get Fred's demand curve; (b) income; (c) the prices of *other* goods and services; (d) the consumer's tastes and habits; and (e) the consumer's expectations about what will happen to the price of the product in the future.

As we set out to derive Fred's demand curve, the only one of these constraints that we will allow to vary is the price of the product itself. All the other constraints we hold constant with the *ceteris paribus* assumption. Changes in them are examined in the Section C of this chapter.

1. The Law of Demand Again

In Chapter 4, we discussed the inverse relationship between the *price* of shirts and the *quantity demanded* of shirts. In fact, we dignified this inverse relationship by calling it a "law"—the law of demand. This law can be stated as follows.

> **Definition:**   The higher the price of a good or service, the smaller the quantity demanded of it, *ceteris paribus*. Conversely, the lower the price, the greater the quantity demanded, again, *ceteris paribus*.

Also in Chapter 4, we accepted this law more or less as common sense. It just seems to make sense that people buy more when price is low and less when price is high. We showed this relationship, too, in the form of a negative-sloped demand curve. Now we want to go beyond the common-sense explanation and explain why the demand curve is downward sloping.

2. Diminishing Marginal Utility and Free Drinks

The shape of the demand curve is closely related to the concept of utility, and we will use Fred to illustrate what this means. More specifically, we want to find Fred's demand curve for colas on a hot Saturday afternoon. To do this, we will further assume that Fred is endowed with the ability to measure in a precise way the utility he gets from consuming each cola. Thus, let's say that he gets 60 *utils* from the first cola he consumes, 12 *utils* from the second, and so on.

Just what are these utils? We really don't know, and we don't need to know. It is probably true that no one can measure utility in such a precise way. But, as we said, it really doesn't matter; we make the assumption simply to get us started in deriving Fred's demand curve for colas. Later we drop the notion of precise measurement and use in its place a more realistic type of measurement.

Here's the setting: It's a hot Saturday afternoon, and Fred has been mowing his rather sizable yard. A good friend, Louie, happens to appear on the scene carrying a cooler full of bottled cola drinks covered with ice. Louie asks Fred if he would like a drink, and since he is so hot and thirsty, Fred happily accepts the offer. As he drinks the cola, he registers a rather large gain in utility. In fact, Figure 16–2 shows that he gets 60 utils from the first bottle. (This is shown by the first bar in Figure 16–2, both panels.) The reason for so many utils is that Fred is so hot and thirsty, and thus the first cola is very satisfying.

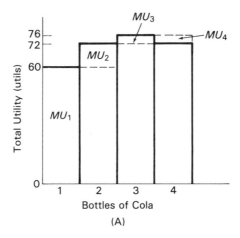

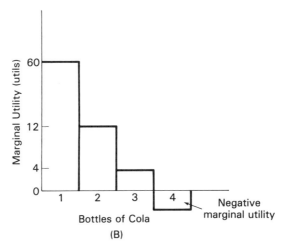

FIGURE 16-2   As the consumer drinks more cola, his or her total utility rises, as shown in panel (A). At least this is true of the first three bottles. But note that total utility increases at a decreasing rate. This is because the marginal utility—shown in panel (B)—diminishes as more bottles are consumed. The fourth bottle represents that the consumer is so saturated with cola that total utility falls—that is, the fourth bottle yields a marginal disutility.

Definition: The utility derived from consuming an additional unit of a good or service is called *marginal utility*.

In our example, the marginal utility Fred derives from the first unit is 60 utils. Fred finishes his cola and Louie offers him another. Still hot and thirsty (but not nearly as much as before), Fred accepts the second bottle. The second cola, however, provides him with less extra utility than before; we assume that he gets only 12 utils from it. This is the marginal utility of the second drink to Fred. The reason why it is less than the marginal utility of the first cola is that the first one has eased his discomfort somewhat and so his need is not as great.

We should note in passing that just because the *marginal* utility Fred gets from drinking another cola diminishes doesn't mean that his *total* utility from colas is also falling. It isn't. To the contrary, it is increasing. With his first cola, Fred's total utility was 60 utils. With the second, it rose to 72—that is, 60 utils from the first + 12 utils from the second = 72 utils. The increasing total utility is shown in the top panel of Figure 16–2. Note that the second bar is greater than the first bar by the amount of the marginal utility derived from the second cola.

Let's get back to the idea of the diminishing marginal utility that Fred is experiencing from his consumption of colas. Will he drink a third one? The answer is yes, as long as he doesn't have to pay for it. As Figure 16–2 shows, the marginal utility of the third cola is still positive, although it isn't very much (4 utils). Remember, he has already consumed two, and he therefore isn't nearly as thirsty and hot as before. Because of this, the third drink yields him only a small marginal utility. Nonetheless, since it is positive, his total utility rises by the 4 utils, as shown in the top part of Figure 16–2.

What might happen if Fred were foolish enough to drink a fourth cola? Recall that he has already consumed three rather quickly, and if he were to drink the fourth one, he would probably experience a *negative* marginal utility. What does this mean? It simply means that Fred may unfortunately get sick, and as a result (as shown by the fourth bar in Figure 16–2), his total utility will decline.

Let's use this example to derive a basic principle of microeconomics.

Conclusion: As the consumer obtains and consumes successive units of a good or service in a given time period, he or she will eventually experience *diminishing marginal utility*. Indeed, if consumption were to be carried far enough, the consumer would experience marginal *disutility*.

Economists believe that this principle holds for all goods and services and for all consumers. Can you think of any exceptions to it?

An important point needs to be made here. An individual need not actually consume the successive units of a product in order to know how much marginal utility falls. Experience is a great aid in this respect. Fred doesn't really have to drink the second cola in order to know that its marginal utility is lower than the marginal utility derived from the first; nor does he have to drink the third in order to estimate that its marginal utility is so low. And, fortunately for him, he doesn't have to experience the marginal disutility of the fourth cola to know whether he wants it.

In fact, consumers are forward looking in making their spending and utility decisions. The relevant question, then, is not "What was the marginal utility of the last unit I consumed?" but rather "What will be the marginal utility of the next unit if I consume it?"

We can now also drop the assumption that Fred, or any consumer, can measure marginal utility precisely in terms of utils (whatever they may be). This is too unrealistic. But dropping this assumption doesn't mean that the consumer doesn't estimate marginal utility in quantitative terms. He does, but now in terms of "more than/less than" and "higher than/lower than."[3] Put otherwise, we assert that Fred can assuredly say that the marginal utility received from the second cola is less than the marginal utility received from the first, but *not* by so many utils. Also, the marginal utility he estimates to have from the third cola is less than that from the second, and so on. Note that Fred is experiencing diminishing marginal utility (as before), but he doesn't ascribe any precise utils to anything.

3. Diminishing Marginal Utility and Priced Drinks

What does this basic "law of diminishing marginal utility" have to do with the downward-sloping demand curve? A great deal, but to see why, let's go back to Fred and ask what he would do if he had to pay for the colas. This makes it harder on Fred, of course, but we will make it even harder and ask him what is the *maximum amount he would be willing to pay for each cola.*

We begin once more with Fred being extremely hot and thirsty. In fact, he is so hot and thirsty that when Louie asks him how much he is willing to pay for the first cola, Fred says $5.00. Why so much? Simply because Fred thinks his thirst is so great and his need to satisfy it so urgent that he is willing to sacrifice $5.00 of other things for that first cola.

Note that we haven't said that Fred actually pays Louie $5.00 for the first bottle of cola. Not at all. We have, indeed, said nothing about what the market price of cola is. We have only said that Fred feels his need is so urgent for the first cola that he is willing to pay a rather high price for it.

This being so, what can be said about the price that Fred is willing to pay for the second unit? Remember, Fred estimates its marginal utility to be lower—that is, there is diminishing marginal utility—and thus he isn't willing to pay $5.00 for it. But, he says, he is willing to pay $1.00 for the second cola. Why such a lower price? Because his need is much less urgent, and this is what the lower marginal utility tells us. The lower price, therefore, reflects the lower marginal utility. From all this, we can draw an important conclusion.

> **Conclusion:** The price that a consumer is *willing* to pay for an additional unit of a good or service reflects (measures?) the satisfaction that the consumer expects from that unit. Moreover, since the consumer experiences diminishing marginal utility from consuming more units of the good or service, then the only way to induce him or her to consume more is to offer the item at a lower price.

[3]These are examples of what is called ordinal measurement. This sort of measurement takes the form of rather loose comparisons—e.g., we can say that George is taller than Mary, but we *don't say by how much.* Cardinal measurement, on the other hand, is precisely making use of whatever unit is necessary (inches, pounds, etc.). Thus we can say that George is one foot, two inches taller than Mary.

Ask Fred how much he is willing to pay for the third cola, and he responds with a price of $0.20. Why so low? Because he estimates that this unit yields but a very small marginal utility to him. He clearly isn't going to spend $5.00 for it, or even $1.00. Indeed, the price he is willing to pay must be less than $1.00, for that price reflects a higher marginal utility than the third cola gives. This is in line with our conclusion above: The lower the marginal utility, the lower the price Fred is willing to pay.

4. Fred's Demand Curve

You may well have anticipated what is to be said in this section. The analysis and example above show that the price that Fred is willing to pay for each successive unit declines because of the diminishing marginal utility he experiences.

> **Conclusion:** Since the price that the consumer is *willing* to pay reflects, or measures, the marginal utility the consumer expects to get from consuming the next unit, we can transform the consumer's marginal utility schedule into a demand curve.

Figure 16–3 shows how this is done. The marginal utility bars here are the same as those in the bottom panel of Figure 16–2. By connecting the marginal utility bars with a smooth continuous curve, we change them into Fred's demand curve for colas on a hot Saturday afternoon. Note how this demand curve *slopes downward from left to right because of diminishing marginal utility*.

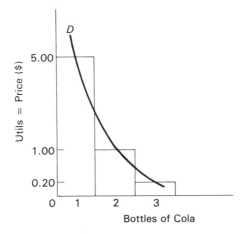

FIGURE 16-3   Here the marginal utility schedule (bars) are used to measure the prices the consumer is willing to pay for different amounts of cola. Since the marginal utility diminishes, the consumer's demand curve has a negative slope.

Conclusion: The law of demand, which postulates an inverse relationship between price and quantity demanded, is itself based on another law, the law of diminishing marginal utility.

You might argue that we have used a very artificial example to draw an important general conclusion. That's true, we have. But the analysis is what matters, and it is general in its applications. Thus we say that demand curves in general have a negative slope because of the law of diminishing marginal utility.

5. Other Persons' Demand Curves

Will all consumers of colas have the same demand curve as the one shown in Figure 16-3? Not likely. This is a particular demand curve of a particular person at a particular time. Most of us will not have the same tastes as Fred, and since each of us is different, we will each have our own demand for colas.

Three other persons' demand curves are shown with Fred's in Figure 16-4(A). Now observe how Louie's demand curve declines very sharply and lies to the left of Fred's. Obviously, Louie doesn't think very much of colas. But Marley's tastes are such that her marginal utility diminishes very slowly, and hence her demand curve has a gently downward slope. Finally, Gerry's demand curve is very much like Marley's except that it lies farther to the right, showing an even stronger preference for cola drinks.

There is, nonetheless, the important similarity that all four of these demand curves have a negative slope. This is because each of the individuals experiences diminishing marginal utility from consuming successive bottles of cola.

6. The Market Demand Curve

For the most part, the sellers aren't concerned with my demand curve for colas, or yours, or Fred's, or any one person's. Instead they are concerned with the *total demand* for colas. We showed back in Chapter 4 how we can move from individual

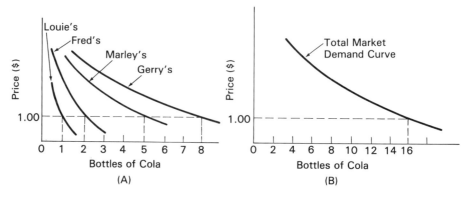

FIGURE 16-4   The market demand curve is obtained by adding together horizontally all the individual demand curves for the good or service.

demand curves to the market demand curve (refer to Figure 4–2 and the accompanying discussion). The identical procedure is shown in Figure 16–4, in which we *add up horizontally* all the individual demand curves in panel (A) to arrive at the market demand curve in panel (B). True, we illustrate this with but four persons' demand curves, but procedurally we can do it for all.

The main thing to observe is that the market demand curve has a negative slope because all the participants' demand curves are also negatively sloped. In this instance, the total is equal to the sum of the parts.

C. CHANGES IN DEMAND

It is now time to return to the constraints we listed above to see what happens to the market demand curve when we relax them one at a time. We begin with the income constraint.

1. A Change in Income

A rise in income obviously reduces the constraint on the ability of consumers to buy. A higher income, in other words, allows them to do either or both of the following things: (a) purchase more of the goods they are already consuming, even at a higher price; (b) buy some items that they felt they couldn't afford at their lower incomes. Let's look at both of these responses, using our friend Fred as a representative consumer.

The first response really means that there is an increase in demand, as shown in Figure 16–5. Here, because of his higher income, Fred finds himself willing to pay $6.00 for the first cola and $4.50 for the second; or he might be willing to buy five colas at $0.20 each rather than only three. In general, then, we say that an

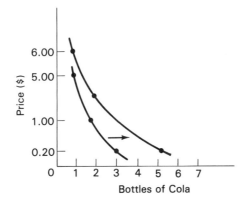

FIGURE 16–5   An increase in income shifts Fred's demand curve for colas to the right. However, as pointed out in the text, this is true only if colas are a normal good for Fred.

increase in income will cause demand to rise. The converse is also true—that is, a decrease in income reduces demand.

This conclusion is true, however, only in the case of normal, or superior, goods. If, on the other hand, the buyers consider the good to be an inferior good, they will react quite differently. Two definitions seem to be in order.

> **Definition:**   A *normal* or *superior good* is one for which the demand *rises* as income rises; the reverse is also true—the demand for a normal or superior good falls as income falls.

> **Definition:**   An *inferior good* is one for which the demand *falls* as income rises; again, the converse is true—the demand for an inferior good rises as income falls.

For example, suppose Fred strongly prefers fruit juice to cola as a thirst quencher, but it is relatively expensive when compared with cola. An increase in his income, however, may alter his situation enough that he will reduce his demand for cola and increase his demand for juice. For Fred, therefore, cola is an inferior good, and he is consuming it only because his income is so low that he feels he can't afford fruit juice. With his now higher income, Fred finds that he can afford the juice, and thus buys more of it and less cola. Hence, to repeat, cola is an inferior good for him, whereas fruit juice is a superior one.

Decreases in income will have the opposite effects. A decrease in income will reduce the demand for a normal good but will increase the purchases of inferior goods.

Let's make an important point here. Normal and inferior are highly subjective qualities that consumers attach to different goods. Thus, what may be a normal good for Fred may be an inferior good for, say, Louie. And what Louie considers to be normal, you may view as inferior. Empirical studies show, however, that there are a few products that consumers in general treat as inferior—e.g., breakfast cereals, beer, and margarine. Can you think of any others?

2. A Change in the Prices of Other Goods

The demand for any commodity is also influenced by changes in the prices of other products. Economists stress two ways in which goods can be related—they can be *substitutes* for one another or they can be *complementary* to each other.

> **Definition:**   Two goods are substitutes for one another when a change in the price of one causes the *demand* for the other to change in the same direction, *ceteris paribus*.

Fred, for example, considers fruit juice and cola as substitutes. Now, if for some reason the price of juice falls so that it is cheaper relative to cola, his *demand* for cola will also fall. The reason is that he now buys more juice, substituting it for cola. In diagrammatic terms, the demand curve for cola shifts to the left. By the same reasoning, a rise in the price of fruit juice would raise his demand for cola— i.e., shift his demand curve for cola to the right.

This relationship between substitute products allows us to explain some fairly complex real-world events. If there were some bad weather on the rangelands so that the supply of beef is reduced, we can safely predict that the prices of pork and chicken will rise. Why? The reduced supply of cattle will raise the price of beef in the supermarkets. In consequence, consumers will switch their demand over to the substitute goods (pork, chicken, fish) and, given the supply of these items, their prices will rise.

Next, what about complementary goods? Another definition is in order.

> **Definition:**   *Complementary goods* are those that must be used together in order for the consumer to get the full benefits of either. Two goods are complementary when a change in the price of one causes the demand for the other to change in the opposite direction.

A few examples are autos and gasoline; beer and pretzels; peanut butter and bread; ham and eggs; golf balls and golf clubs. Many goods we consume have a complementary relationship with others. Note that in our examples, the full benefit of either complementary good is obtained only when the other is consumed along with it.

Let's take an example from the 1970s to illustrate how a change in the price of one good affects the demand for the other. The dramatic rise in the price of gasoline had a significant impact on the demand for automobiles. If *ceteris* had been *paribus* (which they are not in the real world), the demand for automobiles would have fallen. As it was, however, consumers responded by increasing their demand for the smaller, more-efficient automobiles and dramatically reduced their demand for the larger, less-efficient automobiles. This result is consistent with the complementary relationship stated above.

Generally speaking, the increase in the price of a complement decreases the demand for the other good—i.e., shifts the demand curve to the left. To clinch this, what do you think would happen to the demand for golf balls if the price of golf clubs were doubled?

3. Changes in Habits and Tastes

Economists recognize the importance of consumers' habits and tastes as factors affecting demand. By and large, however, they are reluctant to explain how these came about and why they change. They leave that to others.

Nevertheless, economists are much concerned with the consequences of a change in habits and tastes, for these affect demand and hence price. For example, the strong evidence that cigarette smoking is a serious health hazard has undoubt-edly restrained the demand for cigarettes. Also, changing health habits have resulted in many consumers substituting chicken and fish for beef, veal, and pork. And should medical reports next year indicate a causal link between vitamin E and longevity, the demand for E would probably increase substantially.

4. Changes in Expectations of Future Price

Changes in the expected future price of a product can affect the demand for it in the present. Clearly, if buyers for a good suddenly expect the price to rise sharply in the future, they will increase the demand for it today. The reason is simply to buy now at the lower price and thus beat the expected higher price. Similarly, if consumers expect prices to fall in the future, they will postpone their purchases by cutting back on demand today.

D. COMPETITIVE DEMAND AND MARGINAL REVENUE

So far this chapter has explained why the market demand curve is downward sloping and what causes it to rise and fall. Now we need to change direction a bit and consider how the business firms that produce the product view demand.

At one extreme, there is the pure monopolist, that is, the sole supplier of the product. This firm, therefore, faces the total market demand curve.

At the other extreme, there is pure competition, that is, the industry consists of a very large number of small sellers. The remainder of this chapter is concerned solely with the purely competitive market structure. More specifically, we want to examine how the single competitive firm views the demand for its output. (Monopoly demand is discussed in Chapter 19.) Remember, the competitive firm is a very small part of its overall industry. It is atomistic; and since it is so small, whatever it may happen to do has no direct effect on the price of the product it is producing and selling.

If, for example, the firm produces only one-tenth of one percent or less of the industry's total output, it must be considered quite small. What, then, would happen to be industry's total supply if this firm were to go bankrupt? The answer may be obvious. A fall in total supply by the minuscule amount of one-tenth of one percent means that nothing would happen to the market price. Furthermore, if the same firm were to double its output to two-tenths of one percent, or even increase it to one percent, nothing again would happen to the market price. And that's how small the competitive firm is. It has *no direct and immediate impact on the price charged in the market. This truly is atomistic.* Does this mean, however, that the single small competitive firm doesn't merit attention? Hardly!

Actually, the situation here is very much like the one we covered in Chapter 4 and earlier in this chapter. There we discussed your role as a consumer of shirts and pointed out that you are also "atomistic" in the market. You shop around, you try to get the best bargain, you may even try to bargain with the retailer, and yet the bargaining gets you nowhere. You still have to take the market price of shirts as given. Acting alone, you are but a lone cry in the wilderness, a very small cog in a very large wheel. However, you *and all the other consumers* of shirts collectively have a tremendous impact on the market, an impact that affects both the output and the price of shirts. On the one hand, if all of you, for whatever reason, were to reduce your demand, both the price and then the output of shirts would fall. On the other hand, if all of you together were to increase your demand, price and then output would rise. And we concluded that individually, you count for very little in the market, and therefore you take the price as given; you are a *price taker*. Yet, all of you acting together, all of you acting in concert, can exercise a powerful influence.

The same thing is true of the small, single competitive firm. Any one firm cannot influence market price by changing its output, but when most or all in the industry do, market price will certainly change. You can count on it.

> **Conclusion:**   Just as a single consumer is a *price taker* because he or she is so small in the market, so also is the single competitive firm a *price taker*—that is, it takes the prevailing market price as given and set by forces far beyond its control. To repeat, *the single* competitive *firm is a price taker.*

1. The Demand Curve Facing the Competitive Seller

All of this leads us to an important observation about *the demand curve* as it is seen by the individual competitive seller. Note that what we are talking about here isn't the total market demand curve shown in panel (A) of Figure 16-6. Instead, we are concerned with the horizontal line (labeled P_1MR_1) in panel (B), and we also call this a "demand curve."

How can this be? How can there be two demand curves that are so strikingly different? The demand curve in Figure 16-6(A) is indeed the total market demand

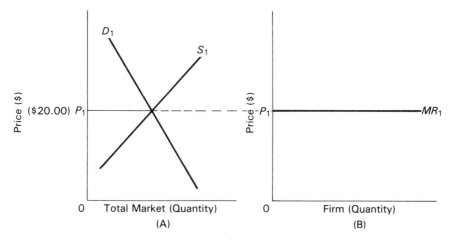

FIGURE 16-6   The Competitive Firm's Perfectly Elastic Demand Curve   The single firm acts as a price taker and thus views the demand for its product as perfectly elastic at the level of the price set in the market. This subjective demand curve is shown in panel (B) as the P_1MR_1 curve. Here P stands for price and MR stands for marginal revenue. The competitive firm considers these two magnitudes equal—i.e., $P = MR$.

curve for the product. It reflects the law of demand by having a negative slope. The equilibrium market price, as we now know, occurs at the level at which the demand curve intersects the supply curve. In this case, the equilibrium market price is P_1 (or, in our example, $20.00).

Let's turn now to panel (B) of Figure 16–6 to see how it is that the horizontal line $P_1 MR_1$ is also a demand curve. Remember that the single firm in panel (B) is a *price taker,* and since it has no control over price, the manager simply views the demand curve for the firm's output as the horizontal line. This is what is called a *perfectly elastic demand curve.* Put otherwise, the perfectly elastic demand curve is what the individual seller *sees,* or *imagines,* as the demand for the firm's output.

Perhaps an example will clear this up better than anything else. This example involves Table 16–1 and Figure 16–7.

In Figure 16–6, we show that the equilibrium market price is $20.00 per shirt, the price that has been set in the market. It reflects the outcome of a myriad of decisions by numerous sellers and consumers. Since the individual seller in our example is only one of hundreds of other sellers, she will have no influence on price at all. She is surely aware of this. Thus the seller knows that when she sells only one shirt at $20.00, or two, or four, or one hundred, or even one thousand, she won't cause the market price of shirts to change. Indeed, she can sell as few or as many as she wants and price remains constant.

She can (if she feels inclined to do so) draw up a schedule like the one in Table 16–1. She can list the price of the product (*P*) in column 1, and output (*Q*) in column 2. Now she can easily compute total revenue (*TR*) in column 3—all she needs to do is multiply $P \times Q$ (that is, multiply column 1 by column 2). The firm's total revenue—we will use *TR* from now on—is listed in column 3.

The data we have so far in Table 16–1 can easily be transferred to Figure 16–7. In that figure, we plot the quantity data *Q* from column 2 on the horizontal axis, and on the vertical axis we plot *TR*. Each point on the resulting *TR* curve is nothing more than a price-quantity relation—that is, $P \times Q$. Thus, at point A, $P \times Q =$

TABLE 16–1   Calculation of the Firm's Total and Marginal Revenue

Price (P) (1)	Quantity (Q) (2)	Total Revenue (TR) (3) = (1) × (2)	Marginal Revenue (MR) (4) = Δ(3)/Δ(2)
$20.00	1	$20.00	$20.00
$20.00	2	$40.00	$20.00
$20.00	3	$60.00	$20.00
$20.00	4	$80.00	$20.00
$20.00	5	$100.00	$20.00
$20.00	500	$10,000.00	$20.00
$20.00	501	$10,020.00	$20.00

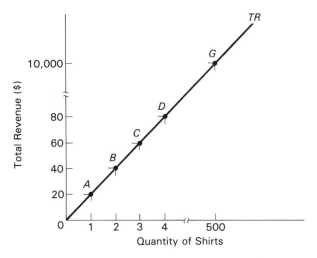

FIGURE 16-7   Total Revenue of the Competitive Firm   Total revenue is calculated by simply multiplying price per unit by the quantity sold at that price. For a purely competitive firm, the total revenue curve (*TR*) is a straight line beginning at 0. The reason for this is that the firm doesn't have to vary price as it sells more or less output.

$20.00 \times 1 = \$20.00$; at point *B*, $P \times Q = \$20.00 \times 2 = \$40.00$; at point *C*, total revenue is $60.00, and so on. If the firm were to increase its output to 500 units, *TR* would equal $10,000.00 at point *G;* and if it were to sell one more, its total revenue at point *H* would be $10,020.00.

2. Marginal Revenue and the Firm's Demand Curve

Note that the *TR* curve is a straight line that begins at the point or origin (0). The reason for this is that, even though $P = \$20.00$, if $Q = 0$, then $TR = \$0.00$. We must stress that every time the firm sells one more unit of output at the given market price of $20.00, *TR* rises by $20.00 as well (we show this in column 3 of Table 16-1). We call this addition to total revenue, this extra revenue whenever another unit is sold, the marginal revenue (*MR*). In our example, the *MR* of each extra unit sold is $20.00.

> **Definition:** *Marginal revenue* is the amount added to total revenue whenever an additional unit of output is sold.

> **Conclusion:** When the firm is a *price taker*—that is, sells each and all units at the prevailing market price—the *marginal revenue* of each additional unit sold *is the same as the price in the market.*

This can be seen in column 3 of Table 16-1. Even when the 501st unit is sold, it adds only $20.00 to total revenue.

We are now ready to draw the firm's demand curve for its product as the decision maker of the firm sees it. It is the horizontal line we drew earlier in panel (B) of Figure 16-6. This is how the decision maker of the competitive firm views it—as a *perfectly elastic* demand curve that exists at the prevailing market price.

3. A Couple of Possible Mistakes

Let's see why this is truly the decision maker's estimate of the demand for the firm's output. There are two points to keep in mind. First, the firm is extraordinarily small. Second, it produces a product that is precisely like the products produced by each firm in the industry (homogeneous products). This second condition means that buyers are interested only in price; they will, if they can, always buy from the lowest-priced seller; they are indifferent between sellers.

You can now see why our decision maker takes the market price as given and sells at that price only. If she were to charge a higher price—say, $21.00—no one would buy from her, not so long as the product could be bought at $20.00 from other sellers. Thus it would be a mistake for the competitive seller to try to sell at a price above the market price. And it would also be a mistake for her to set price below the market price. True, if she charged a lower price, people would hasten to buy from her. But since her firm is so atomistically small, she can actually sell all that she wants at the prevailing price. So there is no need for her to lower the price in order to sell her output.

4. Shifts in the Demand (*MR*) Curve

Does what we say about the demand curve being perfectly elastic at the given market price mean that the firm's demand curve will never change? No. In fact, it may be subject to all sorts of fluctuations because it will shift every time the price of the

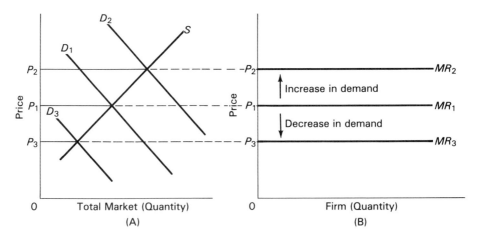

FIGURE 16-8   Changes in Demand for a Competitive Firm's Product   The competitive firm's perfectly elastic demand changes every time market price changes. A rise in market price shifts the firm's demand curve upward; a fall in market price shifts the demand curve down.

product changes in the market. This is shown in Figure 16–8. For example, suppose consumers increase the demand for the product. This is shown by the rightward shift of the *market* demand curve from D_1 to D_2, and accordingly price will rise from P_1 to P_2. Since marginal revenue = price, this also means that the firm's perfectly elastic demand curve has risen from MR, to MR_1. Furthermore, a fall in demand to D_3 will lower market price to P_3 and hence shifts the firm's demand curve to MR_3.

Thus an upward shift of the MR curve facing the single competitor's firm is called a *rise* in demand. If, on the other hand, the MR curve shifts downward, that is called a *fall* in demand. These rises and falls are due to changes in the market price and are *beyond the control of the competitive firm*.

We will have a lot more to say about the competitive firm and industry in the next three chapters.

E. SUMMARY

This chapter (1) explains why the market demand curve is negatively sloped and what causes it to shift, and (2) examines demand as it is viewed subjectively by the competitive firm's decision maker.

The demand curve is negatively sloped because of the law of diminishing marginal utility. This law states that the extra utility a consumer obtains from consuming successive units of the good declines (i.e., total utility increases at a decreasing rate). Because of this, the only way the consumer can be enticed to buy more is by offering more units of the good to him or her at a lower price.

Since the demand curves of consumers slope down from left to right, so does the market demand curve. This latter is simply a horizontal summation of all of the former.

The demand curve is derived on the basis of the *ceteris paribus* assumption— i.e., only the price of the product itself is allowed to vary to see what will happen to quantity demanded. The things that are assumed constant are also constraints on the consumer's behavior. Given these limitations, the individual strives to maximize total utility; and it is assumed that he or she pursues this goal rationally.

A change in any one of these constraints will cause *demand* to change. A rise in income will cause the demand for a normal good to rise and the demand for an inferior good to fall. The reverse of these two propositions also holds.

A fall in the price of a related good will also cause the demand for substitutes to fall, but it causes the demand for complementary goods to rise. The reverse of these two propositions also holds.

Changes in taste will also cause demand to rise or fall, and so will changes in expectations of future price changes. If future prices are expected to rise, present demand will fall. The reverse is also true.

Although the actual market demand curve has a negative slope, the demand as seen by an individual competitive firm is a horizontal line. This is a subjective, perfectly elastic demand curve. It is viewed this way by the firm's management because the firm is so small that it behaves as a price taker.

Marginal revenue is the addition to the firm's total revenue whenever an additional unit of output is sold. In the case of a perfectly elastic demand curve, marginal revenue equals price.

Terms and Concepts to Remember

Marginal utility	Demand curve
Normal good	Diminishing marginal
Inferior good	utility
Total revenue	Substitute goods
Perfectly elastic	Complementary goods
	Marginal revenue

Questions for Review

1. What is meant by *utility?* Is it measurable in any precise way? How can it be estimated?

2. How is it that a consumer can experience *diminishing* marginal utility while his or her total utility is increasing?

3. Explain and illustrate how diminishing marginal utility underlies the negative-sloped demand curve.

4. Explain and illustrate how the demand curve for product X responds to (a) a fall in income, (b) a fall in the price of a substitute good, and (c) a fall in the price of a complementary good. What will happen to the demand for X if all these changes occur at the same time?

5. Why is the demand curve as seen by the purely competitive firm perfectly elastic? Why is this sort of firm a price taker? Elaborate.

6. Define *marginal revenue* and explain why it is equal to price for a purely competitive firm.

Appendix: Price Elasticity of Demand

The law of demand tells us that as the price of the product goes down, the quantity demanded goes up. However, a lot more information than this is needed by many decision makers. A businessperson making a price decision needs to know how much more the consumers will buy at the lower price; and a legislator considering the imposition of an excise tax on, say, cigarettes needs to know how much the consumers will respond to the higher price.

Fortunately, an exact enough measure of these responses is available. It is called price elasticity of demand.

> **Definition:** *Price elasticity of demand* measures the *relative* effect on quantity demanded for a *relative* change in price. More specifically, price elasticity of demand is the percentage change in quantity demanded divided by the percentage change in price. That is:

$$Ep = \frac{\text{Percentage change in quantity demanded}}{\text{Percentage change in price}}$$

where *Ep* stands for *price elasticity coefficient.*

The mathematical sign of *Ep* is negative, reflecting the inverse relationship between price and quantity demanded. For simplicity, we use absolute values in the following discussion.

This measure takes on different values, depending on how sensitive quantity demanded is to a change in price. For example, suppose a 5 percent cut in price leads to a 15 percent increase in quantity demanded. In this event, price elasticity of demand would be 3—that is:

$$Ep = \frac{15\%}{5\%}$$

$$= 3$$

We would say here that quantity demanded is very sensitive (responsive) to a change in price; indeed, the price change leads to a threefold change in quantity demanded. In this case, we say that demand is elastic.

> **Definition:** As long as *Ep* is greater than one (i.e., the percentage change in quantity demanded is greater than the percentage change in price), demand is defined as being *elastic.*

If, on the other, a 5 percent cut in price results in only a 1 percent increase in quantity demanded, the value of the price elasticity coefficient would only be .2, indicating that quantity demanded isn't very responsive (sensitive) to a change in price. In this case, we say that demand is inelastic.

> **Definition:** As long as *Ep* is less than one (i.e., the percentage change in quantity demanded is less than the percentage change in price), demand is defined as being *inelastic.*

Finally, if by some happenstance the 5 percent cut in price leads to a 5 percent increase in quantity demanded, the price elasticity coefficient would be exactly one. In this instance, we say demand has unitary elasticity.

Definition: As long as *Ep* is one (i.e., the percentage change in quantity demanded equals the percentage change in price), demand is defined as being *unitary elastic.*

To sum up, if:

Ep > 1; elastic demand (% change in quantity demanded > % change in price)

Ep < 1; inelastic demand (% change in quantity demanded < % change in price)

Ep = 1; unitary elastic demand (% change in quantity demanded = % change in price).

Let's see how this measure can be useful in business decision making. If we want to calculate price elasticity accurately, we need to have two bits of information: (1) a working formula for the definitions above, and (2) some data on the demand curve or schedule.

We can make the defintion of price elasticity workable by observing that the percentage change in quantity demanded can be stated as $\Delta Q/Q$, and the percentage change in price can be stated as $\Delta P/P$. Therefore the algebraic statement of the price elasticity is

$$Ep = \frac{\Delta Q/Q}{\Delta P/P} = \frac{\Delta Q}{\Delta P} \cdot \frac{P}{Q}$$

This form of the equation indicates that *Ep* equals the change of quantity demanded per unit of price change ($\Delta Q/\Delta P$) *along the demand curve* times the ratio of price to quantity (P/Q) at the point where price elasticity is to be calculated.

Suppose a firm has estimated the demand schedule as follows:

P	Q	TR = (P · Q)
$10	0	$ 0
9	1	9
8	2	16
7	3	21
6	4	24
5	5	25
4	6	24
3	7	21
2	8	16
1	9	9
0	10	0

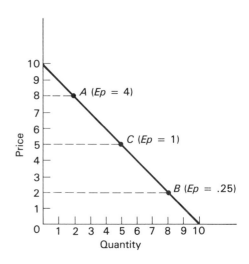

Management desires to know price elasticity of demand at a price of $8 (point *A*), at a price of $2 (point *B*), and at a price of $5 (point *C*). Using the formula, we plug in the relevant number for each point and get the following results. (Note that for each one-unit *Q* change, *P* changes by one unit so that $\Delta Q/\Delta P = 1$ at each point along the demand curve.)

$$\text{Point } A \; Ep = \frac{\Delta Q}{\Delta P} \cdot \frac{P}{Q} = \frac{1}{1} \cdot \frac{8}{2} = 4$$

$$\text{Point } B \; Ep = \frac{\Delta Q}{\Delta P} \cdot \frac{P}{Q} = \frac{1}{1} \cdot \frac{2}{8} = .25$$

$$\text{Point } C \; Ep = \frac{\Delta Q}{\Delta P} \cdot \frac{P}{Q} = \frac{1}{1} \cdot \frac{5}{5} = 1$$

So we see that if we charge a price of $8, we can sell 12 units, and if at that point we cut our price, quantity demanded will respond in greater porportions than the price cut (% change in quantity demanded > % change in price), and so the demand curve is elastic at point *A*.

At point *B*, where price is $2 and quantity is 8, demand is inelastic, since *Ep* = .25. This means that at this point, the percentage change in price is greater than the percentage change in quantity demanded. Therefore demand is inelastic.

At point *C,* at a price of $5, we would have unit price elasticity. Can you see why?

The significance of the price elasticity of demand for decision making, under certain circumstances, can easily be illustrated. Column 3 of the demand schedule calculates total revenue (*TR*) for the seller at each dollar price by taking price times quantity. Careful examination of column 3 shows that as the price is cut from $10 per unit, at first total revenue rises from zero to $25 at a price of $5. If price is lowered below $5, however, total revenue falls, even though unit sales continue to rise. Total revenue is thus maximized at $25 (a price of $5 and selling 5 units).

Now suppose production and sales cost are fixed at some level, say $10. That is, no matter how much or how little is produced, total costs are $10. Under these conditions, would it be wise to produce 2 units and sell them for $8? Well, certainly the firm would make a profit, since total revenue would be $16 and total cost $10, leaving a profit of $6. But note that if the price is reduced from $8 to $5, total revenue rises from $16 to $25. The reason for this rise in total revenue is that the demand curve is elastic over this range. Thus when price is reduced, quantity demand rises by a greater proportion. The effect of the price cut *by itself* is of course to reduce total revenue. However, if unit sales increase by a greater percentage, then total revenue rises. This is only true, we repeat, if the demand curve is elastic. So, if the demand curve is elastic and price is reduced, total revenue rises, and if price is raised, total revenue falls. As price falls below $5, unit sales continue to rise but total revenue falls. The reason is that the demand is inelastic. A fall in price raises quantity demanded by a smaller percentage, so total revenue falls. For example, a price cut from $2 to $1 reduces revenue from $16 to $9. Thus, if demand is inelastic and price is cut, total revenue falls. Conversely, a rise in price with a inelastic demand will raise total revenue. In the final analysis, the producer would be best advised to produce 5 units and sell each one for $5. Total profit would be $15 ($25 of total revenue less $10 of total cost = $15 profit), the greatest possible profit under the circumstances cited. Note at this point that price elasticity of demand is unitary ($Ep = 1$). If the firm prices its products at the point where the price elasticity is unitary, it will maximize total revenue. Under the conditions of this example, this price also maximizes profits. However, that won't be true in all circumstances, as we shall see.

A final note: The concept of elasticity can also be used to measure the impact of the other determinants of demand. As we know, changes in income shift demand curves. Income elasticity (% change in demand/% change in income) measures the direction and strength of this response.

17

Competitive Supply

chapter preview

- Supply and demand together determine price.
- Marginal cost is how much the last unit produced adds to the firm's total costs.
- Management must follow three rules if it is to maximize profits: When marginal revenue exceeds marginal cost, increase production; when marginal cost exceeds marginal revenue, reduce production; when marginal cost equals marginal revenue, maintain production.
- The firm's marginal costs rise because of the presence of diminishing returns.
- The law of diminishing returns states that as successive units of a variable input are applied to fixed inputs, marginal product eventually declines.
- When price is below average total cost but above average variable cost,

the firm will operate where marginal revenue equals marginal cost in order to minimize losses.
- If price falls below average variable cost and management expects it to remain there, the plant should be shut down in order to minimize loses.
- The firm's marginal cost curve above its average variable cost curve is its short-run supply curve.
- A competitive firm must reach optimal size if it is to survive over the long haul.
- Optimal size is achieved when the firm has taken advantage of its economies of size but before diseconomies due to larger size have set in.
- The long-run equilibrium exists when price equals marginal cost equals average total cost at the minimum point of the optimal size cost curve.

The British economist Alfred Marshall pointed out that obviously neither blade of a pair of scissors does the actual cutting. Clearly not; both blades together do the job. By the same token, he argued, demand alone can't determine price. The other side, supply, is just as important. Just like the two blades of a pair of scissors, both supply and demand interact to set price in the market.[1]

The preceding chapter looked at the demand side; this chapter examines supply. The supplies of products come from business firms that, in our society, are privately owned and have one overriding goal—maximum profits. We assume that they always behave with this objective in mind.

Figure 17–1 shows the place of supply in the circular flow of economic activity. The supply curve there (above the business firms box) represents the other supply curves in a competitive economy. The procedure we will follow in getting to the supply curve is the same that we followed in the preceding chapter in deriving the demand curve. There are a number of variables that influence the output of business firms, but we allow only one at a time to change. Thus, in drawing the supply curve in Figure 17–1, we have invoked the *ceteris paribus* assumption and allowed only the price of the product to change. Since the curve has a *positive* slope, it obeys what Chapter 4 called the law of supply.

> **Definition:** The *law of supply* says that the higher the price of the product, the more willing producers are to sell a larger quantity; conversely, the lower the price of the product, the lower the quantity supplied.

A change in any of the variables that are held constant by our assumption will cause the supply curve to shift either to the right (an increase) or to the left (a decrease). All of this, however, comes later. For now, we need to see how we got the Figure 17–1 supply curve in the first place.

A. MARGINAL COST AND MARGINAL REVENUE: AN INTRODUCTION TO THE FIRM'S SUPPLY CURVE

The main message of the last part of the preceding chapter was that the manager of the firm needs to know the marginal revenue that flows from the sale of the firm's output. However, more information is needed if he or she is to make the correct

---

[1]The scissors example is from Alfred Marshall, *Principles of Economics* (New York: Macmillan, 1950), p. 348.

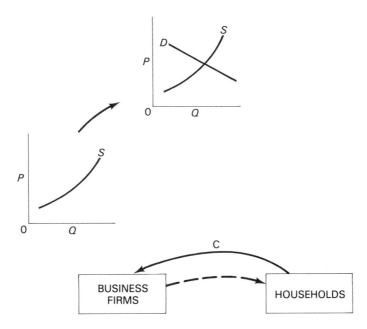

FIGURE 17-1   Supply in the Circular Flow Model   The supply curve here is only one of thousands. It is put up against the demand curve at the top of the diagram. This chapter's main task is to explain why this supply curve has a positive slope.

decision about how much to produce. More specifically, the manager has to have some knowledge of the firm's costs of production. Then, once armed with the proper revenue and cost data, the manager can direct the firm toward the goal of maximum profits. In the process of explaining this, we will derive the firm's supply curve; and once we have done this, we can move on and derive the market supply curve.

1. Two Important Rules

It really doesn't do the manager much good to know how much an extra unit produced and sold adds to the firm's total revenue (i.e., marginal revenue) unless he or she also knows *how much that extra unit adds to total cost* (i.e., marginal cost).

> **Definition:**   *Marginal cost* is the addition to the firm's total costs attributable to the last (or next) unit produced.

As you might sense, the really crucial comparison that the manager must make is that of marginal cost with marginal revenue. Let's take two examples to see how important this comparison is.

It wouldn't be very rational for the manager to decide to produce and sell an extra unit of output that adds, say, $20 to total revenue but, at the same time, adds $50 to total cost. Put in terms we have learned, this means that marginal cost (*MC*) is greater than marginal revenue (*MR*), and the firm would therefore lose $30 *on this unit* if it were produced and sold. In fact, if the firm were to continue operating at outputs at which marginal cost exceeds marginal revenue, the manager should probably be replaced.

Now consider the opposite case, in which marginal cost is less than marginal revenue. Suppose that, as before, the extra unit produced and sold has a marginal revenue of $20 but now has a marginal cost of only $10. In this event, the manager should direct the firm to produce and sell this extra unit. Why? Because it adds more to the firm's total revenue (i.e., *MR* = $20) than it adds to total cost (i.e., *MC* = $10). This particular unit thus *adds* $10 to the firm's total profits if it is produced and sold.

We can now safely generalize from these examples and arrive at two important conclusions about production decisions. These can be stated as rules of behavior.

> **First Conclusion:**   As long as marginal revenue exceeds marginal cost, it is profitable for the firm to produce and sell extra units of output. The reason is that each additional unit adds more to total revenue than it adds to total costs. Thus, as a rule of behavior, whenever *MR* > *MC*, increase output.

> **Second Conclusion:**   As long as marginal revenue is less than marginal cost, it is not worthwhile for the firm to produce and sell extra units of output. In this event, each additional unit adds more to the firm's total costs than it adds to the total revenue. Thus, as a rule of behavior, whenever *MC* > *MR*, reduce output.

Management must always heed these two rules of behavior if the firm is to maximize its profits. It is now time for the next step in our analysis, and here we ask for your patience for a short while.

Figure 17–2 shows a competitive firm's marginal cost curve (*MC*). Note that we have drawn it so that it slopes uphill from left to right (marginal cost increases as output increases), and this is what we ask you to accept for the moment; we will explain this positive slope soon enough. For now we will simply assert that the firm's marginal cost curve slopes upward because of the *law of diminishing returns*.

2. Some More Important Rules and a Supply Curve

Let's bring some things together now. Suppose that, as in Figure 17–2, the prevailing market price as P_1. Since this firm is a *price taker*, management views the demand curve for its product as *perfectly elastic;* the demand curve at this price may be drawn as $P_1 MR_1$. Now, given our two rules above, we can derive a third important guide for management to follow.

When, as in Figure 17–2, the price of the product is P_1, management will elect to produce the output rate of X_1. Why this amount? Let's determine why by asking why management won't produce some other amount. The firm won't produce X_2

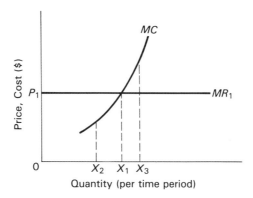

FIGURE 17-2 The Firm's Marginal Cost (MC) Curve Profit maximization means that the firm's management must select that output rate at which marginal cost (*MC*) equals marginal revenue (*MR*). The output rate X_2 doesn't maximize profits because here $MR > MC$, and hence output should be increased. Furthermore, X_2 isn't a profit-maximizing rate of output, for here $MC > MR$, and hence output should be reduced. Only at X_1 does $MC = MR$, and management should select this rate of production to maximize profits.

because at this output marginal revenue exceeds marginal cost, and our first rule tells management that when $MR > MC$, it should increase output. In fact, for all outputs to the left of X_1, each extra unit, if produced, would add more to total revenue than to total cost. Thus management should push production beyond X_2 and all the way up to X_1.

Output, however, should not be pressed beyond X_1. If for some reason it were at X_3, the firm would not be maximizing its profits. At this rate of output, and indeed for all output rates beyond X_1, marginal cost is greater than marginal revenue. Each of these units, in other words, adds more to total cost than to total revenue. Our second rule tells management what to do in this event: If $MC > MR$, cut back on production.

Putting all this together, we can arrive at another important rule of behavior; it flows directly from the other rules.

> **Conclusion:** The firm that is seeking maximum profits will always carry production to the point at which marginal cost equals marginal revenue ($MC = MR$). That is, the firm must push production to the point at which the last unit produced adds as much to total cost as it adds to total revenue.

The same rule applies, as we shall soon see, if the firm is incurring a loss. If it does find itself in such unfortunate straits, management must seek to minimize losses. But more on this later.

So much for Figure 17–2. It has been useful, but we need to move on. Figure 17–3 contains the same information as Figure 17–2 and a little bit more. The P_1 and

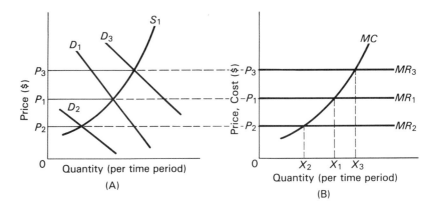

FIGURE 17-3   Changes in Market Prices Cause Shifts in the Firm's Demand Curve   Here we see how changes in market prices induce the competitive firm to adjust output. In each case, however, the firm selects that rate of output at which marginal revenue equals marginal cost.

X_1 in panel (B) are the same as the P_1 and X_1 in Figure 17-2. Panel (A) tells us that P_1 is the market equilibrium price when demand is D_1 and supply is S_1. Now let's introduce a change and have consumers reduce their demand for the product. This is shown by the leftward shift of the demand curve to D_2 in panel (A). The equilibrium market price, therefore, falls to P_2, and this means that the perfectly elastic demand curve facing the firm will also fall, as shown by the lower demand curve P_2MR_2 in panel (B).

How will the firm's management respond to this price reduction? As long as profits remain the overriding goal, the firm's managment must respond by cutting production back to X_2 at which once more marginal cost equals marginal revenue. This is shown in panel (B). Surely the management is not pleased with this lower price and reduced output; but just as surely, the adjustment should be made. Look what would happen if it weren't made. If management persisted in producing the output rate of X_1, the firm would soon be in trouble, for at that output, marginal cost would exceed the *new, lower* marginal revenue. We know the rule of what to do in this case—reduce output. In fact, another rule tells management to adjust production until once again marginal cost equals marginal revenue. When the price of the product is P_2, the equality occurs at the production rate of X_2. Thus we have arrived at another important conclusion.

Conclusion: When market price falls, all other things equal, the competitive firm will cut back on the quantity supplied until again $MC = MR$. Note: the lower the price, the smaller the quantity supplied.

Let's reverse the case and see what happens when demand rises, as shown by the higher demand curve D_3 in Figure 17-3(A). The equilibrium market price will rise to P_3, thus shifting the perfectly elastic demand curve facing the firm upward to P_3MR_3. How will the management react to this? Here the response is a much happier one, for output will be increased until again marginal revenue equals marginal cost. The new equilibrium rate of output will be X_3. Now that price is P_3, all outputs to the left of X_3 have a marginal revenue greater than marginal cost; and our rule says that when $MR > MC$, increase output until $MR = MC$. Therefore we have yet another conclusion.

> **Conclusion:** When market price rises, all other things equal, the competitive firm will increase production until once more $MC = MR$. Note: the higher the price, the greater the quantity supplied.

Look at what has taken place. We have had three different prices and three different corresponding quantities supplied—at P_1 the firm supplies X_1; at P_2 it supplies X_2; and at P_3 it supplies X_3. And each of these price and quantity combinations can be read off of the firm's marginal cost curve. Indeed:

> The competitive firm's supply curve is its marginal cost curve. This supply curve reflects the law of supply—that is, *the higher the price, the greater the quantity supplied; and the lower the price, the smaller the quantity supplied.*

However, we still need to explain the slope of the competitive firm's supply curve, and that's what we turn to now.

B. THE LAW OF DIMINISHING RETURNS

It is because of the law of diminishing returns that the firm's supply (MC) curve has a positive slope. First a definition, then an example, and then back to the marginal cost curve.

1. The Definition

The law of diminishing returns is no stranger to us. We met it much earlier in Chapter 2 when we used it to explain why the economy's production-possibilities curve bows out from the point of origin. We will use the same definition given there.

> **Definition:** As additional units of a variable input (e.g., labor) are added to a fixed amount of other inputs (e.g., capital, land), the *extra* output per *extra* unit of the variable input will eventually decline.

This famous law, it seems, is almost universal. There are few exceptions to it, and it has many implications. For now we want to keep our earlier promise and show why it makes the firm's supply (MC) curve slope upward from left to right.

2. The Example

Mugs Unlimited is a small firm that produces ordinary coffee mugs and has been in business for three years. It has a given amount of space in its plant, and it has the necessary equipment to carry out its production plans. It also has in stock all the essential materials for making coffee mugs. In short, we are assuming here that Mugs Unlimited has a *given amount of capital and space.* These are the "fixed amounts of other inputs" in our definition above. Note that these fixed inputs put an ultimate constraint on how many mugs the firm can produce per day. Column 2 of Table 17-1, in fact, shows us that Mugs Unlimited can produce no more than 67 cases of mugs per day. Perhaps later on the owners may expand its fixed inputs— that is, build a new plant or add on to this one. At the moment, the firm must operate within the physical constraints imposed by its fixed inputs.

Let's assume that business is so brisk that Mugs Unlimited can easily sell all of its output at the prevailing market price. Does this mean, however, that the manager—let's call her Delia—will have the plant produce at maximum capacity? Not necessarily. The amount to be produced per day is determined by the rules we have already developed in this chapter. If Delia follows them (and she should), then she will select the rate of production per day at which $MC = MR$ (or as close as it can be).

We know how Delia calculates marginal revenue. Let's suppose the price per case of mugs is \$8.00. Thus she knows that $P_1 = MR_1 = \$8$. Getting to the marginal cost figure, however, will require a few preliminary steps, and we begin with Table 17-1.

The first three columns of Table 17-1 are what we and Delia need to concentrate on for now. In a sense, they don't tell us anything startling or unusual. In fact, one message they give us is obvious—as more workers are hired, total output goes

TABLE 17-1   Short-Run Production and Cost Data for Mugs Unlimited

Number of Workers (1)	Output per day (2)	Marginal Product (3)	Total Labor Cost (4)	Added Cost per Worker (5)	Marginal Cost (6) = (5)/(3)
0	0	—	—	—	—
1	5	5	\$ 40.00	\$40.00	\$ 8.00
2	16	11	80.00	40.00	3.64
3	31	15	120.00	40.00	2.67
4	41	10	160.00	40.00	4.00
5	50	9	200.00	40.00	4.44
6	57	7	240.00	40.00	5.71
7	62	5	280.00	40.00	8.00
8	65	3	320.00	40.00	13.33
9	67	2	360.00	40.00	20.00
	Full Capacity				
10	67	0	400.00	40.00	—

up. But, as it turns out, there really is something interesting *and important* about how total output behaves: It doesn't increase at a steady pace as more workers are employed. Instead it at first increases very rapidly, and then it continues to increase, but at a decreasing rate. Finally, it tops out at 67 cases per day. Put otherwise, at first there are increasing returns (total output increasing at an increasing rate), which are then followed by diminishing returns (output increasing at a decreasing rate). The range of increasing returns, however, is quite compatible with our definition. Recall that it simply asserts that output will eventually be subject to diminishing returns.

A useful way to distinguish between increasing and diminishing returns and to determine when diminishing returns set in is to look at the behavior of the *marginal product*. (This concept of the marginal product is also essential in the calculation of marginal cost.)

> **Definition:** *Marginal product* is the addition to total output (product) caused by the employment of one more unit of the variable input. Marginal product is calculated by dividing the change in total product (output) by the change in the amount of the variable input.

Marginal product is shown in column 3 of Table 17–1. Note how it first rises, reaches a peak, and then declines. This behavior of marginal product is also traced out in Figure 17–4. The rising portion of the marginal product curve tells us that the firm is experiencing increasing returns. This is the output range from zero to 31 cases when the first three workers are employed.

Yet, as our definition states, diminishing returns will eventually set in; and this

FIGURE 17-4 The Firm's Marginal Product Curve Although marginal product may rise at first, it will eventually begin to decline because of the law of diminishing returns.

is shown by the declining segment of the firm's marginal product curve in Figure 17-4. Diminishing returns set in with the fourth worker and continue until marginal product becomes zero. Remember, as column 2 reminds us, total output continues to increase when there are diminishing returns, but it increases at a decreasing (slower) rate.

Why are increasing returns replaced by diminishing returns? A large part of the answer to this question relates to the idea of division of labor. (Remember Adam Smith's pin factory example back in Chapter 3?) When only one or two workers are employed, their efficiency is quite low. Each has to perform a number of tasks and hence can't be very skilled in any one. Moreover, with only a few workers, the firm's capital equipment can't be used very efficiently. But as more workers are employed things get turned round. There can be more division of labor, and consequently workers become more productive. They themselves work more effectively, and they also work the capital equipment more efficiently. Thus marginal product rises, but only to a point, the point of diminishing returns.

There is, in other words, some limit to the applications and benefits of division of labor. Remember, Mugs Unlimited has only so many square feet in its plant, and it has only so much capital equipment. These are the constraints we mentioned earlier; they are the fixed inputs in our definition of the law of diminishing returns. In our example, these constraints make themselves felt from the fourth worker on. First, the limited amount of equipment becomes overcrowded, and thus it and the workers using it become less efficient. Second, given the size of Mugs Unlimited, there is only so much division of labor that can take place. This would show up clearly and dramatically if the tenth worker were hired: His marginal product would be zero. Obviously, Delia would never employ the tenth worker.

But, in fact, how many workers *will* be employed? Let's turn to the answer to this important question.

3. The Firm's Marginal Cost Curve

Suppose the prevailing market wage for the type of labor that Mugs Unlimited employs is $40 per day and remains constant at that figure. Delia can thus hire as many or as few as she wants at this wage.

The wage cost data that she must consider carefully are given in columns 4 and 5 of Table 17-1. Column 4 shows that total wage outlays rise as more and more workers are employed. Column 5 shows by how much the total wage bill rises whenever Delia hires another worker. In this case, she knows that the total wage bill rises by $40 per day every time another worker is added to the company's payroll.

Finally, we get back to the firm's marginal costs, which are shown in column 6 of Table 17-1. Recall that marginal cost is how much the last unit produced adds to the firm's total cost. It is calculated as

$$MC = \frac{\Delta TC}{MP}$$

that is, marginal cost equals the change in total cost (ΔTC) divided by the corresponding marginal product (MP).

In our example, the change in total cost is always the same as the prevailing daily wage (W) at which Delia can hire new workers—check column 5. In other words, $\Delta TC = W = \$40$, and therefore we can rewrite the marginal cost formula as

$$MC = \frac{W}{MP}$$

Since we have assumed that the wage rate is given, Delia can take the numerator (W) as constant at $40 per day. However, she won't consider the denominator (MP) as constant.

To the contrary, she knows that at first it increases and then subsequently declines. Thus she concludes that at first *marginal cost* must decline, and it does, as shown in column 6 of Table 17-1 and in Figure 17-5. This has to be the case, for she is dividing an increasing MP into a constant W. Therefore MC must decline at first.

However, as the firm presses on into the stage of diminishing returns, marginal cost begins to rise, and Delia knows this. Now she divides a *falling MP* into a constant W. Thus MC must rise, and so it does, as shown in column 6 and in Figure 17-5.

It is mainly this rising portion of the MC curve that we have used as the firm's

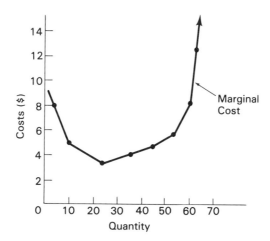

FIGURE 17-5   The Firm's Marginal Cost Curve   The firm's marginal cost curve at first declines because its marginal product curve is rising. Then, with diminishing returns (or falling marginal product), its marginal cost rises. The shape of the firm's marginal cost curve is thus strongly influenced by the shape of its marginal product curve.

supply curve. We ignore the declining segment. But we also don't use all of the rising segment of the curve as the supply curve. To see why, we must look at the other costs of the firm.

C. OTHER COSTS AND THE FIRM'S SUPPLY CURVE

So far we have looked only at wages and marginal cost. But aren't there other costs that the firm must consider? What about rent, interest, depreciation, and similar costs? Surely these must be taken into account.

1. Fixed, Variable, and Total Costs

The other costs that we need to examine are classified according to the type of inputs used by the firm.

First, there are those costs associated with the fixed inputs. These are called *fixed costs.* The important thing to recognize about them is that they don't vary as output changes. Examples are rent, interest on outstanding loans, minimum telephone charges, and utility bills, which must be paid even though output may be zero.

> **Definition:**   *Fixed (sunk) costs* are those costs that are constant and therefore do not change as output is changed. These costs must be paid even if the firm's output is zero.

We have assumed that Mugs Unlimited has fixed costs of $100; see column 2 of Table 17-2.

Some costs, however, do vary as output changes; these are called *variable costs,* and they are associated with the variable inputs used by the firm.

> **Definition:**   *Variable costs* are those costs that change as output changes, rising as output rises, and falling as output falls.

Mugs Unlimited must, in our example, pay a daily wage of $40 per worker. We have already seen how the variable costs are involved in calculating the firm's marginal cost. Mugs Unlimited's total variable costs are listed in column 4 of Table 17-2.

A final definition should present no problem at all.

> **Definition:**   *Total costs* are simply total fixed and total variable costs added together. Total costs will rise as output rises (because of total variable costs) and will fall as output falls (for the same reason).

Total costs are shown in column 7 of Table 17-2. We need to look at each of these costs in a bit more detail.

TABLE 17-2 Short-Run Costs for Mugs Unlimited

Total Output Per Day (1)	Total Fixed Cost (2)	Average Fixed Cost (3) = (2) ÷ (1)	Total Variable Cost (4)	Average Variable Cost (5) = (4) ÷ (1)	Marginal Cost (6)	Total Cost (7)	Average Total Cost (8) = (7) ÷ (1) = (3) + (5)
0	$100.00	$—	$—	$—	$—	$100.00	$—
5	100.00	20.00	40.00	8.00	8.00	140.00	28.00
16	100.00	6.25	80.00	5.00	3.64	180.00	11.25
31	100.00	3.22	120.00	3.87	2.67	220.00	7.10
41	100.00	2.44	160.00	3.90	4.00	260.00	6.34
50	100.00	2.00	200.00	4.00	4.44	300.00	6.00
57	100.00	1.75	240.00	4.21	5.71	340.00	5.96
62	100.00	1.61	280.00	4.52	8.00	380.00	6.13
65	100.00	1.54	320.00	4.92	13.33	420.00	6.46
67	100.00	1.49	360.00	5.37	20.00	460.00	6.86
67	100.00	1.49	400.00	5.97	—	500.00	7.46

2. Fixed (Sunk) Costs

Fixed costs are irrelevant when managment decides on how much or how little to produce. They actually have no bearing on the rule of making marginal revenue and marginal costs equal, and for the simple reason that fixed costs have nothing to do with marginal costs. Recall the formula for marginal cost:

$$MC = \frac{\Delta TC}{MP}$$

However, there can be no ΔTC due to change in total fixed costs when output changes. Fixed costs, remember, are fixed and therefore cannot account for any ΔTC as output varies. The ΔTC in that formula must therefore come from some source other than fixed cost.

> **Conclusion:** Fixed costs are irrelevant to the firm's decision on how much output to produce.

This doesn't mean that management doesn't consider fixed costs. It does. What it does mean is that fixed costs have nothing to do with marginal costs.
It is sometimes useful to convert total fixed costs into average fixed costs. This is done simply by dividing total fixed costs (*TFC*) by total product (*TP*):

$$AFC = \frac{TFC}{TP}$$

Since fixed costs are constant, the numerator (*TFC*) in the formula is also constant. The denominator (*TP*), however, increases as we move from lower to higher outputs. Therefore, as shown in column 3 of Table 17–2, *AFC* declines throughout the range from zero to maximum physical output. This behavior of *AFC* is also seen in Figure 17–6; the *AFC* curve declines throughout, becoming smaller and smaller as total fixed costs are spread over a larger and larger output.

3. Changing Variable Costs

Variable costs, on the other hand, are a different matter. They can't be ignored in the pricing process, and for the simple reason that they are directly related to marginal cost.
Again, it is useful to convert total variable costs into average variable costs. The procedure is to divide total variable costs (*TVC*) by the corresponding total output (*TP*):

$$AVC = \frac{TVC}{TP}$$

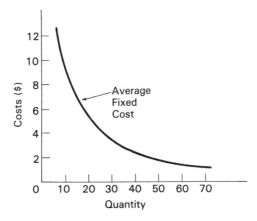

FIGURE 17-6   The Firm's Average Fixed Cost Curve   Average fixed costs continuously decline as output is increased because the total fixed costs are spread over ever larger amounts of output.

The behavior of *AVC* is traced out in column 5 of Table 17-2 and in Figure 17-7.

Note that when Mugs Unlimited employs more workers, two things occur. First, total product rises; and second, so do total variable costs. The behavior of these two things is shown in columns 1 and 4 of Table 17-2. What this means for our formula is that both the numerator (*TVC*) and the denominator (*TP*) are increasing. However, and this is important, they do not increase at the same pace.

At first, when Mugs Unlimited increases production, output rises faster (from 0 to 5 to 16 to 31) than total variable costs (from 0 to $40 to $80 to $120). In this stage of production, therefore, the numerator (*TVC*) in our formula increases more slowly than the denominator (*TP*). Accordingly, *AVC* must decline. However, what happens to *AVC* when the firm pushes production into the stage of diminishing

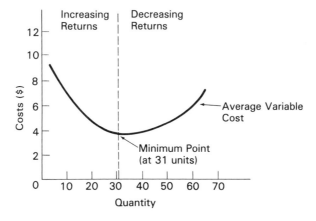

FIGURE 17-7   The Firm's Average Variable Cost Curve   The firm's average variable cost curve takes a U shape because of diminishing returns.

returns? In this stage of production, total output continues to increase, but now at a progressively decreasing rate (from 31 to 41 to 50 to 57, etc.). Total variable costs, on the other hand, continue to rise at the same steady pace (from $120 to $160 to $200, etc.). In terms of our formula, the numerator (*TVC*) is now rising relative to the denominator (*TP*), and hence *AVC* must rise. So, *when the firm is operating in the stage of diminishing returns, average variable costs will rise as output is increased.*

Let's now combine the last two conclusions we have reached into one.

Conclusion: The firm's average variable cost curve takes a U shape. It declines as output passes through the stage of increasing returns, and it rises as output is pushed into the stage of diminishing returns.

The U-shaped *AVC* curve of Mugs Unlimited is shown in Figure 17–7.

4. Average Variable and Marginal Costs

We aren't quite finished with average variable costs, for we need to be aware of the relationships between average variable costs and marginal costs. To show this relationship, we take the *MC* curve of Mugs Unlimited from Figure 17–5 and the U-shaped *AVC* curve from Figure 17–7 and put them together in Figure 17–8. Look carefully at this diagram and study the relationships between the two curves. We will first state a conclusion about these relationships and then explain how we arrived at it.

Conclusion: As long as the firm's marginal cost is less than the average variable cost, then average variable cost declines. This holds true for the

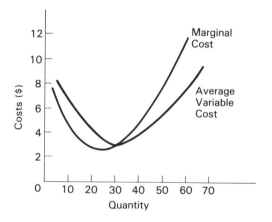

FIGURE 17-8   The Marginal Cost and Average Variable Cost Curves   The behavior of the marginal cost determines the average variable cost. As long as marginal cost is below average variable cost, the latter is falling. If marginal cost is above average variable cost, the latter is rising.

stage of increasing returns. Conversely, as long as the firm's marginal cost is greater than the average variable cost, then average variable cost rises. This holds true for the stage of diminishing returns.

Note how the curves in Figure 17-8 mirror these relationships. In the stage of increasing returns, the *MC* curve lies beneath the *AVC* curve; then in the stage of diminishing returns, the *MC* curve lies above the *AVC* curve. Given these relationships, then the MC curve must cut the *AVC* curve at the latter's lowest point.

What really is at play here is the interaction between an average figure (in our case, *AVC*) and a marginal figure (*MC*). Let's illustrate what is meant with an example that will probably be very clear to you. Suppose you are taking a series of short quizzes in this course, ten in all, each worth 10 points. Your goal is to get the highest possible *average* score. Of course, you know how to calculate the average quiz score. Let's assume that so far you have earned a 10 and a 6. Your average, therefore, is 8. Now, if you want to raise that average, you clearly must score above 8 on your next (i.e., marginal) quiz. Or, to put it a better way, your marginal score must exceed your average if you want to pull the average up. But if you slip and your marginal score is less than the average, then . . . well, you know the consequences. (What happens if your marginal score is equal to your average?)

The relationship between average and marginal grades is precisely the same as that between the firm's average variable and marginal costs. Indeed, it is a relationship that holds generally.

> **Conclusion:** As long as the marginal quantity is less than the average, it will pull the average down. And as long as the marginal exceeds the average, it will pull the average up.

To repeat, the relationship between average and marginal is general. It is as true of a baseball player's batting average as it is of Mugs Unlimited's cost curves. It is also true of a football team's kicker; if he wants to improve his punting average, then his next kick must cover more yards than his average. For now, however, we are concerned only with cost behavior.

5. *AFC* + *AVC* = *ATC*

All the Mugs Unlimited cost curves can be brought together as a family of cost curves. This is done in Figure 17-9, in wich we have the *AFC* curve from Figure 17-6 and the U-shaped *AVC* curve from Figure 17-8. We have also included the *MC* curve.

Note that Figure 17-9 includes another cost curve–the average total cost (ATC) curve. There are two ways of calculating average total cost. One is to divide total cost (*TC*) by total output (*TP*):

$$ATC = \frac{TC}{TP}$$

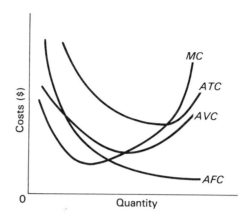

FIGURE 17-9   The Firm's Family of Cost Curves   The complete family of cost curves for Mugs Unlimited.

The resulting *ATC* figures are shown in column 8 of Table 17-2.

The other way is simply to add together the average fixed and average variable cost figures we have already derived:

$$ATC = AFC + AVC$$

Either way of calculating ATC is all right. What we have done in Figure 17-9 is to use the second method—that is, we have added the *AFC* and *AVC* curves *vertically.* Again, check column 8 of Table 17-2.

A final point: The relationship of the *MC* curve to the *ATC* curve is precisely the same as that between *MC* and *AVC.* Thus, as long as *MC* is below *ATC,* it will pull *ATC* down; and as long as *MC* is above *ATC,* it will pull *ATC* up. The reason for this is exactly the same as the reason for relationship between *AVC* and *MC.*

D. THE SUPPLY CURVE, FIRM AND INDUSTRY

At the outset of this chapter, we posited that the firm's marginal cost curve is its supply curve, and we showed this curve in Figure 17-3(B). But then, when we got around to deriving the firm's marginal cost curve, it looked like the *MC* curve in Figures 17-5 and 17-8. In these two diagrams, the *MC* curve has both a decreasing segment and a rising segment. The *MC* curve in Figure 17-3(B) however, has only the rising portion. So which, then, is the firm's supply curve? We will answer this question first and then show how we arrive at the answer.

> **Definition:**   The competitive firm's supply curve is that portion of its marginal cost curve that lies above the average variable cost curve.

Now let's see how we have reached this conclusion.

1. Operating to Maximize Profits

We rely heavily on Figure 17–10 and Table 17–3. Let's assume that the prevailing market price of coffee mugs is $8.00 per case. Thus the firm's perfectly elastic demand curve is $P_{8.00}MR_{8.00}$ in Figure 17–10. Given this marginal revenue curve, the firm will opt to produce an output of 62 cases per day because it is at this output rate that $MR = MC = \$8.00$. Table 17–3 lists the firm's costs of production, its total revenue, and its total profits (or losses, which are shown with a minus sign). Total profits (or losses) are obtained by deducting total costs from total revenue:

$$\text{Total profit} = TR - TC$$

Table 17–3 also has two columns, 7 and 8, that give the marginal cost and marginal revenue figures. When the owner decides to produce at the rate at which $MC = MR$, profits are at their maximum. This can be seen in the last three columns of Table 17–3. When $MR = MC$, profits are $116.00 per day. Any other rate of output yields lower profits because at any other rate $MC \neq MR$. This equilibrium condition is shown by the (P_8, X_{62}) combination in Figure 17–10.[2] Note that in this case, the firm has covered all of its fixed costs and all of its variable costs, and it has a neat profit of $116.00 per day left over.

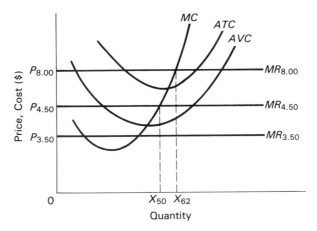

FIGURE 17–10   Profit Maximization and Loss Minimization for the Competitive Firm   When price is above *ATC*, as at $8.00, the firm will maximize the profits by operating where *MR = MC*. When price falls below *ATC* but is still above *AVC*, the firm continues to operate when *MR = MC* in order to minimize losses. Finally, the firm will shut down when price is less than *AVC* in order to minimize losses. Thus the *MC* curve above the *AVC* is the firm's supply curve.

[2]Can you tell why the profit figure for the output of 62 (which is the production rate we select as maximizing profits) is the same as the profit figure for a rate of output of 57? You should be able to. The reason is that the *MC* of the last 5 units produced is $8.00 each; but each sold for $8.00 (i.e., *MR* = $8.00). Thus, for these units, $MR = MC = \$8.00$. Why produce these? Why not? Delia had to go that far to find out indeed that $MR = MC$.

TABLE 17-3 Profit Maximization for Mugs Unlimited When Price is $8.00 per Case

Total Output Per Day (1)	Total Fixed Cost (2)	Total Variable Cost (3)	Total Cost (4)	Total Revenue (5) = (1) × $8.00	Total Profit (6) = (5) − (4)	Marginal Revenue (7)	Marginal Cost (8)
0	$100.00	$—	$100.00	$—	−$100.00	$—	$—
5	100.00	40.00	140.00	40.00	−100.00	8.00	8.00
16	100.00	80.00	180.00	128.00	−52.00	8.00	3.64
31	100.00	120.00	220.00	248.00	28.00	8.00	2.67
41	100.00	160.00	260.00	328.00	68.00	8.00	4.00
50	100.00	200.00	300.00	400.00	100.00	8.00	4.44
57	100.00	240.00	340.00	456.00	116.00	8.00	5.71
62	100.00	280.00	380.00	496.00	116.00	8.00 =	8.00
65	100.00	320.00	420.00	520.00	100.00	8.00	13.33
67	100.00	360.00	460.00	536.00	76.00	8.00	20.00
67	100.00	400.00	500.00	536.00	36.00	—	—

2. Operating to Minimize Losses

Now let's turn to Table 17–4. Would that the firm's good fortune could last, but unfortunately firms are often forced into loss situations. To see what would happen in this event, let's suppose the market demand for coffee mugs falls so that the price per case slumps to $4.50. We show this unpleasant result in Figure 17–10 by dropping the perfectly elastic demand curve down to $P_{4.50}MR_{4.50}$. What will be Delia's response to this? Clearly, it is a very unfortunate situation because at each output, price is less than average total cost. No matter what output is chosen, the firm has a loss.

Don't, however, jump to the conclusion that it is best for the firm to shut down completely. The owner is too experienced to make such a rash decision; she will actually elect to continue operating the plant. Moreover, she will continue to operate according to the $MC = MR$ rule, although this equality now occurs at the output of 50 cases per day and the lower price of $4.50 per case. Really, as columns 7 and 8 of Table 17–4 show, there is no precise, neat equality of marginal revenue and marginal cost; but at 50 cases per day there is an approximate equality ($MR = \$4.50$, $MC = \$4.44$). Column 6 shows that at the output rate of 50 cases per day and $MR = MC$, total *losses are at a minimum.*

Still, wouldn't it be wise to shut down production completely? Not at all, for look at the current situation. Out of the total revenue of $225, the firm is able to pay all of its variable costs of $200 and still have $25 left over to apply to total fixed costs. Since total fixed costs are $100, this means that the losses are $75, as shown in column 6 of Table 17–4. Management, therefore, must dig into reserves (or maybe borrow) to pay the remaining $75 of total fixed costs.

If, however, the firm were shut down, then *all* of total fixed costs would have to be paid out of reserves. Put otherwise, shutting down the plant would increase losses from $75 to $100 per day. The reason, of course, is that *fixed costs must be paid, even though output is zero.* So, in order to minimize losses, the firm should continue to operate at the price of $P_{4.50}$ and output of X_{50} in Figure 17–10.

An important conclusion can be drawn from this example.

> **Conclusion:** As long as price is above average variable costs, even though it is below average total cost, the firm will continue to operate according to the $MC = MR$ rule in order to minimize losses.

Obviously the firm can't operate this way for an extended period of time. If it did, it would eventually go bankrupt (as many firms do). The owners must, in the meanwhile, be looking around for alternatives and (they hope) more profitable uses of their resources. It may be, too, that they feel that the slump in price is only temporary and that they can weather the bad times. But keep in mind that many small firms fail every year in the American economy.

TABLE 17-4   Loss Minimization for Mugs Unlimited by Continuing to Operate (price = \$4.50 per case)

Total Output Per Day (1)	Total Fixed Cost (2)	Total Variable Cost (3)	Total Cost (4)	Total Revenue (5)	Total Profit (6) = (5) − (4)	Marginal Revenue (7)	Marginal Cost (8)
0	\$100.00	\$—	\$100.00	\$—	−\$100.00	\$—	\$—
5	100.00	40.00	140.00	22.50	−117.50	4.50	8.00
16	100.00	80.00	180.00	72.00	−108.00	4.50	3.64
31	100.00	120.00	220.00	139.50	−80.50	4.50	2.67
41	100.00	160.00	260.00	184.50	−75.50	4.50	4.00
50	100.00	200.00	300.00	225.00	−75.00	4.50 ≃	4.44
57	100.00	240.00	340.00	256.50	−83.50	4.50	5.71
62	100.00	280.00	380.00	279.00	−101.00	4.50	8.00
65	100.00	320.00	420.00	292.50	−127.50	4.50	13.33
67	100.00	360.00	460.00	301.50	−158.50	4.50	20.00
67	100.00	400.00	500.00	301.50	−198.50	—	—

3. Shutting Down to Minimize Losses

In this last example, we are going to paint an even bleaker picture for the firm and have demand fall so low that price slumps below average variable cost. This new situation has the very low price of \$3.50 per case, and the new demand curve for the firm is $P_{3.50}MR_{3.50}$ in Figure 17–10.

What will management do now? If you say, "Shut down," you are quite correct. This regretful decision must be made in order, again, to minimize losses. The rule of $MR = MC$ doesn't mean anything here. Table 17–5 shows that new loss picture in column 6. Note that the lowest loss is the \$100 incurred when the plant is closed. Fixed costs, as usual, must be paid. But at any positive output, the loss is greater. Total revenue, in other words, is nowhere great enough to cover the total variable costs shown in column 3. If management unwisely decides to operate, then the firm must pay all the fixed costs and part of the variable costs out of reserves. Hardly a wise choice, is it? So losses are minimized by shutting down.

> **Conclusion:**   Whenever the price of the product is less than average variable cost, losses can be minimized only by shutting operations down.

4. The Firm's Supply Curve

The preceding analysis of this section reveals that the competitive firm will always operate according to the $MC = MR$ as long as price is above average total cost in order to maximize profits; and it follows the same rule when price is between aver-

TABLE 17-5 Loss Minimization for Mugs Unlimited by Closing Down (price = $3.50 per case)

Total Output Per Day (1)	Total Fixed Cost (2)	Total Variable Cost (3)	Total Cost (4)	Total Revenue (5)	Total Profit (6) = (5) − (4)	Marginal Revenue (7)	Marginal Cost (8)
0	$100.00	$—	$100.00	$—	−$100.00	$—	$—
5	100.00	40.00	140.00	17.50	−122.50	3.50	8.00
16	100.00	80.00	180.00	56.00	−124.00	3.50	3.64
31	100.00	120.00	220.00	108.50	−111.50	3.50	2.67
41	100.00	160.00	260.00	143.50	−116.50	3.50	4.00
50	100.00	200.00	300.00	175.00	−125.00	3.50	4.44
57	100.00	240.00	340.00	199.50	−140.50	3.50	5.71
62	100.00	280.00	380.00	217.00	−163.00	3.50	8.00
65	100.00	320.00	420.00	227.50	−192.50	3.50	13.33
67	100.00	360.00	460.00	234.50	−225.50	3.50	20.00
67	100.00	400.00	500.00	234.50	−265.50	—	—

age total and average variable costs in order to minimize losses. In both cases, the firm's *MC* curve is its supply curve. But the firm will never operate at a price below average variable cost, and thus, since it will shut down, the *MC* curve beneath the average variable cost curve is irrelevant. Thus we repeat our earlier conclusion:

> The competitive firm's supply curve is that portion of its marginal cost curve above its average variable cost curve.

And therefore the marginal cost curves we started out with in this chapter were properly drawn. We need only consider the positively sloped segment above average variable cost.

5. The Industry (Market) Supply Curve

Supply and demand analysis, however, isn't really concerned with the supply curve of only one firm like Mugs Unlimited. Instead it is concerned with the total of the supply curves of all the firms in the industry. Thus we must sum up the individual supply curves in order to reach the market supply curve. This is shown in Figure 17-11, in which we have the supply (*MC*) curves of only three firms. There are of course hundreds of firms, but these three will do for the task at hand.

At the market price of P_1, Firm (1) will supply a quantity of three units, for it is at this rate of output that its *MR = MC*. But Firm (2) has its own, different marginal cost curve, and for it, *MR = MC* at four units. Firm (3)'s *MR = MC* at an output of five units. Hence, at the market price of P_1, these three firms will supply a total quantity of twelve units. This gives us point *A* on the market supply

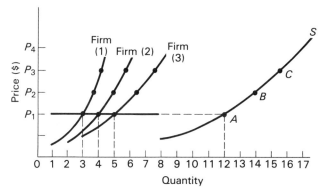

FIGURE 17-11   The Market Supply Curve is the Horizontal Summation of the Individual Supply Curves   The market supply curve is the horizontal summation of the supply curves of all the firms in the industry.

curve *S*. If we were to repeat this procedure for all other prices (P_2, P_3, etc.), we would get other points (*B, C,* etc.) on the market supply curve.

This is the sort of supply curve used in supply and demand analysis. Thus Mugs Unlimited's *MC* curve is lost from view, but we had to derive it in order to get to the market supply curve.

E. CHANGES IN SUPPLY

There is no reason to believe that the supply curve, once we have derived it, is going to remain stable. To the contrary, as we have seen, the supply curve will shift; and it will do so when any of three things occur: (1) there is a change in the price of the variable (not fixed) input; (2) there is a change in the number of firms in the industry; and (3) there is a change in the physical productivity of labor. At times, all of these may change and affect the position of the market supply curve. Let's look at these possibilities.

1. Changes in Costs: Changes in Supply

The market supply curve in Figure 17-11 has been drawn on the assumption that the prices of the variable inputs were given and unchanging. Since the only variable cost we have worked with has been wages, we can be more specific and say that the supply curves used so far have been drawn on the condition that the wage rate is $40 per worker per day.

What, however, would happen to the supply curve if wages were to rise? There is an easy way to answer this question, and that is simply to recalculate the marginal cost of the typical firm, using the new cost figure. Let's suppose the wage has risen from $40 to $60. Thus, using the new data:

$$\text{MC} = \frac{\Delta TC}{MP} = \frac{W}{MP} = \frac{\$60}{MP}$$

Nothing has happened to change the marginal product figures. They are the same that we have been using all along. Table 17–6 shows what happens to average variable cost and marginal cost, however, when the wage rises. (We have to show the average variable cost figure, because only the marginal cost above average variable is relevant for the supply curve.) The old average variable and marginal cost data in columns 5 and 6 are shown by the *AVC* and *MC* curves in Figure 17–12. The new cost figures, reflecting the higher wage, are shown in columns 8 and 9 and as the AVC_2 and MC_2 curves in Figure 17–12. Note how the new supply curve of the firm lies to the left of the old supply curve. In other words, the supply curve of the firm has shifted to the left.

Conclusion: When the price of the variable input rises, the firm's supply curve will shift to the left. In other words, rising variable costs reduce supply.

If this rise in variable costs has affected all firms equally, and we suppose that it does, then rising variable costs cause the market supply curve to shift to the left.

The reverse is also true. A fall in the price of the variable input lowers variable costs and hence will shift the market supply curve to the right—i.e., cause an increase in supply. We haven't provided an example of this, but it would be worth your while to work one out, using, say, a lower wage rate of $30.

It would also be worth your while to investigate what would happen to the firm's supply curve and hence the market supply curve if total fixed costs were to

TABLE 17-6   Consequences of a Rise in the Cost of the Variable Input

Labor (1)	Total Output (2)	Marginal Product (3)	Old Wage (4)	Old AVC (5)	Old MC (6)	New Wage (7)	New AVC (8)	New MC (9)
0	0	0	—	—	—	—	—	—
1	5	5	$40.00	$8.00	$8.00	$60.00	$12.00	$12.00
2	16	11	40.00	5.00	3.64	60.00	7.50	5.45
3	31	15	40.00	3.87	3.67	60.00	5.81	4.00
4	41	10	40.00	3.90	4.00	60.00	5.86	6.00
5	50	9	40.00	4.00	4.44	60.00	6.00	6.67
6	57	7	40.00	4.21	5.71	60.00	6.32	8.57
7	62	5	40.00	4.52	8.00	60.00	6.77	12.00
8	65	3	40.00	4.92	13.33	60.00	7.38	20.00
9	67	2	40.00	5.37	20.00	60.00	8.06	30.00
10	67	0	40.00	5.97	—	60.00	8.96	—

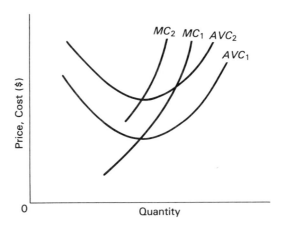

FIGURE 17-12   A Fall in Supply Due to a Rise in Variable Costs   Shifts in the firm's supply curve occur because of changes in the price of the variable input and changes in the productivity of the variable input. If these events are industrywide, the market supply curve will also shift. The market supply curve will also shift as firms enter and exit the industry.

change. Suppose these costs rose from $100 per day to $120 per day. Would this cause a shift in the firm's marginal cost curve? It shouldn't.

2. Changes in the Productivity of Labor

What would happen to the supply curve if there were an improvement in the physical productivity of labor? For example, suppose there is an improvement in the managerial supervision of the work force so that each worker becomes more efficient. In consequence, the marginal productivity of the workers rises. The effect of this on the supply curve can be seen from an examination of our formula:

$$MC = \frac{\Delta TVC}{MP} = \frac{W}{MP}$$

Here the wage remains at its old level of $40.00 and is constant, but the *MP* denominator has risen. Thus the *MC* curve will shift to the right. Let's turn back to Table 17-1 to check this out. If the marginal product of the fifth worker is increased from 9 to 10, then the marginal cost of this additional output falls from $4.44 to $4.00. (You should recalculate some of the other *MC*'s to drive the point home.)

> **Conclusion:**   When labor productivity increases, the firm's supply curve will shift to the right. If the improvements in labor efficiency are industrywide, the market supply curve will shift to the right.

3. Changes in the Number of Firms

Obviously, the greater the number of firms in an industry, the greater the supply; and the fewer the number of firms, the lower the supply.

Suppose, as shown in panel (A) of Figure 17-13, that the market equilibrium price is P_1. The equilibrium for a representative firm is shown in panel (B). In this case, the firms in the industry are operating at a profit, for $MR = MC$ above average total cost. Indeed, *all* costs are covered and the firms are reaping a nice profit.

Now, these profits will attract new entrants into the industry. Recall that the market supply curve is the sum of the MC curves of all the firms in the industry. Since there are more firms in the industry, due to entry, the market supply curve must move to the right.

However, we have allowed a flood of new firms to enter the industry, shifting the supply curve as far to the right as S_2. Market price is driven down to P_2, which lies below average total cost (but above average variable cost). Firms now operate at $MR = MC$ to minimize losses; and accordingly some firms will eventually exit the industry.

Let's suppose that just enough firms leave that the supply curve shifts to S_3 and hence the price settles at P_3. Now there are no inducements for firms to enter the industry or, for that matter, to exit. This is the long-run market equilibrium: long run, in the sense that we have allowed enough time for firms to enter and exit the industry so that price settles at P_3. This price, to repeat, is the long-run equilibrium price, and it occurs where $P = MC = ATC$. Since the ATC curve is U shaped,

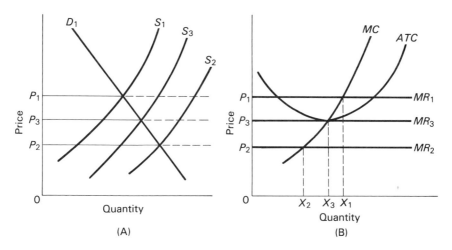

FIGURE 17-13   Entry, Exit, and a Long-Run Equilibrium   The existence of profits attracts new firms into the industry, increasing supply and lowering price and thus eliminating profits. If losses exist, firms will exit reducing supply, raising prices, and eliminating losses for the firms remaining in the industry. Thus equilibrium exists where all firms receive nominal returns.

the only place *P* can equal *ATC* is at the bottom (lowest unit cost) point of the *ATC* curve.

4. The Idea of Normal Returns

The question arises, Why would a business firm want to operate at a price that just covers average total costs? This would mean that total revenue equals total costs, and nothing would be left over for profits. And doesn't this mean that the firm might as well shut down?

   The answer to this question is no. The person who starts a business firm usually has to put two things he or she owns into it: first, the money required for use as capital; and second, labor time. In both cases, there is an opportunity cost. If the owner can work elsewhere at a salary of, say, $40,000, then that should be considered a cost of doing business. The owner hopes, of course, to make at least this amount per year. As for the owner's capital, it too carries an opportunity cost. If it can earn, say, 17 percent elsewhere, then the owner must make at least that rate of return.

   These opportunity costs are called normal returns, and as long as the owner covers them, his or her position can't be improved by moving to another industry.

   These costs are, to repeat, opportunity costs. They are sometimes called implicit costs, but no matter what they are called, they are still costs of doing business, and they are included in the firm's costs of production. Hence, when the firm is in long-run equilibrium ($P = MR = MC = ATC$), the firm is covering these costs as well as all other costs.

> **Conclusion:**   Long-run equilibrium for the competitive firm means that the owner is receiving normal returns. These measure what the owner would obtain by using his or her own resources in their next best use.

F. THE SIZE OF THE FIRM IN THE LONG RUN

This chapter has concentrated mainly on only one decision that the management of the firm must make, and that is to select the profit-maximizing rate of output for *a given size of the firm*. This decision, we now know, is governed by the rule $MC = MR$.

1. What Is the Best Size of the Firm?

Management, however, had to make an earlier and altogether different decision, and that was to determine the best size of the firm. Once that decision had been made and the firm came into being, the dominant question then became how to operate it as profitably as possible. But what we are concerned with now is how the decision was made to determine the best size. This sort of decision is called the long-run decision.

Management of a competitive firm must always strive to reach the optimal size. Just what does the term *optimal size* mean? Well, what it really boils down to is the most efficient size. Figure 17–14 will aid us in this matter. We begin with the size, or scale, of the firm shown by the cost curve ATC_1, which represents a rather small size of a rather small firm. This ATC_1 curve is the same sort of ATC curve we have been using.

Let's look at the next size, as shown by ATC_2. Note that ATC_2 lies below and to the right of ATC_1. We can understand why it lies to the right: It is the cost curve for a larger-size firm. But why below ATC_1? The answer lies in the presence of economies of scale.

Definition: *Economies of scale* are advantages of larger size that lower average total cost of production as the firm grows.

Examples: The larger-size firm can benefit from more extensive division of labor; it can also use more efficient equipment (e.g., a forklift as opposed to manual labor); and it can use more-sophisticated managerial techniques, such as more-efficient inventory or financial control methods.

These economies of scale exist even for the small competitive firm. If they weren't present, the vast majority of products would be produced in basements, garages, and backyards as efficiently as they are actually produced in larger-size plants.

Economies of scale, however, soon run out for the competitive firm and are replaced by diseconomies of scale.

Definition: *Diseconomies of scale* are disadvantages of larger size that raise average total costs of production as the firm continues to grow.

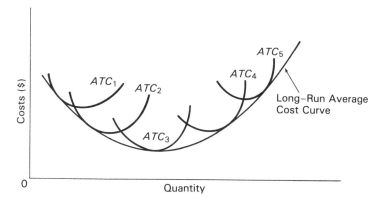

FIGURE 17–14   The Firm's Optimal Size   Economies and diseconomies of scale account for the U shape of the firm's long-run average cost curve. The optimal size of the firm is given by the least-cost point of the curve.

The cost curves ATC_4 and ATC_5 show the consequences of diseconomies of scale. As the firm pushes beyond some particular size, the *optimal size,* increased inefficiency drives costs up. The main reason given for diseconomies of scale for the competitive firm is that the owner-manager is reluctant to share duties and responsibilities, and therefore decisions are made less efficiently.

The important conclusion is that the competitive firm must reach and maintain its optimal size, which is shown by ATC_3 in the diagram. If it doesn't, it will be unable to survive the rigors of competition.

2. Optimality and Survival

Now that we know what optimal size means for the competitive firm, let's see why the firm must attain it if it is to survive the rigors of competition. Figure 17-15 shows us why.

To repeat, each surviving firm in the industry must reach its optimal size. Indeed, each firm is driven by competitive pressures to reduce costs of production as much as possible. This is one of the great benefits of competition; another great benefit is that price will follow costs to their lowest level. Thus, in Figure 17-15, the firm's demand curve is tangent to ATC_3. This tangency can occur only at the minimum point of ATC_3, the optimal size.

But what would have happened if the plant had been pushed to the size ATC_5 or had been stopped at ATC_1? In both cases, the market equilibrium price would be below average total cost; and unless adjustments in scale were made, the firm would fail. If the plant is at ATC_1, the owner-manager may be able to expand to size ATC_3. If, on the other hand, it is at ATC_5, it must contract to ATC_3. In either case, this failure to adjust means death for the firm.

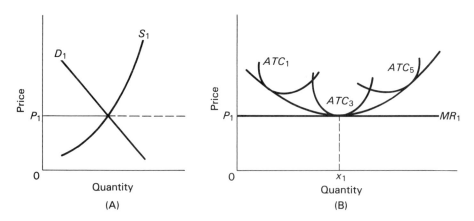

FIGURE 17-15   The Competitive Firm's Long-Run Equilibrium   The long-run equilibrium for the competitive firm exists for the firm at its minimum long-run average total cost. Here $P = MR = MC = ATC$ = long-run ATC. The consumer thus gets the product at a price that just covers the lowest possible average cost of production.

3. An Important Conclusion

In the long run in competitive markets, all firms are forced by competitive pressures
not only to produce the profit-maximizing level of output for a given plant size but
also to adjust the size (or scale) of the firm's operations that allow lowest unit costs
of production. Firms that fail to do this, either by being too small to take advantage
of economies of scale or being too large and experiencing diseconomies, will be
driven out of business by the relentless downward price pressure of competition.
Once the long-run adjustment process settles down, the typical firm remaining in
the industry will have no economic profit; it will be operating at a size that gives
lowest possible unit costs (*ATC*); and it will produce a level of output within that
plant size where price equals marginal cost. In symbol form:

$$P = MC = ATC_{min}$$

Figure 17–15 shows this long-run equilibrium for the typical firm. Panel (A)
shows the total market supply and demand. Panel (B) shows the situation for the
typical firm. Note that the price to the consumer is as low as it could possibly be
and still cover average total costs. Note also that the firm is operating in the most
efficient manner; it has the size that yields the lowest cost curve and operates within
that size at the low cost point (*ATC*$_{min}$).

So we finally arrive at the explanation of why economists in general are so
strongly in favor of competitive market structures. The consumer ends up paying a
price for the product that just covers the cost at the most efficient rate of operation.

G. SUMMARY

Marginal revenue is defined as the additional revenue from producing and selling
one more unit of a product. *Marginal cost* is the additional cost of producing and
selling one more unit of a product. Firms that desire to maximize profits (or minimize losses) should carry production to the point at which marginal cost equals
marginal revenue.

Since the marginal cost rises as more output is produced, if the market price
increases, the firm should increase the quantity supplied along the marginal cost
curve. The marginal cost curve for the competitive firm is the supply curve.

The supply curve slopes up from left to right reflecting the law of supply. The
reason for the upward slope is the law of diminishing returns, which states: As
successive units of a variable input are added to a fixed amount of other inputs, the
extra output per extra unit of the variable input will eventually decline.

Marginal product is the addition to the total output caused by the employment
of one more unit of the variable input. Marginal product declines toward zero when
diminishing returns set in. Total output rises at a decreasing rate until the point of
maximum output is reached. Marginal costs rise because marginal product falls.
When making decisions about the profit-maximizing level of output, only variable

costs are relevant and fixed (sunk) costs aren't relevant in the short run. The reason is that fixed costs have nothing to do with marginal costs. A firm should operate as long as the price is equal to marginal cost and above average variable cost. If price falls below the average variable cost, the firm should close down.

In competition, the industry's total market supply curves are the horizontal sum of the marginal cost curves for all the firms in the industry.

Changes or shifts in supply curves can be caused by changes in the price or cost of factor inputs, changes in the productivity of factors, and changes in the number of firms in the industry. In the long run, the firms within an industry can alter the amounts of the fixed factors as well as the variable. In other words, in the long run, all factors of production are variable.

In the long run, economies of scale are advantages of larger size that lower average total cost as the firm's size expands. Diseconomies of scale raise average total cost as the firm grows.

The process of competition forces firms to be efficient and achieve the size to take advantage of economies of scale and avoid diseconomies of scale. Furthermore, the lack of barriers to entry and exit will ensure that both profits and losses in a competitive industry will be short lived. Long-run equilibrium results when the typical firm in the industry operates at the most efficient size and produces at the lowest possible unit cost and earns no economic profit.

Terms and Concepts to Remember

Marginal cost	Economies of size
Average fixed cost	Diseconomies of size
Average variable cost	Supply curve of the single
Average total cost	firm
Normal returns	Market supply

Questions for Review

1. Why should management do each of the following?
   a. Increase output when marginal revenue is greater than marginal cost
   b. Decrease output when marginal cost exceeds marginal revenue
   c. Maintain production when marginal revenue equals marginal cost

2. Why does the average fixed cost curve decline throughout its length?

3. The shape of the average variable cost curve is determined by the law of diminishing returns. Explain this relationship.

4. Why does the marginal cost curve intersect both the average variable cost curve and the average total cost curve at their respective minimum points?

5. Discuss the operate-shutdown decision that a firm must make. How is this related to the purely competitive firm's short-run supply curve?

6. What are normal returns? Illustrate.

7. If a competitive firm is to survive over the long run, it must seek its optimal size. Explain.

8. Why are economists prone to view the competitive market structure favorably?

18

The Pricing of Productive Services

chapter preview

- The demand for factors of production is ultimately. derived from the consumer demand for goods and services.

- The law of diminishing returns is the foundation for the demand for productive factors as well as output supply.

- Competitive firms hire or acquire additional factor units as long as the added revenue from the use of the factors exceeds the added cost of the factors.

- The marginal renenue product (*MRP*) is defined as the monetary value of the variable input's marginal product and constitutes the demand for that factor.

- The firm's optimal allocation of factors is achieved when the marginal revenue product is equated with the factor price.

- The marginal revenue product of capital is the present value of the future expected net receipts over the useful life of the asset.

- A change in the interest rate changes the present value of the marginal revenue product of capital and therefore the demand for capital.

- Rent is the price of land and also the return to every factor in excess of the next best alternative return for that factor.

- In the aggregate, the supply of land is fixed so that the level of rent is determined by the level of demand for land. The supply of land for different uses is flexible, since land can be shifted among uses.

- In competitive markets, profits (losses) indicate that markets aren't in equilibrium and at the same time provide incentives for the proper reallocation of resources.

The preceding three chapters contain an important message: They show how changes in prices occur and send out signals to all the relevant actors in the economic scene. If, for example, the demand for a product were to rise, we now know what would happen. We know that the price of the product would rise, and that this would signal that consumers not only wanted more of the product, but were also willing to pay more to have it. This signal would in turn lead to two results on the supply side of the market. First, firms already in the industry would increase their *quantity supplied* of the product. Second, new firms, attracted by the prospects of higher profits, would enter the industry and thus increase the *supply* of the product.[1]

All of this is old hat by now, but it has some implications that we need to pursue a bit further in order to close up the circular flow. Figure 18-1 shows what this chapter is concerned with, namely, the pricing of productive services in resource

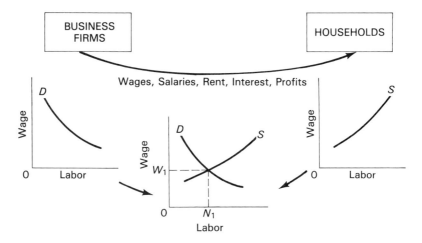

FIGURE 18-1   Resource Markets in the Circular Flow   Here the labor market is used as an illustration of resource markets. The demand curve of business firms interacts with the supply curve of households to yield the equilibrium market wage of W_1, at which the quantity demanded of labor equals the quantity supplied.

[1]Note how we have distinguished between a change in *quantity supplied* (coming from firms already in the industry) and a change in *supply* (coming from new firms entering the industry). The first change is shown as a movement up along the supply curve as the firms already in the industry adjust output to the higher price. The second change is shown as new firms enter the industry and begin producing the product.

markets. It is in these markets, as Figure 18–1 points out, that the demand for and supply of productive services interact to set wages, rent, interest, and profits. This chapter describes how these prices are determined. Section A develops the idea that the demand for productive services is derived from the demand for the products they are used to produce. Section B then explains how the competitive firm makes its employment decision, and Sections C and D extend the analysis to the labor market as a whole. Section E focuses on how physical capital is priced, and Section F focuses on land. Finally, Section G considers the mainstay of all businesses in a capitalist economy, profits.

A. THE IDEA OF DERIVED DEMAND

In our example in the opening paragraph of this chapter, we had firms responding to the higher product price by increasing output. However, in order for them to increase their output, the firms had to raise their demand for productive services— that is, they needed more labor, raw materials, physical capital, and land in order to produce more of the product.

Here we have a basic concept—the idea of *derived demand.* Our example shows clearly that the demand for productive services depends on (i.e., is derived from) the demand for the product. Since we have assumed that the demand for the product has risen, the demand for the labor and other resources needed to produce the product will also rise. This is probably obvious. If the firms are to increase output, they need more resources to do so. Thus their (derived) demand for resources will also rise. On the other hand, if the demand for the product were to slump, the firms would lay off workers and reduce their demand for inputs; their (derived) demand for these productive services would also slump.

> **Definition:** The demand for productive resources is derived from the demand for the goods and services that they are used to produce. Hence the demand for productive services is a derived demand.

Let's look first at the demand for labor.

B. THE COMPETITIVE FIRM AS EMPLOYER

The last chapter stressed how the manager of the firm maximizes profits by producing the output at which marginal cost equals marginal revenue ($MC = MR$). But just what does this mean for the competitive business firm as an employer?

Let's return to our example of Mugs Unlimited and Delia as its manager as we set out to answer this question. Also, let's limit the discussion to labor as the only variable input. We concentrate on labor for two reasons: First, most households receive all, or nearly all, of their incomes by selling their services in the labor market; second, wage costs are the most important cost of doing business, amounting to about two-thirds of total manufacturing costs, and they are especially important in the service sector of the economy.

1. Diminishing Returns Again

Our first step in answering the question of how many workers to employ is to revive the law of diminishing returns. It asserts that as successive units of the variable input (labor) are applied to the firm's fixed inputs (capital and land), the marginal product of the variable input will eventually decline. It may rise at first, but sooner or later it will decline.

The data from Table 17-1 are repeated in the first three columns of Table 18-1. The marginal productivity of labor is shown in column 3. As we shall see, this marginal productivity of labor stands as the foundation of the firm's demand for labor.

2. The Firm as a Wage Taker

So far we have assumed that Mugs Unlimited is in a competitive industry, and therefore, like every other firm in the industry, it is atomistically small. This is also true of its status in the labor market. In fact, we assume that Mugs Unlimited is so very small in the labor market that it acts as a *wage taker*. This means that if the firm, for example, were to double its employment from four to eight workers, the increased demand for labor would have no impact whatsoever on the prevailing wage rate. Furthermore, if Delia were forced to shut the firm down, so that employment fell to zero, the market wage would still be unaffected. In short, the firm's activities are so small that it has absolutely no impact on the market wage.

TABLE 18-1

Labor (L) (1)	Total Output (Q) (2)	Marginal Product (MP) (3)	Price of Product (P) (4)	Marginal Revenue Product (MRP) = (P) × (MP) (5) = (4) × (3)
0	0	0	$8.00	$—
1	5	5	8.00	40.00
2	16	11	8.00	88.00
3	31	15	8.00	120.00
4	41	10	8.00	80.00
5	50	9	8.00	72.00
6	57	7	8.00	56.00
7	62	5	8.00	40.00
8	65	3	8.00	24.00
9	67	2	8.00	16.00
10	67	0	8.00	00.00

This also means that Mugs Unlimited doesn't have to pay a higher wage in order to get more workers on its payroll. Being a wage taker means that it can hire as many or as few workers as Delia sees fit *at the prevailing wage.* In technical terms, the supply curve of labor is seen by management as being *perfectly elastic.* The wage may change, of course, but always because of changes in the labor market, and not because of Mugs Unlimited's hiring policy.

Figure 18-2 shows what we are talking about. The horizontal solid line in Figure 18-2(B) is the perfectly elastic supply curve facing the firm. We have labeled it W_1W_1. In this case, $W_1 = \$40$, and it has been set by the interaction of the market supply and demand curves which are shown as D_1 and S_1 in panel (A). As long as the market wage remains at $W_1 = \$40$, this is the relevant supply curve (W_1W_1) for the firm.

However, like any other price, the price of labor is subject to change. Suppose now that the total demand for coffee mugs rises. Since the demand for labor services is a derived demand, it too will rise so that the new equilibrium market wage is W_2. This change is shown in Figure 18-2(B) as an upward shift of the perfectly elastic supply curve of labor facing Mugs Unlimited. On the other hand, if the equilibrium market wage were to fall to W_3, the perfectly elastic supply curve facing the firm would also fall (to W_3W_3).

For the moment, we must take these changes as they are, but before we finish this chapter, we will be able to explain what causes market wages to rise and fall.

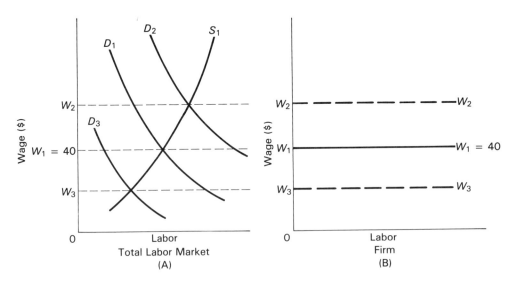

FIGURE 18-2   The Labor Market and the Firm's Labor Supply   The total demand and supply of labor set the wage rate of W_1. Changes in the market wage cause the perfectly elastic supply curve of the firm to shift upward (for a wage increase) or downward (for a wage reduction). In all cases, however, the supply curve remains perfectly elastic for the competitive wage-taker firm.

3. The Marginal Revenue Product

Delia needs to have certain information in order to determine how many workers to hire. The first three columns of Table 18-1 contain some, but not enough, of the data she needs. Two further bits of information are also required—namely (a) the price of the product and (b) the prevailing market wage. But since Delia also has this information, she can make correct decisions about how many workers to employ. However, and this is important, *whatever the number of workers she selects, it must be consistent with the profit-maximizing rate of output given by MC = MR.*

The last three columns of Table 18-1 present all the necessary data, but in a new way. Column 5 is the one that we want to concentrate on. It lists the marginal revenue product of labor.

> **Definition:** The *marginal revenue product* (*MRP*) is simply the *monetary value* of the variable input's marginal physical product. It is calculated by multiplying the marginal physical product (*MP*) by the price of the product (*P*):
>
> $$MRP = P \cdot MP$$
>
> where *MRP* stands for the marginal revenue product.

Actually, *MRP* measures how much the last worker employed adds to the firm's total revenue when his or her marginal output is sold. Suppose the price of the product is $8 per case and that Delia is considering employing the fourth worker, whose marginal product is 10 cases. Since these 10 cases can be sold at $8 each, then, if hired, the fourth worker's employment will add $80 to Mugs Unlimited's total revenue. That is, with *MP* = 10 cases and *P* = $8, then *MRP* = $8 × 10 cases = $80.

The marginal revenue product that Delia needs to know in making her decision is calculated in the last column of Table 18-1; it is also shown as the *MRP* curve in Figure 18-3. This is vital information. The other bit of information that she needs is the wage rate; recall that this is given by the interaction of supply and demand in the labor market.

4. Three Rules of Behavior

To illustrate how Delia's decision is made, let's stay with the assumption that the wage is $40 per worker per day. Figure 18-3 tells us that Delia will hire seven workers at this wage; this is where the downward-sloping marginal revenue product (*MRP*) curve cuts the perfectly elastic supply curve.

Three rules of behavior will show why the employment of seven workers is optimal. These rules are similar to the three rules set out in the last chapter except that they are now applied to the resource side of the firm's operations. In discussing

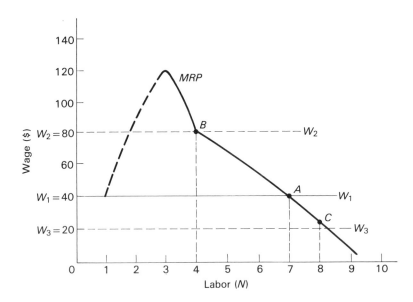

FIGURE 18-3   The Firm's Labor Demand and Optimal Employment   The optimal rate of employment occurs where the firm's demand curve for labor, the downward-sloping part of its *MRP* curve, cuts the perfectly elastic supply curve of labor at point *A*. In this case, the optimal employment rate is seven workers. Whenever the wage rate changes, the firm adjusts employment until once again *W* = *MRP*.

these rules, we must keep two things in mind: First, every time (in our example) a new worker is hired, $40 is added to the firm's total costs; but second, the worker also adds his or her marginal revenue product to the firm's total revenue. Perhaps you can see where we are headed. Whenever a worker's marginal revenue product exceeds the wage, it is worthwhile for the firm to hire that worker. He or she adds more to the firm's total revenue than to total costs. The first rule of behavior, therefore, is this:

> Whenever the marginal revenue product of labor is greater than the wage rage, increase employment.

For example, the fifth worker has a marginal revenue product of $72. Since the firm can acquire his or her services for $40, it is definitely worthwhile for the firm to hire this worker.

However, what if the marginal revenue product of a worker is less than the wage? Consider, for instance, the ninth worker, whose marginal revenue product is only $16. It certainly wouldn't be wise for Delia to hire this worker. Thus our second rule of behavior is this:

> Whenever the marginal revenue product is less than the wage rate, reduce employment.

Putting these two rules together allows us to postulate the third rule, which turns out to be the rule for profit maximization.

> **Conclusion:**   The profit-maximizing firm should always carry employment up to the amount at which the marginal revenue product of the last worker hired is equal to the wage rate paid for the worker's services.

In our example, this means that Delia will employ seven workers. For workers up to that number, the marginal revenue product exceeds the wage rate. And for workers beyond that number, the marginal revenue product is less than the wage rate. This optimal point is shown by the intersection of the *MRP* curve in Figure 18–3 with the perfectly elastic supply curve W_1W_1 (point *A*).

5. Compatible Equilibrium

Does this jibe with what we said in the last chapter about the firm producing the profit-maximizing rate of output? It should, and we can check it out in Table 18–2. This table looks rather formidable, but it really isn't. It simply combines some of the information from an earlier table, Table 17–3, with the information in Table 18–1. It is designed to tell us that when the firm equates the value of the marginal product with the wage (*MRP* = *W*), the output rate is the same as the output at which marginal cost equals marginal revenue (*MC* = *MR*).

> **Conclusion:**   Equilibrium on one side of the competitive firm's operations means that the firm must be in equilibrium on the other side. Put more technically, an equilibrium of *MC* = *MR* in the product market means *W* = *MRP* in the resource market.

In our example, the wage equals the marginal revenue product when seven workers are employed and the rate of output is 62 cases per day. This equality is shown in the last two columns of Table 18–2—that is, *W* = $40 = *MRP* = $40. Note also, as shown in columns 7 and 8, that at this rate of output the price of the product (marginal revenue) equals the marginal cost—that is, *P* = $8 = *MC* = $8. In short, *MC* = *MR* means *W* = *MRP*.

C. TWO DEMAND CURVES: FIRM AND MARKET

Maybe you can see that the declining part of the firm's marginal revenue product curve is its demand curve for labor. We have, in fact, already discovered that when the market wage is $40 per day, the quantity demanded by the firm is seven workers. This wage-quantity demanded combination is shown as point *A* in Figure 18–3.

Suppose now that, for whatever reason, the market wage rises astronomically, doubling from $40 to $80 per day. What will the firm do in response to this change? Well, it definitely must reduce the amount of labor demanded until, once more, *W*

TABLE 18-2

Labor (1)	Total Output (2)	Marginal Product (3)	Total Cost (4)	Total Revenue (5)	Total Profit (6) = (5) − (4)	Price of Product (7)	Marginal Cost (8)	Wage (9)	Marginal Revenue Product (10)
0	0	0	$100.00	$—	$ − 100.00	$8.00	$—	$40.00	$—
1	5	5	140.00	40.00	− 100.00	8.00	8.00	40.00	40.00
2	16	11	180.00	128.00	− 52.00	8.00	3.64	40.00	88.00
3	31	15	220.00	248.00	28.00	8.00	2.67	40.00	120.00
4	41	10	260.00	328.00	68.00	8.00	4.00	40.00	80.00
5	50	9	300.00	400.00	100.00	8.00	4.44	40.00	72.00
6	57	7	340.00	456.00	116.00	8.00	5.71	40.00	56.00
7	62	5	380.00	496.00	116.00	8.00 =	8.00	40.00 =	40.00
8	65	3	420.00	520.00	100.00	8.00	13.33	40.00	24.00
9	67	2	460.00	536.00	76.00	8.00	20.00	40.00	16.00
10	67	0	500.00	536.00	36.00	8.00	00	40.00	00

$= MRP$. This occurs at a quantity demanded of four workers (for it is here that W_2 $= \$80 = MRP = \$80$ at point B). Thus we reach an important conclusion: The higher the wage, the smaller the quantity demanded of labor by the firm. Let's reverse the situation and suppose, again for whatever the reason that the market wage falls drastically to $20 per day. In this event, the firm will increase its quantity demanded of labor to eight workers. Here, the MRP of the eighth worker is $24 and is greater than the wage of $20, but it is the closest approximation in our example (we use $\cong$ to indicate approximate equality). So we have:

$$W_3 = \$20 \cong MRP = \$24$$

Surely the firm wouldn't hire the ninth worker, whose marginal revenue product of $16 is less than the $20 wage. Here we have another conclusion: The lower the wage, the greater the quantity demanded of labor by the firm.

Indeed, we have in our example determined three points on the firm's demand curve for labor; all of these are shown in Figure 18-3. When the wage is $40 per day, the firm will demand a quantity of seven workers (point A); at the wage of $80, it will reduce its quantity demanded to four workers (point B); and at the wage of $20 per day, it will increase its quantity demanded to eight workers (point C).

> **Conclusion:** The MRP is the firm's demand curve for labor. It slopes downward from left to right because of the diminishing marginal physical product of labor. That is, the law of diminishing returns is the basis of the demand for labor.

Each firm in the industry will have a similar negative-sloped demand curve for labor. To get the total demand for labor, we simply sum up horizontally all the individual firm demand curves. The procedure is the same as that in Chapter 16 where we summed up individual consumer demand curves to get the total market demand curve.

D. SUPPLY AND DEMAND TOGETHER

Let's put the market demand curve we have just obtained together with the market supply curve of labor. We have drawn this supply curve in Figure 18-4(A) to be like all other supply curves we have used to be positively sloped. Thus the higher the wage, the greater the number of people willing to work in this particular market. Conversely, the lower the wage, the fewer the people willing to offer their services.

The equilibrium wage rate for both the market and the wage-taker firm is shown in Figure 18-4(B) as $W_1W_1 = \$40$. This is the only wage rate at which quantity demanded equals quantity supplied in the market, at 40,000 workers. Panel (B) shows that the firm is also in equilibrium when, at the wage rate of $40, it employs seven workers; it is here that $W = MRP$.

All of this is essential to understanding how wages are set in competitive mar-

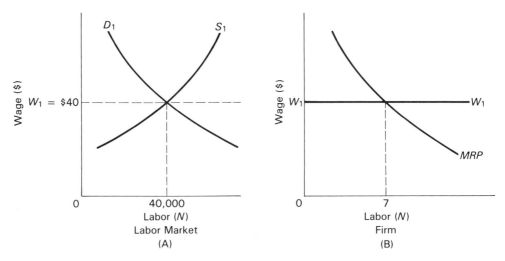

FIGURE 18-4 Equilibrium in the Labor Market This figure shows equilibrium in both the total market for the sort of labor employed by the firm and equilibrium for the firm itself.

kets. It also allows us to predict in general what will happen when supply and demand changes are introduced to upset the equilibrium.

We have stressed that demand for labor is based on the "law of diminishing returns." Specifically, it is the marginal productivity of labor (along with the price of the output produced) that determines the demand schedule for labor. It follows, then, that anything that increased the productivity of the labor force will increase the demand for labor—i.e., shift the labor demand to the right. An increase in demand, given labor supply, would result in higher wage rates and therefore higher incomes and standards of living for households.

The question arises, What factors cause the productivity of labor to rise? Chapter 14 provided the answer. The productivity of any factor is positively affected by the quantities and quality of the cooperating resources used in the production process. For example, the productivity of labor is increased if the labor force works with more capital of a higher quality. Therefore, over the long run, as capital formation (conditioned by technological change) takes place, the demand for labor increases. Under these circumstances, if labor demand increases faster than labor supply, the general level of wages will rise and so will society's standard of living.

There is another problem that we must now consider. The analysis thus far implies that there is a uniform wage rate in the labor market, and yet we know that there are actually real and persistent wage differentials between workers and occupations.

1. Competition Among Markets

To make an important point, let's begin by carrying the analysis to an absurd extreme. Let's assume that *all workers are economically homogeneous.* This means that they are identical in all major respects—education, physical stamina, willingness to work, skill, geographical mobility. Clearly, if this were the case, any one person could be employed as well as any other person for the task at hand. Each worker would be as efficient as any other person in performing any job, whether orthopedic surgery or garbage collection. And if this were true (but only by assumption, remember), employers would be entirely indifferent as to whom they hired.

Would there by any wage-rate differentials in this never-never land? Hardly, for in these circumstances, there could be *only one equilibrium market wage*. To be sure, there might be some wage differentials in the short run, but these would quickly be ironed out as workers moved from the lower-paying to the higher-paying jobs. This is a world of no specialists, no impediments to moving from one location to another, and no nonwage benefits to work. It is a world of no Lee Iacoccas, Walter Paytons, Larry Birds, Itzhak Perlmans, Zubin Mehtas, and Carl Sagans. It would be a world totally unlike its real counterpart.

2. Noncompeting Groups

Such uniformity, of course, doesn't exist, even in a competitive society. For one thing, the work force doesn't consist of a mass of identical people. Instead a number of significant differences among workers exist: Some workers have more formal education, some have more skill and on-the-job training, some have different innate abilities, some are more ambitious, and so on. Differences abound, and they have a direct impact on the wage structure.

How can we take these differences into account? Perhaps the best way is to think in terms of noncompeting groups and to assume further that all the workers *within each group* are more or less the same in terms of economic efficiency. If this were so, then wages *within* each of these groups would tend toward equality (at equilibrium), but wage differentials between groups would occur and persist. Thus we can think of many different labor markets where mobility of labor between the separate markets is difficult if not impossible. Therefore wage differentials may exist and yet be compatible with competitive labor markets. Surgeons, for example, receive higher wages than college professors, who in turn receive higher wages than ministers, who in turn receive higher wages than waitresses.

E. PHYSICAL CAPITAL

The preceding analysis allowed us to draw the important conclusion that when the firm is in equilibrium in the product market, it is also in equilibrium in the labor market. The same conclusion holds for the other productive services, and in this part of the chapter we focus on physical capital.

Throughout this book, we have defined *physical capital* as plants, buildings, machines, tools, and inventories that have been manufactured for the purpose of producing further goods and services. We have also emphasized that since capital is scarce (like any other resource), it has a price tag. This price, however, is a very special one. It is the rate of interest, and as we shall see, the rate of interest is the price that links the present to the future.

1. Saving, Waiting, and the Interest Rate

Let's look first at the supply side of the financial markets. Since business firms have to have *money* capital (loanable funds) in order to obtain the *physical* capital they need for their operations, they typically turn to the financial funds markets to get it. Now, if these funds are to be available, people must be persuaded to save—that is, they must be persuaded to *divert a part of their income from current consumption to future consumption*. They must, in other words, be induced to save and hence provide the loanable funds businesses may borrow. And here we get some insight into the supply side of the market. Economists believe that most people prefer present consumption to future consumption (i.e., present pleasures to future pleasures), and they argue, therefore, that some reward must be given to people in order to induce them to postpone consumption—that is, induce them to save a portion of their current income.

The reward for this "waiting" is the interest rate. For example, a dollar saved today when the interest rate is 10 percent translates into $1.10 worth of goods a year from now.

> **Definition:**   The *interest rate* is the rate at which current demand can be transformed into future demand for consumer goods. In a sense, when people save, they are placing (indefinite) orders for more future consumer goods. This greater amount of future consumption is the reward for postponing current consumption.

Since the interest rate is the price of waiting, the higher the rate of interest, the larger the amount of current income devoted to saving. The reverse is also true. The lower the interest rate, the lower the reward for postponing consumption, and hence a smaller portion of current income is devoted to saving.

> **Conclusion:**   The supply curve of saving is positively sloped, showing a direct relationship between the rate of interest and the quantity supplied of saving.

However, the interest rate is two-edged. Although it may be a reward for the saver, it is, at the same time, a cost for the business firms that borrow these savings to finance investment in capital goods. So, let's turn now to the demand side of the loanable funds market.

2. Capital Productivity: The Broad View

We begin our quest for the demand curve with some rather general views on capital. First, how is it that capital is productive? The answer to this question is easy enough; capital is productive because, like labor or any other factor of production, more can be produced with it than without it. Of course, the production of capital takes time, but once in place, it allows more to be produced.

Conclusion: *New capital* is said to be productive when it is possible to produce more goods and services in the future than would be possible without it.

Let's state another important conclusion, which ties together what we said earlier about the supply of saving and the role of capital.

Conclusion: *Saving* is an order for future consumer goods. Saving also releases resources from the production of current consumer goods so that they are available for the production of more capital goods. The new capital, in turn, becomes the means to produce the additional consumer goods to be demanded in the future.

Now, the expected increase in output as a result of the new capital investment is, in a real sense, the marginal product of the capital. This marginal product can be stated in two different ways: (a) as a dollar value, that is, as capital's *marginal revenue product;* and (b) as a rate of return over cost (expressed as a percentage). And again the law of diminishing returns affects managerial decision making, for as the firm carries out more and more capital formation relative to the use of land and labor, (a) the value of the marginal product of capital will decline and (b) so will the expected rate of return. In what follows we examine the firm's decision to invest in capital from the marginal revenue product perspective.

3. Capital Productivity: The Firm's View

Let's get more specific about the firm's decision-making process. What management must consider here is whether to change the size of the firm's operations, that is, whether to expand the size of plant and equipment. Earlier, when we were discussing the decision as to whether to hire another worker, the employer asked if that worker's marginal revenue product was greater (or less) than the wage rate.

Essentially the same procedure is followed with capital; now the important question is whether an extra machine (or any other capital asset) should be purchased. And the answer should be clear to us: It is worthwhile to purchase the new capital asset only if its marginal revenue product exceeds its cost to the firm.[2]

The purchase price is easy to calculate; it is simply the cost of the machine to the firm. Moreover, since the firm is so small, it acts as much a price taker in the capital goods market as it does in the labor market.

The really difficult task is determining the marginal revenue product, and there is a good reason why this is so difficult. It is because the new output will materialize and be sold *in the future,* and therefore the marginal revenue product also occurs *in the future.*

Here is the dilemma. The cost of the machine must be paid now, whereas the

---

[2]The cost here refers solely to the purchase price of the asset and not the cost of labor and materials needed to run the machine. These latter have their own *MRP*s.

marginal revenue product is something that will occur some time hence. So the big problem is this: How does the firm go about comparing in any satisfactory way a *future* value with a *present* cost? The means of comparison is important, for as we shall soon see, the value of a dollar in the future isn't the same as the value of a dollar today.

There is a way of solving this problem, and that is to *restate the future marginal revenue product in terms of present values.* Once this is done, we can compare the present value of the future marginal revenue product with the present cost of the machine. Again, the three rules we have previously stressed apply here: (a) if the present *MRP* of capital exceeds the cost of the machine, buy the asset; (b) if the present *MRP* is less than the machine's cost, don't buy; and therefore (c) the firm should acquire new capital assets up to the point at which the present *MRP* equals the cost of the last asset bought. An example will help to clarify this important matter.

4. When Is a Dollar Not Worth a Dollar?

This may sound like a dumb question, but it isn't. Let's see why it is important, but let's also be more realistic and ask it about $10,000 instead. When, therefore, is $10,000 not worth $10,000?

The answer is that $10,000 in the future is not worth as much as $10,000 today. It's really quite obvious. If you had a choice, no strings attached, of receiving $10,000 today or the same $10,000 a year from now, which would you take? If you were rational, you would opt for the $10,000 today. If nothing else, you could spend all of it on consumer goods and services and experience your pleasure now. Or you could save it and earn some interest income so that it would be worth more than $10,000 a year from now. For example, if the interest rate is 5 percent, then $10,000 invested today will be worth $10,500 one year from now. The old saying "A bird in the hand is worth two in the bush" has a lot of economic significance.

Let's reverse the question and ask, "When is $10,000 worth more than $10,000?" The preceding paragraph gives us a strong clue: The answer is, "When the $10,000 is used to gain an interest income. At 5 percent, $10,000 is worth $10,500 a year hence."

Still toying with the same idea, what is $10,500 a year from now worth today? Well, we immediately know the answer from our example; it is $10,000. So when we say, "$10,000 is worth $10,500 a year in the future (if the interest rate is 5 percent)," we can also and just as accurately say, "$10,500 one year from now has present value of $10,000 (again, at a 5 percent rate of interest)."

5. Future Values; Present Values

The previous discussion can be stated more formally and more generally. First, suppose we want to know the future value of some present sum. Let PV stand for the present value, and let i stand for the interest rate, while Y_1 represents the future sum (the subscript indicates the number of years the sum PV extends into the future). In our example here, we will use the same numbers as before—that is, PV = $10,000 and $i = .05$. Now, using these symbols and values, we can state the future value of a present sum as

$$PV + PVi = Y_1$$

or, after factoring:

$$PV (1 + i) = Y_1$$

$$\$10,000 (1.05) = \$10,500$$

So we arrive at the same conclusion as before—a present sum of $10,000 is worth $10,500 per year in the future when the rate of interest is .05. We have simply formalized our statement in order to be more general. For instance, what is the $10,000 worth two years from now? The answer:

$$PV (1 + i) + PV (1 + i) (i) = Y_2$$

or, after factoring:

$$PV (1 + i) (1 + i) = Y_2$$

$$PV (1 + i)^2 = Y_2$$

$$\$10,000 (1.1025) = \$11,025$$

So, at 5 percent, $10,000 today compounds to $11,025 two years hence.

Now that you have the general idea, the value of other future sums is easy to get. Three years from now it would be $PV(1 + i)^3$, four years from now it would be $PV(1 + i)^4$, and so on, year after year.

Now let's turn the problem around. Suppose we know (or estimate) a future sum Y_1 and the interst rate i, and we want to find out the present value of this future sum. To get this present value, all we need to do is solve the statements above for PV. For one year, it becomes

$$PV = \frac{Y_1}{(1 + i)}$$

$$PV = \frac{\$10,500}{(1.05)}$$

$$PV = \$10,000$$

For two years, PV is

$$PV = \frac{Y_2}{(1 + i^2)}$$

$$PV = \frac{\$11,025}{(1.05)^2}$$

$$PV = \$10,000$$

In these two expressions, the denominator is called the *discount factor.* Thus, when we find present values, we are *discounting* future sums back to the present. And this is precisely what is needed for the calculation of the marginal revenue product of capital.

6. Capital Budgeting

Any decision to buy a capital asset depends on a comparison of the present value of the future income to be derived from the asset with the purchase price of the asset. Let's see what this means.

Suppose the machine cost $10,000 (*C*) has only a one-year life, and has no scrap value. Furthermore, suppose the machine can be used to produce an output that can be sold for $20,000 in the market over the next year. To produce this output, the firm incurs $6,000 of labor costs and $3,000 of materials costs. Thus the actual net revenue accruing to the firm if it purchases the machine is $11,000 (that is, $20,000 revenue less $6,000 labor cost less $3,000 materials costs). Still assuming that the interest rate is 5 percent, we calculate the present value of the machine as follows:

$$PV = \frac{\$11,000}{1.05} = \$10,476.19$$

In this case, the present value of the machine's output is greater than the purchase price of the machine (*C* = $10,000). Therefore, purchasing the machine would add $476.19 profits to the firm. Indeed, it would be profitable for the firm to buy the machine, or any other capital asset for that matter, as long as the present value of its marginal revenue product exceeds the cost of the asset.

7. A Final Example

Let's make the example a bit more realistic and assume that the machine has an estimated life of three years and that the expected annual values of the marginal product are $11,000. In this event, the present value would read:

$$PV = \frac{Y_1}{(1 + i)} + \frac{Y_2}{(1 + i)^2} + \frac{Y_3}{(1 + i)^3}$$

$$= \frac{\$11,000}{1.05} + \frac{\$11,000}{1.1025} + \frac{\$11,000}{1.1576}$$

$$= \$10,476.19 + \$9,977.32 + \$9,502.42$$

$$= \$29,955.93$$

Now, as long as the machine costs less than this amount, it should be purchased by the firm because the present values of the marginal revenue product exceed the cost of acquisition.

8. The Firm's Demand Curve for Capital

We have already established an important point, but we want to state it again.

Conclusion: As long as the present value of the marginal revenue product of a capital asset exceeds its purchase price (PV > C), then it is profitable to buy the asset.

On the other hand:

If the asset yields a flow of values of the marginal revenue product less than the purchase price of the asset (PV < C), then it isn't profitable to buy the asset.

Finally:

The optimum for the firm exists when physical assets are acquired up to the point at wich the present value of the future marginal revenue product is equal to the cost of the asset.

With these ideas in mind, it is easy to derive a firm's demand curve for capital, like the one in Figure 18–5 which plots the interest rate (*i*) as the price. Now, as long as the interest rate is given, we know that the firm will have many investment projects whose present values of future marginal revenue products are in excess of the purchase prices of the assets. We also know that there are many other projects that the firm will turn down because the present values of their future marginal revenue products are lower than the purchase price of the capital.

All this is true, however, only as long as the interest rate is given. Let's see what happens when the rate of interest changes; here we use the simple one-year present value formula for illustration:

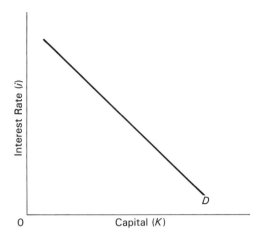

FIGURE 18-5 A Firm's Demand Curve for Capital   The inverse relationship between the demand for new capital and the interest rate exists because reductions in the
interest rate (*i*) raise the present values of projects, making some projects that were
previously unprofitable profitable.

$$PV = \frac{Y_1}{(1 + i)}$$

Suppose the interest rate falls. In this event, the size of the denominator in
our formula also falls. Accordingly, the present value rises. So, we reach a general
conclusion.

> **Conclusion:**   A fall in the rate of interest raises the present values of all
> capital investment projects being considered relative to their costs.

The converse also holds true.

> **Conclusion:**   A rise in the rate of interest reduces the present values of
> all capital investment projects being considered relative to their costs.

Thus the firm's demand curve for capital is negatively sloped. A fall in the
interest rate means that some capital projects formerly unprofitable now become
profitable. Therefore the quantity demanded of capital increases as the interest rate
falls. Furthermore, an increase in the rate of interest makes some projects formerly
considered profitable not worthwhile undertaking at present. Thus, when the interest rate rises, the quantity demanded of capital falls.

> **Conclusion:**   There is an inverse relationship between price (the interest
> rate) and the quantity demanded of capital goods. The law of demand
> holds for capital as well as for other goods and services.

If we were to sum up horizontally all the individual firms' demand curves for capital, we would get the total demand curve (like the one in Figure 18-5).

9. Changes in the Demand for Capital

The demand curve in Figure 18-5 is drawn on the assumption that all the other determinants of capital demand are constant. However, there are a host of factors that, if allowed to changed, will affect the demand for capital. Three very important factors are (a) the wage rate, (b) technology, and (c) expectations. Of these, we will say a few words about expectations. Back in Chapter 10, we saw that investment in new capital can be very volatile over time because of changes in expectations. We are now in a position to see why this is so. For any business to calculate the future values of marginal revenue products requires a leap of faith. Businesses are trying to predict the unknown future, and it doesn't take very much for their expectations of future events to change. Therefore some projects that appear quite sound at a specific time may turn sour as current events change and create a new outlook on the future. The demand for capital, therefore, would fall—i.e., the demand curve in Figure 18-5 would shift to the left. On the other hand, bursts of optimism have the opposite effect, creating a rise in demand for new projects. Thus changes in expectations are a powerful force in determining what happens to the demand for capital goods.

F. THE UNIQUENESS OF LAND (AND OTHER RESOURCES)

When we turn our attention to the pricing of land, we encounter some problems right at the outset. In the first place, land comes in so many varieties, sizes, and locations that it is difficult to make any sound generalizations about the supply of land. To make matters even more complex, economists use the term *rent* to stand for more than simply the payment for the use of land—that is, rent may also be a part of the payments to other productive resources. The economic use of the term *rent* differs from the conventional usage. For the economist, rent means any payment over the opportunity cost of a resource in its next-best use. However, to keep things as simple as possible, we first examine the concept of rent as it pertains to land only. Then we will apply the idea to other productive resources.

1. Land Rent

Rent is the price paid for the use of land. One may, of course, rent other things (e.g., tools, automobiles, apartments), but here we stick to land. Moreover, one may decide to purchase ownership of land rather than rent it; but whether we are concerned with rent (as payment per time period for use of the land) or with the purchase price of the land, the two approaches amount to the same thing.

Land, like capital, yields a flow of returns over time—indeed, very long periods of time—and, as with capital, the prospective buyer should calculate the present values of the future marginal revenue products and compare them with the purchase price of the land. Similarly, the renter of the land should be willing to pay rent per year no greater than the annual marginal revenue product. Whether expressed as a purchase price or as a rental price, however, it is clear that the demand for land is a derived demand. It gets its value from the market value of what it is used to produce.

2. Two Views of the Supply Side

There are two ways of viewing the supply of land. One is to consider land in the aggregate—that is, the total amount of land, which we take as given. The other is to look at parts of this total, parts that have alternative uses.

When we take the first view, land must be treated as fixed in supply. Moreover, since the total amount is fixed, there are no alternative uses, and therefore opportunity costs are zero. As shown in Figure 18-6(A), the supply curve is a vertical line—that is, supply is perfectly inelastic. Therefore no increase in the price of land can elicit an increase in the amount of land; the supply is, to repeat, fixed.

The consequence of this is that the rental price of land is determined solely by the demand. The demand curve in Figure 18-6(A) reflects the annual marginal revenue product, and it sets the rental price at R_1 per year. In this case, then, rents change only as the demand for land changes. For example, as the population grows, the demand for land increases and consequently rent rises. Where land is considered as having no alternative uses, the rent paid to the owner is called *pure economic rent*.

Now we turn to the second case, the one in which the parcel of land in question has alternative uses. This is a more microeconomic view than above where we considered the total supply of land. An example of our present case would be a price of farm land that can be used to produce either wheat or corn. Now, if the price of corn rises relative to the price of wheat, the owner will transfer the land from producing wheat over to producing corn.

The higher price of corn raises the marginal revenue product of corn land relative to wheat land. This rise in the demand for corn land causes the quantity of corn land supplied to increase also. Thus the supply curve of land for growing corn isn't perfectly inelastic; it is, instead, positively sloped, telling us that the higher the relative price of corn, the greater the quantity of corn land supplied.

All of this is shown in Figure 18-6(B), where the increased demand for corn land drives the rental price up from R_1 to R_2. This higher price induces the amount of corn land supplied to rise from L_1 to L_2.

Since the land we are discussing has alternative uses (corn *or* wheat), opportunity costs become important. The opportunity cost to the owner is what land rent will be in the next-best alternative use of the land. Thus if the rent for corn land is $100 per acre, and if the rent for wheat land is $70 per acre, then the *pure economic*

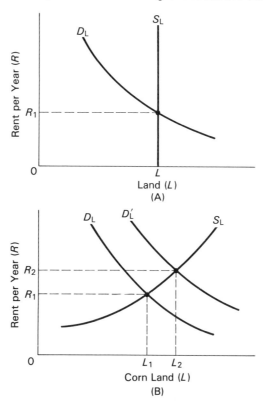

FIGURE 18-6   Rental Price of Land   Panel (A) shows the total demand for and supply of land. Since in the aggregate the supply of land is fixed, rent is determined by demand alone and is pure economic rent, since there is no alternative use for land.

Panel (B) shows supply and demand for corn land. The supply of corn land increases with its rent because, as the value of corn land rises, more land is diverted from other uses.

rent is $30 per acre per year on corn land. This rent reflects the scarcity of corn land relative to wheat land.

3. Rent Payments to Labor and Capital

Rent can actually be "earned" by any "unique" factor of production, whether land, labor, or capital. Whenever a factor of production possesses some specialized marketable attribute, it is able to command an income greater than its opportunity cost. Consider, for example, a person like Lee Iacocca, Chrysler's C.E.O. Although the payment for his services to the corporation would be counted as wages and salaries in the circular flow model, much of his annual income is in the form of economic rent. Let's suppose that his income is $17.0 million per year and that $5.5 million of his income is over what he could get in his next-best alternative employment—then this excess is what we call economic rent. The same situation applies to rock stars, professional athletes, actors, and even some painters and writers.

G. PROFITS

Profits are really a residual component of the circular flow of income, something that remains to the owner (or owners) after *all* costs have been paid.

> **Definition:**   *Profits* are the excess of the firm's revenue over all costs of production, including the opportunity costs of owner-supplied land, labor, and capital (i.e., normal returns).

This definition points up a difference between how the economist and the accountant view profits. The economist includes the opportunity costs mentioned in our definition; the accountant doesn't include them. Therefore the accountant's calculation of profits for a particular firm would be larger than the economist's calculation by the amount of these opportunity costs.

In a very important sense, profits can be viewed as a sign of disequilibrium in competitive markets. It is possible, too, that they are a sign of the presence of monopoly power. But we haven't examined monopoly yet, so let's limit ourselves for the moment to competitive markets.

To repeat, profits (or losses) are a sign of short-run market disequilibrium. For example, a rise in the demand for bread increases the price of wheat. This price increase swells the revenues and profits of wheat growers, and thus they benefit from the rise in demand.

This benefit, however, is short lived. Since there are no barriers to entry, other farmers will, as time passes, switch their resources away from, say, soybeans or corn over to the production of wheat. Thus, again as time passes, the supply of wheat will rise, bringing prices and profits back down to normal returns. We conclude, accordingly, that under the conditions of pure competition, profits (and losses) in any market will be relatively short lived. The absence of barriers to entry is vital to this conclusion.

Profits serve the major function of providing incentives for firms to reallocate resources toward those products for which consumer demand is relatively strong, and away from the production of products for which demand is relatively weak. All of this, if it really existed, would be very beneficial for consumers. However, as the next three chapters argue, many markets are actually far removed from any competitive norm.

H. *FOR WHOM* AGAIN AND SUMMARY
OF THE CHAPTER

As we know, the strength and composition of consumer demand creates a derived demand for labor, capital, and land. But the use of these factors in production is subject to the law of diminishing returns. The marginal revenue product for each factor then becomes the demand for that factor in purely competitive markets over the long run. The supply of each factor available together with demand sets the unit price and quantities of each type of factor employed. Each unit of land, labor, and capital, therefore, earns an income equal to the value of the product of the last unit of that factor used in production. In sum, each factor's income is equal to the value of output produced by that factor.

From the circular flow, we know that households are the ultimate suppliers of factors of production. Therefore each household would receive an income equal to the value of output produced by the land, labor, and capital supplied by that household. So, in pure competition and in the long run, each household receives an income equal to the value of the output produced by the resources supplied by that household. Each household is therefore able to purchase a dollar amount of goods and services equal to the value of its dollar contribution to the total production of society.

Terms and Concepts to Remember

Derived demand	Pure economic rent
Marginal revenue product	Economic profits
Noncompeting groups	Accounting profits
Land rent	Present value

Questions for Review

1. Why is the demand for labor, land, and capital considered to be a derived demand?

2. Define the marginal revenue product of labor. How is it calculated?

3. What would be the general effect on wage rates and employment of an increased immigration of labor into the United States? Would all wage rates be affected alike?

4. How does the marginal revenue product of capital differ from that of labor?

5. Why would a fall in the rate of interest lead to an increase in the quantity of capital demanded? What would happen to household saving if the interest rate fell?

6. How can rent be earned by labor? How would it be different from wages?

7. What role do economic profits play in a competitive society?

19

Monopoly Markets

chapter preview

• A pure monopoly exists when there is only one seller of a product for which no close substitutes are available.

• A monopoly secures its power because entry of rival firms into the market is effectively barred.

• A natural monopoly exists when a single firm is far more efficient at producing the industry's total output than a number of smaller firms would be. Public utilities are good examples of natural monopolies.

• Since the demand curve facing monopolists is the market demand curve, they can affect price by altering the amount produced and sold. Alternatively, monopolists can affect the amount produced by altering the price of a product.

• Monopolists attempt to maximize profits by finding the price and output at which marginal revenue equals marginal cost.

• For monopolists, however, marginal revenue is smaller than price because

of the negatively sloped demand curve facing their firms. As a result, the equality of marginal revenue and marginal cost occurs at some magnitude less than the price of the product.

• Compared with competitive markets, monopolists produce less output and charge higher prices.

• Government policy toward natural monopolies has been either regulation or government operation. In the United States, regulation is favored over operation.

• Government regulates public utilities through average cost pricing.

• There are, however, several serious shortcomings to average cost pricing.

• Large, highly regulated firms have a tendency to become inefficient. This is called X-inefficiency, and it is due to the presence of average cost pricing, a loss of managerial control over workers, and an absence of competitive pressure.

This and the following two chapters take us away from the world of pure competition and into some of the more realistic market structures in the economy. We begin with the idea of *pure monopoly*. Chapter 15 defined a *pure* monopoly as the sole seller in the market for a good or service. Put otherwise, the consumers of the item have no satisfactory substitutes facing them. Let's repeat this in the form of a definition.

> **Definition:** *Pure monopoly* exists when (a) there is but one seller in the market for a good or service, and (b) there are no *available adequate substitutes* from which the buyers may select as they make their purchase decisions.

According to this definition, a pure monopolist has an appreciable impact on the equilibrium market price; in fact, is can change price at its own discretion. The monopolist is, in other words, a *price maker,* a power that can significantly affect the economic well-being of the consumer. One of the dimensions of competition discussed in Chapter 15, that of rivalry between sellers on the same side of the market, is almost totally lacking under pure monopoly. As a result, competition between the supply and demand sides of the market is weighted in favor of the seller.

However, given this definition of pure monopoly, there are few, if any, markets that are truly pure monopoly. For one thing, there must be effective barriers to entry by new firms, and over extended periods of time, this is seldom the case. Such giants as AT&T, Xerox, USX, and IBM have obviously been affected by increasing global competition in recent years. This doesn't mean that they no longer have market clout, but it does mean that any monopoly power achieved at one point in time may be diluted by a number of forces as time passes (see Exhibit 15–1).

Moreover, barriers to entry don't always guarantee a pure monopoly or strong position of power. Consider the case of city-franchised bus systems. Although other firms aren't allowed to compete directly with them, these firms are far from being purely monopolistic. Why? Because, for most people, there are quite a few good transportation substitutes—riding a bicycle, driving one's own car, taking a taxi, and even walking. The existence of substitutes can therefore make the protected bus system a very ineffective monopoly indeed.[1]

---

[1]Except, however, for those who are forced to use it. The impact of substitutes means little to those who don't find them available and/or adequate. Thus some citizens face the bus company as a pure monopoly.

Rarely, it seems, are the dual conditions of *pure* monopoly—effective barriers to entry and absence of adequate substitutes—met in reality. Probably the closest examples one can cite are the public utilities that provide electrical power, natural gas, telephone services, and water. In each of these cases, the single firm is protected by government from potential rivals; and also in each case, the firm supplies a product or service for which there are no good substitutes available. In all these instances, you, as a consumer, find that your range of selection has been severely restricted—that is, you can buy your water from only one source and your electricity from only one seller, and the same applies to natural gas and local telephone services. There is no need to go shopping around for better prices; you face a monopolist seller for each of these products and services.

These examples of actual monopoly are close enough to the extreme to warrant our use of the model of pure monopoly in explaining their behavior. These firms, moreover, are examples of what is called *natural monopoly*. Recall that a natural monopoly exists when a *single* firm is far more efficient producing the industry's total output than a number of smaller firms would be. Indeed, governments have recognized this and have supported natural monopolies by preventing the entry of new firms into the market. But, at the same time, they have reserved the right to regulate these natural monopolies for the benefit of the consumers.

This chapter, therefore, restricts itself to the limiting case of the public utilities that are also natural monopolies. Section A looks closely at the demand and marginal revenue concepts relevant for the monopolist's pricing decision. Remember, however, the firm is a price maker and can thus, unless prevented by regulation, set prices at any level it wants. We assume that the unregulated firm searches for the price that maximizes profits. Section B then shows how the unregulated monopolist goes about maximizing profits; as we shall see, the *MR = MC* rule is relevant but has a quite different meaning here than it has under pure competition. Section C evaluates the government regulation of public utilities. The final section of the chapter discusses a new concept that has created some controversy, the idea of "X-inefficiency."

A. MONOPOLY DEMAND AND MARGINAL REVENUE

We assume that the monopoly has one overriding goal, and that is to make the largest profits possible. In this respect, it is like any other business firm, even a competitive one. It is similar to the competitive firm in yet another important way, that is, in its search for maximum profits, the monopolist must pay close attention to both marginal cost and marginal revenue. Let's see what this means.

1. Those Rules Again

Back in Chapter 17, we postulated three rules that guide the profit-maximizing behavior of the competitive firm. The same three rules are relevant as guides for the monopolist price maker:

  a. When marginal revenue (*MR*) exceeds marginal cost (*MC*), increase production.

  b. When marginal cost (*MC*) exceeds marginal revenue (*MR*), reduce production.

  c. And therefore, set production at the rate at which $MR = MC$ in order to maximize profits.

The application of these rules to monopoly, however, leads to a very different result than under pure competition, since marginal revenue as seen by the monopolist differs considerably from marginal revenue as seen by the competitive firm.

The search for its marginal revenue is really quite simple for the competitive firm. Remember, the firm is so small that it is forced to behave as a *price taker*, and thus the demand as seen by the firm is perfectly elastic. Put otherwise, for the price-taker firm, price equals marginal revenue ($MR = P$), and the search for marginal revenue is therefore completed merely by the manager's observing what the prevailing market price is.

The matter isn't that simple for the pure monopolist—the price maker—who faces a market demand curve that slopes down from left to right.

2. A Declining Marginal Revenue

Let's begin by stating a conclusion and then see how we arrive at it by using an example. We also restate a definition.

> **Definition:**   *Marginal revenue* (*MR*) is the amount added to the firm's total revenue (*TR*) when one more unit of output (*Q*) is sold. It is calculated as

$$MR = \triangle\ TR/\ \triangle\ Q$$

> **Conclusion:**   For a pure monopoly, marginal revenue is less than price, and it falls more rapidly as price is reduced in order to increase sales.

This relationship between price and marginal revenue is shown in Figure 19–1. Since the demand curve obeys the law of demand, it is negatively sloped, but note how the marginal revenue curve lies beneath the demand curve and slopes downward much more rapidly. It is this behavior of marginal revenue that the monopolist must consider in the search for maximum profits.

Let's explain this result by using the example in Figure 19–1 and Table 19–1. Columns 1 and 2 in the table give us the inverse relationship between price and quantity demanded. These data, in turn, are shown as the demand curve in Figure 19–1.

To begin, let's have the monopolist charge a price of $10 *per unit* and consequently sell only one unit. Total revenue, therefore, is $10, as shown in column 3.

Suppose, too, that our monopolist firm is adventurous enough to experiment

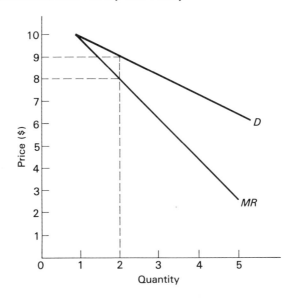

FIGURE 19-1   Monopoly Demand and Marginal Revenue   A monopolist's marginal revenue lies below its demand curve because the price of all units must be reduced in order to sell each additional unit.

with price in order to see what happens to total revenue. In this way, it can estimate what happens to marginal revenue. So, if it cuts price to $9 *per unit,* it (and we) can predict two results: First, there will be an increase in quantity demanded (from 1 to 2); and second, total sales revenue will rise, as shown in Table 19-1, column 3.

These are reasonable predictions, but note what else has happened. When price *per unit* is cut, the second unit is sold at $9, and yet, as column 3 shows, it adds only $8 to total revenue (that is, total revenue rises from $10 to $18). In other words, the marginal revenue of the second unit is only $8. How can this be? An extra unit is sold for $9 but adds only $8 to the firm's total revenue.

This isn't as mysterious as it may first appear. The answer rests with our (unstated) assumption that the monopolist is selling *all units at the same price.* The firm, therefore, sells at a uniform price, and when it changes price, it does so uni-

TABLE 19-1   Monopoly Demand and Marginal Revenue

Price (P) (1)	Quantity (Q) (2)	Total Revenue (TR) (3) = (1) × (2)	Marginal Revenue (MR) = $\Delta TR/\Delta Q$ (4) = $\Delta(3)/\Delta(2)$
$10.00	1	$10.00	$10.00
9.00	2	18.00	8.00
8.00	3	24.00	6.00
7.00	4	28.00	4.00
6.00	5	30.00	2.00

formly. In other words, the monopolist doesn't sell the first unit at $10 and the second at $9; this is a form of price discrimination, and while the monopolist may like to do this, we have assumed that it doesn't or can't.

Thus, in order for the firm to sell the second unit, it must cut price on all units, and this means that it now sells the first unit, not at $10, but at $9. In other words, the monopoly takes a "loss" of $1 on the first unit in order to sell the second at $9. And deducting this $1 "loss" from the $9 sales price of the second unit means that this second unit adds $8 to the firm's total revenue. Thus $MR = \$8$ while $P = \$9$.

Let's do this again for another price cut, this time from $9 to $8 *per unit.* Again the firm must take a "loss' on earlier units if it wants to sell the third unit. Before the price cut, the first two units were priced at $9; now they are priced at $8, and here the monopoly sacrifices $2 on them. The marginal revenue of the third unit is then calculated as follows: It sells for $8, but from this amount must be deducted the $2 "loss." Therefore $MR = \$8$ less $2 = \$6$. Note once more that the marginal revenue is less than the price.

Figure 19–2 shows this procedure graphically. When price is reduced from $9 to $8, the firm sells the third unit at $8. The resulting gain in revenue is shown by

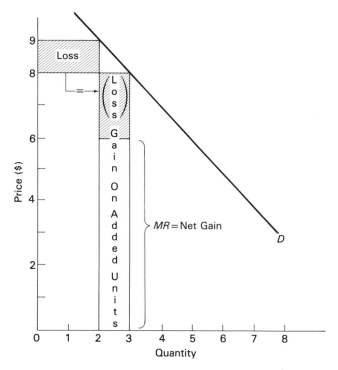

FIGURE 19–2   Calculation of Marginal Revenue   To determine marginal revenue, calculate the added revenue on the additional unit sold, and then subtract from that amount the revenue loss because of lower prices on previous units.

the vertical bar labeled "gain." But instead of selling the first two units at $9 *each,* the firm now sells them at $8 per unit (the new price) and thus incurs a "loss" of $2 on them. This is shown by the horizontal bar labeled "loss." The "net gain," then—that is, the marginal revenue due to the sale of the third unit—is the gain minus the loss ($8 − $2 = $6). This is also shown as the shaded portion of the vertical bar in Figure 19-2.

If we follow the same procedure for every lower price, we end up with the *MR* curve in Figure 19-1, a curve that, to repeat, lies beneath the demand curve for the firm's output. In making its decision about how much to produce and sell, management must pay careful attention to marginal revenue. Let's see why.

B. MONOPOLY PRICE AND OUTPUT

Society has three options or alternatives from which it may choose when it deals with the issue of natural monopolies. First, it may decide to ignore the fact that monopolies price like monopolies and thus give the firms complete freedom in the marketplace. This alternative is examined in this part of the chapter. The second alternative is to allow the natural monopolies to continue being privately owned, and even shield them from potential entry, but to regulate their price-setting powers in order to protect consumers. This is the subject matter of Section C, which also discusses the third alternative, government ownership and operation. And so we begin with seeing how the unfettered pure monopoly goes about seeking maximum profits.

1. The Search for Maximum Profits

It may seem strange, but the pure monopolist doesn't have a supply curve. Remember, the supply curve of the competitive firm is its marginal cost curve, and the supply curve of the competitive industry is the sum of all the firms' supply curves. Such isn't the case for the monopoly firm. The marginal cost curve plays a vital role in the monopolist's decision about how much to produce, but it isn't the monopoly's supply curve.

In making the decision about how much to produce and sell, the monopolist must consider both marginal revenue and marginal cost. As we noted earlier, the rules that apply to the monopoly are the same as those that apply to the competitive firm (see Chapter 17). The main difference is that the monopoly is a price maker, whereas the competitive firm is a price taker. Thus, while the competitive firm accepts the market price as given, the monopoly must search for the price (and corresponding level of output) that maximizes profits.

Figure 19-3 shows how the monopolist can carry out this search. It contains the demand curve, the *MR* curve (which we obtained from above), and the firm's *MC* curve. We will use this figure as we check out the three rules that must be observed if profits are to be maximized.

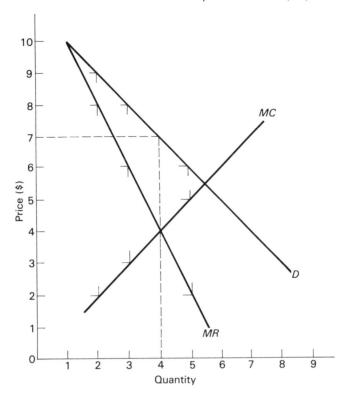

FIGURE 19-3 Optimum Price and Output of Monopolist   A monopolist maximizes profits by producing at the output level where marginal revenue equals marginal cost. Note that price is above marginal cost.

Let's begin the search by having the monopolist charge a price of $9 *per unit* at which two units are sold. This isn't the best position, however, for at that price and output, marginal revenue ($8) exceeds marginal cost (which we have arbitrarily drawn in at $2). Recall that as long as *MR* > *MC,* then each extra unit produced and sold adds more to the firm's total revenue than to its total cost. In this event, the extra output should be produced and sold, for it adds to the firm's total profits.

Since our rule says increase output, the monopolist does just that, pushing it to, say, three units. However, *price must now be cut* in order to sell the additional production; and we assume that price falls to $8. At this price, all three units of output are sold at $8 each, and thus the firm "loses" $2 on them. The marginal revenue has therefore fallen to $6 and, as our *MC* curve shows, marginal cost has risen to $3.

Still, marginal revenue is greater than marginal cost, so the monopolist is induced to increase output even more to, say, four units. Here it must pause and consider its position again. By reducing price to sell this fourth unit, marginal revenue falls to $4, and increasing output that much drives marginal cost up to $4 as well. This is, by our rules, clearly the monopoly firm's equilibrium, for at this output rate $MC = \$4 = MR = \$4$. So we conclude that the firm will establish its price here at \$7 and output at four units.

To verify that this is actually the optimal position, however, the firm may push output up to five units. In doing so, it finds that marginal cost is now greater than marginal revenue—that is, while the fifth unit adds only \$2 to the firm's total revenue, it contributes \$5 to the firm's total cost. This is hardly a desirable position to stay in, at least according to our rules. As long as $MC > MR$, each extra unit produced adds more to the firm's total costs than to its total revenue. In this event, output should be cut back.

In our example, the firm reduces production back to four units, for it is here that total profits are at a maximum (or losses minimized).

Conclusion: The optimal position for the firm is when $MR = MC$, for here the last unit produced adds as much to the firm's total costs as it does to its total revenue.

And so it is that the monopoly firm completes its search for maximum profits. Being a price maker, it can control price, and hence MR, as it seeks out the profit-maximizing rate of output.

2. Profits and Losses

In our discussion of monopoly pricing, we have said nothing about the other costs of production; we have concentrated, and rightly so, on marginal cost. The reason for this is that the monopoly must, as long as it is operating, produce where $MR = MC$ if it is to maximize profits *or minimize losses*.

Let's now introduce the other costs to see how the monopolist may fare. Here we consider three possible cases—one in which the monopoly received profits, one in which it minimizes losses by continuing to operate, and one in which it is so hurt by losses that it shuts down. All three cases may occur for the same monopolist, each at some different point in time.

We begin with the profit situation, which is shown in Figure 19-4(A). Here the firm is acting just as we have postulated it would act; it is maximizing profits at Q_1 and price P_1. However, since P_1 is above average total cost, the monopoly is receiving profits beyond normal returns. Now, if the industry were competitive, these profits would be short lived because new firms, attracted by them, would be drawn into the industry, thus increasing supply and driving price down. Recall that the firms eventually end up operating at their most efficient size and receive only normal returns. Alas, such isn't the case here, for our monopoly is well protected by barriers to entry, and as long as cost and demand remain unchanged, the firm will continue to receive these profits.

However, in a dynamic, ever-changing economy, one in which *ceteris* is never *paribus*, it is misleading to assume that costs and demand conditions remain constant. To the contrary, a host of things may cause them to change, creating different environments in which the monopoly can operate.

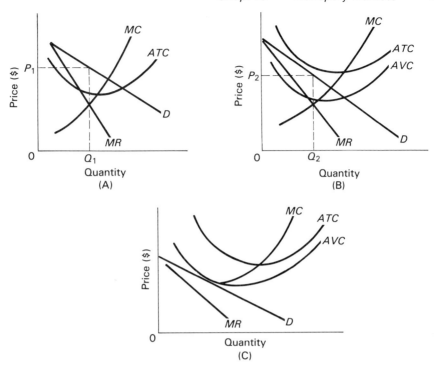

FIGURE 19-4   Monopoly Price and Output in Three Different Situations   In panel (A), the monopolist earns maximum profit because price is above average total cost. In panel (B), the monopolist minimizes losses because price is above average variable cost. When demand is below average variable cost, as in panel (C), the monopolist closes down to restrict losses to fixed cost.

One possible environment is shown in panel (B) of Figure 19-4. Note that in the relevant range, the demand curve is below the firm's average total cost curve but above the average variable cost curve. This situation could have occurred because of a rise in costs or a fall in demand, or both. In any event, the monopolist must operate to minimize losses, and the old rule of $MR = MC$ is as relevant here as it is when the firm operates to maximize profits. Hence the monopolist must restrict output to Q_2 and lower price to P_2 to sell that output—that is, where $MC = MR$. If there is freedom of exit, the owners may be making plans to move to other, better alternatives.

Figure 19-4(C) shows the environment in which the monopoly has but one decision to make and carry out, and that is to *shut down* in order to minimize losses. Here the demand has fallen so much, or costs have risen so high, that the demand curve lies beneath the average variable cost curve at each price. Since no price could yield a total revenue sufficient to cover total variable costs, it would be foolish for the firm to continue operations. The only relevant decision to be made is to shut down.

What could have caused either of the last two situations? Any of a number of factors, some pushing costs up, others causing demand to slump. The point is that monopoly profits aren't necessarily "writ in stone." They may decline—even become negative (losses)—as conditions beyond the control of the monopoly unfold and make themselves felt. For now, however, we want to stick with the pure monopolist shown in panel (A) of Figure 19-4. That is, we want to analyze further the monopolist whose profits aren't threatened now or in the immediate future. Our major conclusion for this firm is that profits are maximized at the level of output at which $MC = MR$.

3. A Comparison of Monopoly and Competition

Our major conclusion, however, must be carefully interpreted. While it is true that the optimal position for both the competitive firm and the monopoly firm can be summarized by $MC = MR$, that equality takes on a different meaning for pure monopoly. As shown in Figures 19-3 and 19-4(A), the equality of MR and MC occurs *beneath the demand curve.* Thus $MC = MR < P$. For the competitive firm, on the other hand, we have $MC = MR = P$; remember, the purely competitive firm is a price taker.

Let's carry this a step further. The usual comparison of monopoly and competition arrives at the conclusion that economists have held since Adam Smith:

> The price of monopoly is upon every occasion the highest price that can be got. The natural price, or the price of free competition, on the contrary, is the lowest which can be taken. . . . The one is upon every occasion the highest which can be squeezed out of the buyers. . . . The other is the lowest which the sellers can afford to take and at the same time continue their business.[2]

Chapter 17 described how the competitive sellers end up taking the lowest price they can and still stay in business. That is, in the long-run equilibrium of the industry, the price settles at the lowest possible average total cost. We show this equilibrium situation in Figure 19-5. The demand curve facing the competitive firms is labeled D_C (ignore the D_M label for the moment). The competitive supply curve is shown as $S_C = \Sigma M_C$, where ΣMC = the sum of the marginal cost curves of all the firms in the competitive industry.

The intersection of the demand (D_C) and competitive supply ($S_{C\,=\,\Sigma M_C}$) curves gives us the equilibrium market price P_C, at which quantity demanded equals quantity supplied at Q_C.

Let's suppose there are five hundred equally small firms making up this industry. In the long-run equilibrium, each of these firms is operating at the minimum point of its average total cost curve. We show this by having the supply and demand curves intersect at the minimum point of the ΣATC_C curve, which is the sum of the ATC curves of all the firms in the industry. This also means that each firm is receiving only normal returns. In Smith's words, this equilibrium price "is the lowest

[2]Adam Smith, *The Wealth of Nations* (New York: Modern Library, 1937) p. 61.

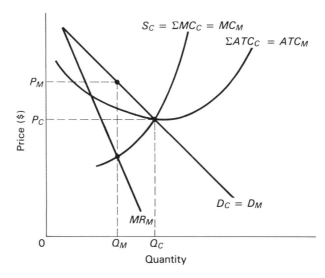

FIGURE 19-5 Monopoly Compared with Pure Competition When compared with a purely competitive industry, a monopolist produces less (Q_M) and sells at a higher price (P_M).

which the sellers can afford to take and at the same time continue their business.''

But suppose one of these firms acquires the rest, so that the industry becomes purely monopolistic. Now we need to relabel the curves in Figure 19–5, as well as add a new one. We thus rename the demand curve as D_M, allowing the subscript M to signify pure monopoly. We relabel as well the ATC_C curve, calling it now the ATC_M curve—that is, it is the average total cost curve of the newly formed monopoly. Furthermore, the competitive supply curve ($S_C = \Sigma MC_C$) becomes the marginal cost curve of the monopolist and is so designated as MC_M.

So far we have merely relabeled the curves used a moment ago to describe the competitive equilibrium. We now have to add a new curve to the picture—namely, the marginal revenue curve as seen by the monopolist. This is drawn in as the MR_M curve, and note the difference it makes. The newly formed monopoly, in its search for maximum profits, will find its optimal position where $MC = MR$, *but* this occurs at the higher price P_M at which a smaller quantity (Q_M) is produced and sold.

This is what Smith concluded when he stated the monopoly price ''is upon every occasion the highest which can be squeezed out of the buyers.'' Smith, of course, didn't even have an inkling of our modern concepts of marginal revenue and marginal cost, but his analysis led him to the same conclusion as ours.

Conclusion: The conventional comparison of pure monopoly and pure competition leads us to the observation that monopoly price is higher than competitive price and, accordingly, monopoly output is less than competitive output. This can be turned round to read that since the monopoly restricts output below the competitive level, it can charge a price higher than the competitive price.

This is a formidable conclusion, and it leads to a number of repercussions.

C. ECONOMIES OF SCALE, NATURAL MONOPOLY, AND GOVERNMENT REGULATION

So far, then, it seems that the policy of simply letting the monopoly alone, so that it can produce and price as it sees fit, does nothing but harm the consumers of the good or service. This, however, doesn't always have to be the case, and we now turn to an important qualification to the preceding analysis.

1. Economies of Scale (or Size)

Natural monopoly provides a serious departure from the conclusion that monopoly hurts the consumer. The preceding comparison is based on a fundamental assumption that we must now question—namely, the cost conditions are the same for both types of market structures. That is, when we had one firm absorb the remaining 499, the cost curves in Figure 19-5 remained unaffected. We didn't allow them to change even slightly when this significant transition from pure competition to pure monopoly took place. Yet there is a strong likelihood that cost conditions will differ between the two market structures. Put otherwise, there is the possibility that rather substantial economies of scale (economies of large size) accrue to the large single firms, a possibility we shouldn't ignore.

Consider the following examples. Now only a few specialists are needed to make a major decision, whereas before there were hundreds of decision makers (one for each firm). This means that there is more effective division of labor at the managerial level. Also, instead of there being numerous small orders for materials, a smaller number of larger orders more efficiently placed will do the trick. The large firm, too, may be able to introduce cost-reducing methods of production, for now there can be a few larger firms instead of hundreds of smaller ones, and therefore management can take advantage of larger, more productive machinery, new types of inventory controls, and more efficient accounting and cash control methods. Note also that a lot of duplication of resources is eliminated when there is one instead of a large number of firms (see Exhibit 19-1).

All told, then, these economies of scale may be so great that the pure monopolist will operate at a more efficient size and at much lower unit costs than a competitive firm ever could. In fact, there is no "may" about it in the case of natural monopoly; compared with competition, the natural monopoly is so efficient (lower unit cost) that there is room for only one firm in the industry.

Figure 19-6 shows the results of these economies of scale. Output Q_M tells us what total output is when there is but the single firm. Note that we have drawn in the price P_M to lie above the long-run unit cost (LRAC) curve, reflecting that the

EXHIBIT 19-1
Why Are Some Natural Monopolies Called Public Utilities?

Natural monopolies are actually the result of economic growth. Railroads in the early history of the United States are a good example; that is, when a railroad was built, it became a monopoly because it was too costly to construct a rival line. Each company, therefore, became a monopoly in its area, and as might be expected, these natural monopolies typically used their economic power in such a way as to hurt the public. In fact, resentment against the obsessive acts of the railroad monopolies became so great that Congress passed the Interstate Commerce Commission Act (ICC) in 1887. The ICC was to prevent all sorts of monopolistic, anticompetitive practices by the railroads that engaged in interstate commerce. Regulation for intrastate commerce was left to each individual state.

As the U.S. economy continued to grow, cities began to dot the landscape, and by 1910 more than half the country's population lived in towns and cities. This development created a rising demand for centralized water, sewage disposal, electricity, natural gas, and urban transportation. As it turned out, the provision of each of these products or services was done more efficiently by a natural monopoly. In each of these activities, as in the case of the railroads, only one firm was required, and duplication of services was to be avoided. Why, for example, have three or four sets of telephone lines when one does the job as well? Why, for another example, have five sewer systems when again only one is needed for the town?

In each of these instances, a natural monopoly served the public more efficiently than did a number of competing firms. And thus the public utility was born. The municipal or state government either operated the enterprise itself or granted monopoly power to the single firm providing the product or service. At the same time the government, at either the state or the local level, regulated the natural monopoly for the public good, or, to use the more common term, the public utility.

monopoly is receiving profits above normal returns. (To keep this diagram simple, we haven't drawn in the short-run cost curves.)

Suppose now that, instead of there being one firm, there are one hundred, all of equal size. The output of *one* of these is shown as Q_C in Figure 19-6. In this case, $Q_C = 1/100$ of Q_M; in other words, all of the hundred smaller firms combined produce the same total output (Q_M) as the monopoly. Note also that we have drawn in their price P_C so that it rests on the long-run unit cost curve. This means that each of the hundred firms is receiving only normal returns.

So here we have a case in which the competitive firms receive only normal returns but sell at a higher price. Under these conditions, therefore, monopoly seems to be preferable to competition, and this is so even if the firm receives monopoly profits. After all, $P_M < P_C$, and this is of benefit to the consumer.

2. Regulation of Natural Monopoly

Governments that have allowed natural monopolies to exist have also usually set about regulating them presumably for further benefit to the consumer. (This is the second option of the three we listed on page 105.) In the United States, the typical procedure is for each state to set up a regulatory commission whose chief aim is to set rates for the utilities to charge their customers. The rates recommended by the commission, however, may be challenged by the utility involved, and consequently lengthy litigation may ensue.

At first glance, this method of regulation seems simple and straightforward enough—the regulatory commission sets a price equal to the monopoly's average total cost. As Figure 19-7 shows, this occurs where the demand curve cuts the monopoly's average total cost curve (point R). The purpose of this regulatory policy is to eliminate the monopoly's profits (beyond normal returns) by forcing the firm to sell a larger output at a price that just covers average total cost.

Figure 19-7 shows how this policy is supposed to work to the benefit of the consumer. In the absence of regulation, the monopoly will produce output Q_1, which it sells at the price P_1. The regulatory commission, however, would have the natural monopoly sell output Q_2 at the regulated price P_R. The benefits to the consumers are obvious—they will now get a larger amount of output at a lower price. And what of the monopoly? It will receive only normal returns, since $P_R = ATC$ (and normal returns are included in the ATC curve). The owners, therefore, have

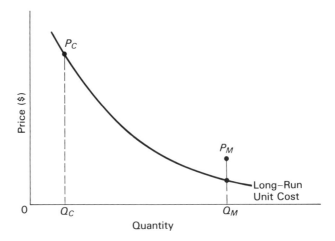

FIGURE 19-6   Comparison of Monopoly and Competitive Price with Economies of Scale   The monopolist firm can produce at low unit cost because of economies of large size. It can sell at lower prices than the competitive firm even with substantial profits.

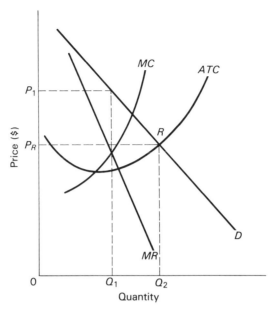

FIGURE 19-7   Monopoly, Price, and Output under Regulation   Regulation of natural monopoly restricts profits to normal returns. The result is a lower price (P_R) and higher output (Q_2) than would occur in the absence of regulations.

no inducement to withdraw their funds and place them elsewhere in some other enterprise.

3. Some Problems of Regulation

Despite the appeal of this regulatory method, and despite its widespread use, it is riddled with problems. Our example above made the process of regulation seem simple enough; indeed, it made it too simple.

First, there is the problem of determining just what "normal returns" are, or to use public utility jargon, what is a "fair rate of return" to the utility. Presumably, the utility must receive enough revenue not only to cover its fixed and variable costs but also to pay the stockholders an amount at least equal to what they could get by using their funds in their next-best alternative. This fair rate of return is usually calculated (estimated may be a better word) as follows: The regulators calculate the average rate of return received by stockholders in comparable-size firms in other, nonregulated industries. They then set a price that will allow the monopoly to pay its owners this rate of return. As you might expect, there could be many ways of estimating this "fair" rate of return.

Second, there can be much dispute over the "rate base"—that is, the total value of the firm's capital—to which the fair rate of return is applied. For instance, should the rate of return be applied as a percentage of the original capital investment? This is one way, but it may not yield enough revenue to pay the stockholders and keep them happy. Suppose the agreed-on rate of return is 12 percent, and it is applied to the original capital investment. But what if there has been substantial inflation in the meantime, so that the funds required to replace the original capital as it wears out are much larger than the original capital investment? Should this larger figure of *replacement investment* be used as the rate base instead of the original investment? It makes a lot of difference to the stockholders, who would clearly prefer replacement investment (in a period of inflation), and the regulatory commission must take this into account when selecting the appropriate rate base.

Third, the utility needs a source of capital funds to finance its expansion. Most utilities rely heavily on undistributed corporate profits as a major source of capital funds. This being the case, there is room for honest debate over what the capital needs may be. Note that the public utility must provide a size of operation sufficient to meet *peak demand*. For example, the peak demand of the electrical public utility is the summer season, and the firm must be large enough to satisfy that peak demand, even though this means much idle capacity for the rest of the year. Now, who can accurately estimate the peak demand, say, a decade from now? Here, as we already mentioned, there is room for honest debate. The firm may estimate a larger future demand than the commission and may thus ask for higher rates than the commission is willing to approve.

Fourth, just because the regulatory commission approves (or disapproves) rates is no sign that the utility's management will agree. Thus there could be (and often are) lengthy, expensive court proceedings before any recommendation is put into effect. This is what is called "regulatory lag."

Finally, there is the potential problem of the ability and motives of the commissioners. Regulators are often ignorant of the technical and economic problems involved in their jobs. Also, it is possible that the regulators may become "captives" of the industry they regulate or "captives" of consumer interest groups. However, it seems more likely that they could become the tool of the large utilities. None of this is meant to impugn the character and morals of regulatory commissioners, but nonetheless, such possibilities exist.

4. Government Ownership and Operation

The third of the three options of what to do with natural monopoly is that the government own and operate it. This alternative isn't unheard of in the United States; there are, for example, the Tennessee Valley Authority (TVA), the U.S. Postal Service, Amtrak, and Conrail. Moreover, many cities own and operate some of the utilities provided to their citizens—i.e., water, natural gas, sewerage systems, and bus transportation.

Is government ownership desirable? The answer depends on how efficiently the government operates as compared with private enterprise, and here there is no clear-cut conclusion. Some studies show that government enterprises have lower costs and have provided the services more cheaply to the consumer. Other studies show the reverse.

In the United States, nonetheless, there is a strong feeling against government ownership and operation of business. So, except for the present instances of government monopolies, there is little likelihood that the government operation alternative will spread.

D. THE MATTER OF X-INEFFICIENCY

One of the major problems of monopoly, particularly monopoly that is protected from potential entry of new rivals, is that the managers of the firm may become very lackadaisical in their performance. They may, in other words, lose their competitive motivation and hence pay less attention to cost efficiency. In a competitive world, remember, each firm must achieve maximum economic efficiency if it is to survive. Not so for the natural monopoly; it faces no direct competition that requires it to strive for maximum efficiency. Hence there is a strong tendency for management to become lax. This tendency is perhaps particularly present in the public utilities, which know that price will be set to cover average total cost no matter how high costs may be. Indeed, one argument can be made (and has been made by the critics of regulation) that regulation of utilities fosters inefficiency in the public utilities.

Moreover, when the firm is large, the owners and top management lose control over the workers below them. Unlike a small firm, in which the owner-manager typically works alongside his or her employees, in a large firm many workers have some control over what has been called the "apqt bundle"—that is, activity, pace, quality, and time.[3] In a large firm, as many natural monopolies are, the methods of production are so complicated that workers have a lot of control over the "apqt bundles," and this raises costs per unit of output. For example, workers often have considerable say-so about how fast they work, the quality of their performance, and even the amount of time they devote to work. It should be pointed out that the managers, too, have their own "apqt bundles" and exercise a lot of control over them.[4] Examples: large entertainment budgets, golf-course conferences, lavishly decorated offices, an excessive number of secretaries, and unnecessary travel—all of these drive costs to unreasonably high levels.

All of this breeds inefficiency in the large firm that doesn't face direct competitive pressures, and these are examples of what Harvey Leibenstein has called X-inefficiency. X-inefficiency is the inefficient use of resources within the firm, and it pushes costs higher than they would otherwise be. Although it may be true that the regulated natural monopoly is charging a price that only yields normal returns, the average total cost curve lies much higher than it need be because of X-inefficiency. Figure 19-8 shows what we mean. The ATC_x curve is higher than the ATC_l curve, which reflects a much more efficient use of resources. Thus the regulated price that

---

[3]Harvey Leibenstein first introduced the idea of X-inefficiency in a journal article in 1966; that article has been reprinted and expanded in his *Beyond Economic Man* (Cambridge, MA: Harvard University Press, 1980). He discusses "apqt bundles" on pages 98–100 of his book.

[4]Ibid., pp. 163–65.

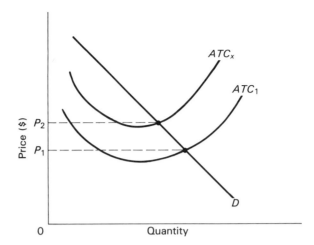

FIGURE 19-8   Effect of X-inefficiency on Unit Cost   In large firms that have complex production processes and are shielded from direct competition, inefficiencies tend to creep in, which raises the average total costs of production.

the consumer pays, P_2, is higher than it needs to be because it has to compensate for managements' X-inefficiency.

Is there any empirical evidence to support Leibenstein's contention that X-inefficiency is widespread enough that it creates much inefficiency in resource use? Leibenstein has estimated that the waste of resources due to X-inefficiency comes close to 10 percent of total output (real GNP). If this estimate is correct, there is a significant amount of wasted resources in our society.

One study dealt with the costs of different electrical power utilities. It so happened that, in the United States, there were forty-nine cities with two or more electric power companies in competition with one another. Primeaux's study of these companies concluded that their average total costs were 11 percent lower than those of electrical utilities in cities that had only one firm. Another study, this one dealing with owner-operated versus manager-operated franchised restaurants, concluded that the owner-operated restaurants were much more efficient than the manager-operated ones. Owners who work directly with the employees have much more control over the workers' "apqt bundles."[5]

We can do no better than to close this chapter with the following example taken from a 1981 newspaper article and discussed in an intermediate microeconomics textbook.[6] Ford Motor Company built two identical plants, one in West Germany and the other in England. In terms of production processes, these two plants were replicas of each other. Yet, look at the figures in Table 19-2. The planned

---

[5]These and a number of other studies are summarized in Leibenstein, *Beyond Economic Man,* pp. 34-44.

[6]H. Kohler, *Intermediate Microeconomics: Theory and Application* (Glenview, IL: Scott, Foresman, 1986), p. 143.

TABLE 19-2   Two Ford Auto Plants Compared

	West Germany	Britain
Daily Output		
Anticipated	1,015 autos	1,015 autos
Actual	1,200 autos	800 autos
Workers employed	7,762	10,400
Labor-hours per individual auto	21	40

production was the same for both plants, but there was a tremendous difference in actual performance.

Ford officials, although they didn't use these terms, observed that the English workers had much more control over their "apqt bundles." They were seen to be reading, eating, even kicking footballs on the job. In contrast, the German workers were highly motivated and worked hard and consistently at their tasks. Where the source of the problem lies, whether in management or unions or both, we don't say. Our only point is that X-inefficiency is probably quite common and harms the consumer who is forced to pay a higher price that covers unnecessary costs.

E. SUMMARY

An industry or market is dominated by pure monopoly when there is only one firm and that firm is protected by barriers to entry and produces a product or service for which there are no available, adequate substitutes. Very few markets meet these two requirements, although the so-called public utilities approximate them very closely.

In it search for maximum profits, the unregulated monopoly firm behaves very much like the competitive firm—the profit-maximizing rate of output for each is set by $MR = MC$. This rule for profit maximization, however, yields different results between the two market structures because, for the monopoly, this equality occurs beneath the demand curve, that is, for monopoly $MC = MR < P$, whereas for the competitive firm $MC = MR = P$. It is because of this that the conventional comparison of the two market structures concludes that price is higher and output is lower if the market is monopolized than would be the case if it were competitive.

In a natural monopoly, however, this conclusion doesn't hold because the firm experiences significant economies of scale. This means that, even if unregulated, the monopoly price would be lower than the competitive price, and therefore monopoly output would be higher than competitive output. The so-called public utilities are natural monopolies—that is, only one firm is allowed in the market because it is so efficient that no other firm could effectively compete against it. Government protects these utilities by preventing entry.

The public utilities, however, are further regulated by government. In the most common type of regulation, the regulatory agency forces the utility to set price equal to average total cost. This method of regulation, however, is often flawed by difficulties involved in setting a "fair rate of return" and determining the rate base.

Another serious problem flowing from regulation of this type is that it breeds X-inefficiency—that is, management has no motivation to use the firm's resources efficiently. Indeed, average-cost pricing may be said to breed X-inefficiency.

Terms and Concepts to Remember

Monopoly   Public utility
Barriers to entry   X-inefficiency
Natural monopoly

Questions for Review

1. Define *pure monopoly*. What conditions form the basis of monopoly power?

2. In what way does the monopolist's demand curve differ from that of the firm in pure competition?

3. Explain why the marginal revenue of the monopolist lies below price on the demand curve.

4. How does the monopolist determine the level of output and price that will maximize profits?

5. Define *natural monopoly*. What factors can create the low-unit costs of large-scale operation that can lead to natural monopoly?

6. Why might large regulated firms, such as public utilities, tend to become inefficient?

20

Monopolistic Competition and Oligopoly

chapter preview

• Firms in monopolistic competition achieve short-run monopoly profits by means of successful product differentiation.

• In the long-run, profits tend to be eliminated in monopolistic competition because of the entry of new firms into the market. This is possible due to the absence of significant barriers to entry.

• The firm in monopolistic competition will receive only normal returns in the long run, for it will operate at an output at which price equals average total cost.

• Yet long-run price will be somewhat higher and output somewhat lower than would be the case under pure competition. Thus there is still some resource misallocation. This conclusion must be qualified, however, since monopolistic competition satisfies consumer demands for differentiated products.

• Market concentration measures the percentage of an industry's sales accounted for by some given number of firms. Oligopolistic industries tend

to have a high degree of market concentration.

• An oligopolistic industry is dominated by a few large firms that must consider feedbacks among themselves in response to price changes. This is called conjectural interdependency.

• Conjectural interdependency tends to result in price rigidity—that is, the firms in the industry are reluctant to change price in response to changing cost and demand conditions. This conclusion holds only in the absence of collusion, however.

• Accordingly, the firms in an oligopolistic industry are inclined to collude in order to allow price flexibility.

• Cartels and different types of price leaderships are examples of collusion over price.

• Collusion is illegal. Covert collusion is definitely in violation of the law. Tacit collution may be in violation of the law, but it is often difficult to prosecute such a collusion successfully.

We now come to the two most important market structures — monopolistic competition and oligopoly. There are few industries that we could characterize as being purely competitive, and as we noted in the last chapter, only a few that could be classified as pure monopoly. Actually, most market structures fall somewhere along the spectrum between the two extremes.

Monopolistic competition lies closer to the competitive end of the spectrum and includes the markets that are normally served by small businesses. Most retail markets tend to fall into this category. Oligopoly, on the other hand, is associated with big business. The steel, automobile, pharmaceutical, chemical, and rubber industries are good examples of this type of market structure.

Firms that serve oligopolistic and monopolistically competitive markets tend to engage in intense personal competition with their industry rivals. Another important similarity is that firms in both types of industries strive to convince consumers that their products are unique and more desirable than their competitors' products. They attempt to reach this goal largely through nonprice competition that involves the use of advertising, promotion, product design, packaging, display, and the like, to achieve strong consumer preference for the product. Basically, each firm strives to distinguish or differentiate its product in the minds of consumers. If the efforts are successful, the firm is able to acquire, at least temporarily, an element of monopoly power and the profits that accompany it.

A. THE THEORY OF MONOPOLISTIC COMPETITION

We look at monopolistic competition first. Most business firms in the United States probably operate in this type of market structure.

Definition: *A monopolistically competitive market* is like a purely competitive industry in all respects but one, which is that the firms produce differentiated (heterogeneous) products.

Since the product of each firm is at least somewhat differentiated from the others, consumers develop preferences for the products of specific producers. Each firm, of course, helps them do this with advertising and other forms of nonprice competition. It is here that the monopoly element enters, for the preference of some consumers for its product gives it a slight monopoly edge. Thus if the firm were to raise price, it would lose some but not all of its customers. The demand curve facing the firm, therefore, has a negative slope, and marginal revenue is therefore less than price (see Figure 20-1).

1. Equilibrium in the Short Run

The short-run analysis of a monopolistically competitive firm is rather straight-forward; it is essentially the same as for pure monopoly, at least as far as the mechanics are concerned. The demand curve facing the firm is shown in Figure 20-1. To maximize its profits, the firm must follow the $MR = MC$ rule, and therefore it will produce Q_1 output and sell it at the price P_1. Given the cost and demand curves of the firm, any other price-output combination would yield less than maximum profits.

In this respect, the short-run theory of a monopolistically competitive firm resembles the short-run theory of pure monopoly. In both market structures, the short-run equilibrium price exceeds marginal cost and marginal revenue because of the negative-sloped demand curve.

The two models, however, differ in a major respect. The demand curve facing the monopolistically competitive firm is not as steeply sloped as the demand curve facing the pure monopolist. This is because in monopolistic competition, the firm faces a lot of rivals who are producing very close substitutes. Thus, if the firm were to raise price, it might not lose all of its customers, but it would certainly lose substantial sales to its rivals. Indeed, because of the similarity of products, the loss of customers could be disastrous. The pure monopolist, on the other hand, has no direct competition from rivals, and therefore it it were to raise price, it would lose

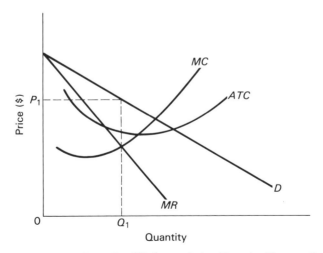

FIGURE 20-1   Short-Run Equilibrium of the Firm in Monopolistic Competition   In the short run, a firm with successful product differentiation maximizes profits by producing and selling that level of output at which marginal revenue equals marginal cost. Note that price is above marginal cost.

some sales, but not necessarily very many. Because of this we conclude that the excess of price over marginal revenue is greater for the pure monopolist than it is for the monopolistically competitive firm.

Nevertheless, as long as the monopolistically competitive firm can successfully differentiate its product in the minds of consumers, it can achieve short-run profits above normal returns. But consumer loyalty is probably quite tenuous, since a number of other sellers are trying to convince buyers of the uniqueness and importance of their products. This, coupled with the absence of barriers to entry, means that the short-run profits are eliminated, and it is here that the resemblance of monopolistic competition to pure monopoly disappears. In the long run, the competitive forces dominate, leaving the firm with only normal returns.

2. Long-Run Adjustments

The long-run adjustments are shown in Figure 20-2, which contains the cost and demand curves for only one firm. We let this single firm represent the behavior of all the others in the market. The number and availability of new substitutes increases as the short-run profits attract more firms into the market. As a result, the market is divided among a larger number of rivals, and this means that the demand for our representative firm's product falls. This is shown by the demand curve in Figure 20-2 shifting to the left from D_1 to D_2. The reduction of demand for the firm's product will, over time, cause product price to fall and eventually eliminate the profits (all other things equal). In fact, if too many firms enter the industry so that market shares are drastically reduced, the demand curve will fall below the firm's average

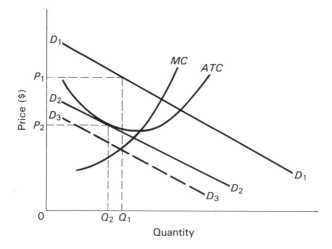

FIGURE 20-2   Long-Run Equilibrium of the Firm in Monopolistic Competition   In the long run, since there are no substantial barriers to entry, the firm's short-run profits are eliminated by the entry of new firms. As market share is lost, the firm's demand curve shifts down from D_1D_1 to D_2D_2, price falls, and profits are eliminated. Too many firms entering (D_3D_3) creates losses, which are eliminated by the exit of firms.

total cost curve. This demand is shown as D_3 in Figure 20-2. In this event, some firms will leave the market. After all these adjustments have taken place, the firm ends up operating at a price equal to average total cost. In this respect, monopolistic competition is similar to pure competition.

> **Conclusion:** In the long run, the monopolistically competitive firm ends up operating at a price equal to average total cost. The reason is clear enough. As long as price is more than average total cost, new firms will enter, thus reducing price. If, on the other hand, price is less than average total cost, firms will exit, thus raising price. It follows, therefore, that in the long run, price must be equal to average total cost.

Note, however, that this equality occurs at the point of tangency of the average total cost curve with the demand curve *to the left of the minimum point of the average total cost curve.* This must be so because the demand curve has a negative slope. Thus we may add to our conclusion above.

> **Conclusion:**   In the long run, the equilibrium price of the monopolistically competitive firm lies above marginal cost and to the left of the minimum average total cost.

3. Resource Misallocation

It would seem that in the long run, even with only normal returns being received, resources aren't allocated in an optimal manner—that is, allocative efficiency isn't being achieved. The reason rests with the nature of demand. Since the demand curve is negatively sloped, the long-run equilibrium price lies both above marginal cost and to the left of the minimum point of the firm's average total cost curve. Consumers, therefore, are not getting the benefit of the lowest possible price which still yields only normal returns. This of course is the long-run competitive equilibrium price that equals minimum average total cost.

This is a thorny issue over which there is no complete agreement among economists. The reason why the long-run monopolistically competitive equilibrium price lies above minimum average total cost is that the firm's demand curve is downward sloping because it produces differentiated products; thus the demand curve is equal to average total cost in the descending segment of the *ATC* curve. But product differentiation is a positive thing; it allows consumers variety and individuality of expression in consumption. Imagine how drab life would be if, for instance, everyone dressed in the same style and color of clothing—i.e., if we had to consume homogeneous products. There is no reason, of course, to expect that consumer satisfaction would be greater if we were compelled to consume identical products. Indeed, there is good reason to expect the contrary effect, that consumer satisfaction would be greater in the face of diversity of goods and services from which to choose.

Therefore, while it may be true that consumers could get products cheaper under pure competition, their desires for diversity of expression would go begging.

Most economists, when considering the trade-off between diversity of product and higher price (monopolistic competition) and homogeneity of product and lower price (pure competition), come down in favor of the former. This is true, however, only if there continues to be a large number of firms in the market, each so small that it has no significant market power in the long run.

B. MARKET CONCENTRATION AND OLIGOPOLY

Now we come to the most important of all the market structures—oligopoly. The very term *oligopoly* means that a few large sellers dominate the market, as in the automobile, spark plug, rubber, and aluminum industries. There is, however, no specific number of firms that must exist in an industry for it to be oligopolistic. Some industries may have only a "Big Three" or "Big Four," others may have a larger number of firms of roughly equal size (say, eight to ten), and still others may have the dominant few surrounded by a number of smaller firms. In all instances, however, there are two marks of oligopoly: First, each of the dominant firms is large enough to be a price maker and thus influence market price; second, each firm must take into account how its actions will affect is rival firms and then how it may react to their reactions. Aside from this, oligopolistic industries vary widely in their characteristics and often in their behavior.

It seems, therefore, that no one single theory of oligopoly can adequately explain oligopolistic price and output patterns. Still, theory or no theory, oligopoly is an important market structure that needs to be examined. It is in oligopolistic settings that we find the corporate giants of capitalism, and these firms have a substantial impact on the economy.

1. The Idea of Market Concentration

We begin this part of the discussion with a definition.

> **Definition:** *Market Concentration* measures the percentage of an industry's total output (or sales) accounted for by some given number of firms, say, the four largest, or the eight largest, or whatever number seems pertinent.

If, for example, the four largest firms produce 95 percent of the industry's output, then the four-firm ratio is 95. Or, if the four largest firms produce only 50 percent of the industry's output, the ratio is 50. Thus the concentration ratio is a measure of the degree of monopoly power in an industry.

Table 20–1 lists the four-firm and eight-firm concentration ratios for some major industries. However, the data presented here must be interpreted carefully. They are misleading in several respects. For one thing, Congress forbids the Census Bureau to disclose information on any single firm, no matter how large or small it

TABLE 20-1   Four- and Eight-Firm Concentration Ratios: Selected Product Groups, 1982 (Percentage of Shipment Value)

S.I.C. No.	Product	4-Firm	8-Firm
2011	Meat Packaging	29	43
2111	Cigarettes	84	—
2026	Fluid Milk	16	27
2711	Newspapers	22	34
3011	Tires and Tubes	66	86
2841	Soap and Detergents	60	73
3251	Brick and Structural Tile	24	35
3325	Steel Foundries	21	31
3334	Primary Aluminum	64	88
3632	Household Refrigerators and Freezers	94	98
3711	Automobiles	92	97
2067	Chewing Gum	95	D
2043	Cereal Breakfast Foods	86	D
3333	Primary Zinc	75	100
2771	Greeting Card Publishing	84	89
3467	Electric Lamps	91	96
3633	Household Laundry Equipment	91	D
3635	Household Vacuum Cleaners	80	96
3241	Cement	31	52

*D signifies withheld to avoid disclosure of undisclosed firm data.
Source: 1982 Census of Manufacturers: Concentration Ratios in Manufacturing, U.S. Department of Commerce, Table 5.

may be. In fact, the concentration ratios must cover no less than four firms, which means that a lot of one-firm and two-firm information is hidden.[1]

Also, the problem of defining an industry correctly is difficult to resolve. The Census Bureau makes use of a "four-digit" classification of industries. Meat packaging, for example, is classified by the four digits 2011, the cigarette industry by 2111, cereal by 2043, and so on. In fact, all the industries listed in Table 20–1 are four-digit industries.

This method of classification, however, can often be misleading. In the first place, it may be too broad. Many four-digit industries consist of firms that produce noncompeting products. A good example is industry 2026, "fluid milk." Lumping all producers of this product under one industry heading implies that they are in competition with one another. Yet, this is hardly the case. The milk producer in Spokane, Washington, is not at all in competition with the milk producer in Tampa, Florida. Each of these firms is operating in its own market area. Some other examples: 2711, newspapers (the *Birmingham Post-Herald* does not compete directly with the *Indianapolis Star*); 3241, cement (the cement plant in Norman, Oklahoma, is

[1]For a discussion of how the data can be interpreted appropriately, see W. G. Shepherd, *Market Power and Economic Welfare: An Introduction* (New York: Random House, 1970).

not concerned with the Atlanta, Georgia, plant); 3251, brick and structural tile; and so on for many other four-digit industries.

The classification scheme also ignores foreign competition, as well as competition from substitutes here at home. The four-digit automobile industry faces stiff competition from abroad, and therefore its concentration ratio of 92 percent is quite misleading. Similarly, the high-concentration ratio for metal cans means little, since the four-digit classification ignores the presence and use of glass and other containers.

All told, therefore, the Census data must be used carefully in assessing the extent of concentration in any particular market. Nonetheless, we can reach some useful conclusions about market concentration. One point of agreement is that in the case of pure monopoly, market concentration is complete; it stands at 100. Another point of agreement is that the concentration ratio in a purely competitive industry is so low as to be meaningless. Atomistic competition means a near zero concentration ratio for four, eight, a dozen, or even more firms. The situation is not much different for monopolistic competition. Oligopolistic industries, however, are characterized by numerous concentration ratios ranging from the 50's to the 90's. Table 20-1, despite its shortcomings, reveals this diversity of ratios.

2. Oligopoly and Mutual Interdependence

The key to whether an industry is oligopolistic is purely subjective and depends on the presence and intensity of conjectural interdependence.

> **Definition:**   If each firm feels that its economic fortunes are directly affected by its rivals' actions and that these rivals, in turn, are directly affected by its own actions, then the industry is oligopolistic.[2]

The firms, therefore are dependent on one another's actions, and they are fully aware of this interdependency. Consequently, their decisions depend largely on their assumptions of how rivals will react. Everything seems to be up in the air, and "casual observation suggests that virtually anything can happen."[3]

How concentrated must an industry or market be for this conjectural interdependence to become so pervasive? Probably when the four-firm ratio is 40 and greater.[4]

3. The Tendency toward Price Rigidity

A major consequence of conjectural interdependence among the firms in an oligopolistic industry is that, in the absence of collusion and under normal economic conditions, it creates a tendency toward price rigidity.

Consider this scenario. There are three or four dominant firms of about the same size and degree of efficiency in the industry. Also, these firms are producing

---

[2]F. M. Scherer, *Industrial Pricing: Theory and Evidence* (Chicago: Rand McNally, 1970), p. 2.
[3]Ibid., p. 3.
[4]Ibid.

products that are close substitutes for one another, and there are effective barriers to entry. Finally, there is no collusion among the firms. With the exception of the last assumption, the cigarette industry is a good example of these conditions.

Let's see what will happen when one firm, say, American Tobacco, considers raising the price of its brands of cigarettes. If it were to raise price, what would happen to the firm's total sales revenue? In this case, revenue would decline, and the reason is that the rival firms, with their close substitutes, probably wouldn't follow the price increase and hence would attract some customers from American. Knowing this (or at least believing this to be the case), the decision makers at American would be reluctant to raise price on their own; *they would fear that their rivals might not follow suit,* and thus they might well lose a substantial share of the market to them.

What, then, of a price reduction? Wouldn't this take sales away from the rival firms and hence raise revenue? The answer is no. If American Tobacco were to cut prices and start to attract new customers from Liggett & Meyers and the others, then it could probably count on the other firms also cutting prices in order to maintain their market shares. Indeed, the rival firms could conceivably undercut American and thus set off a price war. The result, in any event, would be lower prices and lower revenues for all the firms. Again, knowing that this might well be the consequence, the American decision-makers would be reluctant to cut prices; *they would fear that their rivals would follow suit* as all firms strove to maintain market shares.

> **Conclusion:**   In the absence of collusion, each firm in an oligopolistic industry is reluctant to raise or lower prices because of the *presumed* reactions of its rivals. Thus, when collusion is absent, the prices charged by oligopolistic firms tend to be rigid and inflexible.

4. Some Important Implications

Two important implications and an equally important conclusion can be drawn from the preceding analysis. First, there can be no price response to changes in demand (under normal market conditions). Suppose demand for the product rises. Basic supply and demand analysis tells us that price too will rise. This would certainly be the case for pure competition, pure monopoly, and monopolistic competition. Furthermore, if demand were to fall, we would expect that price would also fall. But these predictions prove to be false in the case of noncollusive oligopoly, for each firm, fearful of its rivals' reactions, is afraid to raise or lower price.

Exceptions to this tendency toward price rigidity in noncollusive oligopoly are found in times of severe recession and strong boom. If the industry were to experience a serious and obvious downturn, price cutting would be likely to break out as the individual firms strove to maintain sales volume. There is a sort of "everyone for himself" attitude that prevails among the firms in this serious situation. On the other hand, if there is a very strong and durable demand for the industry's products so that all producers are close to capacity, it is likely that the reluctance to raise price will be overcome. In this event, each firm knows that a price increase won't result in a loss of sales to rivals, since rivals have no excess capacity. Thus, other firms are quick to follow a price boost. Nonetheless, our earlier result holds under normal market conditions—that is, noncollusive oligopoly price doesn't respond to changing demand conditions.

The second implication is that the noncollusive oligopolist firms can't respond to changing cost conditions. If, under normal circumstances, variable costs rise, each firm may want to raise price but is afraid to do so. Similarly, when costs fall, each firm may want to cut price but again is afraid of the anticipated reactions of its rivals.

> **Conclusion:**   Noncollusive oligopolists can't be expected to maximize profits as long as their conjectures of each other's responses result in price rigidity. Price, under these circumstances, isn't changed to reflect changing cost and demand conditions.

Now perhaps we can see why collusion among rival firms is as common as it is in oligopolistic industries. Collusion among firms nearly always has one basic objective, and that is to introduce some degree of price flexibility. This way the firms can respond to changing cost and demand conditions.

C. PATTERNS OF COLLUSION

There are numerous types of collusion; as one student of market concentration put its, "only the bounds of ingenuity" put a limit to the diversity of collusive activity.[5] In this section, we look at a few of the major types of collusion.

1. Joint Profit Maximization (Cartels)

Let's begin with a cartel arrangement that has as its objective the maximization of the *joint profits* of the members of the cartel. To simplify the analysis, suppose there are only two or three firms in the industry producing close substitutes. Also suppose that these firms are quite willing to form a cartel; they feel that it is in their best interests.

> **Definition:**   A *cartel* is a formal agreement among the firms in an industry designed to restrict output, raise price, and hence increase the profits of the member firms.

The term *formal agreement* in the definition means that a cartel can come into being only through an explicit agreement among the firms. One of the first orders of business is for the representatives of each firm to estimate the demand for their combined products. They then decide on the price that they feel will maximize the *combined profits* of the firms. This means that the cartel will pay close attention to

[5]Ibid., p. 30.

the $MC = MR$ rule for profit maximization, but now the rule has a new twist. The MC isn't the same as the one we have been using; rather, it is the horizontal sum of the MC curves of the firms in the industry.

Given the summed MC curve, the joint profit-maximizing price and output are easy to discover, as shown in Figure 20-3. In this case, the maximizing price is P and the equilibrium output is Q. Only at this price-output combination will the combined profits of the cartel members be the greatest.

However, the cartel now faces a serious problem, namely, How are the joint profits to be divided among the firms? We might expect some arguments and disagreements to develop here and thus threaten the stability of the arrangement. Indeed, if any firm decides to improve its profit position by offering hidden price cuts, breakdown is almost assured. On the other hand, if the arrangement is successful, the price charged by the cartel is a pure monopoly price. Consequently, its impact on resource allocation will be the same as under pure monopoly. But if the cartel agreement is ineffective—that is, the greater the tendency of individual firms to break away in order to increase their own profits—the closer will price be to the competitive level.

2. Dominant Firm Price Leadership

Collusion among firms doesn't always have to be based on explicit, overt agreement. In fact, a lot of collusion is implicit or tacit; this is, the firms in the industry tend to agree on a particular pricing policy without even discussing the procedure among

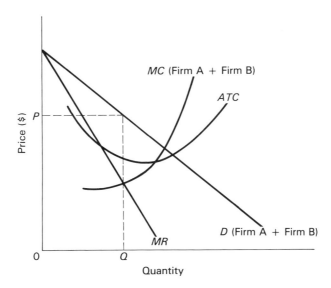

Figure 20-3   Joint Profit Maximization of Two-Firm Oligopoly   Two firms in collusion combine to act as a monopoly. They maximize joint profits by producing the level of output that equates the total market marginal revenue with the combined marginal costs of production of the two firms.

themselves. Price leadership is a common form of this type of collusion. Two major types of price leadership are dominant firm and barometric firm price leadership.

Dominant firm price leadership is found in industries dominated by one large firm. For a long time, the steel industry was considered the prime example of this type of collusion. Another good example is the cigarette industry. Presumably the dominant firm will set the price that maximizes its profits, and the other firms will match that price. There are, however, two problems. First, the dominant firm might be so efficient that its profit-maximizing price would be low enough that the less-efficient firms might not survive. Second, the profit-maximizing price might be high enough to attract new firms into the industry and hence create potential competition.

In both cases, the dominant firm will have to modify its pricing policy. In the fist case, it would have to charge a price higher than the profit-maximizing price in order to place a protective umbrella over the less-efficient firms. Thus, while the dominant firm may be unable to maximize its profits, it can at least avoid the charge of trying to monopolize the industry by driving the less-efficient firms out. In the second case, the dominant firm will have to cut price below the profit-maximizing level in order to prevent entry. The threat of entry, therefore, works in the opposite direction from the threat of antimonopoly litigation.

It is difficult to describe the precise impact of dominant firm price leadership on resource allocation. Although the dominant firm may want to act like a pure monopolist, it can't because it must consider both the other firms in the industry and the threat of potential entrants. So, in the one case it charges a higher price, while in the other it charges a lower price than the profit-maximizing monopoly price. Once again, therefore, we are forced to recognize that no sound generalization can be reached about the impact of monopoly on resource allocation.

3. Barometric Firm Price Leadership

In barometric price leadership, there is no one dominant firm; rather there are a large number of firms (say, ten to fifteen), each being about the same size and having the same degree of efficiency. There may also be a "competitive" fringe of small firms.

Any one of the larger firms may be the price leader, but the one that is generally accepted as the price leader is the firm whose management seems to be adept at anticipating changing market conditions. This superior skill may be due to experience, greater knowledge, or just plain shrewdness. In any event, the price-leader firm is a better barometer of changing market conditions than any of the other firms, and consequently the remaining firms in the industry are content to follow the leader.

One interesting thing about this type of price leadership is that the barometric firm doesn't have its position of leadership guaranteed. As long as the other firms follow its moves, it will continue as leader. But if the followers dissent—if they conclude that the leader has made one too many mistakes—they will refuse to follow, and another firm is apt to emerge as the new leader. All of these changes, however, are quite voluntary; no one firm imposes its will on the rest. Barometric firm price leadership, therefore, is difficult to prosecute in the courts, as are most forms of tacit collusion.

Some economists have argued that it is perhaps unwise to prosecute barometric firm price leadership, since this type of collusion often results in price being set at, or near, the competitive level. In fact, it may be argued that this type of price leadership simply introduces order into an otherwise chaotic situation. When market conditions change, price will be adjusted either up or down; but under barometric firm price leadership, the adjustments are made in an orderly manner.

Other types of tacit collusion take the form of agreement on some sort of cost-plus pricing and other rules of thumb, as well as "gentlemen's agreements."

4. Instability of Collusion

Most collusion among firms tends to be unstable for a number of reasons. The ever-present antitrust laws serve as a major constraint (see Chapter 21). Although these laws have certainly served as deterrents to effective collusive practices, they definitely haven't eliminated them.

Another reason for the instability of collusion is that some firms in the industry may be more efficient than the others. These firms are often tempted to break away from the agreement in order to increase their profits. Hidden discounts and other price concessions are a common means of circumventing the arrangement and attracting more business to the violator firm. Once this becomes known, the collusive arrangement breaks down.

A third reason for the instability of collusion is the threat of potential entry by new firms. In other words, barriers to entry may not be strong enough to prevent new competition from entering the industry when the existing firms adhere to a high-profit collusive price. This may be a strong factor when the potential rivals are already existing foreign firms looking for entry into the American market.

Finally, high rates of innovation breed instability of collusion. New methods of production, as well as the introduction of new products or important product changes, make permanent collusion difficult. When conditions are ever changing, it is almost impossible to maximize joint profits or to adhere to a price leader.

Despite these sources of instability, collusive oligopoly is quite common. Moreover, when it does break down, agreement is often restored very quickly. As long as there are oligopolistic industries, there will be attempts to collude.

D. THE COURTS AND COLLUSIVE BEHAVIOR

The next chapter deals with the antitrust laws at length, but some discussion of them is in order here. Section 1 of the Sherman Act says that all contracts, combinations, and conspiracies in restraint of trade are illegal. These three terms—contracts, combinations, conspiracies—are used interchangeably to refer to any concerted activity among two or more firms to restrain trade or commerce.

The types of collusion that are overt or explicit are more easily prosecuted by government. Exhibit 20-1 provides a good example. What is bothersome for the government is tacit collusion in which no formal agreements are made. In fact, the courts have consistently ruled that identical (or parallel) prices, in and of themselves, don't necessarily imply collusion or illegal conspiracy. Recall that even in the absence of collusion, there is a strong tendency for the firms in an oligopolistic industry to charge identical or parallel prices. In fact, conjectural interdependence means that each firm must consider the policies of its rivals when determining its own policy, and this can hardly be construed as an illegal conspiracy.

In some cases, however, the courts have used price uniformity and uniform price changes over time as evidence against the firms and hence found them in viola-

---

EXHIBIT 20-1
The Electrical Equipment Conspiracy Case

The courts have consistently held that agreements to fix prices violate the Sherman Act and are thus illegal. The Supreme Court took this position as early as 1898 in the *Addington Pipe and Steel Company* case, and it reaffirmed its stand in the *Trenton Potteries* case of 1927. In fact, in the 1940 *Socony-Vaccum* case, the Court stated: "For over forty years the Court has consistently and without deviation adhered to the principle that price fixing agreements are unlawful '*per se*' under the Sherman Act." Of course, the lower courts have recognized the High Court's position.

Much to the embarrassment of the electrical equipment industry twenty-one years later, the courts maintained their steadfastness. The representatives of General Electric, Westinghouse, and two smaller firms met secretly in order to set prices on electrical equipment and to divide the market among themselves. As it turned out, GE got 42 percent of the market, Westinghouse got 38 percent, Allis-Chalmers 11 percent, and ITE 9 percent.

Also as a part of the conspiracy, the firms agreed on a method to rig bids to utilities (both private and public). Their formula relied on the phases of the moon to determine which firm would bid lowest on a contract. From 1950 to 1959 the companies, using this conspiracy, sold $4 billion of equipment to utilities and other customers, of which millions of dollars of profits were excessive.

The federal court responded by imprisoning seven executives, fining the companies $1.9 million, and opening the door to a large number of costly private treble-damage suits by the affected customers.

The moral to be drawn from this ruling is that price-fixing agreements can be costly and embarrassing, especially as long as the courts use the criminal provisions of the laws. Price-fixing conspiracies should definitely be avoided.

tion of the law. In other cases, such circumstantial evidence didn't matter. Clearly, the interpretation of the law continues to be in a state of flux. Our conclusion, then, is quite tentative.

> **Conclusion:**   When it can be shown that price uniformity is the result of overt collusion, the antitrust laws will be used against the colluding firms. However, uniformity of prices in and of itself isn't illegal, although it can be used as circumstantial evidence that some sort of conspiracy does exist.

We have much more to say about the antitrust laws in the next chapter.

E. SUMMARY

Monopolistic competition is similar to pure competition in that there are many buyers and sellers and there are no serious barriers to entry and exit from the industry. The monopoly element is that each firm produces a differentiated product.

Successful product differentiation is the source of profits for monopolistically competitive firms in the short run. In the long run, profits tend to be competed away by the entry of new firms into the market.

Oligopoly exists when a few usually large firms dominate a specific market. The degree of domination is imperfectly measured by concentration ratios, or the percentage of market sales accounted for by the leading firms. Under normal economic conditions and where collusion between firms doesn't exist, prices in oligopolistic markets tend to be relatively stable. Firms thus compete on some basis other than price.

Because of their large size, each firm's pricing policies can dramatically affect the other firms. For that reason, there is a tendency toward collusion between the firms in an industry. Where the law permits, collusion can take the form of cartels, or formal agreements to maximize the joint profits of the competitors. Less-formal forms of collusion include price leadership by either the dominant firm or by the firm most adept at anticipating changing market conditions.

All collusive agreements, whether explicit or tacit, tend to be unstable in the long run.

Terms and Concepts to Remember

Oligopoly	Collusion
Product differentiation	Nonprice competition
Concentration ratios	Cartel
Price leadership	

Questions for Review

1. Using the fast-food industry, give some examples of successful product differentiation. Why are most of these successes temporary?

2. What strategies might monopolistically competitive firms use to fend off long-run competition?

3. Why would an oligopolistic firm be reluctant to raise price on its own? To voluntarily reduce price?

4. Other than price competition, what types of competitive devices are used by oligopolistic firms?

5. List and define the major types of collusion that oligopolists have used.

6. Why are collusive agreements among oligopolists usually short lived?

7. What forces have weakened the Organization of Petroleum Exporting Countries (OPEC) cartel agreement in the past few years?

21

Microeconomic Policy: Big Business, Big Unions

chapter preview

- The merger movement in the United States began in earnest during the late nineteenth century.
- A merger occurs when two or more firms combine into a single firm.
- There are three types of mergers—horizontal, vertical, and conglomerate.
- Mergers lead to substantial deviations from competition.
- The cornerstone of antimonopoly legislation in the United States is the Sherman Act of 1890.
- The Supreme Court ruled in 1911 that large size alone is not illegal. A monopoly, however, may be illegal if unreasonable tactics and methods were used by management in reaching that size.
- This and other early court interpretations of the Sherman Act led to additional legislation over the years, the purpose of which was to prevent monopoly power and abusive actions by business firms.
- Important here are the Clayton Act, the Celler-Kefauver Act, and the Federal Trade Commission Act.
- There is, however, little agreement among economists on how effective this legislation and its enforcement

have been.
- In earlier years, the legal system worked against the union movement in the United States, but by 1945 the movement had the strong support of the law.
- Early unions were organized along craft lines, but the rise of mass production fostered the growth of unions organized along industry lines. In 1946 the craft-oriented A.F.L. and the industry-oriented C.I.O. merged.
- More recent legislation, however, such as the Taft-Hartley Act and the Landrum-Griffin Act, has been less favorable to unions.
- In recent years, union membership as a percentage of the work force has declined. Total membership has also fallen.
- Unions raise the wages of their members by restricting the supply of labor. When successful, this pushes the union wage above the market equilibrium level and creates unemployment for some workers.
- Overall, however, the economic impact of unions seems to have been exaggerated.

Ever since Adam Smith, the idea of the competitive market has appealed to economists (it has probably appealed more to them than to anyone else). Recall that if the competitive market works correctly, it provides the most efficient use of resources and the appropriate mixture of goods for consumers. In the long run, consumers collectively get what they demand at prices at which sellers receive only normal returns. These alone are good reasons for favoring competitive markets.

Yet, as we saw in Chapter 6, the market system doesn't always function properly. In that chapter, we discussed several types of market failures. Here we concentrate on only two—the emergence and growth of big business and big unions. Many economists feel that these concentrations of economic power have seriously affected the functioning of the market system. Government, of course, has responded through legislation. Our purpose here is to describe and evaluate this response.

Section A of this chapter examines American antitrust policies toward business, especially the laws that are supposed to prevent monopoly and encourage competition. Section B reviews legislation with respect to labor unions—a form of labor market monopoly. Finally, Section C examines the economic impact of unions.

A. REGULATION OF BUSINESS MONOPOLY

Business firms have achieved monopoly power in several ways. Control over raw-material supplies and patents, and various forms of governmental protection, have been important. Natural monopolies due to economies of size have also been important. New products and technical innovation in production have proliferated, particularly in more recent times. Probably the most common way in which firms have expanded is through merger, which allows firms to achieve certain types of economies of size. About a century ago, our economy experienced its first big wave of mergers—the first significant step away from a competitive heritage.

A *merger* is simply two or more companies combining into a single organization. It was this first wave of mergers that created a new type of industry structure—one in which the market is dominated by a relatively few large firms (i.e., oligopoly). This was true of a number of industries—steel, sugar, oil, tobacco products, and lead, to name a few. This period was the birth date of U.S. Steel (now USX), Standard Oil (now a number of Standard Oils), American Tobacco, and some other large corporations that are still with us in one form or other (see Exhibit 21–1).

This merger movement created a great deal of public concern. The initial response was the first important antimonopoly legislation, the Sherman Act of 1890.

Before discussing the Sherman Act and subsequent legislation, however, we need to define some important terms.

1. Mergers of Different Types

We defined *merger* as two or more companies combining into a single organization. However, these combinations can be of several types. In fact, three types of mergers have taken place in the American economy (see Figure 21-1). Let's begin with the idea of a horizontal merger.

> **Definition:**   A *horizontal merger* occurs when one company acquires another that sells the same product or service in the same market.

Horizontal mergers were the usual type of combination during the first merger movement in the late 1800s. Through this type of combination, U.S. Steel was born and grew to its eventual dominance. And this was how General Motors came into being; it was an amalgamation of Chevrolet, Oldsmobile, Buick, and Cadillac, all originally separate firms. A modern example was the 1987 merger of Greyhound and Trailways, the two dominant firms in the field of bus transportation.

Other types of mergers have played a major role in the economy.

> **Definition:**   A *vertical merger* takes place when one firm acquires another that is either a supplier or a customer.

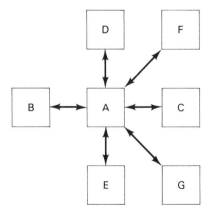

FIGURE 21-1   Different Types of Merger   Firms are motivated to merge by the profit opportunities of doing so. The forms of merger are as follows:
Firms A, B, and C combine—Horizontal Merger
Firms A and D combine—Vertical (downstream) merger
Firms A and E combine—Vertical (Upstream) Merger
Firms A, F, and G combine—Conglomerate Merger

A good example is A&P, the one-time retail grocery giant, which acquired bakeries, canneries, and other food supply firms. This is an example of *backward* (upstream) vertical integration (see Figure 21-1). There is also *forward* (downstream) vertical integration when a supplier acquires a customer firm. For instance, in 1962 the Brown Shoe Company tried to merge with a chain of retail shoe stores. Vertical mergers have been very important in recent years.

Even more important is a quite different type of merger that has dominated the scene in recent decades. Both kinds of mergers we have examined so far involve firms that are related in a direct economic sense. Not so for the next type.

> **Definition:**   A *conglomerate merger* occurs when the merging firms are in completely unrelated industries or markets.

Most of the large corporations in the United States are conglomerates—Xerox, General Foods, Sears Roebuck, USX; indeed, all the major corporations in the United States are now conglomerates. Conglomerate mergers were numerous in the late 1960s and early 1970s. By the mid-1970s, however, many firms found that they had bitten off more than they could chew. They had expanded into areas beyond their expertise of management. Accordingly, many firms divested themselves of some of their previous acquisitions. But then a reversal took place in the 1980s. The conglomerate movement accounted for the fantastic rise in mergers that accompanied the restructuring of the economy in the late 1970s and early 1980s. The law is very murky on conglomerate mergers.

2. The Sherman Act of 1890

As we mentioned above, the first merger movement triggered the passage of the Sherman Act in 1890. (It was one of those rare pieces of legislation that passed both houses of Congress with only one negative vote.) The act stands as the cornerstone of nearly all of our antimonopoly legislation. It is very short, consisting of two brief sections. They are worth quoting:

> Section 1. Every contract, combination in the form of a trust or otherwise, in restraint of trade or commerce among the several states, or with foreign nations, is hereby declared to be illegal. Every person who shall make any contract or engage in such combination, shall be deemed guilty of a misdemeanor. . . .

> Section 2. Every person who shall monopolize, or attempt to monopolize, or combine to conspire with any other person, or persons, to monopolize any part of the trade or commerce among the several states, or with foreign nations, shall be deemed guilty of a misdemeanor. . . . [1]

This wording sounds tough, but how tough it actually is depends on how the courts interpret it. And, as we shall see, the courts have tended to weaken the impact

---

[1]The Sherman Act is reprinted in E.W. Kintner, *An Antitrust Primer* (New York: Macmillan, 1973), pp. 281–283.

of the act in various cases. In fact, some economists argue that court decisions have changed the meaning of the law from the original intent of Congress.

Shortly after passage, the act was used mainly against labor unions and hardly at all against business. When used against business, the penalties imposed were light. During the Taft and Roosevelt administrations (1901–13), enforcement of the act toughened. In 1911, the Supreme Court declared two of the largest industrial concerns—Standard Oil and American Tobacco—to be illegal monopolies.

Critics of big business hailed these two decisions as a major step. They thought that after twenty years, the Court had finally put some teeth into the Sherman Act. After all, two giants had been toppled in the same year.

The two decisions, however, weakened the act instead of putting teeth into it. Why? How? In this way: The Court ruled that American Tobacco and Standard Oil

EXHIBIT 21-1
Why the Sherman Antitrust Act?

As business grew in the latter part of the nineteenth century, a new challenge to competition developed—the trust. A good illustration was the Standard Oil Trust, formed in 1881 under the guiding hand of John D. Rockefeller. The idea was simply for the stockholders of each competing company to assign their voting rights to a central group of "trustees," who would then vote the stock for the benefit of the stockholders. What this procedure did, of course, was to allow the trust to make decisions as a near pure monopoly; all competition among the firms was wiped away. Here was a legal manipulation that replaced competition with monopoly.

The purpose of the Sherman Antitrust Act now becomes clear—it was passed to outlaw all agreements, contracts, and trusts that restrained trade.

The Standard Oil Trust was so successful that it bred a number of others, and interestingly many of these were formed after the Sherman Act was passed. Indeed, some students of the trust movement estimated that, by 1904, trusts controlled about 40 percent of the manufacturing capital in the economy. Around this time, the following trusts were created: Western Union, U.S. Gypsum, Allis-Chalmers, American Can, United Fruit, the Tobacco Trust, U.S. Steel, General Electric, the Sugar Trust, U.S. Rubber, United Shoe, International Salt, International Nickel, Pullman Company, National Biscuit Company, Standard Sanitary, and National Lead.* Many of these names are still important in any list of major corporations in the United States.

Numerous other, but unsuccessful, trusts were formed during these years—e.g., in chewing gum, bicycles, caramels, buttons, and ice.†

*This list is from D. Heminway, *Prices and Choices: Microeconomic Vignettes* (Cambridge, MA: Ballinger Publishing, 1984), p. 187.
†See *ibid* for an interesting discussion of one of these unsuccessful trusts, pp. 187–204.

were monopolies *because of the tactics and activities used in reaching their large size.* To use the Court's own term, they had behaved "unreasonably" in attaining their monopoly positions.[2]

Therefore, and this is what is important, the Court ruled that large size alone isn't illegal; it also ruled that restraints of trade aren't illegal *as long as they are "reasonable."* In other words, the Supreme Court ruled that only "unreasonable" restraints of trade are illegal as far as the Sherman Act is concerned.

Many economists, however, have found this decision off the mark. Our discussion in Chapters 15 and 19 showed that monopoly leads to an inefficient allocation of resources—that is, a monopoly hikes its price by restricting output. The economist is typically opposed to monopolies of all kinds, whether they behave "reasonably" or "unreasonably" according to some legal definition. What matters is that a monopoly is in fact a monopoly, and this in itself is harmful to consumers. Competition is much more desirable.

The "rule of reason" dominated antitrust policy for a quarter of a century, but then there seemed to be a reversal. Beginning with the *Alcoa* case in 1945, the Supreme Court's new attitude seemed to be that "big is bad" and that this is so even if the monopoly power isn't abused by the firm. Thus bigness alone was interpreted as a violation of the Sherman Act. This was a major decision and was applied in a number of important cases—the *American Tobacco* case (1946), the *Griffith Amusement* case (1948), the *A&P* case (1949), and the *United Shoe Machinery* case (1953).

3. The Clayton Act of 1914

The 1911 decision in the Standard Oil and American Tobacco cases stimulated Congress to action once again. Three years later it passed the Clayton Act. Although the Clayton Act is an ammendment to the Sherman Act, the two pieces of legislation differ considerably. Remember that under the 1911 cases, the Sherman Act can be used to challenge monopoly only after it is established and even then only if the methods used to achieve the position were "unreasonable."

The Clayton Act, on the other hand, attempts to be *preventive.* If any business practice is thought to lessen competition, the act can be used to stop it. For example, tie-in contracts, exclusive dealerships, and interlocking directorates are clearly deemed to be illegal. Accordingly, actions can be brought by the Justice Department's Antitrust Division, which enforces the law against violators who aren't already monopolistic on the grounds that their activities may tend to lessen competition and hence create monopoly.

4. Section 7 and the Celler-Kefauver Act

Section 7 of the Clayton Act deserves special mention because of some recent Court decisions. Section 7 makes it illegal for a corporation to purchase the stock of another if the result is to lessen competition. When the act was first passed, most economists felt that it would finally halt monopoly-creating mergers.

[2]See Ibid pp. 17–18 for the Supreme Court's use of the rule of reason in these decisions.

But business firms found an easy way to circumvent Section 7. Since it was illegal to purchase the stock of another firm, they simply purchased the *physical assets* instead. Hence the power of the Clayton Act to prevent undesirable mergers was diluted.

So, just as the Sherman act had been amended by the Clayton Act, the Clayton Act was in turn amended by the Celler-Kefauver Act in 1950. This act makes it illegal for any company to purchase the physical assets of another if "the effect of such an acquisition may be substantively to lessen competition, or to tend to create a monopoly."[3]

How has the Clayton Act, as amended by the Celler-Kefauver Act, been used? During the past two decades or so, some important decisions have been handed down by the courts. Two of these merit a specific look. They are the *Bethlehem-Youngstown* case (1967) and the *Brown Shoe* case (1962).

The *Bethlehem-Youngstown* case is important because it relates to horizontal mergers. In this case, the Court ruled that if Bethlehem and Youngstown merged, they would (as a single firm) control 20 percent of the national market for steel. Twenty percent doesn't sound much like a monopoly, but along with U.S. Steel's 30 percent, this meant that only two firms would control over 50 percent of the national market. The Court felt that these two firms would probably cooperate and act in such a way that competition would be lessened.

In recent years, however, the Justice Department has used another method of determining whether a horizontal merger is allowable. This is the Herfindahl-Hirschman Index (HHI), which is a measure of the degree of concentration or monopoly power in an industry. Generally, the greater the number of firms and the more equal their size, the lower the index. Also, the smaller the number of firms and the more unequal their size, the higher the index.

For our purposes, three rules of thumb are pertinent. First, if any proposed merger results in the HHI being less than 1,000, it won't be challenged. When the index is this low, the market is unconcentrated. Second, when the index stands between 1,000 and 1,800, the market is considered to be moderately concentrated, and any merger that raises the index by 100 points or more will be challenged. Finally, the market is considered to be highly concentrated if the index is already greater than 1,800 points, and the only mergers allowed are those that raise the index by less than 50 points. These increases are quite substantial, and hence the guidelines on horizontal mergers are less strict than in the preceding three decades.

Conglomerate mergers are carried out for various reasons. Since these types of mergers are between firms producing unrelated products or services, the motive of combining may not be obvious at first glance. One motive may be to achieve economies of size in the flows of cash needed to sustain each unit's operations. Centrally pooled cash management can reduce the funds needed below those required for the total of all firms separately. Unrelated business units often complement each other when cash flows are considered seasonally or cyclically. For example, a production unit with cash inflows that are high in winter and low in summer can help finance another unit with opposite seasonal flows. Units whose earnings

[3]Ibid., p. 300.

are sensitive to cyclical swings can be supported by another unit whose earnings are stable over time. Finally, units producing and selling in established mature markets can generate the cash to help finance promising new-product divisions.

We have no specific laws to deal with conglomerate mergers. They fall outside both the Sherman Act and the Clayton Act. In fact, very few conglomerate mergers have been challenged, and the few decisions handed down have followed no general pattern. Some economists, however, argue that Section 7 of the Clayton Act should be further amended so that some control over conglomerate mergers can be established.

What do the recent rulings on conglomerate mergers mean? We will consider this question after we take a look at the Federal Trade Commission Act.

5. The Federal Trade Commission Act (1914)

As with the Clayton Act, the Federal Trade Commission Act stands as a roadblock on the way to monopoly. This act established the Federal Trade Commission (FTC) to enforce the provisions of the law. Any business practice that results in restraint of trade and a lessening of competition falls under the purview of the FTC. Also, many of the practices illegal under the Federal Trade Commission Act are also illegal under the Clayton Act. For example, price discrimination, tie-in contracts, and exclusive dealing contracts are definitely illegal under both laws.

The FTC act, however, goes further. It specifies that commercial bribery, commercial espionage, the pirating of trade secrets, vexatious lawsuits, illegal lottery schemes, and misleading packaging are illegal business practices. Also, and very important, the FTC can take action against all forms of deceptive and misleading advertising. This power was extended in 1958 by the Wheeler-Lea Act.

All told, the FTC act is preventive. As the Supreme Court put it: "[A] major purpose [of the act], as we have frequently said, was to enable the Commission to restrain practices as 'unfair' which, although not yet having grown into Sherman Act dimensions, would most likely do so if left unrestrained."[4] Hence the FTC act serves as another barrier to the growth of monopoly.

6. Where Do We Stand?

What is the future of antimonopoly policy in the United States? There are two schools of thought on this matter. The first school argues that there is really a lot of effective competition among the large firms in our economy. Advocates of this view argue that, for example, USX competes not only with other steel producers but also with the firms in the aluminum, lumber, and plastic industries—all of which produce products that substitute for one another. Furthermore, they assert that in a real sense, all firms are in competition with each other for the consumer's dollar.

This school of thought also argues that advances in technology, as well as rapid introduction of new products and methods of production, eventually tend to

[4]Ibid., p. 116.

destroy or weaken existing monopoly positions. Moreover, large firms do compete intensely with each other in the form of nonprice competition. Style, model changes, and quality improvements promoted through advertising are apparently as important to consumers as price competition. Consumers are interested in quality, style, and the social acceptability of many goods and services that they consume. Hence competition over these things is justified and desirable.

Finally, this school of thought argues that the Sherman, Clayton, and FTC acts are all very much out of date. Large-scale, low-unit-cost production and advanced technology make big business both unavoidable and desirable. In addition, large domestic business units are necessary to compete in today's increasingly global markets. We have long passed the days of the small firm and pure competition; they can't and shouldn't be revived. Therefore the antimonopoly laws should be repealed, and any new laws regulating business should recognize modern technology and the phenomenon of worldwide competition.

The second school of thought disagrees almost completely with the first. Economists in this group argue that big firms are no more efficient (in terms of productive costs) than medium-size and small firms. There are considerable empirical data to support this position. The reason why the big firms are big is that they actively seek monopoly power, perhaps by employing many of the illegal practices proscribed under the Clayton and FTC acts.

These economists also contend that much of the advertising, style changes, and other forms of nonprice competition are wasteful. Procter & Gamble, for example, produces Bold, Bonus, Cheer, Dash, Duz, Oxydol, Dreft, Tide, Salvo, Ivory Snow, Joy, Thrill, Ivory Flakes, Zest, Ivory Liquid, Cascade, Comet, Camay, Lava, Mr. Clean, and Spic and Span—and Procter & Gamble advertises that each of these is superior to others. Wasteful? Perhaps.

This school of thought argues that the antitrust laws should be vigorously enforced to break up big business into smaller more competitive firms. The pendulum has recently swung in favor of the first school of thought. The Reagan administration made it easier for horizontal mergers to occur and also made it easier for vertical and conglomerate mergers. Whether the pendulum will swing back in the future remains to be seen.

7. Price Discrimination

One final area of microeconomic policy, as it pertains to business, needs to be considered. This is price discrimination.

Price discrimination can be defined as charging different prices to customers when those price differences are *not* based on cost differences. Sellers use price discrimination for different reasons. One is that profits can be increased by charging different prices. More important for our purposes is that a seller may discriminate by selling below competitor's prices in one market in order to drive them out of business. Once accomplished, this seller can make up for earlier lost profits by then charging higher prices. Similarly, he can charge high prices in markets where his position is strong enough to cover losses in markets where he is cutting prices.

Price discrimination is illegal under both the Sherman Act and the Federal Trade Commission Act. But there is still another law—the Robinson-Patman Act (1936)—that deals directly with this type of pricing. The Robinson-Patman Act makes price differentials not based on cost differentials illegal. The Supreme Court has been very strict in enforcing this act.

B. LABOR UNIONS AND MICROECONOMIC POLICY

Along with big business and big government, the American economy has big labor unions. Labor unions exercise monopoly power in labor markets. In effect, they represent individual workers in the sale of labor services to employers. The purpose of unions is to improve the general welfare of their members. One way to do so is to raise wages by restricting the supply of labor.

1. The Evolution of Unionism in the United States

Figure 21–2 illustrates several important things about the growth of the union movement in the United States.

First, the union movement isn't a new phenomenon. As the figure shows, it goes back to at least 1900. Actually, union activity of a minimal sort can be traced to colonial times. By the mid-nineteenth century, a concerted labor movement began to develop with the rapid economic expansion of that period. The Noble Order of the Knights of Labor started as a secret organization in 1869. Politically oriented, the Knights of Labor sought public ownership of utilities, an eight-hour day, and equal pay for equal work through the legislative process. More generally, it wanted to replace the existing capitalist system with a society of cooperatives. In the 1880s, internal conflicts weakened the organization. It finally disappeared in 1917.

Second, unions as a mass movement didn't really get under way until the Great Depression of the 1930s and World War II. Union membership rose from about 3 million in the early 1930s to about 15 million in the mid-1940s. This is tremendous growth and will be explained below.

Third, following World War II there was another upsurge in membership, although at a slower pace than the previous growth. As a percentage of the labor force, union membership reached a peak of 25 percent in the postwar period.

In more recent times, union membership has declined both absolutely and as a percentage of the labor force. All of this needs to be evaluated.

2. The Period of Repression

What held back the growth of the union movement until the 1930s? It was simply this: In the struggle between workers and employers, the employers had the upper hand because, in many instances, the courts sided with the employers against the unions.

Employers used several effective devices against the workers' efforts to orga-

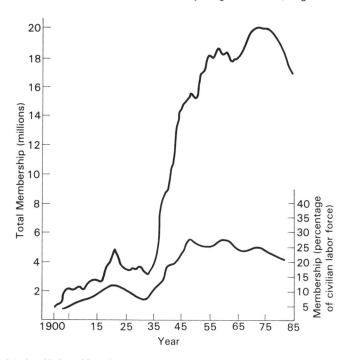

FIGURE 21-2   Union Membership in the United States   Union membership, in both total numbers and as a percentage of the labor force, increased dramatically in the 1930s. By the end of World War II, membership as a percentage of the labor force peaked, although total membership rose until the mid-1970s. Since that time, membership has declined.

nize. One of these was the so-called yellow-dog contract—that is, a contract signed by the worker in which he agrees not to join or help organize a union as long as he is employed by the firm. If a person did either of these things, he was in violation of the contract and could be fired. But why sign such a contract in the first place? Because he couldn't get the job without signing it.

Another device used was, purely and simply, violence. Quite often employers had the support of federal and state officials when it came to force. A famous case in point was the Ludlow Massacre of 1914. Another was the Pullman strike of 1894. Such events were common during the early growth of unionism in the United States.

We mentioned above that the legal system also worked against the formation of unions during the suppression period. Up to the important *Commonwealth of Massachusetts* v. *Hunt* case in 1842, the courts had consistently ruled against unions on the grounds that they were "conspiracies or combinations in restraint of trade." Although the *Hunt* case slowed this action down, it was revived again under the Sherman Act. In fact, most of the early cases under Sherman Act were directed against unions.

Still another legal device used against the union was the injunction. An *injunction* is a court order that restrains a party from some course of action if the result of the action would be damages that can't be recovered. The injunction was used against unions in the following manner. If workers strike, production stops. As a result, there is lost output that can never be sold, and therefore lost revenue that can never be recovered. On the basis of this kind of reasoning, courts were willing to issue injunctions against workers and unions to prevent their striking.

Such devices kept the growth of the union movement slow and faltering until the 1930s. Nonetheless some strides were made. The American Federation of Labor (AFL) was formed in 1886. The AFL was organized along craft lines, under the strong leadership of Samuel Gompers. A *craft union* is an organization of workers with common skills, such as plumbers, brickmasons, or carpenters. For many years, the AFL dominated the union movement in this country.

Gompers introduced three basic principles into the American labor movement: (1) although unions are united through the AFL, each union must have complete control over its special craft; (2) unions must voluntarily cooperate with one another; and (3) unions must emphasize economic objectives—that is, shorter hours, better wages, and better working conditions.

The first two of these objectives meant that the individual craft unions were to communicate and cooperate with each other under the umbrella of the AFL. The third meant that American unionism was to be ''bread-and-butter'' unionism, not political or Socialist like its European counterparts. In fact, Gompers was downright anti-Socialist, and he worked hard to keep unions out of politics.

Despite the tactics used by the employers and the actions of the courts, Gompers's type of unionism dominated the American labor movement for almost fifty years. Indeed, from 1890–1897, more than 90 percent of the cases tried under the Sherman Act involved labor.

Then, in 1914, with the passage of the Clayton Act, unions got some relief. Although the Clayton Act was directed mainly against business, as we saw above, it also specifically stated that unions were not combinations or conspiracies in restraint of trade. As a result, there was a spurt in union membership following the passage of the act (see Figure 21–2). One of the more powerful legal devices used against unions had been eliminated.

3. The Period of Rapid Growth

But it took more than the Clayton Act to allow the union movement to reach the size and strength it had in the post–World War II period. Things dramatically changed with the onslaught of the Great Depression of the 1930s. The administration of Franklin D. Roosevelt and Congress took a favorable stand toward the union movement. In the early thirties, two landmark pieces of legislation were passed.

One of these was the Norris–LaGuardia Act of 1932. It outlawed the yellow-dog contract and also put severe restrictions on the use of injunctions against unions. The other law was the Wagner Act of 1939 (National Labor Relations Act). The Wagner Act also outlawed many of the devices that had been used against unions, but its major contribution was that it guaranteed workers the right to organize and bargain collectively.

Still, laws alone, no matter how favorable, can't account for the tremendous growth of unionism during the 1930s. Two other major forces were involved.

First there was the formation of the Congress of Industrial Organization (CIO). In 1934, six unions broke away from the AFL to organize the CIO. By then the manufacturing sector of the American economy was structured more along industrial than craft lines. The assembly line was present, and new forms of manufacturing had sprung up and spread. The CIO, under the leadership of John L. Lewis, recognized the importance of mass-production industrialization and organized unions in terms of workers in different *industries,* not crafts. This brought great masses of largely unskilled workers into the union movement—workers who had been excluded from the AFL. For the first time, many industries that had been safe from unions as long as the AFL was dominant faced the threat of unionism. The steel industry, meat packing, rubber, chemical, automobile, and numerous other industries were organized for the first time.

The second force stimulating the union movement was the severe Depression itself. At the low point of the 1930s, one of every four workers was unemployed, and not all of the employed had full-time jobs. Hence life was precarious, and the workers often felt that their employers were exerting unreasonable pressures on them. These pressures induced the workers to protect themselves from employer threats, and the logical course was joining the union. And join the unions they did; and they continued to join until by 1946 membership stood at a total of nearly 15 million workers.

Finally, in 1955, the AFL and CIO merged into an uneasy alliance. However, the major power remained with the individual unions.

4. Strikes, Communism, and the Taft-Hartley Act

Things really looked rosy for the union movement in 1946. There was full employment, collective bargaining had legislative support, and most employers had come to accept collective bargaining. All in all, everything pointed toward further growth.

But then problems began to develop, and these problems nearly broke the labor movement. Jurisdictional strikes and similar internal conflicts nearly tore the unions apart. One of the major problems was the infiltration of Communists into the unions. While it is true that there weren't many Communists in leadership positions, they did seem to exercise power beyond their proportional numbers. As a result, public hostility toward unions ran high during the postwar years. Also, immediately after the war unions engaged in numerous strikes, pushing wage costs up in an already inflationary period, and this also roused public hostility. Out of this came two important pieces of union legislation—the Taft-Hartley Act of 1947 and the Landrum-Griffin Act of 1959.

Union proponents referred to the Taft-Hartley Act in such terms as a ''slave labor act'' because it imposed some significant restrictions on union activity. It stipulates, for example, that a union can't force a worker to be a member without his or her consent, that jurisdictional disputes and sympathy strikes are illegal, and that featherbedding and secondary boycotts are illegal.

The act also outlaws the closed shop and specifies that Communists can't hold union offices. Finally, the law gives the president the power to impose an eighty-day injunction (cooling-off period) to stop a strike that in his opinion creates significant dangers for the national health and safety.

The Taft-Hartley Act certainly represented a changed attitude toward unionism. The pendulum had swung from the pro-union Wagner Act and La Guardia Act to a more antiunion stance. The pendulum moved even further with the passage of the Landrum-Griffin Act in 1959. The McClellan Committee investigated union practices from 1957 to 1959 and found that in some unions graft, corruption, bribery, and misuse of union funds were common practices.

The Landrum-Griffin Act is designed to protect union members from these abuses. It requires that financial reports be filed, it protects members who want to sue the union for violations of basic rights, and it provides safeguards for the proper election of union officials. Finally, employers must publicly report any financial dealings with union officials.

5. Recent Troubles and Trends

Today the union movement has matured from the rough-and-tumble days of the early century. At the moment, unions are firmly established institutions on the economic landscape. They still bargain with firms for the benefit of the membership, but as part of the establishment they push a broad social agenda in the halls of Congress and state legislatures. They are strong advocates of liberalization of the minimum wage, social security, and welfare programs. Unions have also been in the forefront of the civil rights movement.

Being an accepted part of society, however, means that unions are affected by the forces of change. Since the mid-1970s, there have been pressures on the movement, as with business in general, to adapt to changing economic conditions. In recent years, union membership has declined not only as a percentage of the work force but also in absolute numbers (see Figure 21–2). Two major factors seem responsible.

First, the growth in total employment during the past two decades has largely been in the service sector of the economy (banking, insurance, information processing, and the like). Employees in this part of the economy have traditionally been white collar and rather antiunion in attitude. As a result, it has been difficult for unions to organize this business sector.

Second, U.S. manufacturing began to lose its competitive position to foreign producers in the 1970s and 1980s. The reasons are clear. Rapid inflation in the 1970s coupled with lagging productivity growth dramatically raised unit costs of production in this country. Then the run-up of the value of the dollar on world currency markets in the 1980s put American manufacturing at a serious competitive disadvantage. As a result, American manufacturing has been forced into a major restructuring. As part of the process, many of the older and inefficient production facilities have been closed, with a heavy loss of jobs for unionized workers. Moreover, workers still employed have, in many cases, been under heavy pressure to accept wage cuts just to keep their jobs.

These changes in the economic environment have forced both unions and management to adapt. For their part, there is some evidence that unions have shifted bargaining demands from higher wages toward more job security for their members. Both management and unions now seem more willing to cooperate than they did in the past. Such cooperation is certainly one ingredient necessary to restore the competitive position of American manufacturing.

C. LABOR UNIONS AS MONOPOLIES

Conventional economic analysis concludes that unions definitely have an impact on wage rates, but just how great that impact is remains controversial. There is no question that wages, on average, are higher in unionized industries; but, at the same time, workers in these industries tend to be more skilled and work with more-efficient capital equipment. These workers, therefore, have a higher marginal productivity, and we would accordingly expect them to receive a higher wage. But how much of the higher wage is due to unionism is arguable.

Let's look at some ways by which unions try to benefit their members.

1. Union Goals

We have assumed that business firms, no matter what the market structure, have one overriding goal and that is to maximize profits. There is no such simple goal for the labor union. It is true that the union leaders would like to get the highest possible income for their members, but since the demand curve for the union's labor is downward sloping, increases in the wage tend to generate some unemployment. Thus there is a trade-off between wages and employment. Let's put this in the form of a general conclusion.

> **Conclusion:**   The union faces a wage-employment trade-off, and this is due to the negative-sloped demand curve for the union's labor services. The result is that if the union wants to get higher wages for its members, it can do so only by having more of its members unemployed. On the other hand, if it wants to create more employment for its members, it can do so only by reducing the wage rate for its members' services.

Once again, opportunity costs make themselves felt.

We suspect that the specific goal of any single union is the outcome of much discussion and controversy *within* the union and reflects some compromise between wages and unemployment. Any such compromise, however, must consider the forces outside both the union and the firm and industry. For example, during a strong expansion of general economic activity, greater emphasis will be placed on higher wages, whereas in a recession or general economic slump, greater emphasis will be placed on employment. The goal of the union, therefore, isn't necessarily fixed and rigid. However, whatever the goal of the union may be, it can be achieved only if the union has some control over the wage rate; and this control can exist only if the union can influence the demand for or the supply of the members' services.

2. Restricting Supply

Some unions, as we have seen, have been organized along craft lines, such as printers, plumbers, and carpenters. Although craft unions aren't nearly as important today as they were in the earlier years of the union movement, the techniques they use are still the same.

Once organized, the union controls the rules and regulations by which new members are admitted. Usually this is done by controlling the number of apprentices and their length of training. Also, this kind of union is going to be effective only if it can force the employers to hire union members.

The result of this type of labor supply restriction is to shift the supply curve of labor services available to the employers to the left; the apprenticeship rules keep it there. Figure 21–3 shows the actual supply curve of, say, printers as S_1. The pertinent union-influenced supply curve, however, is S_2. This curve shows the supply of labor services available after the union-management agreement has been reached. As a consequence, the wage that the employers must pay has been raised from W_1

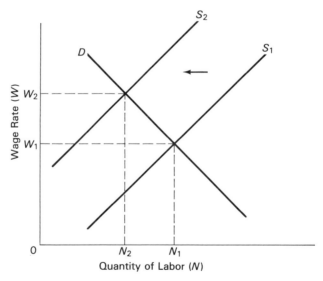

FIGURE 21-3   Labor Market Supply Restrictions   Craft unions can raise their members' wages by restricting the supply of labor. Wages are raised at the cost of some employment.

to W_2, resulting in higher wage costs to the employer. But note the opportunity cost in terms of employment. Labor services employed fall from N_1 to N_2.

We can also use this same type of analysis to explain the high incomes of some special types of workers. Here, however, the direct support of government is sought. States, for example, have licensing requirements for doctors, lawyers, dentists, and other professional types of labor. The standards required to get a license may be modified as a means of controlling supply. If they are made more strict, the supply curve will shift leftward, thus permitting those still in practice to charge higher fees (prices).

Similarly, many towns and cities have building codes that require licenses for plumbers and electricians. These, too, may be used to restrict supply and hence raise the wage incomes of those already possessing licenses.

As noted above, industrial unions, as opposed to craft unions, are made up of semiskilled and unskilled workers organized along industry lines—e.g., the United Steel Workers and the United Auto Workers. This type of union also has a strong effect on the number of workers employed, although it does so by directly manipulating the wage rate rather than by controlling the supply curve. Since industrial unions represent such large numbers of workers, there is no easy way for them to control supply.

Figure 21-4 shows us the result of this control. In the absence of the union, the equilibrium wage rate would be W_1. Under the influence of the union, the wage is set higher at, say, W_2. Thus the workers who are still employed will benefit from

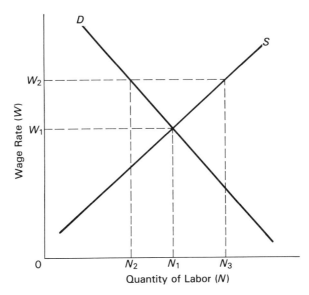

FIGURE 21-4 Industrial unions don't generally raise wages by restricting supply. Instead they push wages above market equilibrium. The result is fewer jobs and unemployment.

the higher wages, but we shouldn't forget the cost of the N_2 - N_3 workers who are now unemployed.

> **Conclusion:**   When the union pushes the wage rate above the equilibrium level through negotiation and the threat of strike, the level of employment will fall.

And this is about all that we can safely say. How high the union will attempt to push the wage depends on its goals. If the union is wage oriented and cares little about the unemployment of its members, it will strive to drive the wage as high as it can. On the other hand, if the union is employment oriented, it will settle for a lower wage in order to maximize the employment of its members. Indeed, unions may take (and some have taken) wage cuts in order to keep employment of members high.

Wage-setting goals are also, of course, influenced by employer resistance, which itself depends to a great extent on general economic conditions.

3. The Economic Impact of Unions

How important have unions been in influencing wages? This question is, unfortunately, difficult to answer. The available studies strongly indicate that the economic impact of unions has been overrated by *both* their proponents and opponents. Let's break the question down into two parts. First, what influence have unions had on the *average level* of real wages? Second, have unions significantly altered the *structure of relative wages?*

As for the first question, the evidence shows that unions achieve significant gains shortly after organizing and from then on more or less hold their own relative to nonunion workers. For the most part, the general rise in real wages that has occurred in the United States is due more to economic growth than to unions.

As for the second question, again the power of unions seems to have been exaggerated. In some cases—e.g., the building trades—unions have had a significant impact on their members' relative wages, but as we saw above, this is as much due to government support as anything else. Take away government licensing requirements and the union impact on wages would be weaker. In other cases—e.g., men's and boys' clothing—unionism seems to have had no appreciable impact on relative wages since World War II.

All in all, unions haven't usually had the distorting and inflationary impacts that their critics contend; nor have they had the power that their advocates argue that they have.

Finally, we shouldn't forget that unions bargain with management for more than wages and employment. Working conditions and the amount and type of fringe benefits (retirement, insurance, etc.) are two of the most important. Improvements in working conditions and more liberal and comprehensive fringe benefits impose added costs on business firms and as a result affect employment. Better fringe benefits, for example, seem to be one way to give a nontaxable wage increase to workers. Therefore, better benefits are probably acquired at the cost of some employment.

D. SUMMARY

With rapid economic growth in the second half of the nineteenth century came the growth of the large business firms in the form of trusts. Size and the economic power it confers could most easily be achieved by merger with other firms. Merger types in historical sequence were horizontal, vertical, and conglomerate.

The growth of monopoly power led to antitrust legislation, the cornerstone of which is the Sherman Antitrust Act of 1890. Initially, the act was ineffective, since the courts ruled that it applied only to monopoly power achieved by unreasonable means, and it was also used as a tool against the struggling union movement. Subsequent legislation attempted to block monopoly power in the process of development as well as outlaw specific business practices used to increase market power. Unions were also made exempt from antitrust legislation.

After an early struggle, the union movement established itself as part of the economic system during the period ranging from the Great Depression to the end of World War II. The economic conditions of the thirties swelled union membership rolls, while prounion legislation forced business firms to bargain in good faith with the workers' representatives.

Unions bargain with management over a wide variety of working conditions. Unions' economic power is most directly used to raise wages essentially by restricting the supply of labor. The cost of raising wages, however, is to reduce the availability of jobs. Increasing global competition in recent years has led unions to seek more job security for members instead of concentrating on higher wages.

Terms and Concepts to Remember

Craft union
Industrial union
Sherman Act of 1890
Clayton Act
Federal Trade Commission
   Act
American Federation of
   Labor
Congress of Industrial Or-
   ganizations
Taft-Hartley Act
Rule of reason

Horizontal merger
Vertical merger
Conglomerate merger
Celler-Kefauver Act
Price discrimination
Yellow-dog contract
Wagner Act
Landrum-Griffin Act

Questions for Review

1. Which of the three types of merger is currently prevalent? In light of the evolution of antitrust law, why might this be the case?

2. What was the first act directed specifically against monopoly? What drawbacks did it have?

3. In what specific ways does the Clayton Act alter the Sherman Act?

4. Some economists believe that a great deal of competition naturally exists in our economy, so that antitrust laws are counterproductive. Do you agree? Why or why not?

5. What factors led to the explosive growth of unions in the 1930–45 period?

6. In what ways can unions raise their members' wages? Has this been the unions' only objective?

Glossary

The numbers following each entry refer to the chapters in which the term or concept is defined and discussed.

Aggregate demand   The summation of consumer demand (*C*), business demand for plant, equipment, and inventory (*I*), government demand (*G*), and net exports or imports (*E* − *M*), which equals gross national product. (8, 9, 10)

Asset   Something that is owned by or is owed to a person, business, or any other economic unit. (11)

Automatic stabilizers   Institutional elements (progressive taxes, unemployment compensation, etc.) that automatically dampen fluctuations in output and employment. (13)

Average fixed cost (AFC)   Total fixed costs divided by the quantity of output. (17)

Average total cost (ATC)   Total costs divided by the quantity of output; same as average fixed cost (*AFC*) and average variable cost (*AVC*). (17)

Average variable cost (AVC)   Total variable costs divided by the quantity of output. (17)

Balance of payments   An accounting statement of the inpayments and outpayments of a country vis-à-vis the rest of the world. (7)

Balance of trade   Relationship between a country's imports and exports; not a very useful concept. (7)

Balance sheet   A statement of an organization's assets and liabilities at a particular point in time, with net worth serving as the balancing item. (11)

Basic balance   Relationship between inpayments and outpayments in both the current and capital accounts of a country. (7)

Built-in stabilizers   See *automatic stabilizers.*

Business cycle   Recurring, but not periodic, fluctuations in the levels of output, employment, and prices that last more than a year. (9)

Capacity, economic   Size of productive organization that yields lowest average total costs of production; a microeconomic concept. (17)

Capital   Productive assets usually in the form of plant, equipment, inventory, and other produced means of production; may be extended to include human beings. (1, 18)

Cartel Form of overt collusion among firms in an oligopolistic industry. (20)

Ceteris paribus Assumption that all variables except one are held constant so that the effects of the one that is allowed to change can be examined. (4)

Collective goods Goods needed by society but provided by government instead of private individuals and businesses. (6)

Command economy Economy in which most decisions are made by centralized authorities; usually contains market and tradition elements. (1)

Comparative advantage Principle that explains how people of different countries benefit from the free flow of goods and services among them. (7)

Complementary goods Two goods that are consumed together (e.g., coffee and cream) so that if the price of one changes, the demand for the other changes in the opposite direction; contrast with substitute goods. (16)

Concentration, ratio The percentage of an industry's output (or sales) accounted for by the few firms that may dominate the industry. (20)

Conglomerate merger A firm merging with another firm producing a completely unrelated product or service. (21)

Consumption function Relationship of households' consumption to disposable income; used in both short-run and long-run analysis. (10)

Demand curve Negative-sloped curve showing different price-quantity demand relationships; a shift of the curve is called a change in demand; a movement along the curve is a change in quantity demanded. (4, 16)

Demand deposits Checking accounts; largest part of money supply; also liabilities of commercial banks. (11)

Depreciation Estimated wearing out of a productive asset over a period of time; considered both as a cost of production and as an internal source of saving. (8)

Derived demand Firm's demand for a productive input as derived from the demand for the firm's product. (18)

Diminishing marginal utility The marginal, or extra, utility derived from consuming successive units of a product diminishes. (16)

Diminishing returns As successive units of a variable input are applied to a fixed input, total output eventually begins to increase at a decreasing rate; may be measured in terms of behavior of marginal product. (2, 17)

Discount rate Interest rate charged by Federal Reserve on loans to member banks. (12)

Diseconomies of size Cost-reducing changes that raise the firm's average costs as it grows. (17)

Disposable income Income of households after personal taxes, but including transfer payments; used for personal consumption and saving. (8, 10)

Economic growth Increase in GNP or per capita GNP over time. (14)

Economies of scale Cost-reducing changes that lower average cost as the firm grows; may be internal or external to the firm. (17, 19)

Entry, barriers to Impediments to entry by new firms into an industry; due to economies of size in natural monopoly, but due usually to advertising, product variation, etc., in oligopoly. (19)

Equilibrium State of rest or balance among counteracting forces that will continue unless upset by a change in one or more of the variables. (4, 10)

Exchange rate Price (or rate) at which the currency of one country exchanges for the currency of another country. (7)

Exchange rates, flexible Prices of currencies in terms of one another when allowed to change freely according to demand and supply conditions. (7)

Fiscal policy, discretionary Arbitrary changes in government spending and taxing to counteract fluctuations in output and employment. (13)

Free good A good so abundant that it has no price. (1)

Full employment Usually defined as employment of total civilian labor force less frictional unemployment. (9)

Full-employment surplus (deficit) Surplus (or deficit) that would prevail, given taxing and and spending programs, if the economy were at full employment. (13)

GNP gap Difference between actual and potential GNPs. (9)

Grants-in-aid Monetary grants, usually earmarked for special uses, from federal government to state-local governments; often made on a partial matching basis. (6)

Gross national product (GNP) Market value of all the final goods and services produced in the economy during a given time period (usually a year); may be calculated in either current dollar or constant dollar terms. (8)

Horizontal integration A firm buying, building, or merging with another firm at the same stage of production of a product. (21)

Import quota Restriction on the amount of a good that may be imported; may be imposed on specific goods or on goods in general. (7)

Indirect business taxes Taxes (e.g., sales and excise) imposed on businesses and included in final selling price of a product; deducted from NNP to arrive at national income. (8)

Inflation General rise in the price level, no matter what the cause; may be cost-push, administered-price, or excess-demand. (9)

Interest rate Payment made for use of borrowed funds. (5, 12)

Investment Capital formation, made up of replacement investment and net investment. (8, 10)

Investment demand curve Curve showing planned investment projects ranked in descending order of profitability; aggregate investment demand is the sum of all individual firms' IDCs. (10, 18)

Joint profit maximization Form of overt collusion in oligopoly; designed to maximize combined profits of all firms in the industry. (20)

Liability   Something owed by a person, business, or other economic unit to some other economic unit. (11)

Long run   A period of time when all inputs are variable. (17)

Marginal cost (*MC*)   Change in total cost (or total variable cost) attributable to producing an extra unit of output; calculated as $\Delta TC/\Delta Q$ or $\Delta TVC/\Delta Q$. (17)

Marginal product (*MP*)   Addition to total output attributable to the last unit of the variable input employed. (17)

Marginal propensity to consume (*MPC*)   Percentage of a change in disposable income devoted to a change in consumption; equals the slope of the consumption function. (10)

Marginal revenue (*MR*)   Change in total revenue attributable to the sale of an extra unit of output; calculated as $\Delta TR/\Delta Q$. (16)

Marginal revenue product (*MRP*)   Firm's marginal revenue times the marginal physical product of variable input; *MRP* curve is the competitive firm's demand curve for the variable input. (18)

Marginal utility (*MU*)   Utility or satisfaction provided by the last unit of a good consumed (in the relevant time period). (16)

Market economy   Economy in which the bulk of economic decisions are made by private individuals and organizations; contains command and tradition elements. (1, 4)

Merger   Two or more firms combining into a single new firm; may be horizontal, vertical, or conglomerate. (21)

Monetarism   School of thought that holds that economic fluctuations are caused by changes in the money supply; hence monetary policy is far more important than fiscal policy. (13)

Monetary policy   Control of money supply and interest rates by the Federal Reserve to counteract fluctuations in output and employment. (11, 12, 13)

Money   Anything generally accepted as a medium of exchange; in the United States, usually defined as privately held coins, currency, and demand deposits outside the banking system. (3, 11)

Money multiplier   Ratio of $1/RR$ that determines the multiple expansion of the money supply, given the reserve base. (11)

Monopolistic competition   Market structure with many small firms selling slightly differentiated products; freedom of entry and exit, no collusion, and both price and nonprice competition. (20)

Multiplier   Ratio by which total output will increase (decrease) as a result of an injection into (withdrawal from) the spending stream. (10)

Multiplier effect   Change in total output, given the multiplier and the initial change in spending. (10)

National debt   Total debt of federal government due to borrowing; represented by outstanding government securities. (6, 13)

National income (at factor cost)   Total income attributable to, but not necessarily received by, owners of factors of production; wages and salaries, rent, interest, and profit. (8)

Near money   Highly liquid financial asset that is a close, but not perfect, substitute for money. (11)

Net national product (NNP)   Gross national product less capital consumption allowances. (8)

Net worth   Difference between an organization's total assets and total liabilities; must always be a positive figure. (11)

Normal returns   Returns that an economic unit must receive on its owned assets in order to keep it in its present employment; determined by earnings of resources in their next-best employments. (16)

Official settlements   Relationship between all inpayments and all outpayments of a country. (7)

Oligopoly   Market structure dominated by a few relatively large firms and characterized by conjectural interdependence, collusion, and much nonprice competition. (20)

Open-market operations   Purchases and sales of government securities by the Federal Reserve in order to control interest rates, reserve base, and money supply. (12)

Opportunity cost   What is given up by doing something, or using a resource, one way rather than another; normal returns are opportunity costs. (2)

Optimum size of firm   The size that yields the lowest long-run average cost of production; lowest point on the LRAC curve. (17)

Personal income   Total income received by households, including transfer payments, but prior to tax payments. (8)

Potential GNP   Level of gross national product that would exist if all growth factors were fully realized; contrast with actual GNP. (9)

Price elasticity of demand   Responsiveness of a change in quantity demanded to a change in product price; calculated as percentage change in quantity demanded divided by percentage change in price. (16)

Price leadership   Form of tacit collusion in which one firm sets price and the other firms in the industry match it; may be dominant-firm or barometric-firm leadership. (20)

Price maker   A firm with enough market power to set price arbitrarily. (15, 19)

Price taker   A firm with so little market power that it takes price as given by market forces beyond its direct control. (15, 16, 17)

Production function, short run   Technological and organizational characteristics of the firm that transform inputs into a finished product when at least one input is fixed in amount. (17, 18)

Production-possibilities curve   Curve that shows various combinations of things the economy can produce with given technology and given, fully employed resources. (2)

Profit   See *normal returns.*

Profit maximization   Selection of rate of output in either the short run or the long run according to the rule *MC* = *MR;* in pure competition, the rule reads *MC* = *MR* = *P.* (17)

Progressive tax   A tax whose rate increases more rapidly than the tax base on which it is levied; for example, personal income tax. (6)

Proportional tax   A tax whose rate maintains the same proportion of the tax base on which it is levied. (6)

Pure competition   Market structure comprised of many small sellers of homogeneous products; has freedom of entry and exit, no collusion, and much price competition; individual firms are price takers. (15, 17)

Pure monopoly   Market structure in which there is only one seller of the good or service. (15, 19)

Quantity demanded   Amount of a commodity demanded at a particular price; one point on a demand curve. (4)

Quantity supplied   Amount of a commodity supplied at a given price; one point on a supply curve. (4)

Quantity theory   Theory that, with velocity (*V*) constant, changes in output (*Q*) and prices (*P*) are due mainly to changes in money supply (*M*). (10, 13)

Range of mutual benefit   Range between economic units within which mutually advantageous exchange takes place. (3)

Rate of return   Anticipated profit rate on planned investment projects; used to equate present value of future revenue to cost of asset. (18)

Regressive tax   Tax whose rate rises less rapidly than the tax base on which it is levied; for example, sales tax. (6)

Rent   Earnings over what a resource can receive in its next-best use; also, payment made for the use of land. (18)

Reserves, excess   Reserve deposits of commercial banks over required reserves: important part of reserve base. (11)

Reserves, required   Specified percentage of demand and time deposits a commercial bank must hold as deposits at the Federal Reserve; vault cash may be counted as part of required reserves. (12)

Saving, business   Saving by business firms in the form of undistributed corporate profits and depreciation charges; often called internal sources of saving. (8)

Saving, personal   Difference between disposable income and personal consumption spending. (8)

Short run   See *production function, short run.*

Social cost   Cost imposed on and borne by society in general as a result of private actions. (6)

Social overhead investment   See *collective goods.*

Substitute goods   Two goods that are substitutes for each other so that if the price of one changes, the demand for the other changes in the same direction; contrast with complementary goods. (16)

Supply curve Positive-sloped curve showing different price-quantity supplied combinations; a shift of the curve is called a change in supply; a movement along the curve is a change in quantity supplied. (4, 17)

Tariff Import duty placed on a product; may be ad valorem or specific. (7)

Technical residual Educational, research, and other institutional forces that contribute to economic growth. (14)

Tradition economy Economy in which most decisions are made on the basis of custom and tradition; usually contains command and market elements. (1)

Transfer payments Payments (usually money) to individuals and businesses; they do not represent productive activity by recipients. (6, 8)

Undistributed corporate profits Profits received by corporations but not declared as dividends to stockholders; an important source of internal saving by business. (8)

Unemployment, frictional Unemployment due to people moving between jobs over very short periods of time; accepted as unavoidable. (9)

Unemployment, involuntary Unemployment of people actively seeking work and able to work but unable to find jobs; excludes frictional unemployment; generally attributed to a shortage of aggregate demand. (9)

Unemployment, structural Unemployment due to mismatched demand for labor and supply of unemployed workers; may last for long periods of time. (9)

Velocity, income Total expenditures *(PQ)* per time period divided by stock of money *(M)* for the same period; rate at which money supply turns over per time period. (10)

Vertical integration Firm buying, building, or merging with another firm in a different stage of producing the same product; may be forward or backward. (21)

X-inefficiency Inefficient use of resources within a firm as a result of loss of managerial control and monopoly power. (19)

Index

V

Velocity
  and aggregate demand, 193–94
  changes in, 195–96
  defined, 194

W

Wages
  and marginal productivity theory,
    382–91
  and noncompeting groups, 381
Wealth, 197, 223–24

X

X-inefficiency, 421–23

Y

Yellow dog contract, 451